Nage Birds

This unusual book describes in detail the relationship between the Nage people of eastern Indonesia and the birds whose environment they share. Based on more than a decade of ethnographic fieldwork, it explores the ways in which a human society interacts with members of another zoological class and attaches particular values to these in a variety of cultural and conceptual contexts. As well as a fascinating study of the local ornithology of the Indonesian island of Flores, *Nage Birds* provides a critical review of current theoretical debate regarding how non-western societies categorize and think about non-human forms of animal life. Ranging from issues of taxonomy and naming to the fascinating subject of birds' prophetic associations and their places in religious representations, myth, poetry and song, **Gregory Forth's** richly detailed work will be invaluable to students of ethnobiology, social and cultural anthropology, folklore, zoology and Southeast Asia.

Gregory Forth is Professor of Anthropology at the University of Alberta. His books include *Dualism and Hierarchy* (2001), *Beneath the Volcano* (1998) and *Space and Place in Eastern Indonesia* (1991).

Studies in environmental anthropology
Edited by Roy Ellen
University of Kent at Canterbury, UK

This series is a vehicle for publishing up-to-date monographs on particular issues in particular places which are sensitive to both sociocultural and ecological factors. Emphasis will be placed on the perception of the environment, indigenous knowledge and the ethnography of environmental issues. While basically anthropological, the series will consider works from authors working in adjacent fields.

Nage Birds

Classification and Symbolism among an Eastern Indonesian people

Gregory Forth

Routledge
Taylor & Francis Group

LONDON AND NEW YORK

First published 2004 by Routledge
2 Park Square, Milton Park, Abingdon, Oxon, OX14 4RN

Simultaneously published in the USA and Canada
by Routledge
711 Third Avenue, New York, NY 10017

Routledge is an imprint of the Taylor & Francis Group

Transferred to Digital Printing 2007

First issued in paperback 2013

Typeset in Galliard by Graphicraft Limited, Hong Kong

British Library Cataloguing in Publication Data
A catalogue record for this book is available from the British Library

Library of Congress Cataloging in Publication Data

Forth, Gregory
  Nage birds : classification and symbolism among an Eastern
Indonesian people / Gregory Forth.
      p. cm. – (Studies in environmental anthropology)
    Includes bibliographical references and index.
    1. Nage (Indonesian people) – Ethnozoology. 2. Birds – Classification.
3. Folk classification – Indonesia. 4. Nage (Indonesian people) – Religion.
I. Title. II. Series.

DS632.N35F67 2003
598.16'3'0899922–dc21   2003046540

ISBN 978-0-415-31827-3 (hbk)
ISBN 978-0-415-86450-3 (pbk)

To my parents

Contents

Illustrations

Plates

Figures

Tables

Maps

Preface

This book is in some sense (and, I hope, the best sense) the work of an amateur. It represents the efforts of a social and cultural anthropologist who came to ethnozoology indirectly, through an investigation of the religious ideas and practices of an eastern Indonesian people – the Nage, who reside in the central part of the island of Flores. In addition to a professional involvement, moreover, the study is guided by a personal interest: a life-long fascination with birds. Nevertheless, following a time-honoured anthropological approach, my objective has been a total view of Nage knowledge of avifauna and their attendant conceptual and practical uses. The work, in other words, aims at a comprehensive understanding of the various ways in which a single human community connects with a single zoological class (the one zoologists label 'Aves'), or, in ethnobiological terms, with a single 'life-form' category. In regard to this specific focus, the book is unusual, at least so far as anthropology is concerned.

The origins of this study lie in two articles (Forth 1996a, 1998b), both based largely on research conducted during four field trips undertaken between 1991 and 1996. In the course of composing these essays, I came to realize that there was rather more I wanted to say about Nage knowledge of birds than space permitted; but in view of the way particular topics I wished to explore connected with other issues, both empirical and theoretical, I was not convinced that additional journal articles would be the best way to do so. In the meantime, I was invited by Dr Pierre Le Roux, then director of the Projet Grand Sud at Prince of Songkla University in Thailand, to contribute a chapter on Nage bird symbolism to a collection exploring the significance of birds in Southeast Asian cultures. I gladly accepted Dr Le Roux's invitation. However, when it later appeared that a publisher might not be found for the collection, I again had to consider possible publishing venues. With this additional paper written, I came to see that by combining newer analyses – not only with topics treated in 1996 and 1998 but also with parts of an earlier essay on a widespread mythological tradition incorporating bird characters (Forth 1992) – a greater whole, and a more creative synthesis, might be realized. Eventually, therefore, I decided to write a proposal for a book-length treatment of 'Nage birds', the product of which is the present volume.

That was early in 2000. About the same time I learned of the availability of unpublished lists of bird terminologies from the languages of the island of Flores and neighbouring islands compiled by the late Father Jilis A.J. Verheijen SVD (1908–97), the foremost authority on the ethnobiology of the eastern Lesser Sunda Islands (the Indonesian province of Nusa Tenggara Timur). Since relatively little has been published on Indonesian folk zoology, I realized that access to Father Verheijen's records could provide a comparative perspective on ethno-ornithological classification and nomenclature paralleling the results of a comparative investigation of myth and symbolism I had undertaken in connection with a monograph on Nage indigenous religion (Forth 1998a) and my essay on eastern Indonesian origin myths (Forth 1992). Further facilitating a monographic treatment of Nage ethno-ornithology was the publication, in 1997, of the first comprehensive field guide of the birds of Wallacea, the biogeographical region of Indonesia that includes Flores island. As both ornithologists and students of Austronesian ethnobiology will immediately realize, I refer to Brian J. Coates and K. David Bishop's magisterial work, *A Guide to the Birds of Wallacea: Sulawesi, the Moluccas and Lesser Sunda Islands, Indonesia*, superbly illustrated by Dana Gardner. Since obtaining a copy in the summer of 1998, the guide has not only made possible a more secure identification of Nage categories, in the sense of relating them to scientific taxa, but has also provided an unparalleled source of information on species morphology, vocalization, behaviour, habitat, and distribution that has contributed to a fuller appreciation of the Nage symbolism of birds.

Drafts of all chapters of this book were completed early in 2001, before I had the opportunity to pay another visit to Flores in July and August of that year. Devoting most of my time and efforts to additional research into Nage ethno-ornithology, including further field observation of central Flores birds, this period – among the most enjoyable and satisfying I have spent in Indonesia – enabled me to fill in a number of blanks and to clarify certain issues that had arisen in the course of drafting the present work.

Although this book draws partly on previously published material, I should point out that no chapter is simply a reprint of an existing publication. In the course of crafting a new analytical whole, I have often found it necessary to incorporate adjustments and refinements, albeit relatively minor ones that do not affect the main thrust of previous arguments. An extended analysis of information on Nage ethno-ornithological classification first presented in the journal *Anthropos* (Forth 1996a) appears below in Chapters 2 and 3. Chapter 4 largely replicates a paper published in the *Journal of Ethnobiology* (Forth 1998b) but also incorporates information from a note published in *Anthropos* (Forth 1999). I am grateful to the editors of both journals for allowing me to employ the substance of these papers in the present work. My gratitude similarly extends to Pierre Le Roux and Bernard Sellato for permission to use the contents of the article to appear in the volume they are editing on aesthetic and symbolic aspects of Southeast

Asian birds. These materials are mostly included in Chapter 5, while some are found in Chapter 6.

A number of scholars, all of them anthropologists, have kindly provided me with information on the naming of birds or other zoological categories in particular eastern Indonesian languages. Among these are Dr R.H. Barnes of the University of Oxford (for the language of Kédang), Professor Roy Ellen of the University of Kent (for Nuaulu), Dr E. Douglas Lewis of the University of Melbourne (for Sikanese), and Dr Takashi Sugishima of Kyoto University (for Lio). Questions of a more general nature, or concerning particular natural kinds, were addressed by Dr Christopher Healey (lately of Northern Territory University) and Dr Peter Dwyer (of the University of Melbourne). To all of these colleagues I am most grateful for responding promptly and generously to both categorical requests for information and more specific enquiries.

With regard to the unpublished terminologies recorded for Flores language by Father Verheijen, I am indebted to Verheijen's biographer, Dr Marie-Antoinette Willemsen who, on my behalf, located these in the Historical Archive of the Koninklijk Instituut voor Taal-, Land- en Volkenkunde (the Royal Institute of Linguistics and Anthropology) in Leiden and in the archive of the Roman Catholic Retirement Home at Teteringen, also in the Netherlands. The most important source of names is contained in the Leiden archive, specifically in a paper entitled 'Vernacular bird names in the Lesser Sunda Islands' (Verheijen n.d.); and in fact all the information included in typescripts found in Teteringen also appears in the Leiden paper, which I have accordingly cited extensively.

The research from which this study derives has been supported from grants awarded by the Social Sciences and Humanities Research Council of Canada, the University of Alberta, and the British Academy. At various times, fieldwork in Indonesia has been sponsored by the Indonesian Institute of Sciences (LIPI) and Nusa Cendana University and Artha Wacana Christian University, both in Kupang. To all of these bodies I am extremely grateful.

My greatest debt, however, remains with the numerous local people, most of them resident in the vicinity of the main Nage village of Bo'a Wae, not only for so generously sharing with me their knowledge of birds but also for their boundless hospitality and friendship. As it is not possible to mention all of them by name, mentioning any incurs the risk of appearing either unduly selective or arbitrary. Nevertheless, I should like especially to acknowledge the help of several regular informants who assisted me repeatedly in a variety of enquiries. These included the late E. Waso Ea (1941–94), T. Cola Bha, M. Dhai Nguza, E. Dhoi Léwa, M. Goa Na'u, C. Kodhi Léjo, F. Laja Ga'e, P. Lape Ga'e, B. Léwa Gisi, T. Mea Béli, J. Méze Bha, A. Nuwa Bupu, and J. Soda Ule.

Finally, a special vote of thanks is due to Donna McKinnon for her splendid drawings which, whatever the merits of my text, have added tremendously to the intelligibility of the analysis and the book's overall appeal.

Note on orthography

Transcription of Nage words is based on standard Indonesian (Bahasa Indonesia). The following examples all refer to Nage bird names included in Table 1.1. Most consonants are pronounced roughly as in English. The sounds written as /bh/ and /dh/ (e.g. *bha*, 'white', in *o ae bha*; and *dhéngi* in *kete dhéngi*) are implosives that contrast phonemically with /b/ and /d/ (e.g. *bopo*, *detu*). The /c/ (e.g. in *céce* and *ceka*) is pronounced as in English /chirp/. The combination /gh/ represents a voiced pharyngal fricative (e.g. *zeghi*). /W/ indicates a sound somewhere between English /w/ and /v/, but closer to the latter in initial positions (e.g. *wi*) and often closer to the former in medial positions (e.g. *lowo* in *wagha lowo*). All vowels are pure. The /é/ is a long 'e' (see *céce*; cf. English 'chain'). Unaccented /e/ represents the schwa at the beginning of words and between consonants (e.g. *bele teka*, *fega*), and a long 'e' in the final position or in monosyllabic words (e.g. the final /e/ in *céce*, and *je*). Glottal stops, which occur both initially (e.g. *'owa*) and in a medial position (e.g. *piko du'a*), are indicated with /'/.

Gregory Forth
Department of Anthropology
University of Alberta
December 2002

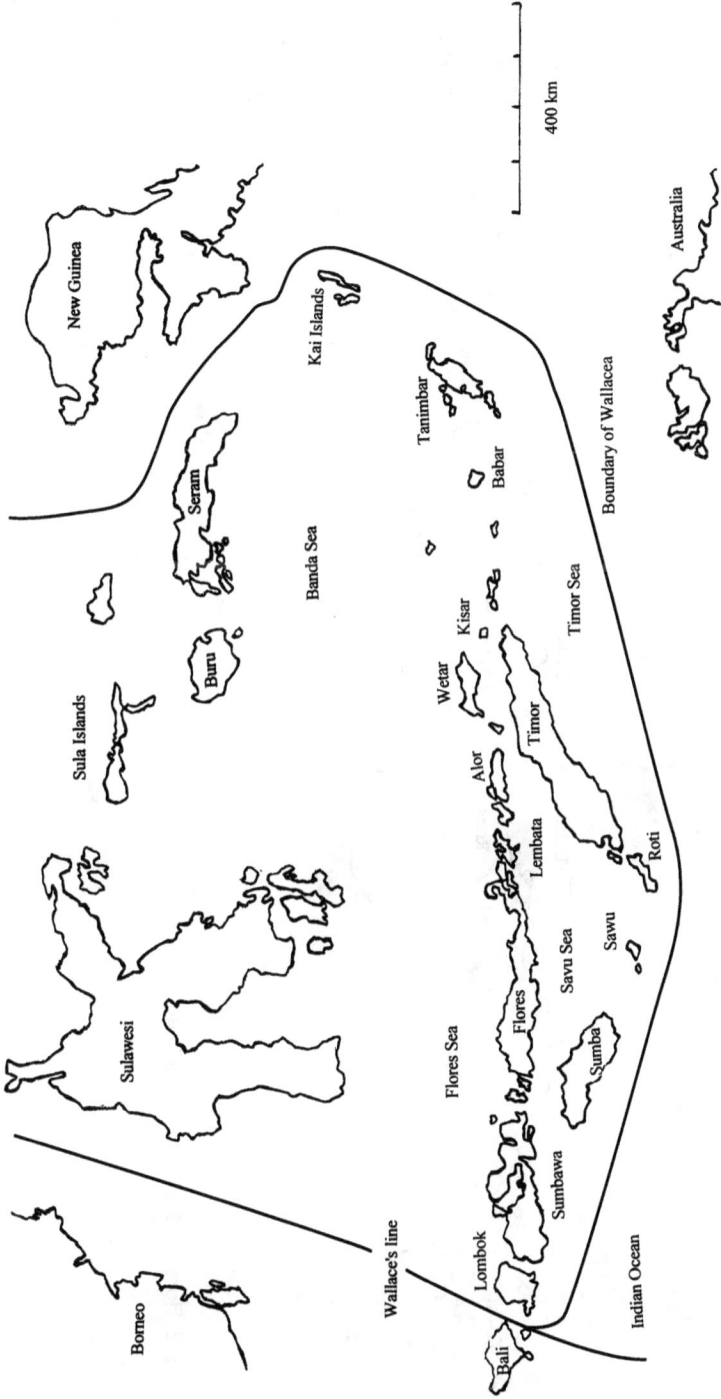

Map 1 Wallacea and eastern Indonesia

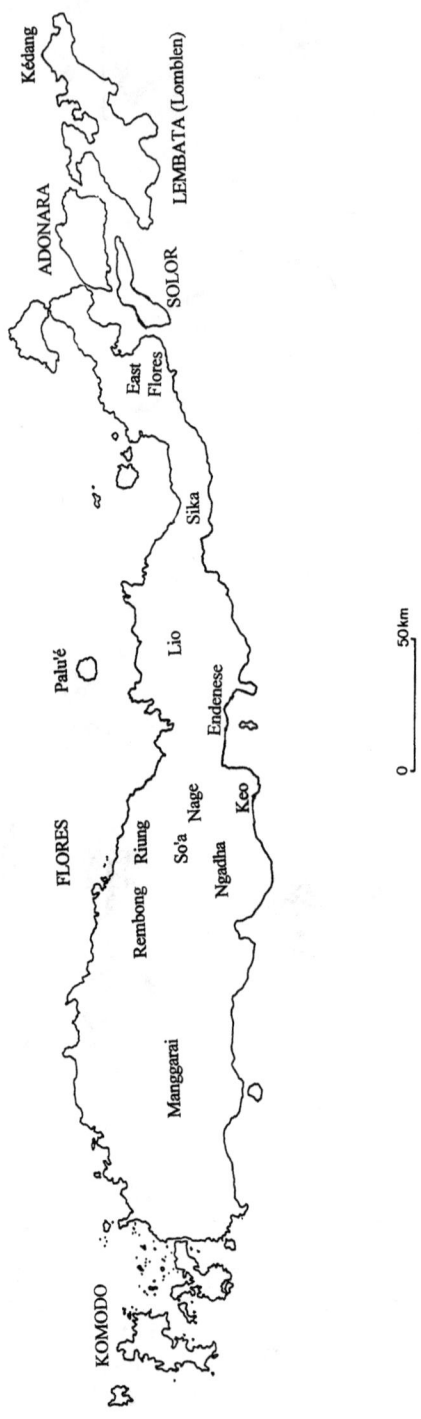

Map 2 Flores and neighbouring islands

Chapter 1

Introduction

This book concerns the Nage, a people inhabiting the central part of the island of Flores in eastern Indonesia, and their knowledge of birds. Although 'Nage' has more restricted applications, in its widest sense the name refers to a population of roughly 50,000 residing in villages to the north and west of the Ebu Lobo volcano (see Forth 1998a, Map 2). Nage dialects are closely related to those spoken in the Ngadha region, to the west, and in the Ende and Lio regions, to the east. All central Flores languages are provisionally classified as members of a Bima-Sumba group (Esser 1938), which forms part of the Central-Malayo-Polynesian branch of the Austronesian family (Blust 1979). In this volume, I refer mostly to the dialect spoken in and around the western Nage village of Bo'a Wae. The immediate vicinity of Bo'a Wae – the residence of the 'rajas' or native rulers of Nage during the period of Dutch colonial administration – has been the main location of my field researches in Nage, and it is to this region that the present work primarily refers (see further pp. 24–26).

Objectives: content and context

A general relevance of this study is the continuing debate about the nature of ethnobiological, or more specifically ethnozoological, classification. For a long time, a crucial question has been whether such classifications fundamentally reflect universal factors of perception and cognition operating directly on discontinuity in the natural world, or whether they are radically shaped by culturally specific values bound up, for example, with economic and religious life. Sometimes identified as 'intellectualists', proponents of the former position (see e.g., Berlin 1992; Atran 1990; Hunn 1976; Bulmer 1974) tend to advance a view of ethnobiological classification as fundamentally similar to modern scientific taxonomy. By contrast, opponents (e.g., Ellen 1993a; Hunn 1982; Randall and Hunn 1984), dubbed as 'functionalists' or 'utilitarianists', adopt a position of cultural relativism, interpreting folk classification as reflecting patterns and principles specific to particular societies.

In recent years, and partly in response to an accumulation of detailed ethnobiological studies of single cultural communities, both sides have refined their positions in ways that accommodate significant findings of their opposites.[1] Indeed, for some time intellectualists have allowed for the existence of 'special purpose' classifications in which folk biological taxa are organized according to criteria that are culturally particular (e.g., Berlin 1992; Hunn 1977: 47). Some have also acknowledged that 'folk generic' categories (typically the smallest named categories, see pp. 5–6) may be linked as members of more inclusive categories (particularly 'intermediate' taxa) on the basis of cultural significance rather than on perceptual grounds (Berlin 1992: 149, 152); and the same allowance has been made for labelled distinctions within folk generic categories (or 'folk specifics'; see Berlin 1992: 120–22). Yet intellectualists still consider special-purpose classifications as constructs quite separate from, and secondary to, 'general purpose' classifications; that is, taxonomic schemes grounded in the perception of natural discontinuities of morphology and behaviour. Most prominent among the factors of perception (or 'percepts') which intellectualists discern in the construction of folk biological taxa are visible features. At the same time, and especially with regard to birds, auditory features – which is to say, characteristic vocalizations – may assume a comparable importance (see Berlin and O'Neill 1981).

As the foregoing may suggest, ethnobiologists of both persuasions have usually spoken in terms of a binary opposition of universal percepts versus cultural particulars, or a contrast of 'perceptual salience' and 'cultural salience'. Recently, however, several scholars have demonstrated how perceptual salience is analysable into several distinct factors. Berlin (1992) thus speaks of 'phenotypic salience' (or 'taxonomic distinctiveness'), 'the *size* of an organism in relation to human beings', and 'the *prevalence* of individual species in the local habitat as well as their relative *ease of observation*' as factors 'determining the likelihood that a particular plant or animal will be named' (1992: 263; emphasis is Berlin's). 'Phenotypic salience' (which has sometimes been used synonymously with perceptual salience) refers to perceptually salient discontinuity, or 'decided gaps' (Hunn 1999: 47), in the natural world, which in principle correspond to taxonomic distance in scientific biology. Even more recently, Hunn has proposed further refinements in the analysis of what he similarly refers to as the 'size factor' and 'ecological salience', as perceptual components that, in addition to phenotypic salience, can affect the likelihood of a natural kind being recognized by folk classifiers (1999: 48). Hunn then contrasts these three factors to a fourth factor, which he calls 'cultural salience' and equates with what others (including Turner 1988: 274; see also Hunn 1982) have termed 'cultural significance'.[2]

If nothing else, these refinements underscore the extent to which pan-human perception and cognition interact in complex ways with patterns of behaviour, interests, and values specific to a particular culture. Yet while analytically separating the factors of size, ecological salience and phenotypic salience advance our understanding of a more general perceptual salience, the concept of 'cultural salience' – a 'variable "interest in" or "attention to" a set of organisms' that differs from one society to another (Hunn 1999: 49) – remains conspicuously undeveloped.[3]

Quite apart from the question of whether 'cultural salience' is properly treated as comparable in this way to the several factors of perceptual salience, it should later become apparent that cultural significance (as I would prefer to call it) has in fact very little influence on either the form of Nage ethnotaxonomy or the definition of its component categories. Nevertheless, if cultural significance is to have any use as a reference to something distinct from pan-human percepts, then, at the very least, one needs to distinguish between utilitarian value (for example, whether an animal or plant is exploited as food or as a source of raw materials) and symbolic significance (for example, whether it is believed to manifest a spiritual being or serves as a metaphor for human qualities or a social status). Noteworthy in this respect is one finding of the present work, that while the majority of Nage bird categories figure in symbolic representations (Chapter 8), very few possess distinctive utilitarian value (see pp. 8–14). The majority of birds can indeed be consumed as food, but this of course does not distinguish one category from another, nor in Nage ethnotaxonomy does it equivocally associate a number of kinds as members of a more inclusive class, the existence of a utilitarian (and non-taxonomic) category of game birds labelled *piko kolo* notwithstanding (see Chapter 3).[4]

As I further demonstrate, both utilitarian and symbolic values of birds are as much grounded in perceptual, and then mostly visual, attributes as is Nage ethno-ornithological taxonomy. Indeed, the basic components of both utilitarian and symbolic associations of individual bird categories can themselves be shown to be, in the first instance, perceptually based units of ethnotaxonomy. The point may be briefly illustrated with reference to diurnal birds of prey, a group that figures prominently in all aspects of Nage ethno-ornithology. With regard to their negative economic significance as predators of domestic fowls, these birds can be conceived as composing a utilitarian class. Yet what defines them as a threat to fowls (and thus lends them a specific utilitarian value) is precisely their physical form and behaviour; and as I show in Chapter 4, the same perceptual features crucially inform their (equally negative) symbolic significance.

In this general connection, in Chapter 2 I introduce a concept of 'simple distinctive features', which comprise locally recognized empirical attributes defining bird categories (or, more particularly, 'folk generics') as the smallest, most exclusive units of a general purpose ethno-ornithological classification. In many instances, these attributes, abstracted from Nage mundane discourse about birds, further provide the focal elements of the symbolic representation of a category (including similative usage). As this may suggest, in regard to their common origin in empirical observation, the difference between ethnotaxonomic and symbolic discourse lies mainly in how percepts are cognitively processed. As I demonstrate in the next two chapters, Nage ethnotaxonomy straightforwardly reflects observation of palpable discontinuity, identifying individual specimens on physical grounds as members of exclusive categories and, in a number of cases, simultaneously classifying two or more such categories together, as members of more inclusive classes – thus giving rise to a taxonomic hierarchy.

By contrast, symbolic representations of birds – including what may be called their 'symbolic classification' – are constructed more selectively, by focusing (Sperber 1975) on particular perceptual features, which may be largely or partly affected by a factor of cultural interest (see, for example, Chapter 4 for the linking of owls, diurnal raptors, and other birds as a function of a pronounced Nage concern with murderous, nocturnally active, and cannibalistic witches). These features further facilitate conceptual linkage with non-ornithological things, so as to create representations of a completely different (that is, non-zoological) sort. In fact, so extensive is the transformation that the resulting classification is arguably one constituted of these essentially non-empirical representations, of which empirical birds appear simply as aspects or components (see pp. 153, 169–71).

A major objective of this book is, accordingly, the demonstration of a distinct kind of symbolic knowledge of birds and hence the existence of a symbolic classification quite separate from ethnotaxonomic relations. As this symbolic classification comprises the same named categories as does the ethno-ornithological taxonomy, it follows that a category like *ha* (Large-billed crow), for example, may be linked with others ethnotaxonomically – in which case it figures as a member of an unnamed intermediate taxon mostly defined morphologically (see Chapter 3) – or it may be conceived symbolically, as one of a number of birds associated on a partly different basis (and particularly with regard to diet rather than dark plumage) as manifestations of spirits. Expressed another way, one can say that a single bird category can figure in more than one classification, and that, while these classifications obviously overlap in respect of shared terms, the content of their component classes (that is, categories identified at a more inclusive level) differs.

As all of the foregoing has a relevance for ethnozoology in general, one might well ask of the substance of this book, 'why only birds?'. Part of the answer is that, in order to control for length, a detailed investigation of Nage knowledge of zoological kinds, including comparison of different forms of Nage knowledge concerning animal categories, requires a concentration on a limited segment of their fauna. The choice of birds might be defended with reference to the large number and variety of ornithological species found in eastern Indonesia (see p. 6). Yet it more directly reflects the concerns of the sort of general ethnographic study in which I have mostly been engaged among Nage. One major interest of this research has been indigenous religion and cosmology, and particularly ideas and practices relating to spiritual beings (see Forth 1998a). To comparativists, it will come as no surprise that birds and other animals figure prominently in Nage ideas regarding both free spirits and the human soul. In connection with certain spiritual representations, it became essential to learn more about the natural kinds in question; yet as this investigation progressed, I encountered details of Nage folk ornithology that were intriguing in their own right, and which bore on issues of classification quite independently of any spiritual associations of the birds in question. In order to advance these other lines of enquiry, therefore, and spurred by a lifelong amateur interest in birds, I decided to pay more systematic attention to Nage ethno-ornithology.

It could fairly be said that, when I began exploring Nage knowledge of birds, my initial approach was that of a cultural relativist. However, as I started to delve into specifically ethnozoological issues, I became more impressed with the veracity of the sort of 'intellectualist' position most closely associated with Brent Berlin and his collaborators. More specifically, I came to realize that Nage do possess a 'general purpose' taxonomy of birds which is grounded in percepts and an observation of morphology and behaviour and is largely unconnected with specific cultural interests. At the same time, this has not been a total conversion; nor, with regard to the room intellectuals evidently allow for the operation of other forms of classification in a single culture, should one expect it to be.

Consistent with an interpretation of ethno-ornithological taxonomy as reflecting a universal perception – or, following Hunn, phenotypical salience mitigated by ecological salience and the size factor – Nage bird categories (or taxa) are readily accommodated to the scheme outlined by Brent Berlin (1992) without distorting the evidence of Nage language or ethnography. The fundamental unit of this scheme is the 'folk generic' taxon, also called a 'basic' category (Taylor

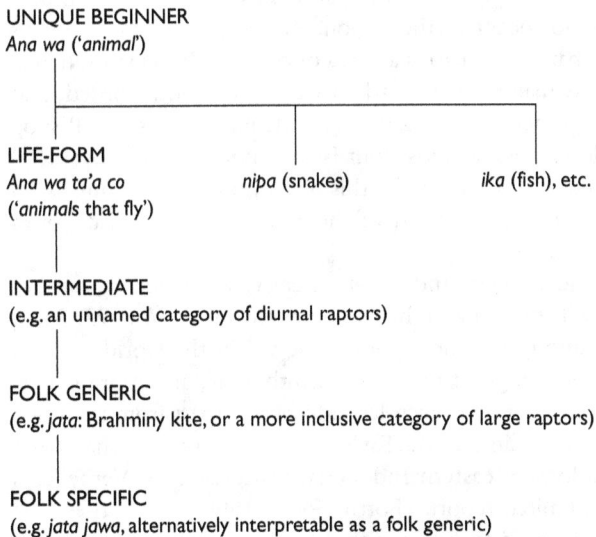

UNIQUE BEGINNER
Ana wa ('animal')

LIFE-FORM
Ana wa ta'a co   *nipa* (snakes)   *ika* (fish), etc.
('animals that fly')

INTERMEDIATE
(e.g. an unnamed category of diurnal raptors)

FOLK GENERIC
(e.g. *jata*: Brahminy kite, or a more inclusive category of large raptors)

FOLK SPECIFIC
(e.g. *jata jawa*, alternatively interpretable as a folk generic)

Figure 1.1 An outline of Nage ethnotaxonomy

1990) and corresponding to the 'basic-level' kinds or 'individuals' of cognitive psychology (see e.g. Rosch 1978; Hall 1993; Hall and Waxman 1993; Lakoff 1987; Malt 1995) and the 'basic level sortals' of logicians (Macnamara 1986: 123). Sometimes, 'generic' categories comprise two or more named or unnamed 'folk specifics' (Berlin 1992: 24), but this is relatively rare.[5]

Comprising the great majority of categories which are named in natural languages, 'folk generics' (or, simply, 'generics') are occasionally combined with a number of other generics, so as to compose 'intermediate' taxa. Intermediate taxa are often 'covert', or unnamed. Both 'intermediates' and 'generics' (the majority of which, typically, are not included in any intermediate taxon) may in turn be identified as instances of more inclusive 'life-form' taxa (a concept treated at length by C.H. Brown; see Brown 1984). Thus, the most inclusive unit of Nage ethno-ornithological taxonomy is the life-form 'bird', designated by the descriptive phrase *ana wa ta'a co* ('animals that fly'). As this expression should suggest, 'bird' and other life-form taxa (e.g., Nage *nipa*, 'snake'; *ika*, 'fish') are then classified as instances of a 'unique beginner' taxon. Although 'unique beginners' are usually unlabelled, Nage designate the category that subsumes birds and other zoological life-forms as *ana wa*, 'animal' (Forth 1995).

The zoological setting

The island of Flores belongs to Wallacea, that part of Indonesia east of Wallace's line, which runs between the islands of Bali and Lombok (see Map 1). A transitional zone wherein oriental fauna give way to Australo-Papuan, Wallacea is home to members of Australian ornithological families that are not found in western Indonesia, while accordingly many Asian birds encountered on Java, Bali, Sumatra, and Borneo do not occur in the region. Although poor in mammals (by far the largest order is bats), Wallacea is an area of considerable environmental and biological diversity. As many as 698 bird species have been recorded, and of these an extraordinary 36 per cent (or 249) are endemic (Coates and Bishop 1997: 39).[6] Although Flores possesses just four island endemics, well over 200 species have been recorded on the island. Of this total, probably as many as 60 per cent occur in Nage country, and most of these are included in categories named by Nage terms (see Table 1.1).

While birds may be the 'largest and most intensively studied' group of vertebrate animals in Nusa Tenggara and the Moluccas (Monk *et al.* 1997: 344), Wallacean birds remain 'among the most poorly known' in the world (Coates and Bishop 1997: 39). Knowledge of the ethno-ornithology, and more generally the ethnozoology, of the region is even less advanced. Apart from the work of Roy Ellen (1993a, 1993b) and P.M. Taylor (1990), very little has been published on the folk zoology of eastern Indonesia, and except for Verheijen's work (1963) and my own limited reports (Forth 1996a, 1999, 2000), there has been nothing specifically devoted to folk ornithology.[7]

The cultural and ecological setting

The Nage are an interior people traditionally practising dry field horticulture and animal husbandry supplemented by hunting and occasional freshwater fishing. Domesticated animals include water buffalo, horses, pigs, goats, dogs, and domestic fowls, recently augmented by cattle introduced during the twentieth century. The major game animals are the Timor deer (*Cervus timorensis floresiensis*) and wild pigs (*Sus celebensis*), although a variety of other wild mammals (including porcupines, *Hystrix javanica*; Flores giant rats, *Papagomys armandvillei*; and Palm civets, *Paradoxurus hermaphroditus*) are also hunted. So too are a variety of birds, as I describe below. Dry field crops include rice, maize, millet, sorghum and Job's tears, as well as various tubers, pulses, and other vegetables. For more than half a century Nage have also cultivated rice in irrigated fields, a technology first introduced in the 1930s.

Nage territory includes areas of lowland monsoon forest, montane forest, savannah woodland, and grassland (see Coates and Bishop, 1997: 24–28, for descriptions of these environments in Wallacea). Since pre-colonial times, travel to both the north and south coasts of central Flores for trade, to contract marriages, and for other purposes has also provided Nage with a limited knowledge of coastal environments and associated natural species. In local terms, the most general environmental contrast is that of *lobo* and *mala*, or 'mountain' (and more specifically, the slopes of the volcano, Ebu Lobo) and 'plain, lowlands'. Although usually described as occupying the higher, southern extremity of the 'plain', the village of Bo'a Wae is actually situated in a transitional zone. Immediately to the south one encounters a series of forested slopes forming the foothills of the great volcano, while to the north the land gradually descends as far as the banks of the river Ae Sésa (also called Ae Bha, 'white water'; see Forth 1998a). Consistent with its transitional location, the distance from Bo'a Wae to the river is roughly the same as from the village to the peak of the volcano.

At present, many large trees grow in the immediate vicinity of Bo'a Wae village; but as Nage point out, many of these (which include fruit-bearing species) were planted in the twentieth century, and formerly the landscape surrounding the village was rather more like that now encountered further to the north. Including the area about Ola Kile, a village subsidiary to Bo'a Wae, this northern region consists mostly of flat grassland and scrub (*mala witu*), interspersed by low hills and scattered single trees or copses. In pre-colonial times, the region was used by Nage of Bo'a Wae (who had probably laid claim to much of it only in the nineteenth century) for pasturing and as a hunting ground. What cultivation was practised involved turning the soil with long sharpened poles (a method called *woka*), contrasting with the swiddening (*'aca, kota 'aca*) practised in more elevated, wooded areas to the south.

Beginning in the colonial era, parts of the northern area covered in marshes and containing small ponds have been converted to irrigated rice fields. Both formerly and at present, it is in this region that one encounters most water birds. As Nage recognize, certain other kinds of birds are mostly found in the forests above (that is to the south of) Bo'a Wae village, and a few, indeed, only on the higher slopes of the Ebu Lobo volcano.

Nage uses of birds

Birds have several economic uses among Nage. Domestic fowls (*manu*) are raised in all villages. Nage regularly consume both the eggs and flesh of domestic fowls, although in the traditional order the birds are killed mainly on ritual occasions, when part of their meat is offered to spiritual beings and their entrails serve as auguries. (Domestic ducks, introduced in the colonial period, are also raised occasionally; but these birds are never used as sacrifices, nor do Nage ever inspect their organs.) Nage use the feathers of domestic fowls as adornment for head-dresses, lances, and parangs employed on ceremonial occasions. Tail plumes of cocks of various colours decorate the headgear of special ceremonial functionaries, while the costume of an accomplished hunter (and, formerly, a warrior) also includes cock feathers.

Apart from the augural use of entrails, domestic fowls have another kind of ceremonial and oracular function. In the rite *pete wole* ('tying the sheaf'), performed in the dry season prior to the annual hunt, Nage attach a sheaf of rice, just before sunrise, to the *ia*, a special wooden pillar located in major villages (see Plate 1.1). People then wait for the fowls to descend from their roosts and peck at the rice. If a cock is the first to peck, this is a sign that the crop will be poor and food will be scarce in the following year. On the other hand, if a hen pecks first then this means that the crop will be plentiful. As to why

Plate 1.1 Figures of domestic fowls, depicting the rite *pete wole*, carved in the ancestral house in Bo'a Wae

it should be a hen that provides the auspicious sign, the only explanation I recorded was that 'it is females that bear children'.

In western Keo, a culturally cognate region located directly south of Nage (see Map 2), people say that if one begins to dig a grave but cannot continue (for example, because the ground proves too hard), then a live fowl must be buried in the cavity – otherwise another human death will occur. Although I seem not to have recorded this notion in Bo'a Wae, the Keo usage appears to be related to the identification, reflected in several Nage idioms, of fowls with humans or, more particularly human souls (*mae*; see Chapter 5). Nage and Keo also inter a small live chicken, together with other young animals, in the cavity in which a new sacrificial post is planted, as do other central Flores peoples (see Molnar 2000: 186, regarding the practice in eastern Ngadha).

Using snares (*modho, modho piko kolo*), Nage capture several kinds of wild birds for local consumption.[8] Although a relatively minor source of protein, bird flesh is a valued food. Some birds intended as food are more usually killed with weapons, including bows, blow-pipes, and slings, and nowadays air rifles and catapults. Nage know no proscriptions on killing birds. Only birds belonging to a symbolic class identified with witches and malevolent spirits, and composed largely of raptorial species, should not be eaten (though they may be killed). Otherwise, Nage will consume virtually any kind of bird flesh. Approximating a class of game birds proper, birds especially favoured as food include pigeons and doves (*bopo, kolo, zawa*), quails and buttonquails (*piko, bewu*), and the junglefowl (*kata*). In fact, I was told that these were the only birds eaten in former times, the Nage diet having become more liberal in recent decades owing in part to improved means of killing (especially air rifles) and the relaxation of some earlier attitudes. According to Nage, the least edible of birds is the friarbird (*koka*), 'because it has too many bones and is very thin'; yet even friarbird flesh is consumed when there is no better fare.[9]

Nage also consume the eggs of wild birds. Again, except for those of raptors, the eggs of any wild bird may be eaten; eggs that Nage find especially tasty include those of quails and junglefowl. The exceptionally large eggs of the scrubfowl (*koko wodo*) are also enjoyed, although for a long time these seem not to have been particularly plentiful in the Bo'a Wae region. Nage say that people whose parents are still living should eat wild eggs only if the mother bird, also, is caught and killed, while only people whose parents are deceased may eat such eggs with impunity. One man, however, dismissed this as a true prohibition, cynically describing it as a means by which older people reserve wild eggs for themselves. While the eggs of raptors are normally considered inedible – if not exactly forbidden (*pie*; see Chapter 6) – spiritual practitioners known as *toa mali* may prescribe these as a cure for certain unspecified illnesses. Otherwise, I never heard of bird parts or products being regularly used as medicines. One qualified exception concerns the blood of flying foxes (*méte*), which Nage classify as birds; when drunk, the blood is claimed to cure sickness affecting the chest.

The one wild bird that Nage kill especially for its feathers is the Black-naped oriole (*leo*), whose brilliant yellow plumage is employed, like fowl's feathers, in the manufacture of ceremonial regalia. In 1991, the carcass of an oriole was purchased for this purpose at a price of 7,500 rupiah (4 or 5 American dollars at the time). Although nowadays Nage seem to exploit only the oriole as a source of feathers, a myth I recorded indicates a former ceremonial use of feathers of the Pale-headed munia (*ana peti jata*), a small bird named after the Brahminy kite (*jata*). No one I questioned had ever encountered this as an actual practice. Nevertheless, it does accord with the inclusion of the munia in a symbolic class of birds identified with malevolent spirits, insofar as the usage described in the myth pertains to decorations worn at rituals focused on the sacrifice of water buffalo, which are similarly identified with such spirits (see Chapter 4; also Forth 1998a: 31, with regard to *wuli tutu jata*).

While birds are caught for other purposes, it is not clear whether keeping birds as pets was ever a regular custom among Nage. One man even suggested that the practice may derive entirely from European influence. During the twentieth century, people have occasionally kept pet birds, but in part at least this appears to have been bound up with the development of an external market in cage birds which Nage bird-trappers came to supply. Kept birds have included cockatoos, mynahs, parrots, Spotted and Barred doves (*kolo* and *kolo dhoro*), quails, and junglefowl. Historically, cockatoos (*kea*) and mynahs (*ie wea*) were the kinds most in demand for export sale. Junglefowl (*kata*) have probably only ever been captured as prospective food; at local weekly markets, one can still occasionally purchase captured junglefowl for consumption. On the other hand, doves and quails, while among the most favoured of game birds, are described as being kept in cages solely for amusement.

A point of interest, and one indicative of the absence of a clearly defined or separate indigenous category of 'pets' among Nage, is that no special prohibitions apply to captured birds kept for amusement. There is no prohibition on killing or eating kept birds, including birds that die in captivity. Nor is there any other taboo that would set them apart from birds killed in the wild. In this regard, Nage practice differs markedly from what Valeri (2000) describes for the Huaulu of Seram who, while regularly partaking of bird flesh, are prohibited from consuming any bird that has been kept as a pet. Indeed, Huaulu even forbid the killing and eating of domestic fowls, since these are similarly raised inside human settlements and in close proximity to humans.[10]

The capture of birds to supply the cage bird trade in other parts of Indonesia and abroad is a decidedly modern development affecting the Nage relationship with avifauna. Early in the twentieth century, the bird most in demand was the Yellow-crested cockatoo (*kea*). Largely as a result, cockatoos are now extinct in the Bo'a Wae region and are very scarce elsewhere in central Flores.[11] A bird that has suffered a similar fate is the Hill mynah (*ie wea*), another species which, like the cockatoo, can be trained to talk. Until the 1970s, both kinds were mostly caught as fledglings. Nage trappers would then raise them locally before taking the mature birds to the port town of Ende, where they could fetch 8–10 thousand rupiah a head. The family of a well-known Nage bird-trapper, now an elderly invalid, described how this man would accumulate 10–15 birds before delivering them to bulk purchasers in Ende. As both cockatoos and mynahs nest in holes in trees, fledglings are captured and raised with relative ease. By contrast, birds trapped when already mature – with snares, or bird lime in the case of cockatoos – do not live long. To the present day, Nage also occasionally catch Barred doves (*kolo dhoro* or *kolo ghodho*), which in 2001 could reputedly fetch a price equivalent to several American dollars each.

In the last few years, Bimanese and Javanese traders visiting Nage territory have created a demand for the Chestnut-capped thrush (*papa*), a bird known for its varied vocal repertoire and, reputedly, an ability to perform tasks such as picking up and carrying away litter.[12] In 2000, local men were paid 100,000 rupiah (about ten American dollars) for a single bird. To facilitate the capture of the birds, traders supply local men with mist-nets which they string between two trees. With relative ease, the low-flying thrushes are then driven into the nets. As an unintended consequence of this practice, other low-flying birds are caught as well. Included among these is the Elegant pitta (*Pitta elegans*; see Plate 1.2), a bird which, despite its brilliant colours and distinctive form, was hitherto unknown to most Nage and, accordingly, lacks a local name.[13]

In July of 2001, I entered the house of a Nage friend of over fifteen years to find the desiccated remains of a paradise-flycatcher (*lawi luja*) decorating a wall. The man mentioned how, like several other local people, he had caught and endeavoured to raise these birds for sale, but without success, as they had always died after a day or two of captivity (see Chapter 7). The same applies to other species, including the aforementioned pitta and kingfishers. To trap birds legally, one is supposed to obtain a permit from the regional government.

Plate 1.2 An Elegant pitta (*Pitta elegans*) accidentally caught in a mist-net

According to local officials, these permits were issued until 1999, but not there-after; hence all bird-trapping in Nage since then has been illegal. Yet, the illegality of the practice appears to have had little effect on its incidence. In the last few years, there has reportedly been a reduction in Nage bird-trapping; but this has probably resulted more from the association of the practice with Islamic outsiders, most notably Bimanese, who have recently suffered persecution at the hands of the predominantly Catholic inhabitants of Flores. In 2000, this found especial expression in suspicions of Bimanese being the cause of a rabies epidemic that resulted in a programme of dog extermination throughout the Nage region.

Also in recent years, some Nage men have occasionally engaged in collecting for sale the nests of the Edible-nest swiftlet (*Collocalia fuciphaga*; see Table 1.1, s.v. *ebu titu*). Two places where such nests are found are caves in the valley of the river Ae Sésa and on the higher slopes of the Ebu Lobo volcano.[14] Eventually exported to fill the demands of the Chinese culinary market, the nests are sold to outsiders, including Bimanese and Makassarese. A Bo'a Wae man described the nests as being used in Chinese medicine, but others said they did not know their use. One man even suggested that the nests were actually useless, and that the whole trade was a hoax.[15]

For Nage, another practical value of birds lies in their significance as chrono-logical indicators. Thus, the calls of the Channel-billed cuckoo (*muta me*) and Common koel (*toe ou*) signal the onset of the rainy season and the start of the agricultural year. More specifically, the cuckoo's cry, which is heard somewhat before that of the koel, indicates that people should begin to prepare their fields for planting. Since the bird orders people to work, as it were, it is epithetically called *mado méze*, the 'great foreman'.[16] The call of the koel, on the other hand, means that the wet season rains are imminent, and that everyone should already be set to plant. Also indicating that rain is near is the nocturnal cry of the 'sky dog' (*lako lizu*), probably a night-heron but also equated with the bird called *kuku raku* (the White-breasted waterhen, see Table 1.1). Hearing the call usually in October, Nage say *lako lizu léghu ae uza*, 'sky dog looks after the rain'. If there is a break in the rains in December, then the nocturnal call of this bird is a sign that rain will soon fall again. Also especially vocal early in the rainy season is the White-breasted waterhen (*kuku raku*), while in a more visual mode, the appearance of large flights of swallows and swifts (*ebu titu*) bears witness to increasingly regular and heavy precipitation. A negative association of a part of the annual cycle with birds is expressed in the phrase *wula kaka ha*, 'month of the cockatoo and crow'. This refers to the time, about late February or early March when, formerly, the two sorts of birds appeared in great numbers to feast on ripening maize and Job's tears.

Although Nage recognize the Pied bushchat (*tute péla*) as the earliest bird to call each day, about half an hour before sunrise, their principal herald of the dawn is the clamorous friarbird (*koka*), whose noisy afternoon calls also predict the approach of sunset. Similar significance is attached to vocalizations of the Imperial pigeon (*zawa*), the friarbird's rival in a myth known throughout eastern Indonesia (Forth 1992; and see Chapter 8), whose call, although heard sometime after the friarbird's cry, is equally reckoned as a 'sign of daylight' (*ola pea da*, 'what points to, predicts daylight'). To mark successive stages of the day about late afternoon, Nage employ the phrases *koka na'u leza* ('friarbird orders, or reserves, the sun') and *zawa ko'a* ('Imperial pigeons alight'). The first expresses the idea that the friarbird, before sunset, arranges with the sun so that they will meet again the following morning. The second refers to the somewhat later time, at the approach of nightfall, when Imperial pigeons begin to call as they 'perch on exposed upper branches and fly between feeding and roosting places' (Coates and Bishop 1997: 326; Schmutz 1977: 32–33).

Like other Indonesians, Nage gauge the nightly passage of time with reference to the crowing of cocks (*manu*). Incidental crowing during the daylight hours, on the other hand, is situationally interpreted as an augury (see Chapter 6). In Bo'a Wae, I recorded the following expressions for the cock crows:

Manu kako tei wula	'cocks crow seeing the moon', heard before sleeping time
Manu kako wunga	'first cock crow', about 12.30–1.00 a.m.
Manu kako kisa	'middle cock crow', 2.00–3.00 a.m.
Manu kako sa pa'u	'cocks crow once', 3.00 a.m.[17]
Manu kako pa'u dhua	'cocks crow twice', 4.00–5.00 a.m.
Manu kako pa'u telu	'cocks crow thrice', 5.30 a.m. (also the time, about dawn, when 'fowls descend from their roosts', *manu pozo*)

While many birds hold a positive value for Nage, in regard to subsistence, others have an entirely negative significance. Munias and similar small birds (*ana peti*) are the most pestilential of avifauna, owing to their consumption of ripening rice. They have, moreover, become all the more so with the increasing importance of rice cultivation, as reliance on other cultigens has decreased and as rice has become a commodity as well as a staple. Doves (*kolo*) and quail (*piko*) consume newly planted rice, and both sorts of birds also feed on new beans and other pulses. But neither do as much damage to ripening crops as do munias and, besides, quails and doves are positively valued as meat. Another, relatively minor threat to wet rice seedlings are ducks (*bébe ae*). These can be kept away from paddies with noise-makers constructed of a bamboo tube which fills with water from a channel until it strikes a stone and then empties, only to be filled again.

To meet the threat of munias, Nage must continuously guard ripening rice, sometimes building special 'bird huts' (*kéka ana peti*) in the centre or at the edge of a field to facilitate their vigilance. The main threat to ripening maize, on the other hand, are the aforementioned flocks of cockatoos and crows. To keep these birds away, Nage build small, smoky fires at the edge of gardens, which indicate human presence. They also employ scarecrows to the same effect.

Large flocks of crows from the north are also associated with seasonal illness among large livestock; but in this context it is the spirits which the birds are believed to manifest, rather than the birds themselves, that threaten Nage material well-being (Chapter 5).

As noted, birds of prey have a negative economic significance as chicken thieves. Nage regard nearly all diurnal raptors (*kua, jata, iki, sizo,* and *bele teka*) as killers of domestic fowls. (The small raptor called *sizo awu*, by contrast, is said to subsist entirely on large insects.) Some Nage also claim that owls (*po*), as well as the night hunter called *je* (see Chapter 7), will seize fowls. Large-billed crows (*ha*), on the other hand, are described as stealing chicken eggs. The relevance of all these recognized or attributed behaviours for Nage classification and symbolism is discussed in later chapters.

Two sorts of avifauna, the friarbird (*koka*) and the sunbird (*tiwe*), will drink arenga palm juice as it emerges from palm stalks cut by tappers. But neither bird consumes so much as to be a serious economic threat. For Nage, the true palm juice thieves are flying foxes (*méte*) and the smaller bats called *gébu*. Both steal larger quantities of juice from containers suspended below palm stalks, as Nage know from occasionally finding drowned bats floating inside the containers. Yet while such chiropterous consumption may be counted as a loss of produce – especially when the bats' appetites cause the juice containers to fall and spill all their contents – Nage, who are quite fond of bat flesh in any case, reckon specimens soaked in palm juice to be among the very tastiest![18]

Factors affecting bird populations

As indicated, trapping birds for sale to outsiders is an obvious cause of reduction in certain species. Another factor, which is affecting a much larger variety of birds, is the air rifle, a modern weapon used not only in hunting but sometimes also in mindless killing. Reduction of habitat, mainly through deforestation connected with agricultural expansion and the cutting of trees for lumber, is a further cause of population decline. In this, another item of modern technology, the chainsaw, has played a major role in the last ten to fifteen years.

Yet another factor affecting some bird populations is the introduction of motor vehicles and roads. A few decades ago, I was told, after the first vehicles were introduced, nightjars (*leba*) were often seen near roads at night, when their eyes would show up in vehicle headlights. Nowadays, however, these nocturnal birds are no longer so common near roadways (see further pp. 130–31). A new hazard for Nage birds, and particularly the Emerald ground-dove (*muke*), are window panes: in Bo'a Wae, a few houses have quite recently been fitted with panes, and the low-flying doves, which are still quite numerous near habitations, fly into these. In 2001, one man told me how seven of the birds had been killed after colliding with window glass he had installed less than a year previously.

Among other birds that have recently become scarce, Nage of Bo'a Wae mention the Imperial pigeon (*zawa*), Channel-billed cuckoo (*muta me*), and dollarbird (*kaka daza*). Interestingly, the first two are birds whose cries mark daily or seasonal change; hence it is understandable that their decrease would be especially registered.[19] The previously mentioned paradise-flycatcher (*lawi luja*) is also said to be less common than formerly, as is the Bare-throated whistler (*kete dhéngi*), in higher regions where the bird was formerly encountered in greater numbers. Quite probably, the extraordinarily long tail of the flycatcher and the remarkable vocalizations of the whistler account for their increasing scarcity being noticed by Nage.[20]

In contrast, Nage describe munias and other finches that feed on rice crops as nowadays being more rather than less common. This they attribute, probably correctly, to new varieties of irrigated rice which they began cultivating in the 1970s, and which produce two or three harvests a year. As Nage explained to me, formerly, when everyone planted and harvested just once a year, they all did so about the same time. Thus, after the harvest, there was nothing left for the munias to eat, so the birds would disappear. Nowadays, when there is always ripening rice available, the birds are present continuously. Also, with the development of irrigation and an expanded production of rice, more land is planted with rice than just a few decades ago.

The introduction and expansion of irrigated fields, especially in the vicinity of Ola Kile, some 5–10 kilometres north of Bo'a Wae village, might be thought to have increased habitats suitable for water birds. Yet Nage claim that, formerly as well, these birds were present in this region, near rivers, streams, ponds, and marshes. Somewhat ironically, herons named *gako tasi* were, according to local reports, more common in Gako – an area several kilometres to the west of Bo'a Wae – before, rather than after, the development of wet-rice cultivation there. As Nage recognize, the name 'Gako' may even refer to the large water birds. The herons are said to have been numerous in this place until the 1960s, when many were shot and consumed; hence they are no longer often seen. Previously, Gako was a marshy area covered in reeds, all of which were cut down to make way for paddy fields.

At present, Nage quite regularly complain about the loss, or potential loss, of avifauna from bird-trapping, habitat reduction, and over-hunting. Although this attitude seems genuine enough, it finds no definite basis in local culture – in spiritual ideas, for example – and may reflect the influence, directly or indirectly, of international or national campaigns for the preservation of wildlife (such as the BirdLife International-Indonesia Programme; see Monk *et al.* 1997). In regard to traditional values, moreover, the drastic reduction of one species, the cockatoo, has in one respect proved beneficial to Nage. For these birds no longer appear in great numbers, as they once did, to feed upon fields of ripening maize. On the other hand, Nage appear to recognize the aesthetic value of the pure white plumage and brilliant yellow crest of the cockatoo, just as they appreciate the splendid tones of the Bare-throated whistler (*kete dhéngi*), the extraordinary tail feathers of the paradise-flycatcher (*lawi luja*), and the brightly coloured plumage of a variety of other birds.

Organization of the volume

Since specific issues of method largely concern classification, and then more particularly ethnotaxonomy, methodology is treated at the beginning of the next chapter. Matters of ethnotaxonomy are further dealt with in Chapter 3. The next three chapters (4, 5, and 6) are all devoted to Nage symbolic thought and practice regarding birds. Chapter 7, which considers the possible empirical and other origins of a variety of Nage ideas, partly continues this theme, but also bears upon the topic of ethno-ornithological classification. While a concern with language permeates this book, Chapter 8 deals specifically with the use of bird categories in Nage figurative discourse. As such, it provides an introduction to the appearance of birds in Nage myth. Building on generalizations established earlier, Chapter 9 provides a detailed exploration of a particular mythical tradition and extends the discussion of bird symbolism and classification. Chapter 10 then summarizes the entire discussion and considers possible directions for comparative study of eastern Indonesian ethno-ornithology.

Table 1.1 Nage bird names (Bo'a Wae dialect)

The following is a list of names rather than distinct, named taxa; thus in some instances, two names refer to the same bird categories. Where there are two variants of a name, the more common is listed first. This information draws on Forth (1996a, 1999), and on field research conducted by the author in 2001. Identifications given here supersede those included in Forth (1996a, 1999). The key below employs a modified version of the notation used by Verheijen (1963). Orthographic conventions are described in the Preface.

Key:

C&B	Coates and Bishop (1997)
ON	Wholly onomatopoeic name
On	Binary name where the first component is onomatopoeic
oN	Binary name where the second component is onomatopoeic
V	Name describing a visible or other perceptible feature (morphological, behavioural, or environmental) of the bird designated. Includes names describing vocalizations (as distinct from onomatopoeia)
v	Binary name, part of which describes a visible or other perceptible feature. The number 1 or 2 after the /v/ indicates whether this concerns the first or second component
NA	Name, no part of which is analysable (i.e. as a reference to a perceptible feature or as an onomatopoeia)

1   *ana go.* Identification uncertain, but local descriptions suggest the Singing bushlark (Australasian Bushlark, C&B), *Mirafra javanica* or a pipit (*Anthus gustavi*, the Pechora pipit, or *A. novaeseelandiae*, Richard's pipit). *Go*, 'gong', appears not to be relevant to the bird name. (NA)

2   *ana peti jata* or *peti jata*, Pale-headed munia, *Lonchura pallida*. Translatable as 'Brahminy kite munia', the name refers to the similarity of plumage between this bird and the Brahminy kite (*jata*). (v2)

3   *awe uza.* Synonymous with the more common *ebu titu* (swallows, swifts; see below). The term means 'summoner of rain' (cf. Nage *ana uza* and Keo *ana ura*, 'rain creature') and refers to the appearance of the birds in large numbers before a fall of rain.[1] (V)

4   *bama* or *bama cea*, Russet-capped tesia, *Tesia everetti*. *Cea* reproduces the bird's characteristic call. (oN)

5   *bébe ae*, wild ducks, *Anas* and *Dendrocygna*. Also applied to cormorants (*Phalacrocorax* spp.) occasionally encountered by Nage in coastal areas. *Ae* is 'water'. (v2)

6   *bele teka*, a falcon. Probably the Peregrine falcon, *Falco peregrinus*, or the Australian hobby, *Falco longipennis*. The name means 'sharp wing'. (V)

7   *bewu*, buttonquail, *Turnix* spp. Two species of *Turnix* occur on Flores: *T. maculosa*, the Red-backed buttonquail, and *T. suscitator powelli*, the Barred buttonquail. (NA)

8   *bi* or *ana bi*, Red-cheeked parrot, *Geoffroyus geoffroyi*. The identification is based on informants' descriptions (2001) and Verheijen's listing (n.d.). Confined to higher elevations and inhabiting the tops of tall trees, the bird is rarely seen by Nage of Bo'a Wae. (NA)

9   *bio*, one or more species of *Lonchura* and other Estrildine finches (cf. *ana peti jata* and *naka bo*). In view of local descriptions of *bio* as a small red bird, the term probably includes the Red avadavat, *Amandava amandava*. (NA)

10   *bopo* or *bopo soi*, one or more kinds of fruit-doves (*Ptilinopus* spp.) and the Flores green pigeon (*Treron floris*). *Soi* is locally explained as the name of a tuber with bright yellow flesh. The plumage of all Flores species of *Ptilinopus* includes prominent yellow parts. A few people distinguished between *bopo soi* and a larger kind named simply *bopo* or *bopo méze* ('large *bopo*'). This may specify *T. floris*, which is indeed significantly larger than two of the three *Ptilinopus* species that occur on Flores (*P. melanospila*, *P. regina*, and *P. cinctus*; the last is slightly larger than the *Treron* species). (v2)

11   *céce*, Wallacean drongo, *Dicrurus densus*. (The sub-species that occurs on Flores is *D. h. bimaensis*.) Nage recognize the name as resembling one of the bird's vocalizations. (ON)

12   *ceka*, fantail, *Rhipidura* sp. Two fantails occur on Flores, the Brown-capped fantail, *R. diluta diluta*, and Rufous species *R. rufifrons semicollaris*. In view of the locally recognized onomatopoeic character of the Nage name (/c/ corresponds to English /ch/ while /e/ represents the schwa), the more likely reference is the Brown-capped fantail, whose voice includes sounds which C&B reproduce as 'tchk' and 'chingk'. (ON)

13   *cici ko'i*, Tree sparrow, *Passer montanus*. According to C&B, the species first appeared on Flores in 1954. Although not widely known, the name may derive from a wholly or partly onomatopoeic term describing sounds of a person drinking from a spout, which the bird's chattering is thought to resemble. *Ko'i* may be understood in the sense of 'to scratch or peck open', thus possibly (but not certainly) referring to a behaviour. (On)

14   *cio woza*, cuckoo-shrike, more particularly *Coracina novaehollandiae*, the Large or Black-faced cuckoo-shrike. Other species of *Coracina* present on Flores include the Wallacean cuckoo-shrike (*C. personata*) and the generally uncommon Pale-shouldered cicadabird (*C. dohertyi*, C&B). However, only *C. novaehollandiae* exhibits the 'strongly undulating flight' (C&B), which for Nage is the bird's most characteristic feature. *Cio* refers specifically to a rising and descending 'ciooo-ciooo', also locally rendered as 'chee-upp'. One man claimed that *woza*, a word otherwise meaning 'foam, froth', referred to the bird's greyish plumage, but since *woza* is not a usual colour term, this remains uncertain.[2] (On)

15   *detu* or *detu dalu*, Sunda pygmy woodpecker, *Dendrocopos moluccensis* (formerly *Picoides moluccensis*). *Detu*, 'to tap, rap', obviously refers to a characteristic behaviour; *dalu* is a kind of tree (perhaps *Albizia procera*) said to be favoured by the bird. (V)

16   *deza kela*. Unidentified. The name is known only to a minority of Nage who describe it as a small bird whose poignant song manifests souls of the dead in need. (One man's statement that most, but not all, birds so named lack tails suggests that more than one species may be involved. At the same time, the name is not synonymous with *bama*, a bird that Nage describe as 'tailless'.) *Deza kela*, 'enters among giant reeds', refers to the bird's reputed habit of disappearing into thick vegetation. (V)

17   *ebu titu*, swallows, *Hirundinidae*, and swifts, *Apodidae*. Birds thus named are regularly described as inhabiting caves and making nests of saliva which are in demand by foreign traders. This suggests *Collocalia fuciphaga*, the Edible-nest swiftlet, as a focus of the category. *Ebu*, 'grandparent, ancestor', does not definitely motivate the name, although one commentator – imaginatively but probably idiosyncratically – linked it with the birds' living in caves that are also inhabited by spirits (*nitu*). *Titu*, replicating a twittering sound, is probably onomatopoeic in origin but is not locally recognized as such.[3] (NA)

18   *fega*, kingfisher. The name is invariably described as designating a red-billed bird and refers equally to *Halcyon capensis*, the Stork-billed kingfisher, and *Caridonax fulgidus*, the White-rumped kingfisher. The term, however, can also be applied to *Halcyon chloris* which, in contrast to the other two species, lacks a red bill. Occasionally, Nage distinguish *Caridonax* and *H. capensis* as *fega wolo* and *fega ae*, 'hill *fega*' and 'water *fega*'. This accords both with recognized differences of diet and the fact that the former is found in more elevated, forested areas (including places above Bo'a Wae) whereas the latter is typically encountered at lower elevations, near rivers and streams. (NA)

19   *feni*, parrot. More commonly applied to *Tanygnathus megalorhynchos*, the Great-billed parrot, the term also refers to the smaller and less common Rainbow lorikeet, *Trichoglossus haematodus*. As Nage correctly observe, *Trichoglossus* has red eyes, and hence can be distinguished as *feni mata to*. *Tanygnathus* is then described as *feni mata mite* ('black-eyed *feni*). In regard to its association with higher elevations, the smaller species is further distinguished as *feni lobo* (*lobo*, 'summit', also a specific reference to the volcano Ebu Lobo). (NA)

20   *gako tasi*. One or more large black and white herons, probably including the White-faced heron (*Egretta novaehollandiae*) and Purple heron (*Ardea purpurea*). As a modifier, *tasi* can be understood as 'sea' (cf. *angi tasi*, 'wind from the sea'; Malay/Indonesian (Bahasa Indonesia) *tasik*, eastern Sumbanese *tahiku, tehiku*, 'sea'), thus indicating an association with coastal regions. (v2)

21   *ha*, Large-billed crow, *Corvus macrorhynchos*. (ON)

22   *héga hea*, Flores crow, *Corvus florensis* (a Flores endemic). Although a few people described *hea* as onomatopoeic, the majority thought it was not. Indeed, the bird's characteristic vocalization is rendered as *kela kela*. (According to Verheijen, n.d., *kela* is a common form of the bird's name in western Flores.) On the other hand, Verheijen (1963) lists the Manggarai names for this bird, *léa* and *éa* (in *kaka-éa*), as onomatopoeic. Arndt describes in the same way the Ngadha variant he transcribes as *xéga réca* (1954: 448). One man explained *héga* as a form of *hega*, which he glossed as 'to feel frightened'. Although this accords with the ominous portent of the bird's call, the interpretation is not confirmed. (NA)

23 *ie wea* or *io wea*, Hill mynah, *Gracula religiosa*. *Wea* ('gold, golden pendant') refers to the bird's bright yellow lappets. *Ie* denotes a whining or whinnying sound, and refers to a vocalization of the bird. So too does the variant *io*, which corresponds to the frequent, whistled and slightly nasal sound recorded by C&B as 'tchi-ong'. (On, v2)

24 *iki* or *iki titi*, Moluccan kestrel, *Falco moluccensis*. Nage describe both *iki* and *titi* as onomatopoeic. (ON)

25 *'iri ae* or *riri ae*, another name for the wagtail (see *wagha lowo*); *ae* is 'water'. (v2)

26 *jata*, Brahminy kite, *Haliastur indus*. *Jata* also means 'to turn, wind; spinning wheel' and describes the bird's circling flight. In Bo'a Wae, one occasionally hears the dialectal names *ulu bha* ('white head') and *jata ulu bha*. (V)

27 *jata jawa*, one or more large, high-flying diurnal raptors with speckled or variegated (*ke'o*) plumage. The term may be applied to larger hawks such as the Brown or Variable goshawk, *Accipiter fasciatus* or *A. novaehollandiae* (but see *sizo* below). *Jawa* means 'Javanese, foreign', and 'soy bean'. As a modifier of *jata*, the term may be understood in the more specific sense of 'strange, unusual', contrasting the bird with the more common and differently coloured Brahminy kite (*jata*). (V?)

28 *je*, a nocturnal or diurnal raptor. Most local descriptions of the bird's appearance match the Brown hawk-owl, *Ninox scutulata* (sub-species *japonica*). Others suggest a small Falconiforme. Although regularly described by Nage, behaviours attributed to the *je* do not, however, correspond to those of any species reported in the ornithological literature. Nage say the bird will alight on branches near roosting hens, imitate the piping of a chick, and steal up on their unsuspecting young. The voice of the Australian hobby (*Falco longipennis*), described by C&B as a 'rather weak, high pitched, rapid *ki-ki-ki-ki*', is somewhat reminiscent of Nage accounts of the vocalization; the hobby is moreover reported as preying mainly on birds and often hunting at dusk (C&B: 259). It is from *je*, 'to advance slowly toward, to creep up on', that the Nage category takes its name. (V)

29 *kaka daza*, Common dollarbird, *Eurystomus orientalis*. The first part of the name reproduces the bird's call, locally rendered as *ka ka ka ka*. It is not certain whether *daza*, possibly related to words meaning 'bright, light', refers to the round, silvery or light-blue wing patches that give the bird its English name.[4] Nage themselves seem not to recognize any such meaning. (On)

30 *kata*, Green junglefowl, *Gallus varius*. (NA)

31 *kea* or *kaka kea*, Yellow-crested cockatoo, *Cacatua sulphurea*. Nage associate the name with *kea* in the sense of 'to shout, scream, call out', which indeed describes the bird's strident cry. In view of cognates of *kea* employed for the cockatoo in other languages of Flores (e.g., *kéka*, however, the name is unlikely to be a true onomatopoeia (cf. Verheijen 1963: 687). Similar uncertainty surrounds the optional element *kaka*, a possible reflex of a protoform occurring in other eastern Indonesian languages (see Indonesian *kakatua*, from Ambonese). When it is compounded with *ha*, denoting the Large-billed crow, the name of the cockatoo becomes reduced to *kaka* (see *kaka ha*, p. 52). As Nage remark, some specimens of *Cacatua sulphurea* have red eyes. Although especially valued by bird-catchers, these are not regarded as a separate kind. (NA)

32 *kete dhéngi*, Bare-throated whistler, *Pachycephala nudigula*. The species is endemic to Flores and Sumbawa; the sub-species endemic to Flores in *P.n. nudigula*. Like the Latin *nudigula*, the English name refers to a bare patch which expands during vocalization, a feature of this rarely seen highland bird of which Nage seem unaware. The Nage name comprises *kete*, 'cool, cold', and *dhéngi*, glossed in this context as 'lamenting, sorrowful' or 'pathetic, pitiful'. Nage also describe the second element as corresponding to one of the birds calls, alternatively reproduced as *dhéng dhéng*. (A few informants thought the entire name might be onomatopoeic, but this could reflect influence from a popular song in which the bird is referred to as *ana kete dhéngi dhéngi*.) While *kete* alludes to the high, relatively cool altitudes where the bird is encountered, the name is also illuminated by a mythological association of the species. (v1, oN)

33 *koa ka*, a night bird, probably the same species as *héga hea*; but the term may sometimes be applied to a cry of the Common koel (*toe ou*). The name replicates a nocturnal vocalization. (ON)

34 *koka*, Helmeted friarbird, *Philemon buceroides*. (ON)

35 *koko wodo* or *wodo*, Orange-footed scrubfowl (Reinwardt's scrubfowl), *Megapodius reinwardt*. *Koko* is described as onomatopoeic. *Wodo* in the sense of 'to perch, sit like a domestic fowl' is probably a homonym. (On)

36   *kolo* or *kolo méze*, Spotted dove (Spotted turtle-dove), *Streptopelia chinensis. Méze* is 'big'. (v2)

37   *kolo dasi*, Domestic pigeon (Rock pigeon), *Columba livia.* An introduced species. (NA)

38   *kolo dhoro* (or *kolo dhuru*) or *kolo ghodho*, Barred dove, *Geopelia maugei. Dhoro* is onomatopoeic. *Ghodho* refers to the bird's manner of walking with its head lowered.[5] (oN in regard to *dhoro*, v2 in regard to *ghodho*)

39   *kua* or *kua méze*, eagle. Often described as denoting a crested raptor. Possible applications include the Changeable hawk-eagle (*Spizaetus cirrhatus*), Bonelli's eagle (*Hieraaetus fasciatus*), and the Short-toed eagle (*Circaetus gallicus*). Being almost exclusively coastal, the White-bellied sea-eagle (*Haliaeetus leucogaster*) is probably rarely if ever seen by the Nage of Bo'a Wae. *Méze*, 'big', is an optional component of the name. (v2)

40   *kuku raku*, White-breasted waterhen, *Amaurornis phoenicurus.* The onomatopoeic name corresponds most closely to vocalizations described for *Amaurornis* both by Nage and western ornithologists, but it may further be applied to other water birds, such as the watercock, *Gallicrex cinerea*, and (following information from the western Nage district of Rowa) even the Purple swamphen, *Porphyrio porphyrio*. According to Verheijen (n.d.), in several parts of central Flores, including Bo'a Wae, the term refers to a Night heron (*Nycticorax* sp.; see *lako lizu*, below). (ON)

41   *lako lizu*. Nage identify this term primarily as the name of the Oriental mole cricket (*Gryllotalpa orientalis*). In accordance with its literal meaning, 'sky dog', the term also refers to an apparently much larger creature known only from its nocturnal vocalization, which resembles a baying dog and is heard only during the wet season. Although the creature is never seen, some Nage infer that it is a bird (rather than an insect), and several people identified it specifically as the bird otherwise called *kuku raku*. Verheijen (n.d.) lists both *lako lizu* and *kuku raku* as Bo'a Wae terms for a night-heron (*Nycticorax* sp.). On Flores, this is most likely to be *Nycticorax caledonicus*, the Rufous night-heron, whose vocalization C&B describe as 'a single loud kyok or kwok, given in flight'. Although the name refers to a vocal feature, and thus a kind of perceptible behaviour, it is obviously not onomatopoeic. (V)

42   *lawi luja*, Asian paradise-flycatcher, *Terpsiphone paradisi*. According to Schmutz (1977: 80), the very similar Manggarai (western Flores) variant of the name, *lawelujang*, comprises a word meaning 'thread, string' (*lawe*) and the name of a climbing plant with long, hairlike tendrils (*lujang*), both referring to the bird's extraordinarily long tail. Nage do not, however, interpret the term in this way. Variants of the name appear in other languages of central and western Flores. In Nage, *luja* denotes a kind of worm occurring in large swarms, but this is not obviously relevant to the name of the bird. (NA)

43   *leba*, Savannah nightjar, *Caprimulgus affinis*. The other species of *Caprimulgus* present on Flores, *C. macrurus*, the Large-tailed Nightjar, appears not to be present in the Bo'a Wae region. If *leba* in the sense of 'to beat, thrash; to shake out (a mat or damp cloth), crack (a whip, length of rope)' is relevant to the bird's name, it conceivably refers to the general nightjar habit of communicating by clapping the wings together (Cameron and Harrison 1978: 138), a behaviour of which at least one Nage appeared to be aware. (V?)

44   *leo* or *leo te'a* or *leo wea*, Black-naped oriole, *Oriolus chinensis. Leo* in the sense of 'to go, travel, wander' is unlikely to be related to the bird's name which, although not recognized as such by Nage, is probably onomatopoeic. *Te'a*, 'ripe', also refers to the yellowish colour of ripe fruit and hence to the bird's plumage. *Wea*, 'gold', also refers to the plumage. (v2)

45   *manu*, Domestic fowl, *Gallus gallus*. (NA)

46   *manu ghebhe*. Unidentified. Known to just two Nage, whose descriptions suggested a pipit (*Anthus* sp.; see *ana go*). Others thought the name might refer to the Orange-footed scrubfowl (see *koko wodo*). The name means 'hidden, hiding, disappearing fowl', referring to an attributed behaviour. (v2)

47   *manu ke'o*, a fantastic creature with a snake's body and cock's head. The name translates as 'speckled fowl'. (v2)

48   *manu mesi*. Identification uncertain. Meaning 'sea fowl', the term is often described as a poetic usage without any particular avifaunal denotatum or as a general reference to coastal birds that irregularly occur near inland waters. If applied to empirical birds, the term is likely to refer to herons, bitterns, or other large wading birds. (Verheijen, n.d., lists the term as an eastern Nage

name for egrets or the Woolly-necked stork, *Ciconia episcopus*.) In Keo, *manu mesi* denotes sand-pipers and similar shorebirds. (v2)

49   *manu miu*. Spoken of by some Nage as a particular, although unknown, kind of night bird that is never seen. Others describe it as a nocturnal sound produced by various birds and other animals. The sound resembles *miu*, 'you (second person plural pronoun)'. (oN)

50   *manu wodu*. Unidentified and probably imaginary. Described as a forest bird that resembles a domestic fowl (*manu*), particularly a hen, with dark plumage, and with a crest instead of a cox-comb. The modifier *wodu* apparently derives from *odu*, 'crest, crested'. (v2)

51   *mata to*. A kind of rail or crake that inhabits forest as well as watery areas. The name means 'red eyes'. Local descriptions consistently indicate the Red-legged crake, *Rallina fasciata*. (V)

52   *mele witu*. Informants' descriptions strongly suggest *Cisticola* spp. The name, 'disappears into long grass, undergrowth', refers to a characteristic behaviour. The bird is said to terminate its flight by diving into long grass and not appearing again. The particular reference may be to the song-flight of the male of *Cisticola juncidis* (*fuscicapilla*), the Zitting cisticola (C&B: 439). Hails and Jarvis (1987: 137) similarly describe this bird as diving into long grass when danger threatens. The other member of the genus found on Flores is *C. exilis lineocapilla*, the Golden-headed cisticola. (V)

53   *muke*, Emerald ground-dove, *Chalcophaps indica*. (NA)

54   *mu ki* or *mulu ki*, Blue-breasted quail, *Coturnix chinensis*. The bird is locally recognized by its red underparts and small size relative to other quails and buttonquails. The more common variant of the name is a contraction of the longer form, *mulu ki*. Comprising *mulu*, 'to assemble', and *ki*, '*Imperata* grass, grassland', the name refers to the bird's habitat. (V)

55   *muta me*, Channel-billed cuckoo, *Scythrops novaehollandiae*, but possibly applied also to the Common koel, *Eudynamys scolopacea* (see *toe ou*, below).[6] Both are large cuckoos that parasitize crows. The name comprises *muta*, 'to vomit', and *me*, 'to bleat (of a goat), retching sound', and describes the bird's call, particularly when it invades crows' nests and is driven away by reluctant hosts. (V)

56   *naka bo* or *ana naka bo*, one or more kinds of munia (*Lonchura*). The commonest referent appears to be *Lonchura punctulata*, the Scaly-breasted munia; another possibility is the Black-faced munia, *L. molucca*. The name means 'steals from granaries'. (V)

57   *o ae*, herons and egrets (*Ardea*; family Ardeidae), probably including the Great-billed heron, *A. sumatrana*. *Ae* is 'water'. The taxon is not conceived to include *gako tasi* (see above). (v2)

58   *o ae bha*, 'white *o ae*', predominantly or entirely white members of the Ardeidae, particularly egrets. Also described as smaller than birds simply named *oe ae*. Corresponding Flores species include the Great egret (*Egretta alba*), Little egret (*E. garzetta*), Pacific reef-egret (*E. sacra*), and the Cattle egret (*Bubulcus ibis*). (v2, in respect of both *ae* and *bha*)

59   '*owa*, Cuckoo-dove, *Macropygia* spp. Species present on Flores include *Macropygia ruficeps* (the Little cuckoo-dove), *M. unchall*, and *M. emiliana*. Although the name is not locally regarded as ono-matopoeic, it is nevertheless interesting that C&B reproduce the cries of *M. unchall*, the Barred Cuckoo-dove, as including 'whoo-ooo' and 'u-wa', which rather resemble '*owa*. (NA)

60   *papa* or *ana papa*, Chestnut-capped thrush, *Zoothera interpres*. The name is attributed to one of its calls, more elaborately rendered as *poa pa, po apa*.[7] (ON)

61   *piko*, Brown quail, *Coturnix ypsilophora*. Verheijen (n.d.) gives the Bo'a Wae term for this bird as *piko tawu*, a name he also lists for the Wogo dialect of Ngadha. Although a couple of Nage claimed to have heard the term, most people I questioned were unfamiliar with it. (NA)

62   *piko du'a*. An unidentified bird known only by its nocturnal call, usually described as a high-pitched and rapid series of piping sounds heard near villages. Despite the name, Nage do not definitely regard the bird as a variety of 'quail' (*piko*). *Du'a* means 'highland, interior, hinterland'. (v2)

63   *po*, owls, including scops-owls (*Otus*, spp.) and Barn owls (*Tyto* spp.). More elaborate terms for owls, which do not however distinguish kinds or varieties, are *po koba*, *po kua*, and *po tadu*. The modifiers mean respectively 'vine', 'eagle (or eagle-like)', and 'horn(ed)'. Members of the genus *Otus* recorded on Flores are the Moluccan scops-owl (*Otus magicus albiventris*), Wallace's scops-owl (*O. silvicola*, which is endemic to Flores and Sumbawa), and the Flores scops-owl (*O. alfredi*, a Flores endemic). The Tytonidae are represented by two species, the Barn owl (*Tyto alba javanica*) and the Eastern grass owl (*T. longimembris*). (ON)

64   sizo, a relatively small hawk or goshawk, probably of the genus *Accipiter*. Species present on Flores include the Chinese goshawk (*A. soloensis*), Brown goshawk (*A. fasciatus*), Variable goshawk (*A. novae-hollandiae*), and Japanese goshawk (*A. gularis*). Referring to a characteristic behaviour of the bird, *sizo* means 'to sweep down on and seize'. (V)

65   *sizo awu*, a diurnal raptor, about the size of the Moluccan kestrel (see *iki*) and smaller than the kind simply named as *sizo*. The modifier, *awu*, 'earth, soil', is explained as referring either to the bird's colour or an association with the ground. Local descriptions mostly suggest the Black-winged kite, *Elanus caeruleus*, but some details, including suggestions that the bird is insectivorous, contradict this identification. (V)

66   *tiwe* or *tiwe te'a*, sunbird. The most common referent appears to be the Olive-backed sunbird, *Nectarinia jugularis*. The term may also be applied to other sunbirds and to small honey-eaters (*Lichmera* spp.). *Te'a* denotes a yellowish colour (see *leo te'a*, above). (v2)

67   *toe ou* or *to ou*, *ko ou*, Common koel, *Eudynamys scolopacea*. The name replicates its call. (ON)

68   *toto*, Lesser coucal, *Centropus bengalensis*. The name is based on a particular vocalization, locally imitated as *to to toto*. Nage alternatively reproduce the call as *tum, tum* or *gum, gum*. Another vocal-ization is rendered as *tuku koa*. (ON)

69   *tute péla*, Pied bushchat, *Saxicola caprata*. No local exegesis was obtained for either *tute* or *péla*. *Péla* might be understood in the sense of 'to interrupt' or 'to place crosswise', in which case it could conceivably refer to the bird's significance as a hunting omen. The word can also mean 'to transgress (sexually)'. (NA)

70   *wagha lowo*, wagtail, *Motacilla* spp.; the Yellow wagtail (*M. flava*) or Grey Wagtail (*M. cinerea*). *Wagha* describes the typical vertical movement of the bird's tail; *lowo* is 'river, stream'. Another variant is *weghu wadho*, the first component of which is synonymous with *wagha*. (The meaning of *wadho* is not clear.)[8] (V)

71   *wi*, Buff-banded rail, *Gallirallus philippensis*, and similar members of the Rallidae (rails and crakes). Some Nage also apply the name to the Common moorhen, *Gallinula chloropus*.[9] (NA)

72   *witu tui*. Identification uncertain. Some descriptions of the bird's behaviour and appearance sug-gest the Great tit, *Parus major*. However, Nage imitations of the call replicated in the onomatopoeic name, as well as other descriptions, suggest a somewhat larger bird. The vocalization and its local imitation are quite similar to a whistled 'wee-te hea' attributed by C&B to *Pitta elegans maria*, a sub-species of the Elegant pitta found in southern Flores. One local expert, moreover, identified a live specimen of *Pitta elegans* as *witu tui*; but no one else questioned about the name of the specimen, or the species, made this identification.[10]

73   *wole wa*, a diurnal raptor. Most descriptions suggest a large raptor, and some Nage regard the term as an alternative name for *jata jawa* (see above). Meaning 'plays with (in the) wind', however, *wole wa* refers to the bird's habit of hovering motionless. Together with informants' descriptions of the plumage as white or light in colour, this is more suggestive of the smaller Black-winged kite, *Elanus caeruleus*. Verheijen (n.d.) appears to associate a dialectal form of the name with *Elanus*. (V)

74   *zawa*, Green imperial pigeon, *Ducula aenea*. The commonest Imperial pigeon in lowlands and foothills, the Flores sub-species is *D. a. polia*. Otherwise understood as a collective compound, *bopo zawa* is also interepreted as a specific reference to this bird. (NA)

75   *zawa ngongo*. A Columbiforme and probably a member of the *Ducula*, but otherwise unidentified. The name means 'mute, silent *zawa*'. Local descriptions suggest another species of *Ducula*, especially *D. lacernulata*, the Dark-backed imperial pigeon. But while the bird is described as larger than the *zawa*, the latter species does not differ significantly in size from *D. aenea*. Apparently the largest member of the genus present on Flores is *D. rosacea*, the Pink-headed imperial pigeon. An alternative name is *zawa hingo*, 'deaf *zawa*'. (v2)

76   *zeghi*, *jeghi* or *ceghi*, Blue-tailed bee-eater, *Merops superciliosus* (= *M. philippinus*). The name repro-duces the call described by C&B as 'a liquid chrrrip' (p. 383). (Contrary to my earlier impression (Forth 1996a), *jeghi* now seems a more common pronounciation in Bo'a Wae than does *zeghi*.) *M. superciliosus* is the only bee-eater that breeds on Flores. A migrant species to which the term could also be applied is *M. ornatus*, the Rainbow bee-eater, but since Nage describe the bird nesting in earthen burrows the principal referent is apparently *M. superciliosus*. (ON)

Addendum: bats

77   *gébu*, a medium-sized bat. (NA)

78   *'ighu*, a small bat. (NA)

79   *méte*, Fruit bat, flying fox (*Pteropus* spp., *Dobsonia* spp.). Nage distinguish two varieties: a larger and darker sort called *méte ha* (crow *méte*) and a smaller, shorter-winged sort, with light-coloured patches of fur, named *méte wula* (moon *méte*) or *méte uwa* (*uwa*, 'grey or white-haired'). (NA)

Notes

1   The name *ana uza* was recorded just once in Bo'a Wae. Only one person described *awe uza* as referring to a bird different from *ebu titu*, and this was claimed to differ only by being somewhat larger.

2   The idea that *woza* refers to a colour may reflect confusion with *wuza*, denoting a pale grey. Two regular informants from the village of Ola Kile, some 6 kilometres to the north of Bo'a Wae, gave the cuckoo-shrike's name as *mole sio*, a term Verheijen (n.d.) also records for dialects of eastern Nage and Ende. *Sio* is a dialectal variant of *cio*.

3   An idiolectal variant of the name, *ebu uza*, recorded just once, is apparently influenced by the synonymous *awe uza* or *ana uza*.

4   For Ngadha, Arndt lists *kaka daza* as a bird name (1961, s.v. *kaka*), and *daza* as 'to become light, bright'; thus the word is evidently related to Ngadha *dara*, 'bright, light, shining'. Similarly, Lio *kaka ndara*, 'a dark, black bird', should be considered in relation to *dara* and *ndara*, both of which mean 'transparent, trans-lucent' and 'bright, light' (Arndt 1933). The relevance of these comparative data for the Nage name is how-ever complicated by the fact that the Nage cognate of *dara* and *ndara* is *da* rather than *daza*.

5   The distinction of *Streptopelia chinensis* and *Geopelia maugei* respectively as *kolo* (or *kolo méze*) and *kolo dhoro/kolo ghodho* revises earlier information (Forth 1996a) suggesting that these terms applied indiscriminately to both species.

6   Influenced by informants' initial descriptions of *muta me* as a dark-coloured bird about the same size as a crow, I previously identified the term exclusively with the Common koel (Forth 1996a, 1998c). For Nage dialects, Verheijen (n.d.) gives it only as the name of the Channel-billed cuckoo.

7   In earlier publications, I described the identification of this name as uncertain (Forth 1996a, 1999). In 2001, a recently initiated practice of capturing these birds for the export market allowed me to observe a num-ber of specimens. By that time, the name *papa*, or *ana papa*, had, for the same reason, become widely known in the Bo'a Wae region, whereas previously I had encountered only one man who both knew the name and was able to provide a comprehensive description of the bird to which it referred.

8   Verheijen (n.d.) records the Bo'a Wae name for wagtails as *wagha wedho* (*wedho* here may mean 'to beat, pulsate', also referring to the motion of the tail). For the Nage dialect of Wudu, spoken just to the east of Bo'a Wae, Verheijen lists the same term as referring to sandpipers.

9   Two men provisionally described what may have been female specimens of the watercock (*Gallicrex cinerea*) as *wi kune*, 'yellow *wi*'.

10   None of numerous Nage I asked knew *'oko*, which Verheijen (n.d.) gives as the Bo'a Wae term for the Elegant pitta. Another term that seemed not to be known was *su tana*, listed by Verheijen as the name of a snipe (*Gallinago* spp.). The only member of this genus occurring on Flores is *G. stenura*, the Pintail snipe, described by C&B as an uncommon winter visitor.

Chapter 2

Ethno-ornithological classification: generic categories and ethnotaxonomy*

Methods

Information on Nage ethno-ornithology derives from discussions conducted over a period of some 15 years with a variety of informants, the majority of whom reside in or near the western Nage village of Bo'a Wae. More intensive investigations of Nage naming and classification of birds, involving interviews and the eliciting of lists of bird names, were conducted with 24 individuals from the Bo'a Wae region. In central Flores, terms for birds can vary within quite short distances. In what follows, I occasionally mention other parts of the Nage region, and also western Keo (see Map 2); but unless otherwise specified my reference is to the Nage of Bo'a Wae. Throughout Nage and Keo, investigations were conducted partly in the local language and partly in the Indonesian national language, Bahasa Indonesia.

Free recall lists were generated by asking the 24 individuals to name, in the Nage language, all the birds they knew, to begin with any kind they chose, and to continue in any order they liked. Informants were able to give between 15 and 61 bird names without further prompting.[1] After informants had exhausted names recollected completely freely, prompts were used to elicit further names. Afterwards, the same individuals were asked about names they had not mentioned, in order to discover whether they were familiar with these names and, if so, what sorts of birds they designated.[2]

Originally, I employed the recall procedure in order to generate a comprehensive register of local names. Comparing informants' lists, however, I quickly discovered patterns, whereby certain categories tended to appear earlier or later and to cluster with other categories. Implications of these apparent tendencies are discussed below. As birds which appeared on other grounds to be better known were usually mentioned earlier in the lists, they approximate the 'best examples', or relatively central members, of a category (in this case 'bird')

---

* Most of the material discussed in this chapter and in Chapter 3 has previously appeared in articles I published in the journal *Anthropos* in 1996 and 1999. This material is reproduced here with the permission of the editors.

generated by other kinds of elicitation procedure. Nevertheless, I did not directly question Nage about 'best examples', nor did I ask them to mention 'best examples' before other birds. Also, I do not interpret late mention in the lists as a necessary indication of ambiguity with regard to the inclusion of a particular category in the larger category of 'bird'.

As both Berlin (1992) and Ellen (1993a) have demonstrated, informant knowledge can vary according to the factors of sex and age. Owing partly to the main themes of my general ethnographic research, the majority of Nage with whom I had regular dealings were middle-aged or elderly men. Of the 24 Bo'a Wae people who provided free recall lists, just four were women. Efforts to engage more females proved unsuccessful owing to factors such as shyness, lack of confidence, and difficulty in communicating the purpose of the exercise (cf. Berlin, Boster and O'Neill 1981: 97). Nevertheless, my general impression is that, among Nage, sex is less important a differential in regard to knowledge of bird categories than one might expect from reports of other societies. Two of my most regular male informants, a man and his son, not only insisted that women were less knowledgeable about birds than were men, but suggested that it was pointless to consult them at all. At the same time, from this assessment the father exempted his wife and daughter – two of my most knowledgeable sources by any standard – and so did the son! What is more, other male informants disagreed with their low assessment of female knowledge of local avifauna. While on the whole women probably do know less about birds than men, there appears to be no systematic difference between the sexes in regard to the kinds of birds each is more or less familiar with.

In a similar way, people in their late teens and early twenties generally appeared competent in the use of indigenous ethno-ornithological categories, and in some cases seemed more knowledgeable than their parents. Of the 24 individuals who participated in the free recall procedure, five were below middle-age, and two of these were women. Youngsters compared favourably with older people in spite of increasing access, during the last few decades, to modern education conducted entirely in the national language and the gradual expansion in the use of Bahasa Indonesia at the expense of the local language.

Insofar as young adults may be equal to or better than their elders in naming and describing birds, this circumstance may be accounted for by a factor of 'ecological salience' (Hunn 1999), more particularly the amount of time people spend in the villages as opposed to cultivated fields, rice paddies, and forests. While older folk, and probably more women than men, spend a greater portion of their time in or near permanent settlements some distance from gardens and wooded areas, young people often spend longer periods in precisely these places, where certain birds are only, or are most commonly, found. In this connection, social rank also comes into play. Thus, while many high-ranking members of the leading clan Deu, centred in the village of Bo'a Wae, live most of the time in or near this village, most members of lower rank reside in Ola Kile, a large settlement to the north, located close to wet rice fields and major rivers (including the Ae Sésa and Lowo Léle). Consistent with this difference, Ola Kile people are noticeably more familiar with the names of birds found near water, or otherwise at lower elevations, than are people in Bo'a Wae.

Naming and identification

Table 1.1 comprises a total of 79 names recorded in the vicinity of Bo'a Wae. Most of these label folk generic categories (see pp. 1–6). While 76 of these refer to members of the ornithological class of Aves ('birds'), three denote bats. It needs to be stressed that Table 1.1 comprises a list of *names*, not categories (or taxa). Three names are by all indications synonyms of other names. In addition, two names (*héga hea* and *koa ka*), though not definitely recognized by Nage as labels for the same species, appear to designate the same bird (*Corvus florensis*), while at least another three evidently refer to non-empirical creatures (*manu ke'o, manu miu, manu wodu*). If one excludes bats as well, the names in Table 1.1 thus pertain to some 69 empirical bird categories.[3]

While one can never claim that such a list is absolutely complete, the names included in Table 1.1 nevertheless provide a comprehensive representation of labelled ethnotaxa mostly at the folk generic level. (The question of unnamed, or 'covert' taxa is discussed at the end of this chapter.) The total of 69, it should be noted, compares well with the total of 54 terms recorded for the Nuaulu of the eastern Indonesian island of Seram (Ellen 1993b), and the total of 51 (excluding synonyms and names of bats) for eastern Sumba (Forth 2000).[4] For the western Flores region of Manggarai, Verheijen's list (1963) suggests that each Manggarai dialect may contain as many as one hundred terms for birds. But this rather larger total can be ascribed to the size and ecological diversity of the region and the richness of Manggarai avifauna relative to more easterly parts of Flores (Verheijen 1963: 678). With reference to the region's greater vegetation cover, Verheijen claims that all Flores birds are found in Manggarai, while Verhoeye and Holmes (1999: 3) remark how, on Flores, 'the diversity of the avifauna varies according to the vegetation cover, which is why it is the western districts that have received the most attention from ornithologists'. Apparently in accordance with this contrast, in his unpublished lists, Verheijen (n.d.) records 61 bird terms for the Ngadha region of Wogo, to the west of Nage, and between 52 and 55 for dialects of Solor, East Flores, and Sika, all located well to the east.[5]

According to Coates and Bishop (1997), 232 species of birds have been recorded on Flores. How many of these occur in the Nage region, or more specifically in the vicinity of the village of Bo'a Wae, is not known; but it is unlikely to be more than two-thirds. Thus, if Verheijen is correct and all or most Flores birds occur in Manggarai, it is probable that Nage name roughly the same proportion of their avifauna (69 – the total that excludes bats and non-empirical categories – of approximately 150), as do speakers of any given Manggarai dialect (approximately 100 of 232).

In identifying ornithological species associated with Nage categories listed in Table 1.1, I have relied on informant's descriptions as well as my own observations in the field. Observations were sometimes assisted by Nage pointing out instances of bird categories or applying names to birds jointly encountered by ethnographer and informant. Neither preserved specimens nor sound recordings could be used, but questioning with live birds was possible in several instances. In the later stages of the research, I was able to make some use of colour illustrations of scientific species from Mason and Jarvis (1989) and Coates and Bishop (1997). The success of this particular method was however limited. Among other things, Nage were often overzealous in applying local names to pictures of birds I knew to be absent from Flores. Problems with the use of illustrations in ethnozoological research are already well known (see Gardner 1976: 448; Hunn 1992) and require no further discussion here.

While simultaneous field observation may seem an ideal, even essential, method of linking local categories with local birds, even this procedure does not guarantee correct identification. For one thing, such observation tends to be opportunistic, and to that extent unsystematic. For another, it does not completely resolve the issue of whether researchers and local people are observing, and identifying, the same thing. By the same token, simultaneous observation works only to the extent that the ethnographer is able to provide an accurate scientific identification for the bird that both he and his local collaborator have observed; and then there is the question of the veracity of scientific taxonomy itself.

Although it cannot be considered a god's eye view of things, as it exists at any given point in time, scientific biological taxonomy at least provides a universal language and standard against which other classifications can usefully be compared. But while the value of linking local categories with scientific taxa can hardly be questioned, what I wish to stress in this discussion is the importance of other, 'more ethnographic' kinds of identification which shed light on the ways folk ornithologists link a category with other ethno-ornithological categories, as well as the particular ways in which they distinguish one category from another.

An uncritical reliance on local descriptions as the sole or major means of linking indigenous categories with scientific taxa entails obvious risks. Such descriptions can be vague or incomplete, overemphasize or ignore particular features, or otherwise produce a distorted representation. Similarly problematic are local descriptions or replications of bird vocalizations. Standard ways of imitating bird calls may bear little correspondence to what the researcher might actually hear, or indeed anything that one might read in the usual ornithological field guides, and this may apply with special force where vocalizations are associated with onomatopoeic names.[6]

In spite of problems involved in the use of informants' descriptions, common ways of describing birds nevertheless have value in their own right, since they may reveal features of folk biological knowledge – local ways of knowing living kinds – that are not discoverable from other methods. How people talk about birds can reveal much about how they conceive of relations among different bird categories and about processes of bird classification in a given society. It goes without saying, then, that as much can be gained from familiarity with local languages as from zoological knowledge of local avifauna. Nage conversations about birds reveal a number of standard criteria by which they define named kinds, or distinguish them from others. Prominent among these are overall size and shape; colour of plumage; bill length, shape, and colour; tail length; and habitat (e.g. birds found in forests as opposed to cultivated areas or watery environments; birds that live in tree tops as opposed to ground-dwelling species). Other criteria include diet, nesting habits, and characteristic vocalizations.

Local ethno-ornithological discourse further reveals that Nage tend to conceive of bird taxa, more particularly folk generics, with reference to what may be called 'simple distinctive features'. These are, for the most part, morphological features which Nage regularly mention when talking about a particular bird. A comprehensive list is provided in Table 2.1. Apart from serving as a means of defining and identifying bird kinds, as I later demonstrate, many of these features are also the foci of symbolic or metaphorical elaboration, including standard similes.

Simple distinctive features recall, and arguably lend some support to, Ghiselin's argument that 'biological species' are not

> kinds, or classes, of organisms, or of anything else. They are wholes composed of organisms, or to put it in slightly different terms, they are individuals at a supraorganismal level.
>
> (Ghiselin 1999: 448)

Noting that 'individual' here reflects the ontological sense of a 'concrete particular' (ibid.), Ghiselin further describes scientific species, conceived as individuals, as having diagnostic rather than defining properties (ibid. 452), a claim which also accords with the nature of simple distinctive features of folk generic taxa articulated by Nage. Also relevant here is Waxman's characterization (1999: 236) of 'basic level names' (which may be equated with named folk generics) as providing 'criteria for object individuation and object identity'.[7]

If not literally, then with reasonable accuracy, all descriptions given in Table 2.1 translate typical Nage statements about birds. To the categories listed in the table one may reasonably add the names of other birds distinguished by their calls, insofar as these calls themselves constitute distinctive features. In some instances, the vocalization is reproduced in an onomatopoeic name (e.g. *koa ka, kuku raku, manu miu, papa, po, toe ou, zeghi*); in another case, a name, *lako lizu* ('sky dog'), makes indirect reference to the call (which in this instance resembles that of a dog). As the example of *po* ('owl') illustrates, a kind distinguished by its vocalization, and onomatopoeically designated, may additionally be defined by other, visible attributes. Indeed, the notion of 'simple distinctive

Table 2.1 Simple distinctive features associated with named folk generic categories

Nage categories are listed alphabetically; for full ornithological identifications, see Table 1.1. (While each category is described in the singular, this does not mean that each name refers to a single species, or even that Nage themselves do not recognize divisions within named categories.)

Ana go (bushlark or pipit), the bird with small, very thin legs

Ana peti jata (Pale-headed munia), the small bird whose plumage is identical to the Brahminy kite (*jata*)

Bele teka (falcon, probably the Peregrine falcon), the bird that decapitates fowls with its sharp wing

Bama cea (tesia, or stubtail), the bird without a tail (*weo mona*)

Céce (drongo), the black bird with a forked tail

Ceka (fantail), the bird with the spreading tail

Cio woza (cuckoo-shrike), the bird with an undulating flight

Detu (woodpecker), the bird that taps on trees

Deza kela, the bird whose mournful song manifests a deceased soul in need

Ebu titu (or *'awe uza*, swallow or swift), the bird that nests in caves and makes a nest of saliva

Fega (kingfisher), the bird with a long red bill

Feni (coloured parrot), the (green) bird with a large, peculiarly shaped (i.e. psittacine) bill. (While it is recognized that the cockatoo, *kaka kea*, has the same form of bill, the cockatoo is better known for its pure white plumage, which evidently distinguishes it radically from other psittaciformes.)

Gako tasi (large pied heron), the tallest of birds, or the bird with the longest legs. (Long-leggedness is also a defining feature of *o ae* and *kuku raku*; see Table 1.1.)

Ha (Large-billed crow), the black bird par excellence (or the blackest of birds)

Héga hea (Flores crow), the bird that looks like a crow (*ha*) but is smaller and has a distinct voice

Ie wea (mynah), the bird with golden 'ear pendants' (lappets)

Jata, the raptor with a white head (*ulu bha*, an expression sometimes used to name the *jata*)

Jata jawa (big hawk), the large raptorial bird that flies extremely high

Je (unidentified raptor), the bird that mimics fowls in order to seize chicks

Kaka daza (dollarbird), the bird with a raucous call (like wild laughter), and with a round, light-coloured mark on the wings

Kaka kea (cockatoo), the white bird par excellence

Kata, the wild bird that looks just like a domestic fowl (*manu*)

Kete dhéngi (Bare-throated whistler), the bird which is an extraordinary mimic and songster, and is heard but never seen (*mona tei*)

Koka (friarbird), the bird whose early morning cries herald the dawn; also the scrawniest and noisiest of birds

Koko wodo (scrubfowl), the bird that 'lays eggs on the ground but hatches them up in a tree'. (The phrase refers to the fact that the bird lays its eggs in a heap of plant debris, with which it further covers them, producing a large, distinctive mound. The bird thus does not sit on its eggs, like other birds; rather these hatch while the parent birds 'remain sitting in a tree'.)

Kua méze (eagle), the largest of birds

Lawi luja (paradise-flycatcher), the bird with an exceptionally long tail (also claimed never to alight or defecate on the ground; cf. *piko*)

Leba (nightjar), the bird with no legs (*taga mona*)

Leo (oriole), the yellow bird par excellence

Manu wodu, the bird resembling a domestic fowl but with a crest (rather than a coxcomb). (The category is, however, probably non-empirical.)

Mata to (Red-legged crake), the bird with very red eyes, and also red legs

Mele witu (*Cisticola* spp.), the bird that dives into undergrowth

Méte (flying fox), the 'bird' that lacks an anus. (To a lesser degree this feature is also attributed to the bat kind named *gébu*.)

Muta me (Channel-billed cuckoo), the bird that is raised by crows, or that is 'the child of crows' (*ana ko'o ha*)

Naka bo (Scaly-breasted munia or other munia), the small bird that steals from granaries

Piko (quail), the bird that never alights or defecates in trees (cf. *lawi luja*)

Piko du'a (unidentified), an unseen nocturnal bird with a distinctive cry (which indicates the presence of thieves)

Po (owl), the bird with a face and eyes like a cat

Tiwe (sunbird), the smallest of birds

Toto (coucal), the bird with the 'rotten anus' (*'obo mou*)

Tute péla (bushchat), the small bird that calls before sunrise in advance of the friarbird

Wagha lowo (or *iri ae*, wagtail), the bird with the wagging tail

Witu tui (unidentified), the restless bird that never stays still (also claimed to steal human hair clippings)

Wole wa (a diurnal raptor), the bird that hovers motionless

---

features' refers to a minimal principle, whereby Nage regularly describe and define a bird by at least one perceptible characteristic. It should also be noted that some birds with onomatopoeic names (for example, *ceka, toto, witu tui*) are known at least as well by other, visible features.

Nevertheless, there is a minority of generic categories that Nage seem not to distinguish with reference to simple distinctive features, even though many of the birds in question are well known. Prominent among these are Columbiformes (doves and pigeons) and Falconiformes (diurnal birds of prey, specifically *iki, sizo, sizo awu*). In fact, none of the eight named Columbiformes is clearly associated with a regularly articulated distinctive feature.[8] This circumstance may be explained by a representation of these two sets of birds – the largest and most salient of intermediate groupings (see Chapter 3) – with reference to shared and multiple, rather than single, features. In other words, the most salient traits of 'pigeons' and 'hawks' may well be perceptible features which members of each group possess in common. The same analysis applies to the buttonquail, *bewu*, and the Blue-breasted quail, *mu ki* (both of which Nage regularly compare to the Brown quail, *piko*), as well as to the bats named *gébu* and *'ighu*. None of these categories, it will be noted, is listed in Table 2.1.

As for the remainder of the terms absent from Table 2.1, some apply to categories that are non-empirical, or not fully empirical (e.g. *manu ke'o*).[9] Others are birds whose names are known only to a minority of Nage (*bi, bio, cici ko'i, manu ghebhe*). Where they are known, they are mostly described as resembling other, better-known kinds; e.g., parrots called *bi* are compared to *feni*. The bird named *wi* is usually defined by reference to *kuku raku* (another member of the Rallidae, or rail family) which it is conceived closely to resemble. The same observation can be made with regard to the herons *o ae* and *o ae bha*, in relation to large pied herons named *gako tasi*.

This leaves only ducks (*bébe ae*) and the domestic fowl (*manu*). Arguably, fowls could be absolutely defined as the one bird that is domesticated, domestic ducks and other poultry being a very recent innovation. However, not only do Nage evidently not feel the need to mention this, but it is questionable whether they classify *manu* as a 'bird' at all – that is, as a member of a larger category that also includes wild birds. Somewhat recalling the status attributed to the cassowary in New Guinea (Bulmer 1967), this negative characteristic might itself be counted as the distinctive feature of the domestic fowl. Yet probably the main point is that the distinctiveness of *manu* is multifaceted (rather than simple), and in that sense even overdetermined. Much the same may apply to ducks and similar birds (*bébe ae*); although Nage certainly classify ducks as birds, they are so manifestly different from other birds that their difference is both difficult and unnecessary to articulate.

The extent to which named folk generics are defined by simple distinctive (and moreover physical) features obviously lends support to Berlin's claim (1992; see especially pp. 25, 62) that generic taxa – both 'folk' and 'scientific' – are basic to, in the sense that they represent the logical point of departure for, any ethnobiological classification. Folk generics, Berlin argues, represent the most exclusive taxa that are perceptually distinct and hence salient. Simple distinctive features, it may then be argued, are what minimally, or synoptically, articulate this salience. Also noteworthy is the number of instances in which such features are reflected in bird nomenclature (see e.g. *bele teka*, 'sharp wing'; also Table 1.1, see *ulu bha* as an alternative name for *jata*; *mata to*; *naka bo*; *wagha lowo*).

At the same time, the stereotypical characterizations illustrated in Table 2.1 provide obvious aids to memory (X is a bird with Y), as well as an economical means of describing a particular bird kind and locating it within the wider folk classification. Although most descriptions of this sort are empirically beyond dispute, some refer to relative rather than absolute distinctions (e.g., the crow defined as the blackest of birds). A few others involve palpable exaggerations. For example, notionally 'legless' nightjars do possess legs and feet (albeit tiny and inconspicuous ones), while the tesia (*bama cea*) does have a tail (although a very short one). Also, since *fega* (kingfisher) can include the Collared kingfisher, not all birds thus classified actually have red bills. Conversely, not always are features represented as distinctive actually exclusive to the category in question. Thus, several birds besides kingfishers – for example, some parrots, the oriole, and the dollarbird – have red bills, and not only *feni* (coloured parrots) have psittacine bills.[10] As regards the 'red-billed' kingfisher, it is probably the relatively large size and length of certain kingfisher bills (*Halcyon capensis*, especially, has a massive bill) that are crucial to the representation. Therefore, what Hunn (1999) calls the 'size factor' may partly account for more widespread features being consciously associated only with particular categories.[11]

The value of simple distinctive features for Nage bird classification is not compromised by a recognition of manifest similarities among single kinds. Phenomenal features shared with birds included in other named categories, moreover, qualify certain kinds as standards of comparison. As only attention to actual language use can reveal, Nage descriptions of birds commonly include statements such as '(bird) X is like (bird) Y, only darker and smaller' or 'X has a bill shaped like, or has plumage of a similar colour to, that of Y'. Prominent among these standard kinds are birds labelled as *ana peti* (or *peti*, small passerine birds, especially munias) and *kolo* (small doves). As I show further below, the selection of these as objects of comparison appears significant in the light of the use of an expression combining the two names in a sense approaching that of 'bird (in general)'. Other birds commonly selected as standards of comparison include medium-sized kinds such as the *koka* (friarbird), *leo* (oriole), and *céce* (drongo). Larger black birds are regularly compared to the *ha* (Large-billed crow).

It should be clear how attention to distinctive features in defining individual named folk generics is connected with this sort of comparative method in Nage classification. Of course, not all such standards of comparison are readily conceived in terms of simple distinctive features. With the friarbird, oriole, and doves, it is medium size, and to some degree shape as well as common occurrence, that motivates comparative reference. Otherwise, what is truly distinctive about the oriole, for example, is its yellow plumage, while the distinctiveness of the friarbird (a bird that could not possibly be mistaken for any other) is rather more complex. As will be demonstrated presently, distinctive features of two or more kinds that are nevertheless similar (for example, the prominent tails of the paradise-flycatcher and drongo, and the yellow lappets of the hill mynah which Nage link with the yellow plumage of the oriole) may contribute to the development of certain covert intermediate groupings. At the same time, of course, by no means all birds recognized as comparable are associated to this extent.

Identification and taxonomy

The form of an ethnobiological classification can be described and analysed in the absence of certainty as to the scientific species to which all component terms refer. Whatever the state of the investigator's knowledge, it is in any case unlikely that members of a community will completely agree in the way they apply the terms, so that associations between local categories and scientific taxa must always be considered probabilistic. Nevertheless, in determining the extent to which non-western classifications correspond to perceptible discontinuity in the natural world, one needs to compare their components with the classes of scientific ornithology, which strives explicitly to reflect such discontinuity.

In investigating what it is precisely that non-western bird names name, one must remember that many birds are rarely or never seen by folk ornithologists. Others are usually observed in conditions where they do no show themselves clearly (Feld 1982; Hunn 1992), which of course is one factor limiting the utility of illustrations and vouchers in ethnobiological field research. The other side of this coin is that some birds are known mostly, if not entirely, from vocalizations, rather than from their visible forms or behaviours. Thus, since certain birds possess several quite distinct calls, sometimes associated with different parts of the 24-hour cycle or the year, two or more designations may in fact refer to one and the same ornithological species, particularly where one or more names are onomatopoeic. Among Nage, probable examples include the names *koa ka* and *héga hea*, and *kuku raku* and *lako lizu* (see Table 1.1).

In these instances, distinct names obviously exceed distinct species. In effect, the same follows where names have no definite empirical referents at all. For example, *manu ke'o* and *manu miu* refer respectively to visible and auditory manifestations of spiritual beings and, whatever their ornithological motivation, most Nage do not regard them as references to actual birds. In a similar vein, some people characterize *manu mesi* as merely a poetic device rather than the name of a particular bird, and the empirical status of the category *manu wodu* is in at least equal doubt. One might therefore question whether these designations should be treated as components of a Nage classification of birds. I do so because Nage do sometimes speak of them as birds; *manu miu* and *manu wodu* were mentioned in free recall, while *manu mesi* was once described as an alternative name for *o ae bha*. Also, partly because all four terms are binomials incorporating the name for the domestic fowl (*manu*), it is useful to retain them for the purpose of nomenclatural comparison.

Leaving aside probable non-empirical instances, the names listed in Table 1.1 generally refer to folk generic taxa that are terminal, in the sense that they do not further comprise named kinds. Possible exceptions are *fega*, *feni*, and *méte*, since a minority of Nage recognize named varieties within these generics (see *fega ae* and *fega wolo*; *feni mata mite* and *feni mata to*, or *feni lobo*; *méte ha* and *méte wula*). That one is not dealing with pairs of folk generics is suggested by the fact that the distinction of the two sorts of kingfishers and of the two kinds of parrots emerged only from directed questioning, and at a late stage of research. With regard to the two parrot terms, however, it should be noted that the 'black-eyed' variety (*feni mata mite*), which is the larger Great-billed parrot (*Tanygnathus mega-lorhynchos*), is alternatively designated as *feni méze* ('big *feni*'), or, more often, simply as *feni*. In this context, the other, 'red-eyed' type (*feni mata to*) is usually designated as *feni lobo*. The resulting contrast of *feni* and *feni lobo* is of course identical to several others described in Table 1.1, including *jata/jata jawa*, *o ae/o ae bha*, *piko/piko du'a*, *sizo/sizo awu*, and *zawa/zawa ngongo*.[12] Another instance is the pair *kolo* (*kolo méze*) and *kolo dhoro* (or *kolo ghodho*), since *kolo dasi*, referring to the Rock pigeon, is evidently a recent innovation.[13]

On the whole, Nage appear to treat pairs like *kolo* and *kolo dhoro*, *o ae* and *o ae bha*, and so on, as pertaining to taxa at the same level of contrast. Especially where the binomial (e.g. *kolo dhoro*) frequently occurs in free recall or everyday discourse, one might moreover be inclined to regard both terms of a pair as folk generics. However, since *kolo*, for example, may also be used in a general sense, thus implicitly subsuming a binomially designated type, it is arguable that terms like *kolo dhoro* (and indeed *kolo*, where the reference is specifically to the larger sort, *kolo méze*) may contextually be conceived as designating folk specifics. As is consistent with my previous application of a notion of encompassment to such terminological contrasts (1995), therefore, the taxonomic status of these terms appears ambiguous. Further issues pertaining to the form of nomenclature exemplified in all these binary contrasts are discussed in Chapter 3. Nevertheless, the general form of Nage ethnozoological taxonomy, particularly as it pertains to birds, can be summarized as in Figure 1.1.

As might be expected, a number of Nage categories include birds belonging to more than one scientific species or genera, while others are applied to members of different ornithological families. Excluding the three bat categories, Table 1.1 contains 72 terms (including synonyms) that refer to empirical kinds. Of these, nine (or 12.5 per cent), cannot be securely identified.[14] This, then, leaves a total of 63, or 87.5 per cent, which can be linked, with a high degree of confidence, with particular scientific species or genera, thus providing a sufficient basis for determining the extent to which Nage employ these terms for one or more than one ornithologically distinct kind.

At least 38 of the 63 identified terms – or over 60 per cent – refer to single species. Of the remaining 25, nine (or 14.3 per cent of 63) denote two or more species belonging to the same scientific genus. Just two of these nine terms – *'iri ae* and *wagha lowo* – are synonymous. Another 11 terms (17.5 per cent) are applied to two or more species belong to different genera but to the same ornithological family. Just five terms (7.9 per cent) designate species belonging to different families, and two of these (*awe uza* and *ebu titu*) are synonyms. All include birds which, in terms of size, shape, behaviour and habitat, are rather similar. This observation applies with even more force to the 11 terms which each encompass species assigned to different scientific genera but belonging to the same family.

A case in point is *po*. As applied to an ethno-ornithological taxon, the term, which Nage describe as the name of a single kind (see Chapter 4), designates owl species belonging to two families, the Strigidae (which includes the genus Otus) and the Tytonidae, or Barn owls. For Nage, however, as for most people, owls – or Strigiformes – are sufficiently similar one to another, and sufficiently distinct from all other sorts of birds, that their subsumption under a single term is hardly surprising. The only possible Strigiforme known by a separate name is *je*; yet the identity of this bird – which the majority of Nage have never seen – remains unclear, and the name, which refers to an attributed behaviour rather than the bird's physical appearance or vocalization, may alternatively refer to a Falconiforme.

Combining the figures for single species categories (38) and terms exclusive to species of a single scientific genera (nine), we see that nearly 75 per cent (47 of 63) of identifiable Nage categories, the majority of which are 'folk generics', correspond to scientific species or genera. It is evident, then, that distinctions reflected in the terms listed in Table 1.1 closely accord with those of scientific taxonomy. Where two or more species of a scientific genus occur in Nage territory, their terminology of birds marks these sub-generic distinctions in at least 11 instances (see *ana peti jata/bio/naka bo*, *bele teka/iki*, *ha/héga hea*, *kata/manu*, and *mu ki/piko* in relation, respectively, to the genera Lonchura, Falco, Corvus, Gallus, and Coturnix). To these might be added a further seven terms whose referents are not scientifically specific or whose identification is less clear-cut (see *gako tasi/o ae/o ae bha*, *jata jawa/sizo*, and *zawa/zawa ngongo* in respect of the genera Egretta and Ardea, Accipiter, and Ducula). Clearly, where local nature provides further contrasts, Nage folk generics do not always coincide with either scientific genera or species. At the same time, the majority of terminological distinctions appear to be based on perceptual factors rather than values that are culturally specific. With regard to members of the same scientific genera, the only arguable exceptions concern the contrast of *kata* and *manu* in regard to the latter's domestication, and the species of Lonchura named *ana peti jata* with reference to its resemblance to that of the Brahminy kite (*jata*), a bird that is culturally conceived as a spiritual manifestation.

In cases where a term is associated with several scientific species (whether these belong to the same genus or not), it is not always clear whether one can be called focal or prototypical, or whether the term can be said to be 'extended' so as to incorporate one or more other species as peripheral members (see Hunn 1991: 139). Apparent examples of focality and extension include *feni*, *naka bo*, *tiwe*, and *wi* (in respect of the Great-billed parrot, Scaly-breasted munia, Olive-backed sunbird, and Buff-banded rail). Similarly, evidence relating to calls linked with the onomatopoeic name *po* (see Chapter 4), as well as the local surmise that 'horned' (that is, 'eared') owls may be the male members of a single kind, suggest that Scops owls (genus Otus) may be the prototype of the category *po*.

Of course, in all of these instances, possible focality pertains to a local discrimination only to the extent that informants recognize (but do not articulate terminologically) variation within a single named kind. Otherwise, the distinction of focal and peripheral instances, or applications, of a category is an artifact of external observation and analysis, grounded in a statistical preponderance of instances in which an undivided term is used to designate one scientific species rather than others. Nevertheless, there is evidence to suggest that, sometimes, this sort of hierarchy is cognitively real, especially where the common representation of a local category evidenced by local descriptions, and more particularly still by simple distinctive features, draws from one designated species rather than others.

A good illustration of this last point is the category *fega* ('kingfisher'). As noted, for Nage the most salient feature of birds thus named is a red bill. Indeed, in repeated questioning, Nage claimed that all *fega* (and not just certain varieties, or one gender) had red bills. From this one can infer that the focus of this category comprises the two large, red-billed kingfishers, *Caridonax fuldigus* (the White-rumped kingfisher) and *Halcyon capensis* (the Stork-billed kingfisher). In addition, from regular descriptions of *fega* as birds with dark plumage, it would further appear that the first species, *Caridonax fuldigus*, is more focal than the second. Nevertheless, as I have myself observed, Nage also apply the name *fega* to *Halcyon chloris*, the Collared kingfisher, which possesses a dark grey, or 'black', rather than a red bill. All the same, when questioned, Nage will usually deny that there are any black-billed kingfishers.

What this suggests is a representation labelled *fega* which incorporates only features of red-billed kingfishers even though, situationally, Nage – implicitly recognizing features that these birds share in common with kingfishers that lack red bills – will also apply *fega* to the Collared kingfisher. On the other hand, the harsh cries Nage attribute to *fega* may largely reflect the vocal habits of the Collared kingfisher, thus suggesting what I have previously called a 'blended' representation (Forth 1996a: 93). Relevant here is an overlap in habitat between *Halcyon chloris* and the other two kingfishers, which Bo'a Wae people regularly describe as occupying habitats around or above the village and well below the village respectively. Accordingly, the previously mentioned contrast of 'hill kingfisher' (*fega wolo*) and 'water kingfisher' (*fega ae*) normally distinguishes the two kinds of red-billed kingfishers (see Table 1.1), not these and the Collared kingfisher.[15]

Taxonomic relations

Nage regard all birds, thus all named taxa listed in Table 1.1, as instances of the category *ana wa*, 'animal' (Forth 1995) and furthermore as members of a covert life-form taxon 'bird'. The latter in turn comprises several, mostly unnamed intermediate groupings. These intermediates then subsume a sizeable minority of the folk generics listed in Table 1.1. Other generic terms do not belong to any intermediate group, being directly subsumed in the 'bird' taxon.

By describing 'bird' as a covert life-form taxon, I refer to the fact that, although it is not named with any single indigenous term, it nevertheless appears to be a category of Nage thought (see Berlin, Breedlove and Raven 1968; Berlin 1992: 176–78; Taylor 1984, 1990: 42–51; Ellen 1993a: 119–20). Nowadays, Nage often refer to birds by employing Malay and Bahasa Indonesia *burung*, a term which, in their usage as in that of other Indonesians, includes bats. In their own language, they can also resort to the descriptive phrases *ana wa ta'a co*, 'creatures that fly', and *ana wa ta'a ne'e bele*, 'animals with wings'. While in both cases other animals, such as flying insects, could logically be included as well, birds are the prototype, if not the sole members, of these descriptive categories, and context usually excludes non-birds as possible referents. So too does the additional phrase *zéta lizu*, 'up in the sky', sometimes placed after 'creatures that fly', since this excludes insects, most of which are characteristically encountered flying close to the ground.[16]

Observed usage reveals another means by which Nage make general reference to birds. In its most specific sense, the term *ana peti* denotes a number of small, separately named passerine birds which are commonly found near cultivated fields (especially, nowadays, rice paddies) and feed on ripening crops. The largest number of these are munias and other Estrildine finches, and the principal member of the category, and the only one whose name incorporates *ana peti*, is the previously mentioned 'Brahminy kite munia' (*ana peti jata*; *Lonchura pallida*). Other generic taxa that Nage regularly classify as *ana peti* include *naka bo* (or *ana naka bo*) and *bio*. However, while Estrildine finches are the focus of *ana peti*, in a more inclusive usage the same term refers to a larger class of small birds, a grouping evidently similar to the 'dicky-birds' identified by Hunn (1991: 139) for Sahaptin. In this broader sense, Nage often classify such small birds as *ana go* (pipit or bushlark), *bama* (tesia), *ceka* (fantail), *cici ko'i* (Tree sparrow), *detu* (Pygmy woodpecker), *tiwe* (sunbird), and *tute péla* (bushchat) as instances of *ana peti*. When asked, Nage were less certain about larger birds such as *céce* and *leba*, though some informants thought that even these should be included among the *ana peti*.[17] A methodological point is in order here. When Nage are directly questioned as to whether a particular folk generic kind is an *ana peti*, they will frequently understand the latter term in its strictest sense, thereby often denying classifications that are evident from observed speech (see Forth 1996a: 93, note 4; and cf. Forth 1998a: 328, regarding Nage spirit classification).

The foregoing examples are by no means exhaustive; for as Nage themselves remark, and as I myself have often observed, people will apply *ana peti* to any small bird for which they, individually, are unable to apply a special name or which they do not recognize. In this regard, Nage use of *ana peti* resembles the application, by the ornithologically ill-informed, of English terms like 'sparrow' to any small and plain passerine bird; or 'duck' to other swimmers like grebes and gallinules; or 'hawk' to all Falconiformes. By the same token, species of small birds, which are unremarkable or which Nage rarely see, are known by no other name than *ana peti*. In this case, Nage also speak of *ana peti bholo*, 'plain *ana peti*', denoting a residual category comprising small birds which, in the words of one Nage man, 'do not have a name' (senses of *bholo* are further discussed in Chapter 3, note 11). The question of nameless, yet recognizably distinct, birds is taken up towards the end of this chapter.

As the foregoing may suggest, in its widest acceptation, *ana peti* tends to cover a notional half of the Nage bird population: the half comprising smaller as opposed to larger birds. Owing partly to this general sense, but also because the term especially refers to small seed-eaters, *ana peti* – or more often, the short form of the name, *peti* – is conjoined with *kolo* (dove) to form *peti kolo*. Commonly, Nage use this compound when referring to birds that habitually consume ripening crops. When questioned directly, Nage sometimes define the expression as an exclusive reference to birds named *ana peti* (in the sense of small seed-eating birds) and *kolo* (doves). Yet, as with different senses of *ana peti*, observed usage tends to contradict this interpretation. Like similar phrases combining the names of two ethnozoological kinds, *peti kolo* ('munia-dove') operates as a dual synecdoche, naming a larger, though not always precisely definable, class of avifauna.

In fact, Nage occasionally employ *peti kolo* in something approaching the general sense of 'bird'. For example, describing the procedure followed when obtaining a *hebu* tree (*Cassia fistula*) to make a sacrificial post, Nage explain how, before sticking a lance into the trunk, one should wait until a bird, of any kind, has alighted in the branches. Representing the spirit of the tree which should be retained, this bird is referred to as *peti kolo* (or, in one particular instance, as '*kolo* (or) *ana peti*, . . . *ne'e kolo ko, ne'e ana peti ko* . . .'). At the same time, Nage insist that, in this ritual context, any sort of bird will do. It is also noteworthy that the spirit of a *hebu* tree is most closely associated not with small diurnal birds but with owls (see Chapter 4). Another illustration of the completely general use of *peti kolo* is the phrase *supi peti kolo*, referring to the hunting of birds with a blow-gun.

The occurrence of *peti* in a compound contextually denoting birds in general is largely explained by inclusive uses of the longer form, *ana peti*. *Kolo*, on the other hand, is less readily accounted for, although birds thus named are of a medium size and common. It is noteworthy as well that, in other eastern Indonesian languages, cognates of *kolo* are employed alone as equally general terms for 'bird', thus suggesting a possible residue of an earlier, more inclusive sense of the Nage name.

The foregoing usages recall features of bird classification in other parts of the world. For example, as a name specifically designating various warblers, sparrows, and juncos, Shoshoni *huittsuu* also resembles *ana peti* in its further application to small birds in general. Similarly, Aguaruna (Jivaroan) *pishak*, 'small bird', is sometimes applied to all birds, in which respect it can subsume the contrasting term, *chigki*, 'large game bird' (Berlin, Boster and O'Neill 1981: 99). In the latter regard, the Aguaruna usage may more closely resemble Nage uses of *peti kolo*. Even so, it is doubtful whether 'birds in general', or 'all birds', ever occurs as the unequivocal sense of the Nage compound. Actual usage suggests that *peti kolo* is better understood in the sense of 'any bird', or in the more restricted acceptation, 'any (relatively small) grain-eating bird'.

If this is correct, then *peti kolo* cannot strictly be said to name a taxon. That it does not function as a taxon is further indicated by the fact that it is not enumerable. Thus, unlike the names of individual folk generic terms, the compound cannot be articulated with *éko*, the number classifier used for all kinds of animals (*ana wa*). One can say, for example, *kolo éko dhua*, 'two doves', or even *ana peti éko telu*, 'three small birds'. But one cannot say 'four (seed-eating) birds' (*peti kolo éko wutu*; see further, Forth 1995). While the use of *peti kolo* to refer to a bird or birds of no particular kind does point to the existence of 'bird' as a covert category in Nage folk zoology, therefore, the phrase does not unequivocally designate this category.

As noted earlier, modern Nage often use the national language term *burung* ('bird'). Insofar as they do so even when speaking their own language, *burung* could be accurately described as a loan word. Observed usage, however, reveals that Nage sometimes employ the term to refer more particularly to larger birds, in contrast to *ana peti*, understood as a general reference to small passerine birds. On several occasions, the contrast was quite explicit. For example, once when I asked whether the drongo (*céce*) could be classified as an *ana peti*, one man, responding in the negative, remarked that, owing to its relatively large size, the drongo must be counted instead as a *burung*. Another informant suggested that the same bird might be considered as intermediate between *ana peti* and *burung*.

From this, one should not conclude that all modern Nage uses of *burung* exclude small passerine birds. Nevertheless, small birds would appear to be marginal to the adopted category, while larger birds are evidently central. The implicit Nage contrast of *ana peti* and *burung* suggests an intriguing comparison with the aforementioned Shoshoni classification. In Shoshoni, *kwinaa*, designating a category of eagles, hawks, and falcons, further serves as the term for 'large birds' and can moreover designate birds in general (Hage and Miller 1976). At the same time, Shoshoni *huittsuu* specifies an intermediate taxon of small birds, so that this term and *kwinaa* together subsume all local avifauna.

Especially in the context of the Shoshoni comparison, the centrality of larger birds in regard to observed Nage uses of the category *burung* might further suggest a particular prominence attaching to larger kinds within the covert life-form taxon 'bird'. Relevant here is the frequency with which diurnal raptors (interestingly enough, the most specific referents of Shoshoni *kwinaa*), were mentioned at or near the beginning of free recall lists (see Chapter 3). On the other hand, there can be no question that, in its broadest sense, *ana peti* ('small birds') also occupies a large conceptual space within the unnamed 'bird' category. Indeed, the combination of the reduced form *peti* and *kolo* (dove) – *peti kolo* – virtually approximates a label for this covert taxon.

The prominence of both small and large kinds among Nage birds, as apparently among birds classified in Shoshoni (and also in Aguaruna where, as noted, a term for small birds when used in the general sense of 'bird' can subsume members of a category of 'large game birds') may at first seem curious. Yet the inclusion in the focus, or prototype, of a class of members possessing quite distinct, even opposed, attributes appears in fact to be quite common. To cite a more familiar comparison, in English vernacular classification, 'robin' and 'eagle' both tend to be cited as good examples of the category 'bird' (Rosch 1973: 133).[18] Similarly, in regard to functional categories (as opposed to ethnotaxa), dogs and cats both occupy a prominent place within the English category 'pets', their opposite natures in western symbolism notwithstanding.

Reflecting Proto-Malayo-Polynesian **manuk*, 'chicken, bird, fowl' (Zorc 1994: 583), cognates of Nage *manu* occur as the general term for 'bird' in eastern Indonesian languages belonging to Esser's 'Ambon Timor' group (Esser 1938, Blad 9b). In other eastern Indonesian languages, including Nage, the same term specifically denotes the domestic fowl. Nage terminology also contains five compounds that incorporate *manu* plus a modifier (*manu ghebhe, manu ke'o, manu mesi, manu miu, manu wodu*); but from these it can hardly be inferred that, in Nage, *manu* retains the general sense of the Malayo-Polynesian proto-form. In fact, in all five compounds, the word is better understood as a metaphorical use of the term for 'domestic fowl'. Noteworthy in this regard is the unproductive character of the five binomials; for in none does the modifier define a taxon as an instance of a more inclusive category labelled *manu* (see e.g. English 'nighthawk', 'titmouse', 'silverfish'), or refer to a bird conceived as a type of domestic fowl.

Consistent with their unproductive character, in the view of most Nage, three of these terms (*manu ke'o, manu mesi, manu miu*), do not refer to empirical birds at all. In a similar vein, local descriptions of *manu wodu*, a category that does not correspond to any known species, suggest a spiritually powerful creature somewhat comparable to the *manu ke'o* (see Chapter 7). A question arises, then, as to why *manu* ('domestic fowl') should occur in the names of creatures which, although bird-like in some particulars, do not unambiguously constitute empirically definable categories of birds.[19] Part of the answer may be found in indications that, for Nage, domestic fowls themselves are not really birds. Despite the ubiquity of domestic fowls in Nage villages, just three respondents listed *manu* in free recall, while two of these mentioned the term with reluctance or hesitation. Yet another man was reluctant to list *kata*, referring to the junglefowl (*Gallus varius*), a bird of the same genus as the domestic fowl. He explained his reluctance with reference to the close physical resemblance between the two birds. In addition, one man remarked that 'bird' (*burung*) should properly subsume only wild creatures and not domestic fowls, which live inside villages.

The foregoing might suggest that Nage are not entirely in agreement as to what constitutes a 'bird'. Yet this does not contradict the psychological reality of some covert taxon translated by the English term. Also relevant to the definition of the category is the status of bats (which Nage name with three folk generic terms) in Nage ethnozoology. Although Nage, like many folk ornithologists, speak of bats as birds, the inclusion of bats in the unnamed bird taxon requires some qualification. Certainly, bats qualify as 'winged animals' and 'animals that fly' (the glosses of two expressions Nage use when speaking generally of birds). On the other hand, if questioned directly no Nage will recognize bats as an instance of *peti kolo*; but this would apply to many (especially larger) aviformes as well. Nage also count bats as creatures to which the adopted Indonesian term *burung* applies. At the same time, they express ambivalence regarding the classificatory status of the Chiroptera, noting that, unlike aviformes, bats facially resemble dogs and Palm civets, and that members of two bat categories (*méte* and *gébu*) give birth live (see further Chapter 7). It would appear, therefore, that although bats are subsumed within an unnamed Nage category of 'birds', they constitute its most marginal members.

Despite the evident marginality of certain members, the unnamed life-form taxon 'bird' is a bounded category. That is, Nage include none of the individual bird categories simultaneously as instances of 'bird' and of another life-form taxon (such as 'snake' or 'fish'). An exception might be suggested by their use of *kea* to name both the Yellow-crested cockatoo and marine turtles. The evidence of related languages and dialects, however, confirms that the two applications reflect different protoforms (see, e.g., Keo and Ngadha *kéka*, Lio *véka*, 'cockatoo', by contrast to Keo *kea*, Ngadha and Lio *kéra*, 'turtle'; Arndt 1933, 1961). What is more, Nage often distinguish the cockatoo as *kaka kea*, and turtles as *kea mesi* ('sea *kea*'). It is quite clear, then, that the two uses of *kea* constitute a homonymy, and do not reflect a classification of turtles and cockatoos as common members of any ethnotaxon (other than, of course, *ana wa*, 'animal'). Interestingly enough, two female informants, a woman and her daughter, gave *kea mesi* (turtle) as the name of a bird in free recall. Yet later questioning revealed that both thought that the term referred to an ornithological kind, and not a marine reptile.[20]

A similar case concerns the term *lako lizu* (literally 'sky dog'; see Table 1.1). Among the Nage of Bo'a Wae, the name refers both to a mole cricket and a much larger creature that utters a nocturnal call, rather like a dog. While the latter appears to be either a night heron (*Nycticorax* spp.) or waterhen (*kuku raku*), people often express uncertainty as to whether this is a bird of any sort. Nevertheless, Nage do not classify the insect as a bird, nor the night-calling creature as an insect. And they most certainly regard neither as a kind of dog (*lako*).[21]

Covert generics and double naming

As exemplified by the Nage 'bird' taxon, covert categories have usually been recognized at higher levels of ethnotaxonomies, notably in regard to unique beginner, life-form, and intermediate taxa. Yet, if Berlin's principle that 'absence of a label does not necessarily imply the absence of a category' (Berlin 1992: 27) is taken to apply to any level of taxonomy, then it should follow that folk generics, as well, can be covert (cf. Ellen 1993a: 70). Indeed, there are several birds that Nage know and can describe in detail, but which they do name. Since they evidently recognize these as distinct kinds (in fact, employing the Indonesian national language, informants sometimes describe them exactly in this way), they may be called 'covert generics'.

The most striking example concerns the Black-naped monarch flycatcher (*Hypothymis azurea*), a brilliant blue bird with a dark ridge at the back of the head that is quite unmistakable. Other cases include sandpipers, which Nage occasionally encounter near water courses, and several types of seabirds which Keo people distinguished with reference to behaviour and morphology but could not name. Nage first mentioned the Black-naped monarch spontaneously, when I was discussing ways of asking about kinds of birds in the local language. Three men described the monarch quite accurately and, a little later, identified a picture (in Mason and Jarvis 1989) as the bird in question. Later still, others, including a bird-trapper who had caught a specimen, said they were familiar with the bird when I described it to them.

One man with whom I first discussed the Black-naped monarch stated that he had asked several local people about its name, but no one knew it. Many people, he claimed, had noticed the bird, although they 'had not paid it too much attention' (perhaps meaning that they had not thought about it as much as he had). These remarks are important, as they reveal a local notion that the bird might have a name – indeed, that it possesses an unknown name – a supposition which, in itself, arguably defines it as occupying a separate folk generic taxon. In other words, in regard to ethnotaxonomic status, the idea that the bird might be named is arguably tantamount to its possession of an actual name.[22] Similarly noteworthy in this connection is the number of times Nage, when giving free recall lists, described a named bird that they knew but whose name they did not know or could not recall. (Sometimes, they later thought of the name; or, on the basis of a description, someone else nearby did so.) Occasionally, Nage would also ask me if I had heard others mention a bird's name; for example, when the nameless Elegant pitta (*Pitta elegans*) suddenly became familiar in Bo'a Wae, owing to the activities of Nage bird-trappers.

All my enquiries convinced me that Nage really do *not* name the Black-naped monarch. But if the bird is as distinctive as they evidently recognize it to be, one must ask why this should be so. A functionalist might reply: because it has no special utilitarian or symbolic value. Yet this equally applies to any number of other generic taxa (for example, those comprising parrots and ducks) which are indeed named. A more likely hypothesis is that the Black-naped monarch 'has yet to be named', perhaps because it is new to the region or its numbers have recently increased. However, I have found nothing to suggest that the bird has recently become more available to Nage observers, or has acquired greater 'ecological salience' (Hunn 1999). The extension of wet-rice cultivation may account for the recent appearance, or 'discovery', of birds like the Common moorhen, which Nage in Bo'a Wae claimed to be new to their region.[23] But this cannot apply to the monarch flycatcher, since the bird is often encountered in more elevated places, far away from paddies.[24]

If there are folk generics that are unnamed, then Nage bird classification also reveals the converse: two separate terms that denote what, from a western ornithological view, designate one and the same bird. Here, I refer not to simple synonyms which Nage themselves recognize as having an identical referent, but to instances where different perceptual manifestations of a bird are named separately. One case has already been mentioned. The names *héga hea* and *koa ka* both appear to refer to the Flores crow (*Corvus florensis*); however, while the first is usually applied to the visible bird, the second name replicates a nocturnal vocalization. Another instance concerns the Bare-throated whistler, a bird known to western ornithologists as both a superb songster and a versatile mimic. Nage in the Bo'a Wae region call the bird *kete dhéngi*. Yet some describe *kete dhéngi* only as the name of a songster and dissociate the term from the representation of the mimic, with which they are familiar but regard as an unnamed category. Furthermore, people in south-western Nage (notably in the modern administrative division of Légu Déru) apply a distinct name, *mapa bewa*, to the mimic while reserving *kete dhéngi* for the songster.[25]

What may be called 'double naming' of birds suggests the converse not only of 'covert generics', but also of instances where morphological, behavioural, and vocal features of two ornithological kinds are apparently combined in the representation of a single ethnotaxon (see p. 35 regarding *fega*, and Chapter 7 in respect of *je* and *witu tui*). Yet none of these phenomena compromises a view of Nage bird classification as an ethnotaxonomy firmly grounded in a universal perception of natural discontinuity. In all cases, the features defining folk taxa are obviously perceptual. Their association with particular named categories can most readily be attributed to disjunction or conjunction arising from an insufficiency of observation that would allow Nage to connect distinct perceptual features (especially visual and auditory ones) as manifestations of a single ornithological kind or (in the case of 'blended' representations) distinguish features belonging to different kinds. What is more, it is difficult to see how either of these classificatory procedures or the deficient or unsystematic observation to which they can be ascribed, could be positively connected with cultural values of either a symbolic or utilitarian kind (see further Chapter 7).

Chapter 3

Intermediate categories, binary associations, and nomenclature

In the previous chapter I dealt mostly with named folk generics and the covert life-form taxon 'bird'. In this chapter I discuss ways in which Nage represent the most exclusive named taxa as combining to form larger groupings intermediate between the life-form and the generic level. I then extend the discussion of names initiated in several places earlier, in order to consider general characteristics of bird nomenclature, and conclude with a summary of fundamental features of Nage ethno-ornithological taxonomy.

Intermediate classes

As demonstrated earlier, *ana peti* designates a category intermediate between the covert taxon 'bird' and named generic kinds. Sometimes referring particularly to munias and similar small seed-eating birds, and other times to a much larger class of small birds, the extension of the category is variable. Nevertheless, particularly with reference to the first, more exclusive grouping, *ana peti* can be described as the only intermediate taxon that is named by Nage. Accordingly, it was the only such category mentioned in the recall lists. Of 24 respondents, as many as 14 gave *ana peti* in free recall. Either immediately afterwards or at a later point, however, 11 of the 14 added spontaneously that there was more than one kind of *ana peti*, by far the most frequently specified being *ana peti jata* and *naka bo* (or *ana naka bo*).

The recall lists also provide evidence for several unnamed intermediates, revealed in a tendency to mention two or more named bird kinds in succession. The result is a series of clusters subsuming nearly 40 per cent of the categories listed in Table 1.1.[1] Exemplifying such a cluster is one informant's list, which included – in succession – the terms for eagles, the Brahminy kite, large hawks, (one or more) smaller hawks, and (larger) falcons. Indeed, Falconiformes, or diurnal birds of prey, compose one of the larger intermediate groupings. The others are pigeons and doves (Columbiformes, and all members of the family Columbidae), quails and buttonquails, a group I label 'crow-like birds', and bats. In an earlier discussion (Forth 1996a) I suggested that 'water birds' may, in a qualified sense, form another such grouping. Following in part the evidence of more recent field research, my view is now that Nage regularly recognize associations only between pairs of folk generics comprising water birds (see pp. 51–54).[2]

The most firmly attested of Nage intermediate groupings are Falconiformes and Columbiformes – or 'hawks and pigeons', as these might synoptically be described. In both cases, serial linking in free recall was very consistent. Of 24 respondents, all but one mentioned two or more of the eight generic terms for diurnal raptors in succession, while 16 people successively mentioned three or more. With regard to the eight generic terms for Columbiformes, 18 of 24 informants listed two or more terms in succession, and of these, 12 listed three or more. Seven people listed at least four. Additional support for the psychological reality of the two categories is found in the recall list provided by the informant mentioned in note 2 above. Employing Indonesian (Bahasa Indonesia) terms, he explicitly grouped together six Nage generics as 'hawk kinds (Falconiformes)' (*bangsa elang*; *bangsa* is 'category, kind'), and another five as 'kinds of pigeons (or doves)' (*bangsa merpati*).

The intermediate grouping of quails and buttonquails is much smaller than the foregoing, comprising just three folk generics (*bewu, mu ki, piko*). Twelve people mentioned just two of these successively in free recall; another listed all three together. In every case, one of the kinds was *piko*, while in most instances the second term was *bewu*. While the ethnotaxa I have glossed as Falconiformes and Columbiformes correspond exactly to the scientific groups thus labelled, the association of these three generics varies in an interesting way from scientific taxonomy. *Piko* and *mu ki* denote quails (genus Coturnix), thus members of the scientific family Phasianidae, while *bewu* denotes members of the Turnicidae, which are distantly related but manifestly similar buttonquails. At the same time, included with quails in the Phasianidae is the scientific genus Gallus, the two Florenese members of which are designated as *kata* (junglefowl) and *manu* (domestic fowl).

Of the 24 respondents, eight mentioned *kata* immediately before or after *piko, bewu*, or *mu ki*, which of course is fewer than the dozen who mentioned two or more of the quails and buttonquails together. Since just 14 people mentioned *kata* at all, however, these eight amount to 57 per cent of this total. Also, the educated informant referred to above listed the Brown quail and a buttonquail (*piko, bewu*) with *kata* in a category he labelled 'ground-dwelling birds' (Indonesian: *burung yang di tanah*). Arguably, therefore, there is a further association of the junglefowl (*kata*) with quails and buttonquails. Yet, rather than an inclusion of *kata* within the same intermediate taxon, what we seem to be dealing with here is a recognized affinity of the junglefowl, on the one hand, with *piko, bewu*, and *mu ki*, on the other, considered as a single group. Also noteworthy in this connection is the regular binary connection of *kata* and *piko* in poetic idioms (see Appendix 1). Accordingly, where one of the three quail or buttonquail terms was mentioned with *kata* in free recall, in the majority of cases this was *piko*.

The evident focality of *piko* within the intermediate grouping of quails and buttonquails is further demonstrated by the regular Nage translation of Indonesian *puyuh* ('quail') as *piko*, combined with the application of the Indonesian term to *bewu* and *mu ki* as well. One man even spoke of there being two sorts of *piko*, namely *piko* and *bewu*, a representation reminiscent of bird classification in Ngadha (Wogo) and So'a (Verheijen n.d.), where *piko* occurs in compounds denoting the three categories Nage distinguish as *piko*, *mu ki* and *bewu*. Also relevant is the circumstance that, of the three categories, only *piko* is the subject of symbolic elaboration, appearing not only in figurative language but also, in one phenomenal context, as an ominous sign of a particular sort of danger (see Chapter 6).

As only two of 24 respondents mentioned *manu* in free recall (and then with reluctance), it is not surprising that none of the lists reveals any association of this term with either *kata* or *piko*, *bewu*, and *mu ki*. As also noted in the previous chapter, the status of the domestic category within the Nage life-form taxon 'bird' is in any case equivocal.

In an earlier analysis (1996a), I described an intermediate group of crow-like birds. This includes two members of the scientific genus *Corvus* (*ha* and *héga hea*), as well as *muta me* and *toe ou*, both large cuckoos that are brood parasites of crows. To these I would now add *koa ka*, previously treated as a member of a category of 'night birds' (Forth 1996a: 108). The male *toe ou* (Common koel) is black like the two crows; and although Nage describe the *koa ka* as a bird that is never seen, they also say that it too is black. (In fact, this onomatopoeic name may refer to no more than a nocturnal manifestation of the Flores crow, otherwise known as *héga hea*.) Although Nage speak of the *muta me*, the Channel-billed cuckoo, as another dark-coloured bird, its plumage is actually light grey. The bird's notional darkness might therefore be ascribed to the fact that it is usually seen in silhouette, flying high and being mobbed by crows. However that may be, its association with crows is sufficiently grounded in its parasitism, or more exactly in the Nage representation of this behaviour (see Chapter 7).

All together, 12, thus exactly half, of 24 informants named two or more of the 'crow-like' generics in succession in free recall. Just four people mentioned three of the five terms. Given the remarkable similarity of the two actual crows it is perhaps surprising that, where just two names were associated, these belonged to the Flores crow (*héga hea*) and Large-billed crow (*ha*) in just three instances (or 25 per cent of 12, and 37.5 per cent of 8). Also noteworthy in this connection is one man's statement that the *héga hea* 'is actually a *ha*', which I take to mean that the two are instances of a single category which may also be labelled as *ha*.

Although the drongo (*céce*) is dark-coloured like most of the crow-like birds, and although it is associated with the crows *ha* and *héga hea* on symbolic grounds, only in two (of 24) instances was *céce* mentioned before or after one of these terms. In part this can be attributed to the drongo's peculiar tail – its 'simple distinctive feature' (see Table 2.1; Figure 3.1) – as well as its smaller size. In the same number of cases, the drongo was listed with *tute péla* (Pied bushchat), a much smaller bird, the male of which, however, is predominantly black. In fact, in free recall, the drongo shows a greater association with the Asian paradise-flycatcher (*lawi luja*), another bird which, as Nage themselves explicate, also possesses a distinctive tail (see Figure 7.1).

Previously, and in a provisional way, I suggested the possible existence of an intermediate grouping of 'night birds', including bats (Forth 1996a). The evidence of more recent field research, however, suggests that Nage thought tends to associate, on the one hand, the three named bat taxa (*méte, gébu,* and *'ighu*) and, on the other *po* (owl) and *je* (which some Nage describe as another nocturnal raptor). Not just bats but all nocturnal categories, including nocturnal birds of prey, are peripheral to the life-form taxon of 'bird'. Accordingly, when their names were freely recalled, owls, bats, and other nocturnal kinds were mentioned towards the end of the lists. In this regard, nocturnal raptors contrast strongly with diurnal raptors, birds which on the contrary appear to be the most exemplary kinds of Nage avifauna. On the other hand, while distant ethnotaxonomically (and in scientific taxonomy as well), the two groups are closely associated in Nage spiritual or symbolic thought (see Chapter 4). Indeed, in this context, both sorts of raptors jointly occupy what I describe as a symbolic class, a class which, it is worth emphasizing, does *not* include bats.

That Nage should conceive of the three bat categories as a single taxon is consistent not only with their manifest physical resemblance but also with the marginal status of bats in general in relation to the 'bird' taxon. In free recall, just 13 of 24 informants mentioned any of the bat terms. Of the 13, six listed two or more of the three terms in succession, while three of these six listed all three terms. Mostly employing Indonesian terms, Nage themselves often describe the three bat generics as composing a single 'kind' (Bahasa Indonesia *bangsa*). Also relevant in this connection is the fact that, in response to questioning, Nage always gave *méte* (flying fox) as the local equivalent of Indonesian *kelawar*, a term which has the general sense of 'bat' and which Nage themselves apply to instances of all three of the local categories. *Méte* was also the first bat term I encountered in the field, even before directly questioning Nage about 'birds'. It is not surprising, then, that in free recall all 13 Nage who mentioned at least one bat category mentioned *méte*, while only six mentioned *'ighu*, and only three *gébu*.[3] Other ideas linking the three Nage bat categories, notably the idea that all three can transform into other kinds, are discussed in Chapter 7.

All of the foregoing attests to the focality of *méte* within the unnamed intermediate taxon that can be labelled as 'bats'. As demonstrated earlier, precisely the same status is occupied by *piko* in respect of the trio of quails and button-quails. Not surprisingly, the focal member of the group of crow-like birds is the Large-billed crow (*ha*). As many as 22 of 24 Nage mentioned *ha* in free recall. The figures for *héga hea* and *muta me* were both 12, while the total for *toe ou* was 11. In contrast, *koa ka*, which Nage describe as an exclusively nocturnal bird known only by its onomatopoeic – and ominous – cry, was mentioned by just five informants. Interestingly, the Large-billed crow is not in fact the largest member of this group. This position is held by the Channel-billed cuckoo (*muta me*); nevertheless, most Nage describe this bird as being the same size as the crow.

Among the *ana peti* (small seed-eating passerines), the focal member, or prototype, is evidently the Pale-headed munia (*ana peti jata*), not least because it
is the only folk generic that actually incorporates *ana peti* in its name. Of 24
respondents, 18 mentioned *ana peti jata* in free recall. Eleven listed *naka bo* (or
ana naka bo), another generic referring to munias, and all but two of these mentioned the term immediately before or after *ana peti jata*. In contrast, only three
mentioned *bio* and only one man mentioned *cici ko'i*, the two other terms
subordinate to *ana peti* in its most specific sense. Consistent with this evidence
is a mostly binary representation of this sense of *ana peti*, explicated in the
commonly expressed idea that there are just two kinds. As this should suggest,
bio and *cici ko'i* (applied to the recently arrived Tree sparrow) are known only
to a minority of Nage in the Bo'a Wae region.

Focality within other intermediate groupings is more complex. In free recall,
all but one of 24 Nage mentioned both *jata* (Brahminy kite) and *kua* (or *kua
méze*, eagles), mostly within longer series of diurnal birds of prey. A close third
was *iki* (Moluccan kestrel), mentioned by 20 informants.[4] Thus, the focus of
the ethnotaxon I gloss as 'Falconiformes' would appear to be occupied by three
folk generics. At the same time, the sequence in which Falconiformes were
mentioned may be significant, since in most cases *kua* and *jata* – the largest of
the diurnal raptors – were named before any other kind. In fact, diurnal birds
of prey were mentioned right at the beginning of nearly half (11 of 24) of the
free recall lists. Other 'leaders', as they might be called, included the names of
Columbiformes and, to a much lesser extent, common or well-known birds such
as the friarbird (*koka*) and cockatoo (*kea, kaka kea*), and *ana peti*. The fact that
ana peti was not mentioned more often at the beginning of free recall lists may
seem surprising in view of the inclusive use of this term with reference to a large
variety of smaller birds. However, it may be precisely the birds' small size that
explains this. Raptors, of course, are among the largest of birds, although there
are many birds that are as large or larger than the smaller raptors.

With the two tripartite intermediate taxa comprising quails and buttonquails,
and bats, the member of each that is clearly the prototype is also the largest.
Although *kua* and *jata* denote the largest Falconiformes, the fact that *iki* – denoting the smallest of diurnal raptors – is almost as well known qualifies the importance of size in regard to focal status within this group. In free recall, *jata* and
kua were mentioned together in 16 of 23 instances, while *iki* was mentioned
before or after *jata* in 10 of 20 instances. As much as anything, these associations appear to reflect two standard compounds which Nage employ when referring generally, or synecdochally, to diurnal birds of prey, namely *kua jata* and
iki jata (see pp. 52–54). On the other hand, in response to my questioning,
Nage gave either *jata* or *kua*, and not *iki*, as local equivalents of Indonesian
elang ('hawk', 'large raptor').

Although not similarly explicable on linguistic grounds, a comparable conceptual pairing is suggested for the medium-sized and otherwise similar *bele teka*
(large falcon) and *sizo* (goshawk), which Nage mentioned in succession nine out

of 12 times. On another occasion, *sizo*, *sizo awu*, and *bele teka* were spoken of as three members of a single kind, thus suggesting a sub-category of the inter-mediate taxon comprising all Falconiformes. Interestingly, while *sizo* denotes goshawks (family Accipitridae), *iki*, denoting a small falcon, was associated in free recall with *bele teka*, a reference to one or more larger members of the Falconidae, in just two instances. Designating an unidentified small raptor, *sizo awu* was rarely mentioned at all in the recall lists.

With regard to focality or prototypicality, Columbiformes reveal even less internal stratification than diurnal birds of prey. In free recall, *muke* was mentioned by 16 informants, *zawa* (or the synonymous *bopo zawa*) by 14, *'owa* by ten, *kolo* by nine, and *kolo dhoro* (or *kolo ghodho*) by seven. *Bopo* was listed by 11 Nage and *bopo soi* by nine; but as noted earlier, Nage usually describe these terms as synonyms, and it may well be that people who mentioned both were thinking of the same bird. The only obviously peripheral members of the inter-mediate Columbiforme taxon are *zawa ngongo* and *kolo dasi* (the recently introduced Rock pigeon), although some Nage who listed *kolo* may have intended this to subsume *kolo dasi* as well.

In several places above, I indicated how size may influence focality within some, but by no means all, intermediate taxa. Another principle arguably affecting the composition and representation of at least two intermediates is what may be called 'size seriality'. Thus, Nage explicitly describe both the three bats and members of the trio of quails and buttonquails as comprising large, medium, and small kinds. From largest to smallest the respective series are *méte*, *gébu*, *'ighu* and *piko*, *bewu*, *mu ki*. As noted, in each series, the largest member is moreover the prototype or focus of the taxon. Although they do not compose such a distinct grouping as bats and the group of quails and buttonquails, Nage also compare the smaller raptors *bele teka*, *sizo*, and *iki* as similarly descending in size. In addition, the medium-sized *sizo* was once described as having plumage that is a 'mixture' of the plumage of the other two.[5]

General findings regarding Nage intermediate groupings may be summarized as follows:

1   There are six groupings of Nage bird generics that correspond to inter-mediate taxa as described by Berlin (1992: 24, 25; 139ff.). All but one of these (*ana peti*) are unnamed and therefore 'covert'. An important source of evidence for the six taxa is free recall lists which reveal clusters of folk generic terms. Yet these lists are by no means the only support for the cognitive reality of such groups.

2   Like the covert life-form 'bird', Nage intermediates are discrete and clearly bounded categories. Nage do not conceive of folk generic taxa as belonging to more than one intermediate grouping (cf. Ellen, 1993a: 119, who describes certain Nuaulu intermediate categories as not being mutually exclusive, and therefore as 'untaxonomic'). In regard to boundedness, one possible qualifica-tion concerns the polysemous character of *ana peti*. As an intermediate, *ana*

peti can be interpreted as including just three or four folk generics. Yet the same term can also designate a much more inclusive class of smaller, passerine birds; and as Nage vary in regard to which birds might be included as *ana peti*, this variability challenges the discreteness of the category when thus employed.

On the other hand, no evidence suggests that *ana peti*, in either of its senses, overlaps with any of the other five intermediate taxa described above. As I demonstrate below, Nage associate the drongo with the paradise-flycatcher in regard to the birds' prominent tails; and insofar as this pair might be conceived as a further intermediate category, then it should be recalled that a few Nage judged the drongo (*céce*) to be, in the broadest sense, an instance of *ana peti*. Nevertheless, it is questionable whether *ana peti*, when applied in the more inclusive way, actually labels a taxon, even though this sense, too, is logically 'intermediate' between 'bird' and the folk generic categories.

3   All six Nage intermediates appear to be perceptually salient; that is, firmly grounded in empirically given similarities and differences of morphology, plumage and, to a lesser degree, behaviour. Consistent with this is the extent to which they correspond to distinctions enshrined in scientific taxonomy. Although Berlin (1992: 149) suggests that the definition of intermediate taxa may involve culturally specific factors, this seems not to apply to the six groups described above. Also noteworthy is evidence supporting a common occurrence of Falconiformes and Columbiformes, especially, as recognized intermediate groupings in ethnotaxonomies the world over; for example, 'hawks and falcons' and 'doves' compose two of four 'mid-level complexes' named by the South American Aguaruna (Jivaro: Berlin, Boster and O'Neill 1981: 102).

Of course, several intermediate categories are indeed associated with particular utilitarian values, bound up with Nage cultivation (most notably, in this context, of rice) and raising of domestic fowls. Nage thus partly conceive of diurnal raptors as chicken thieves. The small birds that compose the *ana peti* (in the exclusive sense) are the most serious of avian crop pests, while two of the three bats – *méte* and *gébu* – are renowned among Nage tappers as stealers of palm juice. Also, the quails and buttonquails, and the Columbiformes, are especially favoured as food. Nevertheless, the fact is that these utilitarian or economic specifications, most of which are negative, do not exactly coincide with the intermediate classes of Nage ethnotaxonomy. Thus, although Falconiformes are largely chicken thieves, one (the *sizo awu*) is not, while, in the Nage view, nocturnal raptors (*po*) also kill fowls. Similarly, it is not just munias and other small seed-eaters (*ana peti*) that do damage to crops; as noted in Chapter 1, doves (*kolo*) and quail (*piko*) are also considered agricultural pests. Finally, while Columbiformes and the quails and buttonquails are preferred as food, these kinds account for only a part of the variety of wild bird flesh consumed by Nage.

To the extent that perceptual and utilitarian features do somewhat coincide, moreover, birds possess values of the latter sort only by virtue of quite specific, and easily recognizable, morphological features (such as sharp bills and talons, in the case of raptorial birds). It is thus only in a secondary and derivative sense that the six intermediate categories might be conceived as utilitarian or symbolic groupings and, to that extent, culturally particular. How far perceptual features coincide with and inform symbolic values among Nage, for example as manifestations of spirits or as omens, is discussed in the next chapter.

4   According to Berlin, 'taxa of intermediate rank . . . are comprised of small numbers of folk generics' (1992: 24). As shown, the six Nage categories each subsume between three and eight generics, the largest number belonging to the ethnotaxon coinciding with Columbiformes. Whether eight could still be considered a 'small number' is moot. As has also been demonstrated, most, if not all, intermediate groups have obvious focal members, or prototypes (see Berlin 1992: 152). Prototypicality is most equivocal among the two largest groups, the diurnal raptors and the Columbiformes. Where focal status is unambiguous, in two instances (quails and buttonquails, and bats) it is the generic category associated with the largest member that is the prototype, but this is not the case with *ana peti* (small seed-eaters). As indicated earlier, within the class of crow-like birds the significance of size is complicated by local size comparisons that are inaccurate.

5   The best attested of Nage intermediate categories are also the largest clearly defined groupings, coinciding with the scientific taxa of Falconiformes and Columbiformes. As noted, such birds are also the earliest mentioned in free recall lists, a circumstance suggesting that, for Nage, they are among the most typical, or exemplary, of birds. That this characterization applies more to Falconiformes than to Columbiformes is consistent with the relatively large size of diurnal raptors, as well as their visibility entailed in a capacity for high flight, possibly supplemented by the economic danger they pose as stealers of domestic fowls. Members of the *ana peti*, the taxon of quails and buttonquails, and crow-like birds are also well represented early in the recall lists. There is, then, some evidence for a correspondence between membership of intermediate taxa and relative focality within the covert life-form taxon 'bird'.[6]

The one exception of course is bats which, when mentioned in free recall, tended to appear towards the end of informants' lists. Yet this circumstance is entirely in accord with various other respects in which bats are exceptional 'birds'. Also noteworthy in this connection is the peripherality of nocturnal aviformes – including owls (*po*), nightjars (*leba*), and the unidentified *je* – within the 'bird' taxon. It should be recalled as well that the most peripheral member of the intermediate category of crow-like birds, *koa ka*, is the only one represented as exclusively nocturnal.

6   Not only do Falconiformes and Columbiformes compose the most clearly defined of Nage intermediates, they also appear to be the most internally homogeneous. The characterization is consistent with their lack of obvious

Figure 3.1 Wallacean drongo (Céce)

single prototypes. Also, as noted earlier, unlike the majority of birds, most members of the two groups are not identifiable by way of the standard representations I call simple distinctive features (see Table 2.1). At the same time, diurnal birds of prey are not so similar to one another that they can be lumped in a single generic taxon. The same of course applies to pigeons and doves.

Binary associations

In addition to the six intermediate categories described above, Nage discourse reveals other associations, or combinations, of folk generics. Virtually all of these are binary in form.

Nage thus describe the Black-naped oriole (*leo*) and the Hill mynah (*ie wea* or *io wea*) as a pair of yellow birds, referring in the second case to the yellow lappets (identified as *wea*, 'gold, golden ornaments') of the mynah. This visible resemblance is further brought out in the alternative naming of the oriole as *leo wea* – that is, 'gold(en) oriole' (see also *leo te'a*, Table 1.1; cf. the English vernacular 'Golden oriole', referring to *Oriolus oriolus*).[7] In much the same way, Nage link the Asian paradise-flycatcher (*lawi luja*) and drongo (*céce*) as two birds distinguished from all others by their long, forked tails.[8]

Previously I characterized these two pairs as further instances of intermediate groupings (Forth 1996a: 108). I have no reason to change my opinion now. Rather more doubtful candidates, however, are several other, more implicit pairings, discernible in Nage statements to the effect of one bird being 'a kind of' another, which is mostly to be understood as the two being 'of a (single) kind'. This sort of idea is often expressed by using Indonesian *jenis* ('kind, type', but also a reference to simple resemblance; cf. Forth 1995: 56–58, regarding Nage *bhia ko'o*). For example, one man spoke of the two Columbiformes *muke* (emerald-dove) and *'owa* (cuckoo-dove) as being of the same kind but differing in colour. Similar statements were recorded regarding *fega* and *zeghi* (kingfisher and bee-eater), *ha* and *muta me* (two members of the crow-like birds), the rails *kuku raku* and *wi* and, as noted earlier, *ha* and *héga hea* (two members of the scientific genus Corvus).[9] In these instances, too, the paired kinds are morphologically quite similar. For example, although kingfishers and bee-eaters belong to different ornithological families, they are both colourful birds which, as Nage commonly remark, nest in earthen holes, often in river banks. The respective families (Halcyonidae and Meropidae) are, moreover, closely related phylogenetically (see Chapter 2, note 15).

Another type of binary association of folk generics is demonstrated by several standard compound terms (see also Forth 1995: 61). One of these has already been discussed – namely, *peti kolo* ('munia-dove') which, in its most inclusive sense, serves contextually as a general term for birds.[10] Other usages include the following:

bopo zawa	larger pigeons and doves (or, sometimes, Columbiformes in general)
gako tasi o ae	herons and egrets, long-legged water birds
iki jata	diurnal raptors
kua jata	diurnal raptors (perhaps, more specifically, larger raptors)
kaka ha	cockatoos (*kea*, *kaka kea*) and crows (*ha*), as large flocking birds that consume ripening maize.
piko kolo	(smaller) game birds

Most of these pairs quite obviously reflect morphological resemblance. Yet many also pertain to utilitarian values; for example, *piko kolo* comprises two categories associated as agricultural pests, as well as birds exploited as game. In regard to the first association, it should be noted as well that Nage further combine *piko* with the name of a mammalian category, *dhéke* (mouse, rat), when referring to creatures that do harm to crops (Forth 1995: 49). Although also linked by shared behaviours (notably, flocking and harsh cries), cockatoos and crows (*kaka ha*) are largely associated in Nage thought by their common habit of invading fields of ripening maize in large numbers, a phenomenon that provides the basis of metaphorical uses of *kaka ha*.

Implicitly, most if not all of the compounds listed above refer to groupings more inclusive than the two kinds named; they are instances of dual synecdoche, whereby two members represent the entirety of a larger category. Yet, as I pointed out in the previous chapter with regard to *peti kolo*, none of the compounds actually names a taxon, since none is numerable with the classifier *éko*. Thus, when referring generally to diurnal raptors, for example, one cannot say 'two eagles (and/or) kites' (*kua jata éko dhua*). Rather, *kua jata* refers only to raptors in the abstract or to a specimen whose identity is undetermined. Expressed another way, the compounds may provide further support for the psychological reality of such intermediate taxa as Falconiformes among Nage, but they do not actually label them.

The non-taxonomic character of such compound expressions is moreover in accord with their largely utilitarian, or culturally particular, quality – a feature further distinguishing them from the six, mostly covert intermediate categories described earlier. The evidence of recall lists is also relevant in this respect. Where standard compounds concern birds belonging to large intermediate groupings (e.g. the Columbiformes), then clustering of recalled names can of course be attributed to the more inclusive association. The pairing of morphologically similar heron kinds (*gako tasi, o ae*) appears to find some reflection in free recall. In contrast, the more culturally dependent associations of *piko* and *kolo* and *kaka* (= *kea, kaka kea*) and *ha* were not so clearly reflected. Thus, whereas the two heron generics were listed together in ten of 24 lists (or 19 where at least one term was mentioned), for the other two pairs the figures were respectively six of 24 or 20, and four of 24 or 22. In fact, rather than the cockatoo, the crow (*ha*) was more often mentioned with one of the diurnal raptor generics (in seven of 24 or 21 instances), a circumstance consistent with the Nage identification of crows as meat-eaters. With regard to compounded terms with a partly utilitarian definition, it is also noteworthy that, in free recall, *peti* (or *ana peti*) and *kolo* were listed together just four out of a possible 24 times. Nage myth, song, and ritual speech reveal a pairing of bird terms that is mostly different from the binary compounds described above. Yet distinct combinations occurring in these genres also appear to have at best a marginal influence on associations evidenced in free recall, as I further discuss in Chapter 8.

Another, less formal variety of binary association is discernible in the several nomenclatural contrasts discussed in the previous chapter, where a category is labelled with the name of another plus a modifier (e.g., *jata/jata jawa*, *kolo/kolo dhoro*). With just one exception (*piko/piko du'a*, where the second term is ornithologically unidentified), the contrasting terms denote birds that resemble one another morphologically or behaviourally, but are nevertheless distinguishable on other perceptual grounds. For example, several unmodified terms (*feni, kolo, sizo*) denote birds that are larger than those identified with their modified contrasts (*feni lobo, kolo dhoro, sizo awu*); thus, when necessary, these can be specified with the adjective *méze*, 'big' (see *kolo* = *kolo méze*, and *sizo* = *sizo méze*). Nage also describe herons or egrets labelled *o ae* as bigger than the smaller and shorter-legged *o ae bha* ('white *o ae*'). Yet another means of distinguishing the normally unmodified member of a pair is *bholo* ('only, alone', 'just', 'ordinary, common'; see *zawa bholo*, as opposed to *zawa ngongo*).[11]

As stated earlier, pairs like *jata/jata jawa* and *kolo/kolo dhoro* are ambiguous in regard to the taxonomic status of their components. If, however, the components of the first pair, for example, are construed as two folk generic categories distinguishing two kinds of diurnal raptors, a question arises as to whether both should then be interpreted as taxa equally subordinated to a more inclusive taxon also labelled *jata* – and moreover, whether in that case, *jata* should not be interpreted as occupying another 'intermediate' level of Nage bird taxonomy – more precisely a 'sub-intermediate' rank – between the folk generics and the unlabelled intermediate category comprising all diurnal birds of prey previously identified (see pp. 43–44). The same question, of course, can be posed in regard to the categories named *sizo* and *sizo awu* and, in respect of Columbiformes, the other large unnamed intermediate ethnotaxon, the pairs *kolo/kolo dhoro* and *zawa/zawa ngongo*.

I would not entirely rule out the possibility of more than one intermediate rank intervening between folk generics and life-forms (cf. Waddy 1988: 77, 87, on Groote Eylandt aboriginal classification of fish). Earlier, for example, I mentioned evidence pointing to a group of smaller Falconiformes (*bele teka*, *iki*, *sizo*), as a sub-grouping within the Nage taxon definable as diurnal birds of prey. Yet to view nomenclatural contrasts such as *jata/jata jawa* as instances of intermediate taxa would surely be exaggerating an aspect of Nage classificatory thought and unduly forcing the evidence into a taxonomic mould. It is, I suggest, the very ambiguity of the relation of categories like *jata* and *jata jawa* that precludes an unequivocal interpretation of the first term as clearly defining an intermediate, or 'sub-intermediate', taxon comprised of just two members (cf. Hunn and French 1984, with regard to what they call 'polysemy').

As indicated in the previous chapter, this sort of relation is best conceived as an instance of 'encompassment' (Forth 1995: 58–59; cf. Dumont 1979). By this I mean that one term of a pair – always, evidently, the one denoting a kind more focal within any attested intermediate taxon, or simply a better-known bird – subsumes the other only contextually and implicitly (and thus, in a sense, incompletely), rather than by way of a truly taxonomic inclusion. Neither this, however, nor the non-taxonomic, or quasi-taxonomic, character imputed to designations like *piko kolo* or *kua jata*, compromises the taxonomic features of other parts of Nage ethno-ornithological classification. The relation between *jata* and the covert intermediate category that subsumes all diurnal birds of prey is, I would maintain, straightforwardly one of taxonomic inclusion. Nor, as I have suggested elsewhere, are taxonomy and encompassment absolutely opposed principles (Forth 1995: 59).

Nomenclature

The crucial importance of nomenclature for the study of ethnobiological classification has been noted by Berlin, who observes that ethnobiological nomenclature 'reveals much about the way people conceptualize the living things in their environment' (1992: 26). The link between naming and conceptualization is borne out by the number of times nomenclatural issues have necessarily been raised in the discussion above.

Before proceeding, a couple of points should be registered concerning phonological features of bird names employed in Bo'a Wae. Although /r/ has virtually disappeared from most Nage dialects, not only is it retained in song but it occurs as well in three bird names, *kolo dhoro, kuku raku*, are *'iri ae* (or *riri ae*). Since both *dhoro* and *raku* are locally regarded as onomatopoeia, the retention of /r/ in these contexts may be ascribed to its imitative quality. The onomatopoeic character of the first name may also explain alternative pronunciation of *dhoro* as *dhuru* (cf. Verheijen 1963: 707).[12] On the other hand, onomatopoeia does not appear to account for *'iri ae*, one of the less well-known names for wagtails (also called *wagha lowo*).

Of 79 names appearing in Table 1.1, 41 consist of two independent lexemes (see e.g. *ana go*). To these may be added another 11, which do so optionally (see e.g. *bama* or *bama cea*). Such binomials are not of course to be confused with the binary compounds described in the previous section, composed of the names of two folk generics. The total of 52 binomials includes *o ae bha* and *ana peti jata*, since the primary component of each (*o ae* and *ana peti*), although itself apparently comprising two parts, expresses a unitary sense. Accordingly, *o* does not possess an independent ornithological referent, while as previously shown, *ana peti* can be reduced to *peti* without any change of meaning.[13]

Of the 52 Nage binomials, only *ana peti jata* is straightforwardly productive. Terms like *jata jawa* (see also *kolo dhoro, o ae bha, sizo awu, zawa ngongo*) may also be construed as productive binomials, although as discussed in the previous chapter, they do not unambiguously denote 'kinds of' a category designated by the qualified term (e.g. *jawa, kolo*), at least not in the sense that the binomial specifies a taxon occurring at a level subordinate to the referent of the former.

The unproductive character of *manu*, which occurs in five compound terms, was demonstrated earlier. Similarly unproductive is *kaka*, included in *kaka kea* and *kaka daza*, the names of the Yellow-crested cockatoo and dollarbird. While *kaka* in the second term is a locally recognized onomatopoeia, the same element occurring in first term is not. Questioning also confirmed that, despite the similarity of names, Nage do not in any way associate these two empirically quite different birds. The unproductiveness of *kaka* in the two bird terms is borne out by the further appearance of the lexeme in four other animal terms: *kaka hika*, the 'flying' lizard (*Draco* sp.); *kaka koda*, Praying mantis; *kaka meo*, a large spider; and *kaka watu*, a kind of freshwater fish. It is clear, therefore, that, either in respect of birds or a larger congeries of animals, *kaka* does not name a bird taxon any more than does 'mouse' in English 'titmouse' (a vernacular term for the Paridae). By the same token, there is no question of an inclusion of members of different life-forms in single taxa.

Yet another instance of unproductive binomials concerns the appearance of *ana* ('child', 'small or young animal') in *ana go* (pipit or bushlark). Although

the component also occurs in *ana peti*, this term of course names an intermediate category rather than a generic. At the same time, *ana* evidently refers in
both instances to the relatively small size of the birds denoted. While *ana* is
essential to the term *ana go* (in contrast to *ana peti*, which is reducible to *peti*),
however, names of several other birds can optionally be prefixed by *ana*, as for
example in *ana bama, ana bi*, and *ana ceka*. Other instances include *ana kete
dhéngi, ana koka, ana kolo, ana mele witu, ana papa*, and *ana naka bo*.

Although this seems mostly to be done with reference to small birds, *ana* can
in fact be placed before the name of virtually any bird, especially as a way of
singularizing the kind, or speaking of a species as though it were an individual.
Relevant here is the further use of *ana* in the question *ana apa ke*? (or *ke ana
apa*?), 'what bird is that?', where according to a local interpretation *ana* is to
be understood as a contraction of *ana wa* ('animal'). *Ana* may be used when
enquiring about any sort of animal, although, as was pointed out to me, with
nipa, 'snakes', one of the Nage named life-forms, one would normally use the
life-form term instead.

Locally interpreted as 'children (or people) of the wind' (Forth 1989), *ana
wa* ('animal') exemplifies exactly the same form of naming as bird binomials incorporating *ana*, a form which further occurs in terms denoting particular animals
other than birds, and especially small ones.[14] Despite the fact that *ana* can mean
'child, child of', its appearance in these contexts does not entail a representation of ethnozoological taxa as being connected by kinship, as is found in some
other societies (Berlin 1992: 145, citing Bulmer 1974). In fact, kin terms as
such are entirely absent from Nage ethnozoological nomenclature.[15]

The last point is further borne out by the name *ebu titu* (swallows and swifts).
The commonest sense of *ebu* is 'grandparent, grandchild; ancestor'. Yet this
meaning is not obviously relevant to its occurrence in the bird term. One man
suggested that, in the sense of 'ancestor', *ebu* might be connected in this
context with the birds' inhabiting caves also haunted by free spirits (*nitu*); he
then mentioned the association of such spirits with ancestral spirits (*ame ebu*;
Forth 1998a). Yet while it accords with a general association of the top of
the volcano Ebu Lobo with both free spirits and spirits of the dead, and with
a representation of the top of the volcano as a place where swifts and swallows
are thought to hibernate during part of the year (see Chapter 7), this interpretation appeared to be no more than a fanciful extemporization. Whatever its
worth, moreover, like *ana*, the component *ebu* in the bird name does not imply
any particular relationship to any other ethno-ornithological category.

As may already be apparent, relations between the components of binomials
are various. In a few instances, the second component modifies the first, as in
detu dalu ('*dalu* tree *detu*'), *kua méze* ('large *kua*'), *tiwe te'a* ('yellow *tiwe*'),
and *leo wea* ('golden *leo*'), but without contrasting the taxon so named with
any other designated by the same primary term. Indeed, in all four of the names
just cited, the modifier is optional. A comparable pattern occurs in the more
elaborate names for 'owls' (*po*), listed in Table 1.1. Contrasting with all of the

foregoing are *ie wea* ('golden *ie*'), *o ae* ('water *o*'), and *wagha lowo* ('river *wagha*'), since in no instance can the first component stand alone as a bird name.[16]

Being almost entirely monosyllabic or disyllabic, Nage lexemes entail a high degree of homonymy; hence the second element in many binomials can be seen to serve the purpose of disambiguation. Relevant here is the fact that, by themselves, the terms *detu*, *ie*, *leo*, *po*, and *wagha*, incorporated in the afore-mentioned names of woodpeckers, mynahs, orioles, owls and wagtails, possess distinct meanings (e.g. *leo* means 'to travel, wander'). The analysis also applies where two lexemes appear simply as paired components of a single term rather than as substantive and modifier. Examples include *ebu titu*, *iki titi*, *kaka kea*, *kete dhéngi*, and *muta me* (see Table 1.1).

In contrast to all of the foregoing, the components of other Nage binomials produce a unitary description of visible, mostly behavioural features attributed to the bird in question. Among these are *bele teka* ('sharp wing'), *mata to* ('red eyes'), *mele witu* ('disappears into undergrowth'), *naka bo* ('steals from granaries'), and *wole wa* ('plays with wind'). Further possible instances include *manu ghebhe* ('hidden, disappearing fowl') and *manu ke'o* ('speckled fowl'), although the last name, evidently a euphemism, refers to an imaginary creature. Several monolex-emic names, also, are descriptive of behavioural features. Examples include the names of the raptors *jata* ('to turn, wind'), *je* ('to steal up on'), and *sizo* ('to sweep down and seize'). In regard to the earlier discussion of intermediate taxa and their bases in perception, it may be noted that two of the fully descriptive binomials – *bele teka* and *wole wa* – are also names of diurnal birds of prey (see also *ulu bha* as an occasional reference to *jata*, the Brahminy kite).

Of the 79 names for birds (including bats) listed in Table 1.1, 57, or over 72 per cent, are at least partly analysable. Since the large majority, if not all, of the terms in Table 1.1 can be considered as denoting folk generics, this finding contradicts the characterization of such taxa by Coley *et al.* (1999: 208) as being designated by unanalysable names, or 'primary lexemes' (but see Berlin 1992: 29, for a more qualified account). Further challenging this generalization is the fact, registered above, that over half (41 of 79) of the terms in Table 1.1 comprise two independent lexemes. Analysable bird names among Nage include terms that refer, either entirely or in part, to perceptible, and then mostly visible features (a bird's form, behaviour, or habitat), as well as terms that are entirely or partly onomatopoeic. The remaining 22 names (which include all three of the names for bats), are unanalysable either because the name has no other known meaning or appears to be a homonym of an unrelated word (e.g. *go* in *ana go*).

As many as 18 of the analysable names refer entirely to visible or other perceptible features. The total includes two names which refer to vocal features, or vocal behaviour of birds, but are not actually onomatopoeia (see *lako lizu*, *muta me*). Also included in the total of 18 are two names (*jata jawa*, *leba*) where there is uncertainty regarding which other senses may be linked with the use of the term in bird nomenclature. Another set of 18 names includes terms com-prising two lexemes, just one of which (but in nearly every case the second) refers to a visible feature (see e.g. *bébe ae*, where *ae*, 'water' refers to an environmental association), thus bringing the number of analysable, non-onomatopoeic names to 36, or 46 per cent of the total of 79, and over 63 per cent of the 57 analysable names.

In determining instances of onomatopoeia, I have relied on informants' judgements supplemented by imitations and descriptions of bird calls. Some names thus described by Nage may be false onomatopoeia. One example is *kea*, details of which are given Table 1.1. In this respect, it should be noted that reputedly onomatopoeic names are sometimes distinct from standard renditions of one or more of a bird's vocalizations. For example, while *koka* (friarbird) is considered an onomatopoeia, the bird's characteristic cry is regularly designated as *iko ako*. In addition, Nage describe the friarbird as producing an unlimited variety of meaningful cries (see Chapter 6).

The fact that a few reputedly imitative bird names are cognates of forms that are widespread in eastern Indonesian languages (e.g., *iki* and, indeed, *koka*) might also call into question their onomatopoeic status. On the other hand, ornithological descriptions of vocalizations of the Black-naped oriole (*leo*) seem to correspond closely to the Nage name; for example, McKinnon (1991: 252) reproduces the bird's whistling as 'leeuw' and 'klee-lee-tee-leeuw (see also 'uLIEUW' and other sounds recorded by Coates and Bishop, 1997: 413). Yet Nage do not consider *leo* an onomatopoeic name.[17]

Among the onomatopoeic names in Table 1.1, 12 are entirely onomatopoeic, while another nine contain onomatopoeic components (see entries marked On and oN). The former total includes seven single lexemes (e.g. *céce*) as well as five binomials, both of whose components are onomatopoeic, reproducing either two different vocalizations or a single vocalization reckoned to consist of three or more syllables (see *iki titi, koa ka, kuku raku, toe ou,* and *witu tui*). In nearly all of the partly onomatopoeic binomials, the other component is not analysable. The exception is *ie wea*, where the second element refers to a visible feature, the 'golden' (*wea*) lappets of the Hill mynah. Also exemplifying this sort of combination are the three owl terms listed in Table 1.1 (s.v. *po*).

From the foregoing computations, it is quite clear that, of the 57 terms that are at least partly motivated and analysable, only 22 (or 38.5 per cent) include onomatopoeic components. The majority, therefore, which comprise 36 (or over 63 per cent), are non-onomatopoeic names referring to perceptual, and then mostly visible, features of birds.[18] In relation to the total of 79 names, the proportions are 27 and 73 per cent respectively. These findings thus tend to weigh against suggestions (see Feld 1982) that, in non-western cultures, birds are generally better known by – or, indeed, as – sounds than by visual features. (The figures, it may be noted, are not significantly affected if the two names describing, rather than imitating, vocal behaviour are added to the number of onomatopoeia.)

In regard to entirely or partly onomatopoeic names constituting just 27 per cent of all Nage bird names, it should also be noted that this figure is considerably lower than Verheijen's estimate of onomatopoeic bird names in Manggarai, which he gives as nearly 40 per cent (1963: 713). The Nage total is also lower than the 34 or 38 per cent given by Berlin and O'Neill (1981: 240) for two South American (Jivaroan) languages, figures which for these authors signal a 'pervasiveness' of onomatopoeia in the nomenclatures concerned. Interestingly, the Manggarai figure is very close to the 39 per cent given by Feld for the New Guinean Kaluli (1982) and figures of 37 per cent cited for both Selepet (Papua New Guinea) and Canadian Delaware (Berlin and O'Neill 1981: 259). The figure Hunn (1977: 84) provides for the Tzeltal Maya is a quite remarkable 50 per cent. These comparisons suggest, then, that the incidence of onomatopoeia among Nage bird names is noticeably less than what one finds in the languages of other small-scale, traditional societies. On the other hand, whether the Nage figure of 27 per cent (or indeed 37 per cent if only analysable cases are counted) might yet be sufficient to constitute 'pervasive' onomatopoeia, following the usage of Berlin and his collaborators, remains an open question.

A final note concerns names that refer to culturally particular associations, or rather the virtual absence of such names from Nage bird nomenclature. Just two terms might be interpreted in this way, and both of them simultaneously reflect frequently remarked behavioural features of the birds in question. One is *kete dhéngi* which, although also explained partly as an onomatopoeia and by the bird's usual habitat, may allude to a mythical association of the Bare-throated whistler (see Table 1.1; also Chapter 8). The other is *awe uza*, 'rain summoner', a name that may be taken as a particular cultural gloss on the preponderant appearance of the birds so named during rainy weather. Even though *lako lizu*, 'sky dog', accurately captures the quality of a bird's vocalization, the name is of course a metaphor, and so to that extent differs from straightforward descriptive names (e.g. *mata to*, 'red eyes'); hence it might be counted as a further example.

General features of Nage bird classification

This chapter and the previous chapter have served to establish the general outlines of Nage ethno-ornithological taxonomy and patterns of bird nomenclature:

1   Implicit in Nage classification of birds is a taxonomic structure constituted of relations of inclusion. All folk generics, named and unnamed, are considered instances of 'bird', understood as a covert life-form taxon, which in turn is included in the category of 'animal' (*ana wa*). Separately, as well, all individual bird generics are classified as *ana wa*. Between 'bird' and the generic terms, moreover, one encounters a named intermediate taxon (*ana peti*) and several unnamed intermediates. Given the further occurrence of a few terms which, contextually at any rate, may be interpreted as folk specific taxa, Nage bird classification forms part of an ethnozoological taxonomy comprising five levels.

None of the foregoing is contradicted by a previously documented linguistic ambiguity regarding relations of inclusion (Forth 1995). Although the Nage expression *bhia ko'o* does not always unequivocally specify the inclusion of X in Y (in the statement 'X is a 'kind of' (*bhia ko'o*) Y'), this sort of relation is nevertheless a demonstrated property of Nage cognition regarding natural kinds. Apart from evidence presented above, further support is found in other areas of Nage ethnozoological classification, particularly in regard to the named life-form taxa *nipa* (snake) and *ika* (fish; Forth 1995). Nor is the representation of Nage bird classification as a taxonomic order contradicted or superseded by the possible accommodation of certain categories to a 'focus and extension' model, whereby one term can be seen as focal, or central, to a category (either an intermediate taxon or the life-form 'bird'), in relation to which other terms are relatively peripheral.

2   Named taxa, especially Nage folk generics, reveal a high degree of correspondence to scientific taxa. Thus, for the very most part, generic terms designate either ornithological species, or birds belonging to the same scientific genera or closely related genera. Similarly, the most firmly attested of the unnamed intermediate categories – 'hawks' and 'pigeons' – coincide with the ornithological orders of Falconiformes and Columbiformes.

3   As the second conclusion should suggest, Nage ethno-ornithological classification is pervasively grounded in perceptual criteria. Accordingly, where folk taxa are definitely at variance with scientific taxa, the former are nevertheless based on observable, physical resemblances. For example, Nage placing of members of the distinct, and phylogenetically distant, families Hirundinidae and Apodidae (swallows and swifts) in a single folk taxon (*ebu titu*, alternatively called *awe uza*) is most readily explained by manifest morphological and behavioural similarities. Another illustration concerns the inclusion in a single covert intermediate category of both true quails and distantly related but manifestly similar buttonquails.

4   Mostly covert intermediate taxa suggested by Nage discourse about birds (including lists of bird terms generated in free recall) should not be confused with partly utilitarian categories regularly designated with binary compounds (e.g. *bopo zawa*, *kaka ha*, *piko kolo*). At first glance, this distinction might be construed as a contrast of nomenclature and classification. Yet, while analytically distinguishable, naming and classifying cannot in practice be so simply disengaged.

What is most compelling about Nage compounding of names of ethnozoological taxa (and, to a lesser extent, more variable instances of binary association among folk generics) is the way these conform to a pervasive social and conceptual dualism, whereby unities of various kinds are conceived in terms of a combination of two parts. Indeed, it is precisely in this respect that Nage representations of birds and other natural kinds appear mostly to correspond to general principles of culture and social structure, as distinct from universal factors of perception. Recently, I explored this pervasive social and cultural dualism in a monograph on western Keo society (Forth 2001), and much of what I demonstrated there in regard to Keo applies to Nage as well. The force of these observations is somewhat qualified by the fact that Nage social dualism itself parallels a widespread binary tendency of the Nage language in general, where in ordinary speech nominal, verbal, and other usages are regularly combined in pairs expressing a unitary sense (Forth 1996b). It also needs to be reiterated that compound expressions involving birds do not really define units of Nage ethnotaxonomy. Rather, they reveal further ways of thinking and talking about birds that both reflect and, in a sense, extend this taxonomy.

5   While the Nage ethnotaxonomy of birds is thoroughly grounded in perceptual features, vision is the sense mostly involved in discriminations on which this form of order is based. Consistent with this is the predominance of names that refer to visible attributes of empirical birds. This finding would also seem to accord with Ong's suggestion of a special link between the visual sense and a taxonomic ordering of species (a word derived, as he notes, from Latin *specio*, 'to look at, behold', 1977: 139). Yet onomatopoeic names are also numerous among Nage bird terms, even though they seem to be less pervasive than in the nomenclatures of other non-western societies.

As motivations of names designating taxonomic units, vocalizations can be understood as metonymies, or parts that stand for larger, physical and visible wholes. As imitations of auditory behaviour, onomatopoeic names can further be interpreted as indices of perceptually grounded wholes, not essentially different from visible behaviours or even visible morphological traits. At the same time, for Nage, similarities of sound apparently do not connect birds as members of the same folk generics, or of intermediate categories, in the same way or to the same extent as does visible resemblance, even though birds that look similar (for example, Columbiformes) often sound similar as well.

6   Just one or two bird names can be linked with culturally specific values attaching to particular birds. Yet values of this sort, whether conceived as 'symbolic' or 'utilitarian', are not necessarily basic to the formation of either generic or intermediate taxa. The several named taxa of small seed-eating birds classified together as *ana peti* (the one named intermediate category) do possess a common utilitarian character of sorts, albeit a negative one, insofar as all do damage to crops. Yet such folk generic taxa are at least equally identifiable on grounds of morphology and behaviour. The more general point is that utilitarian and symbolic values can rarely be divorced from perceptible physical features. In regard to the several named kinds whose vocalizations serve as chronological indicators, or signs of seasonal change (for example, *kuku raku, lako lizu, muta me*, and *toe ou*; see Chapter 1), the point can be extended to include natural auditory features – one might even say auditory behaviours. Even so, it is noteworthy that these birds generally do not share the same covert, intermediate taxa, which are defined instead by visible factors, and so in this respect are more comparable to birds associated on the basis of symbolic, or mystical, significance.

The fact that Nage generally do not name birds with reference to symbolic values does not mean that birds among Nage are not linked with such values. On the contrary, as I demonstrate in the next several chapters, the majority are. Nage bird categories may compose a taxonomic order grounded largely in perceptual features; yet Nage representations reveal other ways in which units of this classification, more particularly folk generics, are regularly associated. In this regard, one might even speak of symbolic classes, contrasting with cognitively distinct taxonomic classes. In the following chapter, I explore the most prominent instance of such a symbolic class, one comprising birds that Nage credit with the ability to emit sounds considered as manifestations of malevolent spiritual beings.

Chapter 4

Things that go *po* in the night: ethnotaxonomy and symbolic classification*

In what follows, I employ the phrase 'symbolic classification' advisedly, not least because, in his book of this title, Needham (whose name is most closely associated with the term) admits that 'we do not yet know what exactly we are talking about when we discuss symbolic classification' (1979: 56). For present purposes, 'classification' refers simply to a regular conceptual treatment of two or more terms as instances of a more inclusive class. 'Symbolic', on the other hand, indicates that instances of the class are associated on grounds that are not attributable to simple empirical observation but are thought to be linked, for example, by virtue of their supposed possession of common spiritual, or mystical, properties.

Otherwise, the sense of 'symbolic classification' can best be illustrated through the detailed investigation of a single, hypothetical instance. The case I explore in this chapter concerns birds associated with the Nage category *po*. Although in Nage ethnotaxonomy this is the term for 'owl', in symbolic contexts the same term links owls with several other, distinctly named folk generic taxa comprising birds which, Nage say, 'can *po*' (*ngala po*); that is, produce sounds designated – or, indeed, classified – as *po*. In these contexts, then, the term pertains more to sounds than to empirical, which is mostly to say, visible, birds. Thus, insofar as *po* refers to a classificatory concept apparently displaying features of a taxonomy (most notably, inclusion), its components are terms labelling sounds identified primarily with various manifestations of spiritual beings. As this should suggest, it is the 'spiritual' nature of the category that largely motivates my distinguishing this use of *po* as an instance of a symbolic classification.

Po as a reference to birds

As a reference to birds and sounds respectively, *po* participates in two series of compound terms, shown in Table 4.1. Although distinguished from

* This chapter is drawn from my article entitled 'Things that go *po* in the night: the classification of birds, sounds, and spirits among the Nage of eastern Indonesia', which appeared in *Journal of Ethnobiology* (18 (2): 189–209, 1998). It appears here with minor, mostly augmentative, revisions.

Figure 4.1 Wallace's scops owl (*Po*)

Table 4.1 Terms incorporating *po*

1 Terms denoting owls	
Po koba	'Vine *po*'
Po kua	'Eagle *po*'
Po tadu	'Horn(ed) *po*'
2 Terms denoting nocturnal sounds	
Po polo	'Witch *po*'
Po bapu	'*Bapu* (malevolent free spirit) *po*'
Po tadu bhada	'Buffalo horn *po*'
Po keo	'*Po* that sounds *keo*'
Po uci	'*Po* that sounds *uci*', 'Whistling *po*'
Po ci	'*Po* that sounds *ci*', 'Hissing *po*'
Po lobo	'Volcano *po*'

non-ornithological uses by the optional inclusion of one of three modifiers, the bird terms, in section (a) of the table, nevertheless designate what for Nage is an indivisible folk generic taxon minimally labelled as *po* and glossable as 'owl'.

In an earlier article (1996a), I discussed whether Nage bird classification subsumed an intermediate grouping that could be labelled 'night birds'. Doubts as to the psychological reality of such a group were raised in the previous chapter. Whatever the status of the hypothetical category, however, nocturnal birds are cognitively quite distinct from the far more clearly circumscribed, although also unnamed, complex of Falconiformes, or diurnal birds of prey.

As already shown, the conceptual unity of the Falconiformes (diurnal raptors) is clearly revealed in free recall; in contrast, the term for owls (*po*) – Strigiformes or nocturnal raptors – was mentioned far less often, and rarely in close proximity to names of Falconiformes.[1] In part, this can be ascribed to the peripherality of night birds in general, and the fact that, whereas diurnal birds of prey were commonly named early in the lists – thus suggesting a prototypical status in relation to the life-form taxon 'bird' – nocturnal kinds, if mentioned at all, were usually named much later.

This ethnotaxonomic separation of daytime from night-time birds of prey is important, for in Nage religious discourse *po* defines an essentially mystical class which includes both nocturnal and diurnal raptors. Also subsumed by this grouping – entities that 'are able to produce *po* sounds' (*ngala po*) – are certain material objects, more particularly trophy horns of sacrificial buffalo and certain manufactured items of *hebu* wood (*Cassia fistula*). At the same time, Nage believe that the sounds, whether initially identified with birds or with objects, emanate ultimately from malevolent spirits. In this way, Nage classification of birds and sounds implicates a classification of spiritual beings. As will also become clear, while daytime birds of prey are unequivocally central to the ethno-ornithological category 'bird', and while night birds, including owls, are peripheral, in this other, spiritual context, the relation is inverted, and it is owls that occupy the more central place.

Also crucial to this contextual contrast of nocturnal and diurnal birds is the circumstance that, in ethnotaxonomic discourse, as in free recall, Nage associate owls not with diurnal raptors but, if anything, then with other night birds. Moreover, none of these other nocturnal kinds belongs to the mystical category of things believed to produce *po* sounds. Conversely, Nage generally do not identify eagles, hawks or falcons as night birds, even though diurnal raptors too are reputed to emit nocturnal sounds classified as *po*.[2] Nocturnal kinds which Nage say 'do not *po*' (*mona po*) include the Savannah nightjar (*leba*), the birds named *koa ka* and *piko du'a*, and the three bat categories (*gébu*, *'ighu*, and *méte*; see Table 1.1). All this attests to the perceptual, and more specifically visual, basis of the Nage bird ethnotaxonomy, as it indicates how Falconiformes are separated from Strigiformes by virtue of visible, behavioural features, and particularly the fact that they are seen flying during the day. By the same token, by separating night birds from day birds, in their construction of a general purpose classification of avifaunal kinds, Nage evidently do not attach significance to a bird's supposed ability to produce *po* sounds.

As listed in Table 4.1, the three synonymous terms Nage apply exclusively to owls are *po koba*, *po tadu* and *po kua*. In each, the second element modifies *po*, understood as a substantive. As *koba* means 'creeping or climbing plant, vine',

Nage explain the first name as an allusion to the common daytime sighting of roosting owls, perched on or near large forest vines. *Po tadu*, 'horn(ed) po', refers to the 'horns', or ears, some owls are recognized to possess (see Figure 4.1). According to Nage statements, *po kua* is motivated by the resemblance in plumage between owls and eagles (*kua*, or *kua méze*), although conceivably other similarities between the two bird kinds might play a part as well. In free recall, many informants simply mentioned *po* while others gave a binomial, or sometimes more than one. In the latter instances, *po kua* was listed six times, *po koba* twice, and *po tadu* once. (I can find no obvious explanation for the preponderance of *po kua* in this context.)

It is important to stress that the three modifiers refer not to different kinds of owls, but rather to features of what Nage regard as a single indivisible generic. Although there are probably three or four owl species present in Nage territory (see Table 1.1), including both eared owls (genus *Otus*, family Strigidae) and Barn owls (Tytonidae), Nage deny with quite remarkable consistency that the three terms distinguish three distinct owl kinds, describing them instead as alternative names for the same bird which focus on different physical or behavioural features. While Nage are aware that not all owls possess 'horns', some informants thus explain these as a possible sexual characteristic – speculating that only the males are horned – rather than as a trait marking a separate owl taxon. The synonymy of the three names is further indicated by the remark of one man, who referred to owls as *po kua* ('eagle po') but immediately added that these are recognized, and distinguished from eagles (*kua*), by their 'horns'.[3]

All the same, the three modifiers of *po* evidently do refer to visual features of empirical species. For example, *po tadu* ('horned' po) undoubtedly refers to the two or three species of *Otus*, all of which, in contrast to other genera of owls, possess 'horns' (or 'ears'). While the reference of the term cannot be identified conclusively, the motivation of *po koba* recalls a description of *Otus silvicola* as perching 'high in a tall tree or in a concealed position' (Coates and Bishop 1997: 361). Also, in regard to the contrasting lighter under parts and darker upper parts of the Tytonidae, and their greater size than *Otus* species, the empirical referent of *po kua* ('eagle *po*') is probably *Tyto alba* or *T. longimembris*. (Possible ornithological correspondences of the terms referring primarily to nocturnal sounds, listed in Table 4.1, section (b), will be discussed presently.)

As the term for 'owl', *po* is an onomatopoeic name, replicating a nocturnal vocalization that Nage themselves identify as one of a number of sounds characteristically produced by owls. Owls are thus one of several of birds Nage describe as 'saying their own name'. Following Jespersen's strict definition of onomatopoeia, *po* can further be characterized as an 'echoic word [which] designates the being that produces the sound' (1921: 399; cited in Berlin and O'Neill 1981: 239). As is often the case with such names (cf. English 'crow' and 'cuckoo'), *po* further refers to the sound itself, or rather, in a more general Nage usage, a series of sounds so classified, and to the act of producing the sound or sounds.

Yet as already noted, Nage claim that not only owls (*po*) are capable of producing sounds they classify as *po*, since they consider a number of other raptorial birds (and even certain material objects) as capable of doing so as well. With one exception, other birds credited with this ability are diurnal birds of prey, including *bele teka*, *iki*, *jata*, *jata jawa*, and *sizo* (see Table 1.1). All of these categories, then, are separately named, and none is designated with a name incorporating the lexeme *po*.[4] The one non-raptorial bird sometimes classified as a *po*-sounder is the Pale-headed munia, or 'Brahminy kite munia' (*ana peti jata*; see Figure 4.2). So named because its plumage closely resembles that of the white-headed, but otherwise rusty red Brahminy kite (*jata*), the inclusion of this little bird among kinds that produce *po* sounds (including the sound more specifically labelled as *uci*, which I describe below) provides one indication of the significance of visual, and morphological, criteria in defining the otherwise auditory category, a matter I take up further below. It is similarly noteworthy that some informants doubted whether the munia can really produce *po* sounds, adducing its small size – thus another visual criterion – as the reason for their scepticism.

It is perhaps ironic that some Nage were also unsure whether another raptorial bird is able 'to *po*'. This is the *je*, which many local descriptions indicate may be a Strigiforme (more specifically, the Brown hawk-owl, *Ninox scutulata*). Other Nage accounts, however, suggest a partly nocturnal, or crepuscular, Falconiforme. The status of *je* in relation to the category of things that manifest *po* sounds is thus ambiguous, just as it is in regard to the ornithological distinction of the two families of raptorial birds. Nevertheless, the fact that *je*, when mentioned in free recall, was most often listed with *po* provides further evidence

Figure 4.2 Pale-headed munia (*Ana peti jata*) and Brahminy kite (*Jata*)

that, in the context of Nage ethno-ornithological taxonomy, nocturnal birds are associated primarily on the basis of visual criteria (morphology and observable behaviour) rather than their common membership in the auditorially conceived mystical category.[5]

Because Nage do not normally speak of raptorial birds other than owls as 'kinds of *po*',[6] when used as a substantive *po* does not unambiguously *designate* a class of birds (or, more generally, entities) that can produce *po* sounds. At the same time, all things thought to emit these sounds evidently constitute some sort of covert grouping, which is to say, one unnamed by any single lexeme. What is more, for Nage this grouping and the ethnotaxon named *po* (denoting exclusively Strigiformes), while distinct, are conceptually close. As the epitome of things that produce *po* sounds, owls constitute the focus of the unnamed class. Pertinent here is the Nage claim that they have only ever seen owls actually making the sounds. The idea that other birds can do so as well, while maintained with considerable conviction, is therefore not well grounded in experience. As one man expressed the matter, it may simply be an 'inference' or 'interpretation' (Indonesian/Bahasa Indonesia *tafsiran*).

Since reputed *po*-sounding birds other than Strigiformes are, with one exception, all diurnal raptors, the fact that owls are nevertheless the prototype points to another peculiarity of the unlabelled symbolic class. For this prototypical status accords with the previously mentioned inversion of the normal pattern whereby creatures of the daytime are considered typical and unmarked, while night creatures are atypical and marked. The obvious ground for this pattern is the fact that diurnal creatures are more often seen and therefore far more familiar than are night creatures (cf. Bulmer 1979: 67). In the present case, however, the inversion also confirms the primacy of auditory over visual values in the symbolic classification of entities linked with the category *po*.

The *po* sounds

The other binomial use of *po* concerns the series of names incorporating this term which designate sounds heard at night (see Table 4.1). Formally, the series is identical to the set of three names that denote birds. Whereas the bird terms all refer synonymously to a single ethno-ornithological taxon, however, these terms distinguish several varieties of nocturnal vocalizations. Since all of the named *po* sounds are attributed to all of the birds Nage credit with the ability 'to *po*', there is, furthermore, no systematic matching of kinds of *po*-sounding birds – that is, the various Nage generic taxa encompassing Strigiformes and Falconiformes – with kinds of *po* sounds.[7]

Particularly when encountered near habitations, all of the *po* sounds are regarded as portentous. Two of these, *po polo* and *po bapu*, refer specifically to sounds that manifest different kinds of spiritual beings. *Polo*, the modifier of the first term, means 'witch' and refers to a person believed to operate as a maleficent spirit, attacking human victims by mystical means, typically at night.

Although *polo* thus refers to a type of human being as well as a malevolent spiritual force, witches are distinguished from other humans on specifically spiritual grounds; hence *polo* can be treated as a kind of spiritual being. Also relevant in this connection is the fact that Nage sometimes speak of *po* – referring both to sounds and birds – as a form more specifically assumed by the *wa*, the maleficent spirit, of a witch (see Forth 1993a).

As another modifier of *po*, the term *bapu* denotes varieties of malevolent autochthonous free spirits associated with uninhabited places. In part because some of these spirits are regarded as the source of a witch's powers, *polo* and *bapu* are closely linked concepts in Nage cosmology. Nevertheless, the spiritual entities to which the terms refer are distinct. Accordingly, *po* sounds identified with each, though equally inauspicious, are distinguished by different auditory qualities. Vocalizations identified as *po polo* ('witch *po*') include an uneven number of 'soft' or 'weak' calls. Another manifestation is a call heard coming from the ground at night, just in front of a house or beneath a raised house floor. Indicating that a witch is extremely angry at someone living in the house, such an event foreshadows certain disaster unless ritual measures are taken to ward off the witch's wrath.[8]

Calls which, by their number or quality, are otherwise interpretable as *po polo* can alternatively be understood as simple omens without any explicit spiritual attribution. Thus a *po* sound repeated eight times can indicate an imminent theft. An informant from the Keo region, to the south of Nage, stated that *po* repeated four times is a bad omen for one's own group, while five times means that the bad news is for 'other people'. Although consistent with the auspicious and inauspicious significance both Nage and Keo attach to odd and even numbers respectively (Forth 1993b), this notion appears inconsistent with the Nage representation of *po polo* as comprising an uneven number of cries. The same informant further stated that a harsh call is an omen for men whereas a soft call is ominous for women.

Not surprisingly, sounds classed as *po* are not invariably interpreted as omens of any sort. In fact, so often are they heard in the night that the sounds seem to acquire determinate mystical significance mostly situationally – for example when they are heard unusually close by, or repeatedly, or occur in conjunction with other inauspicious signs or unfavourable circumstances. Describing the auditory phenomenon known as *po uci*, one Nage man suggested that, whereas a combination of *po* and *uci* sounds (which I describe just below) indicates the presence of a witch, *po* sounds heard alone might be nothing more than the nocturnal cry of a bird. More often than not, however, Nage identify *po* sounds as portents that are at least potentially inauspicious. What is more, they usually take them to indicate the presence of a witch (*polo*), even to the extent that *po polo* can be characterized as the prototypical variety of all *po* sounds.

In contrast to *po polo*, Nage describe *po bapu* ('malevolent free spirit *po*') as a loud, penetrating cry that carries far, often taking the form of a series of long, drawn-out or continuous hoots. The local description is somewhat reminiscent of the 'drawn-out shriek' of *Tyto alba* (Coates and Bishop 1997: 357), but vocalizations of other Strigiformes, also, are likely to be interpreted as instances of *po bapu*. Occasionally, I recorded *po bapu* as a reference not simply to a sound but directly to a *bapu* spirit, a usage that is fully in accord with a close connection between *po* sounds and malevolent spiritual forces generally. Sometimes Nage further distinguish a particular variant of *po bapu* called *po tadu bhada*, 'buffalo horn *po*'. This refers to a representation of sacrificial water buffalo as embodiments of mountain-dwelling spirits, also classified as *bapu*, which continue to be identified with the trophy horns of slaughtered buffalo (Forth 1998a). Nage describe this buffalo horn *po* as a soft, faint noise like a 'puff' or quiet 'pop', a description that recalls vocalizations of Wallace's scops-owl (*Otus silvicola*), and especially the 'deep *hwomph*' mentioned by Coates and Bishop (1997: 361). As the sound is taken to mean that trophy horns have not been properly cared for, when it is heard a fowl should be slaughtered and some of its blood smeared on the horns in order to avert illness or other misfortune.[9]

Nage regularly speak as though the buffalo horn *po* emanates directly from old trophy horns. On the other hand, one informant explained that the sound was more likely produced by a bird calling just outside a building in which horns are stored. This sort of disagreement suggests that, unlike birds, and especially owls, material objects are marginal to the set of entities that Nage say 'can *po*'. Nevertheless, one cannot on this ground exclude these objects from the unlabelled grouping, any more than one can, in this same context, distinguish sharply between nocturnal and diurnal birds.

In contrast to the buffalo horn *po*, the other sort of *po bapu* sound – the common or unmarked variety – is often interpreted as a sign that a *bapu* is demanding that a human client reciprocate favours bestowed by the spirit. A particularly famous spirit of this sort inhabits a large boulder called Ebu 'Egu (Forth 1998a); hence its auditory manifestation is sometimes specified as *po Ebu 'Egu*. Nage further associate *po* sounds, and more particularly *po bapu*, with the *hebu* (*Cassia fistula*), a hardwood tree possessing an especially powerful *bapu* spirit. Should anyone build a house or field hut close to such a tree, the occupants are therefore likely to be constantly bothered by *po* sounds. Also relevant in this connection is the use of *hebu* wood in the construction of forked sacrificial posts (*peo*), wooden statuary (*ana deo*), and the principal post, or 'hearth post' (*posa lapu*), of special ceremonial buildings, or 'cult houses' (*sa'o waja*). All of the foregoing are items of ritual importance which, if not treated properly, can similarly express their anger by way of *po* sounds.

Also illuminating the common association of objects of *hebu* wood and buffalo horns with both the auditory category *po* and the spiritual category *bapu* is the use of forked *hebu* posts (*peo*) for tethering sacrificial buffalo. In addition, wooden statues and house posts of *hebu* are exclusive to cult houses, buildings in which trophy horns are also found. Not surprisingly, therefore, the sound of *po bapu* heard repeatedly near a cult house can be interpreted as reflecting the displeasure of a *bapu* spirit – in this context represented as a negative component or aspect of the otherwise tutelary 'house spirit' (*ga'e sa'o*) – caused by the house owners having allowed the building to fall into disrepair or having transgressed rules of proper use. Nage commentators mostly linked *po bapu* in these circumstances with the *hebu* wood used to construct such a house. Nevertheless, the connection with buffalo horns, which Nage also identify with the guardian spirit of a cult house, is equally germane. Although the association of *po* sounds and buffalo horns may recall the term *po tadu* ('horn(ed) *po*') as a specific reference to owls, it is worth stressing that neither trophy horns nor sounds called *po bapu* are associated with any particular kind of physical bird. Rather, buffalo horns, the *hebu* tree, all *po* sounds, and all *po*-sounding birds figure as components of an intricate representation of malevolent spirits, the two named varieties of which are *bapu* and *polo*.

A further idea connecting *bapu* with both buffalo and raptorial birds is the belief that *bapu* spirits residing atop the volcano Ebu Lobo assume the guise of a Brahminy kite (*jata*) or a large, high-flying hawk (*jata jawa*) when searching for human victims, whom they characteristically kill in the form of spirit buffalo. In contrast to the general pattern, in this instance a particular kind of spirit is indeed identified with a particular bird taxon (or taxa, if *jata* and *jata jawa* are construed as two contrasting categories). Yet in this case it appears significant that the manifestation is not auditory but visual, a distinction to which I return later on.

In addition to *po polo* and *po bapu*, Nage distinguish two other types of *po* sounds: *po keo* and *po uci*. Unlike the former varieties, in these instances the modifiers of *po* are onomatopoeic references to auditory phenomena rather than the names of spirits, and each can accordingly be designated simply as *keo* or *uci*. Even so, *po keo* and *po uci* are equally regarded as manifestations of both malevolent spirits (*bapu*) and witches (*polo*). *Po keo* describes a harsh call locally reproduced as 'keo, keo', or as 'ko, ko, ko, ko, ko, keo', a cry somewhat reminiscent of the 'high-pitched, hoarse, drawn-out shriek' that Coates and Bishop (1997: 357) record for the Barn owl (*Tyto alba*). At the same time, one cannot rule out 'mechanical sounding' vocalizations of the Eastern grass owl (*T. longimembris*) and croaking and quacking sounds described for the Moluccan scops-owl (*Otus magicus*). Unlike other *po* sounds, Nage consider *po keo* a partly auspicious omen. Heard in the night before the annual hunt (*to'a lako*), *po keo* indicates that wild pigs, or other large game, will be killed on the following day. Although mostly regarded as a simple augury – and a positive one at that – a link between *po keo* and *bapu* spirits is nevertheless discernible in the belief that spirits of *hebu* trees can manifest themselves as wild pigs, as well as in the idea that nature spirits generally (*nitu*, a category that can subsume *bapu*) are the owners of game animals.

This latter belief also helps explain why the *keo* sound is sometimes regarded as auspicious. Although it may manifest potentially harmful free spirits, it does so in a way that reveals the presence of their livestock, which humans wish to appropriate. Instead of foretelling a successful hunt, the cry of *keo* at other times can reveal a witch (*polo*) out hunting for humans victims, a notion that links *po keo*, like other *po* sounds, with spiritual malevolence. In this regard, the auspiciousness of the *keo* sound during the annual hunt might further be attributed to the fact that, on this single occasion, human hunters – sleeping outside in the wild, staying awake until late into the night, and attacking and killing, if not wild spirits, then their livestock – themselves resemble man-hunting witches.

A more elaborate version of the augury of *po keo* links the cry with the nocturnal sound of a grasshopper named *poi ce*. Whereas *keo* heard in the context of the hunt indicates that pigs will be killed on the following day, the sound of the grasshopper presages the killing of deer, the other major game animal. Also, when the insect is heard in or near a village, at night, this can indicate the presence of a witch, just as can the *keo* sound.[10]

The other major category incorporating *po* and referring to ominous nocturnal sounds is *po uci*. Although *uci* refers to a high-pitched whistle (cf. the 'thin whistle' attributed by Coates and Bishop to the Eastern grass owl, *Tyto longimembris*), Nage speculate that the sound may be produced by a bird's wing rather than by vocal means.[11] When placed after *po*, *uci* can be construed either as a modifier or as a paired term, the two words in combination – and in accordance with the widespread pattern of binary compounding illustrated in the previous chapter – then referring more generally, or synecdochally, to inauspicious nocturnal sounds. As accords with the second interpretation, sounds identified as *uci* are sometimes heard in combination with vocalizations more specifically classified as *po* (the hoots and other softer calls usually distinguished as *po bapu* or *po polo*).[12]

That the sounds sometimes occur in succession of course suggests that *po* and *uci* derive from the same avifaunal source. In one instance, several people reported hearing the *uci* sound repeated three times followed by a double cry of *po*. This was heard close to the grave of a man who had died ten days previously, and was counted as one of several indications that he had been killed by a witch. Whether or not the sounds occur in succession, *uci* is attributed to exactly the same birds that give voice to other *po* sounds. Some local interpretations link the sound more closely with diurnal raptors than with owls (the Brahminy kite and eagles being mentioned most often in this connection), an association that may seem curious in view of the coupling of the *uci* sound with *po* and the special, though not exclusive, linking of *po* with owls. One man, for example, said he could not be sure whether owls could '*uci* as well as *po*'; but he was certain that kites, eagles, and falcons could do so. Whatever is to be made of this, the fact is that all Nage regard *uci*, like the *po* sound, as a manifestation of a malevolent being, and most often, if not invariably, of a witch (*polo*).

An association comparable, and in a sense perhaps complementary, to a closer connection between *uci* and diurnal raptors may be found in evidence suggesting that *po keo* is associated with owls rather than with diurnal birds of prey. In fact, seeming to contradict the representation of the term as a reference to a variety of sounds made by all owls, a few Nage described a physical distinction between birds called *po keo* and others simply designated as *po*, or more specifically as *po tadu*, 'horned *po*'. The clearest account comes from a young man who claimed to have shot an owl with an air rifle, while it was calling *keo* in the night. Discovering that the bird did not have 'horns', he concluded that *po keo* and *po tadu* are distinct kinds of owls. Two other men made statements to the same effect. Quite possibly, the harsh cry Nage call *keo* is the 'high-pitched, hoarse, drawn-out shriek' that Coates and Bishop (1997) describe for the Barn owl (*Tyto alba javanica*), which unlike other Flores owls does indeed lack 'horns'. Nevertheless, Nage also claim that, to quote another man, 'there is only one "form" of *po* and that is the horned *po*'.[13] Interestingly, one of the two men who distinguished *po keo* from the *po* with horns implicitly linked this with a partial moral contrast. As he noted, the cry of the *keo*, in the context of the annual hunt, is a good sign, while the call of the horned *po* is always a bad sign. As noted above, Nage also attribute the presence or absence of 'horns' in physical birds called *po* to a difference of gender.

It is by now quite clear that Nage vary somewhat in their accounts of *po*-sounding birds, particularly in regard to the symbolic interpretation of specific manifestations. Nevertheless, it is worth reiterating that, in their associations with malevolent spiritual beings, all manifestations of *po* sounds (including *keo* and *uci*) belong ultimately to a single symbolic category. Distinctions articulated by some Nage commentators, in regard to relations between audial differences and physical contrasts among birds, are therefore of secondary importance to the construction and representation of this category.

Further possible distinctions among *po* sounds are signalled with the terms *po ci* and *po lobo*. On purely vocalic grounds, some Nage distinguish *po ci*, a reference to a hissing or rasping sound reminiscent of sounds made by the Tytonidae (Coates and Bishop 1997: 358), from the high-pitched whistle they call *uci*. People in the Keo region use *po lobo* (roughly, 'volcano *po*') to refer to the cry of a night bird that begins as a small, soft voice and gets progressively louder. Although this term seems not to be known among Nage in Bo'a Wae, it nevertheless accords with other Nage representations of raptorial birds. For Keo say the *po lobo* manifests a being from the Ebu Lobo volcano out searching for buffalo, which is to say human victims, and thus reveals a spirit of the sort Nage classify as *bapu*.[14]

As should by now be clear, whereas *keo*, *uci*, and *ci* refer to quite specific sounds, *po* can denote a wide variety of bird vocalizations. Yet as an onomatopoeic term, *po* reproduces only particular instances of this class. Thus it may be understood as a synecdoche and a prototype of a more inclusive auditory category, paralleling the prototypical status of owls in relation to the entire class of birds and other things thought capable of producing the *po* sounds. Although, among birds, only owls are unambiguously denoted by *po*, this formal similarity provides an important clue to the association of the onomatopoeic term, and the sounds it designates, with the larger, mystical category of *po*-sounding entities.

As further accords with the special connection between *po* sounds and owls, Nage speak of the sounds (including *uci* and *keo*) as the only calls made by Strigiformes. By contrast, they recognize diurnal birds of prey as producing vocalizations other than ones classified as *po*. Unlike *po* sounds, these cries are normally heard during the daytime. They are also not considered ominous in the same way as is *po*, and they do not, in themselves, connect the birds with malevolent spirits. The kestrel (*iki*), for example, cries 'ki ki ki ki', as, following some accounts, does the falcon named *bele teka*, although this bird is also described as emitting an ascending 'wiiii'.[15] The term *ie* refers, onomatopoeically, to a call of kites (*jata*); it further denotes the whinnying of a horse (cf. also *ie wea*, the Hill mynah, *Gracula religiosa*). The high-pitched shriek of eagles (*kua*) sounds something like 'ji ji ji jiii' according to several informants. In addition, Nage employ a special term, *no'i*, to refer to the crying of eagles, but this appears not to be onomatopoeic. *Io*, apparently a variant of *ie*, also denotes a raptor's cry (see Appendix 1, text 24).

Sounds, spirits, and Strigiformes

Both as a reference to owls and to a series of sounds, *po* can be understood as an onomatopoeic term. While the first, ethnotaxonomic sense is distinguished by modifiers which refer not to sound, but to visible features of physical birds (see Table 4.1), sound nevertheless figures crucially in defining the mystical category of birds and other things that 'can *po*'. As the only birds that Nage straightforwardly designate as *po*, owls are the most central members of this grouping just as they are the sole members of the ethno-ornithological taxon of the same name. In addition, it is on the whole the nocturnal Strigiformes, rather than the diurnal Falconiformes, that are more closely associated with the several separately named kinds of *po* sounds, as well as with the malevolent spiritual beings considered their ultimate source.

The central position of owls in all three contexts owes something to auditory experience. As noted, Nage claim to have seen only Strigiformes emitting *po* sounds. At the same time, the fact that these sounds are heard at night means that their producers cannot normally be seen; hence their possible attribution to a variety of otherwise visible things, including what westerners would regard as inanimate objects as well as diurnal raptors. What has yet to be considered, however, is why Nage should think that diurnal birds of prey also make sounds empirically attributable only to owls. The answer requires consideration of factors additional to actual vocal properties that bear upon the focality of owls within the several classificatory domains in which *po* participates.

While *po* strictly speaking denotes only owls and sounds, crucial to a proper understanding of its function in defining a wider class of perceptible things is a third term connecting birds, material objects, and auditory phenomena in a way that, for Nage, creates a unitary configuration of meaning. This third term is malevolent spirits. All physical things associated with *po* sounds, whether birds or material objects, are considered as visible, or potentially visible, manifestations of dangerous spirits. Also, while Nage statements sometimes suggest that the sounds are produced by birds serving as physical media of witches and *bapu* spirits, other evidence points to a representation in which the sounds, on the one hand, and visible birds and objects, on the other, are equally signs of malevolent anthropomorphous beings which are spiritual and hence essentially invisible.

Consistent with the second interpretation are occasional Nage claims that *po* sounds, inasmuch as they manifest the anger of spiritual beings, are not made by birds at all. Here, one is reminded of the remark of Feld's Kaluli informant, who asserted that what westerners call birds, New Guinean Kaluli regard as ancestral voices (1982: 45).[16] The Nage statement might be understood simply as a claim that spirits, not birds, are the ultimate source of the sounds. Yet it also suggests a distinction between sounds whose derivation from the mouths of birds, if not incidental, is of secondary significance, and physical birds that can be conceived non-spiritually. The distinction of course accords with evidence suggesting that Nage conceive of owls and other *po*-sounding birds in two quite separate ways: as components of an ethnotaxonomy based on visible features, and as focal members of an unlabelled mystical grouping defined by auditory phenomena ineluctably associated with – and simultaneously attributed to – malevolent spiritual beings. In this connection, Nage statements regarding *po* bear comparison with remarks by Geddes on the Fijian association of guardian spirits called *vu* and a bird called *kikau*. The spirit, Geddes claims, 'is not considered to be resident in the *kikau* nor even that the *kikau* signals his presence [*sic*]. It is merely that the sound is identical' (1945: 43).

While the mystical class of *po*-sounding entities is defined by sound, and particularly sounds known to be produced by owls, other members, especially daytime birds of prey, are evidently included on the basis not of auditory, but of visual (that is, morphological and behavioural) features. These of course are also the principal bases of Nage ethno-ornithological taxonomy. Yet the symbolic class identified with *po* sounds is not simply based on perceptual grounds – or the fact that diurnal raptors sufficiently resemble owls to be classed with the onomatopoeically designated nocturnal raptors. For this would fail to explain why night-time and daytime birds of prey are not classified together in Nage ethnotaxonomy. Rather, inextricably bound up in their symbolic association – and consolidating their relationship in this context – are also local ideas regarding malevolent spirits.

It is beyond question that the participation of diurnal raptors in representations of murderous witches and malevolent *bapu* spirits derives from their predatory and carnivorous habits combined with their possession of sharp bills and talons. As I discuss more fully in the next chapter, relevant in this regard is the Nage characterization of all flesh-eating birds – both scavengers and predators – as 'witch birds' (Indonesian: *burung suangi*) or, in their own language, simply as *polo*, 'witches'. This is a larger mystical class which also includes crows (*ha* and *héga hea*), the drongo, and unidentified night birds (*koa ka*, *manu miu*).[17] As will be demonstrated in the next chapter, implicitly reflecting varying combinations of plumage and other morphological traits, behavioural criteria, diet, and vocalic features, this is also a polythetic class.

Obviously, the 'witch birds' are more inclusive than the group of *po*-sounding birds, a category which (with the obvious exception of the White-headed munia) applies only to predators. On the other hand, non-birds which also 'can *po*' (e.g., the trophy horns of buffalo) are obviously not included among the 'witch birds' (see Forth 1998b: 202 s.v. Fig. 1).

Although 'witch birds' are largely defined by visual features, it is worth reiterating that *po*-sounding birds, while identified with reference to auditory phenomena, are nevertheless more central to the class than are other bird categories. Especially diurnal birds of prey share a definitive behavioural trait with witches, and in a sense with anthropomorphous *bapu* spirits as well. This is their habit of killing and eating other birds, most notably domestic fowls, a characteristic that parallels the anthropophagous proclivities of Nage witches (Forth 1993a). Also relevant is the identification, in Nage symbolism, of domestic fowls with human beings, and of human souls as chickens belonging to the divinity which, in one conception of death, are ultimately returned to God when humans die (see pp. 89–90; also Chapter 9). Owls are generally less given to preying on other birds than are Falconiformes. Nevertheless, some Nage claim that owls (*po*) as well as diurnal raptors 'steal domestic fowls' (*naka manu*). What is more, in other respects the night-time predators are even more closely linked with witches and *bapu* spirits than are diurnal birds of prey. Apart from their nocturnal habits, owls alone possess visual features which associate them with these malevolent anthropomorphous spirits. Thus, just as witches and *bapu* possess an ability to manifest themselves as a variety of creatures, and to partake of both human and animal characters, so, as Nage frequently observe, the round facial discs of Strigiformes resemble human faces. Nage also describe the form of owls' heads, and especially their 'ears' (or 'horns'), as lending them the appearance of cats, an evaluation suggesting that they are birds which, rather anomalously, exhibit features of non-birds. Yet another connection concerns the reputed ability of human witches, in accordance with their generally inverted character, to rotate their heads 180 degrees, just as Nage know owls to do.

Just as sounds labelled *po* are the prototype of an identically named broader auditory class that includes other named vocalizations, so owls (*po*) are therefore the prototype of the complex of things associated with the auditory category labelled *po*. At the same time, the identification of Strigiformes with witches and *bapu* spirits clearly derives in considerable measure from visual traits of birds that, for Nage, recall malevolent anthropomorphous beings. Sharing the same empirical features with Strigiformes, diurnal birds of prey are then assumed by Nage to share also in the vocal habits of both owls and maleficent spirits (cf. Lakoff 1987: 86, citing Rips 1975). With objects such as buffalo horns and things made of *hebu* wood, the spiritual connection appears rather more ideological than perceptual, or at least to be based on other sorts of empirical criteria (including the red colour of *hebu*). Yet the connection is evidently sufficient to associate these material objects, indirectly, with owls (and hence with other raptorial birds) as things that 'can *po*'. This circumstance moreover confirms how an identification with malevolent spirits provides the common link among all things, birds and non-birds and nocturnal as well as diurnal avifauna, belonging to the class of *po*-sounding entities.

Yet while an identification of *po* sounds with witches and other harmful spirits is crucial to the inclusion of diurnal raptors in the class of *po*-sounding entities, a question remains as to the origin of the identification itself. Occasional experience of the sound emanating from physical birds whose form reminds Nage of malevolent spirits would seem an inadequate explanation. An additional factor may therefore be intrinsic qualities of the sounds – their eeriness or a sense of mystery they evoke. In this regard, Nage ideas about *po* may lend support to the thesis of an inextricable link between particular kinds of sound and varieties of experience contributory to the development or maintenance of spiritual or religious representations (see Tuzin 1984). Recalling that spirits the world over tend to be conceived as essentially invisible (or, at least, bound to no particular visible form), also relevant here are Walter Ong's observations on the 'interiority of sound' and the 'exteriority of vision', and the special relation of the former to what Ong calls 'the sacral' (1982: 71–75).

Although pertaining more to features of language than directly apprehended sound, a resemblance between *po* and *polo* ('witch'), a non-onomatopoeic term with a quite separate derivation (cf. Indonesian/Bahasa Indonesia *polong*, 'evil spirit'), may also contribute to an evaluation of *po* sounds as manifestations of spiritual malevolence. Similarly suggestive is the homonym *po* ('to cut, to be cut down'), which in the idiom *mata po* (*mata*, 'to die') specifies a premature death. Not only is this a frequently cited form of retribution by witches and other angry spirits, but an untimely death is also a possible consequence of failed attempts to derive special powers from *bapu* spirits, an alternative outcome of which is transformation into a witch (*polo*).[18] As well as inherent qualities, therefore, the Nage identification of *po* sounds with witches and other harmful spirits may owe something to their resemblance to human words and voices, particularly as they issue from a nocturnal, invisible – and seemingly disembodied – presence.

Concluding remarks

Nage uses of *po* support several general conclusions regarding the relation between ethnotaxonomy and symbolic categories. In the sense of 'owl', *po* denotes a peripheral taxon in an ethno-ornithological classification based primarily on visual criteria, in regard to which diurnal raptors are decidedly focal. Conversely, owls are central, and day birds relatively marginal, to the category of *po* understood as a reference to a series of nocturnal sounds and as the defining quality of a spiritual class. Thus when auditory percepts are valorized over visual ones, what may be called the taxonomic precedence of diurnal over nocturnal birds is overturned.

Although owls and other raptors are both identified as instances of *po*-sounding birds, this obviously does not constitute a discrete ethno-ornithological taxon since their identification is subsumed within a broader spiritual class that further includes non-birds and objects westerners would consider inanimate. By the same token, the seemingly heterogeneous composition of this symbolic category can hardly be adduced in support of the view that folk classifications of natural kinds are radically different from scientific taxonomies or display significant cultural relativity. As demonstrated in previous chapters, Nage do possess an ethnotaxonomy of birds; but this operates quite separately from the symbolic complex in which *po* figures as a spiritual category. That is, while the series of *po* sounds and entities thought to manifest these sounds are indeed connected by a common link with powerful spirits, spiritual associations play no discernible part in Nage ethno-ornithological taxonomy. As I describe in the next chapter, although several mostly diurnal birds with dark plumage are identified as 'witch birds', the fact that many (but not all) are coincidentally further associated as members of an unnamed intermediate group in folk ornithology (see Chapter 3) turns on a salient visual feature – their resemblance to crows – rather than on any auditory or other similarities (such as dietary habits or nocturnal behaviour) which could further identify them spiritually. As noted in the previous chapter, one of the witch birds, the drongo (*céce*) is not a member of this intermediate taxon of 'crow-like' birds because, regardless of its symbolic identity, it differs from the other birds in both size and morphology. On the other hand, two members of the crow-like taxon (*muta me* and *toe ou*), the second of which is moreover sometimes described as nocturnal (Forth 1998b), are not considered witch birds.

Separating *po*-sounding night birds from *po*-sounding day birds, Nage bird taxonomy is thus grounded in perceptual criteria that reflect natural discontinuities that are independent of culture. As shown, the symbolic identification of nocturnal and diurnal birds is also grounded in such criteria. Yet in this instance, as with symbolism in general, empiricism is partial and selective. As noted, the idea that diurnal raptors are *po*-sounders, like owls, is empirically not well founded, as even Nage themselves recognize. Conversely, the representation of owls killing domestic fowls, like diurnal birds of prey, is similarly suspect ornithologically, and is more readily ascribed to the symbolic identification of both sorts of birds as manifestations of malevolent spirits, and of fowls as the souls of ordinary mortals.[19]

That beliefs regarding which birds produce *po* sounds have no direct bearing on Nage bird taxonomy turns partly on a nomenclatural feature: the fact that, unlike owls, diurnal raptors are not actually named as *po*. Auditory features are of course implicated in this taxonomy, but only insofar as several component terms, including of course *po* as the label for 'owl', are onomatopoeic. Yet, in the present case at least, onomatopoeia pertains to nomenclature rather than to classification per se. There is a classification of *po* sounds, but this is not at all articulated with a classification of birds. By the same token, birds figure in a class of *po*-sounding entities (as distinct from the class of *po* sounds) only to the extent that owls and other avian kinds are considered as partial, physical manifestations of things that are essentially non-physical, invisible and, indeed, non-ornithological. These are of course kinds of malevolent spirits. Expressing this another way, one can say that spirits compose an auditorially defined whole of which certain birds form a part. Accordingly, while there are contexts where Nage identify physical birds (such as high-flying hawks) with harmful spirits, it is nevertheless the *po* sounds that they regard as their most immediate manifestation. Thus Nage are able to experience nocturnal sounds directly as manifestations of spirits, rather than as cries of owls and other birds rationalized as visible embodiments of these spirits.

In Nage ethno-ornithological classification, this part–whole relation between auditory and visual percepts is of course reversed, as indeed it is in western vernacular and scientific nomenclatures where onomatopoeic designations (see, e.g., 'crow', 'cuckoo', and indeed 'owl') are similarly applied to natural kinds identified on non-auditory grounds.[20] Thus, in this domain, the auditorially motivated (or onomatopoeic) name *po* figures as the part arbitrarily designating a visible whole; that is, a taxon defined primarily by visual criteria.[21] It is by now well established that a single term referring to a natural kind, even one whose empirical referents remain partly constant over a variety of contexts, can figure in more than one classificatory schema (cf. Forth 1995). *Po* provides a particularly clear example of this general possibility. As the only visible entities actually denoted by *po*, owls form a discrete taxon in a perceptually based folk ornithology while remaining focal to a culturally specific, symbolic complex of 'things that go *po* in the night'.

Chapter 5

Spiritual birds*

In the preceding chapter I introduced the subject of symbolic classification by way of an examination of one symbolic class – birds which, according to Nage, can produce sounds they call *po*. As noted there, being considered manifestations of witches (*polo*), these birds, which except for the Pale-headed munia (*ana peti jata*) are all nocturnal or diurnal raptors, are counted among the 'witch birds', a larger symbolic grouping that also includes birds which 'do not *po*'. Yet there is an even more inclusive congeries of ethno-ornithological categories that Nage identify with beings of the sort conventionally called 'spiritual'. Nage ideas accommodate an analytical distinction of two kinds of spiritual birds. First, there are birds identified with 'free spirits'; secondly, there are those which Nage associate with human souls, more particularly souls of the dead.[1] Almost without exception, birds of both sorts are ominous in the general sense that, either as auditory or visible manifestations of spiritual entities, they can reveal to humans otherwise hidden knowledge.

Birds associated with free spirits

I use the term 'free spirits' to refer to normally unseen beings possessing extraordinary powers which, unlike 'souls', have never existed in human form. Among Nage, such spirits are most inclusively labelled as *nitu*. As I have demonstrated elsewhere (Forth 1998a), however, implicitly subsumed by this category is a variety of other terms referring to more specific spirit kinds, most notably *bapu* and *noa*. Although witches (*polo*) are identified with individual human beings (and particular humans are identified as witches), Nage witches closely resemble free spirits, with whom they are moreover related both ontologically

*   Much of the information presented in this chapter is drawn from my essay entitled 'Sounds, spirits, symbols and signs: birds in Nage cosmology', which is included in *Les Messagers divins. Aspects esthétiques et symboliques des oiseaux en Asie du Sud-Est*, edited by Pierre Le Roux and Bernard Sellato (Paris/Marseille, Seven Orients/Presses de l'Université de Provence, 2002). Other parts of the same essay inform Chapter 6. I am grateful to the publishers for allowing me to use this material.

and ontogenetically. Accordingly, the spirit of a witch (*wa, wa polo*), the malefi-cent quality that makes a person a witch, behaves in all essential respect like a free spirit. For these reasons, witches can be understood as instances of the general category of 'free spirits'. As previously shown, all birds that Nage identify as producers of nocturnal *po* sounds are equally considered as manifestations of both witches and free spirits called *bapu*; and whether such sounds are inter-preted as instances of one or the other spiritual category is entirely a matter of their length, pitch, or other auditory qualities. Indeed, virtually all kinds of birds that Nage identify with categories of free spirits are equally regarded as possible manifestations of witches (*polo*), and vice versa. Thus, the symbolic category of 'witch birds' is virtually conterminous with the series of birds Nage associate with varieties of free spirits.[2]

As mentioned, apart from the previously described *po*-sounding raptors, witch birds include two kinds of crow, the drongo, and unidentified kinds called *koa ka* and *manu miu*. In what follows, I review Nage ideas concerning each of these, in alphabetical order according to their local names.

Céce (*Wallacean drongo*, Dicrurus densus; see Figure 3.1)

A diurnal species, the glossy black drongo is identified as a witch, and hence as a bird of ill-omen, specifically when it calls at night. Nevertheless, Nage also describe the bird as providing negative signs visually, and in the daytime.

A story I recorded in Bo'a Wae (the main Nage village defining the centre of the region where most of my research was conducted) concerned an incident in which a *céce* was seen flying noisily in circles and calling persistently – a habit referred to as *céce ghaba gheo* – around a slightly raised patch of ground. Observing this, one man later inspected the spot and discovered a shallow grave which, when excavated, revealed a fully formed foetus. The police were then called, and their enquiries revealed the foetus to have been the fruit of an illicit relationship that a desperate woman had clandestinely buried. The tale illustrates the drongo's association with corpses. Yet an identification with witches is strongly implied as well, for Nage represent human witches as grave robbers and corpse-eaters (Forth 1993a, 1998a: 58). In a similar vein, another man explained the prohibition on eating drongo flesh – a taboo (*pie*) that in fact applies to all 'witch birds' – with reference to the idea that the bird calls riotously because it has seen a bird of prey or because it has detected the smell of human blood or a corpse.[3] Not only does this further link the drongo with human deaths, but it also connects the species with *po*-sounding raptorial birds, the kinds that Nage most closely associate with witches.

Other evidence links the drongo with malevolent free spirits called *noa* and *bapu*. In a myth, the bird appears as a form taken by a *noa* spirit, a being more closely identified with crows (*ha*, see below). The drongo then devours a man whom the spirit has previously punished by reducing him to a tiny size (see further Chapter 8). People in Keo, to the south of Nage, spoke of *bapu* spirits manifesting not just as owls (*po*), but as drongos and crows as well (Forth 1998a: 152, note 2). On a more empirical note, the negative reputation of the drongo may be explained by its dark plumage and its noisy and aggressive nature (cf. Coates and Bishop 1997: 408). Although Nage seem not to regard drongos as flesh-eaters, both Ellen (1993b: 75) and MacKinnon (1991: 250) describe members of the genus *Dicrurus* occasionally feeding on carrion or small lizards. Like the names of many Nage omen birds, *céce* replicates the drongo's characteristic vocalization.

Ha (Large-billed crow, Corvus macrorhynchos)

Another onomatopoeically named bird, the *ha* is associated with witches not so much because of its call – which Nage do not often speak of as a distinct omen – but in regard to its inauspicious appearance, particularly in large numbers. Pertinent here are the bird's scavenging, carnivorous habits and tendency to flock. Nage also describe crows as stealing chicken eggs, a habit which, in the local view, links them, as 'chicken thieves' (*naka manu*), with both diurnal and nocturnal birds of prey (thus the producers of ominous *po* sounds). In the same vein, one man expressly compared crows to carnivorous raptors in regard to their feeding on animal carcasses and pecking at wounds of large livestock.

Although classified as a 'witch bird', Nage more often represent the *ha* as a visible form assumed by malevolent free spirits called *noa*. Crows also embody very similar spirits called *u boe* (Forth 1998a: 99–100). Characterized as bearers of disease afflicting livestock, large flocks of crows suddenly appearing from the north are thus taken as a sign of the approach of these spirits, and hence sickness and death among buffalo and horses. A more benign manifestation of the *noa* concerns large-scale buffalo sacrifices, when flocks of crows, attracted by the numerous carcasses left lying in the village plaza (Forth 1998a: 99), descend on a village to feed on the congealed blood and other waste from slaughtered beasts.

Héga hea (Flores crow, Corvus florensis)

A Flores endemic resembling a smaller version of the Large-billed crow (*ha*), the *héga hea* reveals the presence of dangerous spirits by way of a harsh cry reproduced as 'kela kela'. The bird sometimes calls at night as well as in the daytime, but Nage do not usually describe it as a nocturnal bird. Somewhat recalling ideas concerning the drongo, the cry of the *héga hea* is more specifically identified as a sign that the bird has smelt the blood of a 'buffalo' which is actually a human being recently slaughtered by witches. Alternatively, Nage identify the killers as malevolent mountain spirits (*ata zéle lobo*, 'people on top of the volcano'), an instance of the spirit category *bapu* (Forth 1998a: 149–52).

Upon hearing the call of a *héga hea*, a person should exclaim 'do it (instead) to your mothers and fathers' (*tau we'e wai ine kau, ema kau*) or 'death to your fathers and mothers' (*mata we'e wai ema kau, ine kau*), in order to deflect the threat onto the kin of whoever or whatever the perpetrator might be. According to this representation, it is not the bird itself that embodies a witch or harmful spirit, or poses the threat. In fact, by way of its cries – which might even be characterized as a useful warning – the *héga hea* merely responds to an act of violence committed by a spiritual being. Nevertheless, Nage still speak of the bird as though it were itself a witch, evidently because of the negative import of its call and the affliction which may yet follow it.

Although most Nage do not interpret the name *héga hea* as onomatopoeic, their Keo neighbours describe *yea* (a dialectal variant of *hea*) in this way. Also, Verheijen (1963) lists the Manggarai terms for the same bird, *léa* and *éa* (as a component of *kaka-éa*), as onomatopoeia. In Rembong (in the extreme north-western part of central Flores), the Flores crow is named *kelaq*, obviously a variant of the term which in Nage describes its call.

Koa ka (most likely the Flores crow, Corvus florensis)

The *koa ka* is known mostly as a nocturnal vocalization. Although the name is onomatopoeic, Nage also reproduced the bird's call as 'kha, kha', or 'waa, waa, waa', an imitation that resembles a vocalization of the Flores crow (*héga hea*).[4] Local descriptions of the bird's size and dark plumage also accord with the endemic corvine. Always heard at night, the sound of *koa ka* is a sure sign that someone will shortly die. Nage further say that if the call is heard near the landward end, or 'head', of a village, then a death will occur in a house located in the seaward or 'tail' section, and vice versa. Similarly, if it comes from the right (the direction called *mena*), then someone residing on the left side of the settlement will meet his end, and if from the left (*zale*) then someone on the right.

These ideas immediately recall Nage representations of free spirits, witches, and even human souls as entities characterized by several sorts of inversion (Forth 1998a: 52, 56–58, 70–72). Inversion is also encountered in portents involving other kinds of animals. Thus, if Nage observe a tiny spider descending on a web all the way to the ground, this can presage the death of an adult, whereas if the same behaviour is displayed by a larger spider, the death of a child is indicated. Similarly, a nocturnal moaning sound that is loud and deep reveals the soul of a child being led away by a witch, but if the sound is soft and high-pitched then the victim is an older person. In much the same vein, Nage say that the call of a cricket named *meci*, another manifestation of a witch, is always heard to emanate from a direction contrary to the insect's actual location.

Manu miu (unidentified)

Nage describe *manu miu* as an unseen creature that utters a sound resembling *miu* ('you', the Nage second person plural pronoun) in the night. When people hear this, they should either keep silent or respond with phrases that deflect any intended harm onto the ultimate source of the *miu* sound, rather as one should do upon hearing a Flores crow (*héga hea*). Such a response might be *miu wai ine kau, ema kau, azi kau, . . .* 'you with your mother, your father, your younger siblings (and other relatives)'. On the other hand, if the hearer should answer with 'who are you?' (*miu sai?*), as one might be inclined to do since the sound resembles a human voice, then the answer might be *miu toto kéka*, 'the whole field hut (houseful) of you'. In that case, not just the unwary questioner but his entire family may suffer illness, death, and thus eventual extinction.

Manu miu differs from previous categories in two respects. First, although *manu* is 'domestic fowl', most Nage doubt whether the term names a distinct bird. People of this opinion state that the *miu* sound can be made by a variety of birds – including small birds (*kolo, ana peti*), kites (*jata*), and eagles (*kua*) – and by horses as well. Secondly, although the sound is definitely ominous, negative effects follow only if it is answered.[5] Nevertheless, like other bird categories described above, Nage identify the *manu miu* as a manifestation of a witch, and more particularly as something that is 'commanded by witches' (*polo watu*). Consistent with this, the dangers of answering the sound are reminiscent of the Nage belief that talking to animals can transform a person into a witch (Forth 1989).

Other avifaunal manifestations of free spirits

While the 'witch birds' described above, like the *po*-sounding raptors, reveal free spirits largely through their vocalizations, in a few instances birds can also manifest such spirits in an entirely visual mode. A contextually positive revelation pertains to the procedure followed when Nage obtain a *hebu* tree (*Cassia fistula*) to fashion into a sacrificial post, when a functionary waits until a bird, of any sort, alights in the branches, before plunging a lance into the trunk. According to one local interpretation, this act (which I described in another context on p. 37) ensures that a necessary connection is retained between the tree and its spirit, a being classified as *ga'e* or *bapu* (Forth 1998a: 118–19). As I have demonstrated elsewhere, this representation ultimately implicates free spirits of the same general sort as those that manifest themselves negatively as nocturnal *po* sounds. What is interesting in this context is not only the desirability of the bird's appearance – a positive omen bound up with the purpose of capturing and controlling powerful spirits that otherwise cause harm – but the fact that, here, any kind of bird provides the required augury.

A partly comparable set of ideas informs Nage practices when felling large trees in order to clear an area of land. In this case, the object is not to retain but to remove free spirits (in this context typically specified as *nitu*). Nage usually say that, if procedures are properly performed, such a spirit can be observed leaving the tree in the guise of a snake. On one occasion, however, men of the Nage village of 'Abu set about felling a large banyan tree at the landward end of their settlement. Although they performed the requisite ritual, the chain-saw they were using would not initially cut through the main trunk. Just then a pair of woodpeckers (*detu dalu*) flew out of the tree, after which the villagers claimed to be able to fell the trunk with ease. Later, in response to my question, they identified the birds as the spirits (*nitu*) that had been requested to leave the tree.

With regard to links between birds and spirits in general, this incident is instructive. Previously I had never heard of such tree spirits taking the form of birds, only snakes. Identifying the woodpeckers in this way thus suggests an opportunistic interpretation in which representations are adjusted, temporarily though perhaps in the longer run permanently, to fit experience. At the same time, ideas regarding *hebu* trees and the sacrificial posts made from these trees do provide a prototype (and, perhaps, a sort of internal motivation) for the interpretation. For although the spirit of a *hebu*, one sort of being able to manifest as nocturnal *po* sounds, is distinct from other free spirits, all can ultimately be understood as variants of a single image, or complex of images (Forth 1998a).

As mentioned in the previous chapter, another purely visual indication of the activity of free spirits is the appearance of a Brahminy kite (*jata*) or another large hawk (*jata jawa*) hovering high over human settlements. Since this betokens a *bapu* spirit of the sort that dwells on top of the Ebu Lobo volcano searching for a human victim, Nage then take ritual precautions in order to protect themselves from harm (see Forth 1998a: 151). A somewhat more diffuse death omen, involving raptorial birds of the same kind, is a gathering of three or four kites (*jata loka*; *loka*, 'to assemble, place of assembly') in the air or in a tree, which can mean that malevolent beings have come together to plan someone's demise. On the other hand, such a raptorial gathering can sometimes be interpreted in other ways.[6]

Birds of prey designated as *jata* and *jata jawa* are of course members of the group that produce *po* sounds and therefore count as instances of the larger collection of witch birds. Classified more specifically as *bapu*, moreover, the free spirits they can manifest visibly are ultimately of the same kind as those associated with *hebu* trees. It is noteworthy that, unlike some other eastern Indonesians, Nage do not identify large birds of prey as participants in the creation of the world. Nor, by the same token, do they associate any bird with their supreme being (Ga'e Déwa). In this respect, the Nage contrast with other eastern Indonesians, including their Ngadha neighbours, who identify eagles, the Brahminy kite, and other large raptors with higher forms of divinity. Arndt (1960: 120–24; cf. Arndt 1954: 194) also records a myth concerning a Ngadha clan ancestor named Kua who takes the form of an 'eagle' (cf. Nage *kua*, Table 1.1).[7] How far Nage ideas regarding large raptors as visible embodiments of *bapu* spirits can be construed as an echo of the Ngadha association of such birds with deities is moot (see Chapter 9, note 7). As I explain later, the only birds appearing in Nage myths concerning the creation of the world are the friarbird and Imperial pigeon (Forth 1992), and neither of these is explicitly identified with a spirit or deity.

Finally, a partly avifaunal association of birds with free spirits is found in the Nage representation of the *manu ke'o* (literally, 'speckled fowl'), a mystically powerful winged creature with a cock's head and the body of a large snake.[8] As I have explained elsewhere (Forth 1998a), Nage describe the *manu ke'o* as an instance of the spirit category *nitu*, understood in a general sense. Despite the common element *manu* (domestic fowl) in their names, there is no special connection between the designation *manu ke'o* and either the previously described *manu miu* or the *manu mesi* ('sea fowl') which I treat in the next section. On the other hand, it may be recalled that, if not all, then the majority of Nage categories labelled with binomials incorporating *manu* (see also *manu wodu*, described in Chapter 7) appear to refer to imaginary beings at best only partially linked with particular empirical birds (see pp. 32–33).

Birds associated with human souls

Birds associated in one or another way with human souls (*mae*) are rather fewer than those identified with free spirits. The following describes the several kinds encountered in Bo'a Wae, again in alphabetical order.

Cio woza (Black-faced cuckoo-shrike, Coracina novaehollandiae)

The cuckoo-shrike is one of just two birds whose cries Nage speak of as a manifestation of a dead soul. The first part of the name, *cio*, replicates this vocalization, a rising and descending cry locally imitated as 'ciooo-cioooo' or 'chee-up'. Interpreted as the soul of a dead relative come to call another to death, this can be a sign that someone has died or is about to die, an idea that illuminates poetic references to the *cio woza*'s cry as evoking sorrow (see Appendix 1, text 32; also text 24, regarding the dialectal name *mole sio*).[9] The omen has especial force when the bird flies directly over a house, and if it does so at midday. Impending death is indicated as well when a *cio woza* calls from the back of a sick person's house. On the other hand, if the bird calls from the front, then Nage say the sufferer has a good chance of recovery. According to a modern variant of these ideas, a cuckoo-shrike calling from the back of a clinic, just as one enters to obtain treatment, is an inauspicious portent. But if the call is heard from the front, then the sign is good, or at least not negative.

Nage qualify the meaning of the cuckoo-shrike's cry in yet other ways. If heard simply in the vicinity of a settlement, the call can indicate the impending arrival of a guest. According to a similar idea, if one hears a cuckoo-shrike while travelling, it means that something either positive or negative is about to happen, or that on returning home one will receive either good or bad news. One man further opined that the sign is bad if the bird calls in front of the traveller and good if it calls from behind. As I have myself observed, the cry of a *cio woza* heard on a journey may render a Nage traveller noticeably anxious. It is not taken as a definite indication that one should directly return home. Nevertheless, within a day or two, Nage say, one will certainly receive news of an occurrence of some importance.

When a cuckoo-shrike's cry is heard near a settlement, residents may attempt to silence the bird – or the deceased human soul it embodies – by casting a little food in its direction and proclaiming 'there, you hungry one, eat a little of this' (*kéna kau ta'a mange, ka nge'e sa éno*). Alternatively, people may simply hope that the bird's appearance holds the more positive significance of the arrival of an unexpected visitor, an instance of the general Nage belief that souls of the dead are able to reveal knowledge of things hidden, including the location of lost objects (Forth 1998a: 246–47). Apart from the quality of its call, visual features that may link the cuckoo-shrike with souls of the dead include the black face, or mask, referred to in the complete English name and, possibly, its distinctive, undulating flight – a commonly remarked characteristic which can be construed as the bird's 'simple distinctive feature' (see Chapter 2).

Deza kela *(unidentified)*

Deza kela is the label some Nage specify as the proper name of a very small bird known to most people only as 'soul of a dead person' (*mae ata mata, mae mango ata mata*). The bird is rarely, or, according to some, never seen. But its sad and pathetic song, heard during the daytime and comprising a long, drawn-out trill recalling a soft ascending wail or moan, reveals to Nage the presence of the soul of a deceased kinsman who is hungry and has come to request food (or, perhaps, some other necessity, like tobacco or betel and areca). If the sound is heard by people inside a house, as it often is, then they should cast a little uncooked rice (*wéca zea*) in one corner of the building. Otherwise, so that the bird might desist, they may simply throw cooked food in the direction of the mournful song, much as people do on hearing a cuckoo-shrike (*cio woza*). The dead soul manifest as a *deza kela* may be that of either a recently deceased or a long-dead person, whose precise identity might therefore not be inferred. Nevertheless, Christian Nage, disturbed by the experience, may on the following day hold a prayer service for deceased relatives.

Interestingly, the very few descriptions I recorded of the physical appearance of the *deza kela* included mention of the back of its head, or neck, being black, a detail that recalls the dark face of the cuckoo-shrike. Pertaining to a regular colour symbolism, this feature appears to link the two 'soul birds' with several of the 'witch birds', or birds associated with free spirits rather than human souls. The shared colour attribute may therefore provide a further illustration of an aspect of Nage cosmology that I have discussed elsewhere – namely, how the distinction between such spirits and deceased souls is by no means absolute (Forth 1998a: 47–53, 259–65).

Kete dhéngi *(Bare-throated whistler,* Pachycephala nudigula; *see Figure 5.1)*

Although the whistler is also identified with human souls, by contrast to the previous two kinds, neither the bird's appearance nor its vocalizations are regarded as ominous, or a manifestation of a particular spirit. Nage identify both the souls of infants who die in early childhood and aborted foetuses (or perhaps the spiritual aspect of these) with the *kete dhéngi*. Both associations are illuminated by a mythical representation of the Bare-throated whistler as a transformation of a little girl who is neglected and mistreated by her mother. After being cast out of the house into the cold and rain, the child turns into a whistler and, as a bird, flies away; all that remains is the sound of her voice gradually disappearing up the side of the mountain (specifically, the volcano, Ebu Lobo).

This last detail relates to the standard image of the *kete dhéngi*, an extraordinary songster and a superb mimic, as a highland bird that is never seen and exists, as it were, only as a voice. This representation of the whistler as a disembodied sound may in itself be sufficient to link the bird with a spiritual being. The poignant quality that Nage recognize in the whistler's song may then identify the bird more specifically with the soul of a small, unwanted child (or, indeed, a foetus). Possibly also relevant to the representation is the bird's name. *Kete*, 'cold, to feel cold', recalls a detail of the myth as well as the characteristically cool elevations inhabited by the Bare-throated whistler, while *dhéngi* can apparently mean 'lamenting, sorrowful'. On the other hand, Nage describe both components of the name, but especially the second, as onomatopoeic, reproducing the bird's melancholy song.

It may be relevant as well that the higher elevations, where the whistler is found, are relatively wet as well as cool. Not only does this recall the rainy day mentioned in the myth but also possibly connects with a general association of infant souls with water or wet or watery things or places, both among Nage (who describe infant souls as 'searching for dew' on the broad leaves of the *sule* tree, a kind of banyan) and more generally (Forth 1981: 194–95, 195 note 57; van Gennep 1960: 52). However that may be, the association of the Bare-throated whistler with infants' souls, and the mythical identification with a neglected child, illuminates a ritual practice. Thus, as part of a traditional procedure for inducing an abortion (called *tetu loja ne'e ana*), a female therapist (*lima mali*) massages the woman's abdomen, taps lightly on it with a small stone, and proclaims 'you (i.e., the foetus) turn into a whistler' (*kau bale bhia kete dhéngi*). In a more general vein, Nage further describe the souls of young children ascending after death to higher elevations and there becoming manifest as *kete dhéngi*.

From a comparative perspective, it may be significant that the male Bare-throated whistler has a black head and neck. But while in this respect it resembles other spiritual birds (including the cuckoo-shrike), it is unclear how relevant the visible feature may be, since most Nage have never seen the bird and none I talked to was able to provide more than a partial or perfunctory description of its plumage. (No one, for example, seemed aware of the bare, expanding throat which gives the bird its Latin and English names.) The fact that the bird is found only in higher elevations above the territory of the Nage of Bo'a Wae may explain why the whistler has no particular augural significance. Probably also pertinent in this connection is the circumstance that, just as small children have little influence in life, so after death they have little effect on the living.

Figure 5.1 Bare-throated whistler (*Kete dhéngi*)

Manu mesi *(unidentified)* and manu *(domestic fowl)*

If the association of infant souls with the Bare-throated whistler inheres in myth and ritual rather than in everyday augural thought and practice, then the identification of deceased souls in general with the *manu mesi*, or 'sea fowl', appears to derive entirely from a particular poetic idiom. Indeed, most evidence indicates that Nage do not consider this a particular kind of bird, and to the extent that the term may refer to something empirical, it designates nothing more specific than coastal birds (perhaps including especially members of the Ardeidae) which, unusually, are sighted far inland.[10]

The usage in question is a song of lament which includes the refrain *ana manu mesi, polu kasi weki*, 'the sea fowl calls pitying himself' (see Appendix 1, text 26).[11] In this connection, Nage commentators explained 'sea fowl' as an allusion to the human soul as analogous to a seabird which, for a time, frequents inland places but must inevitably return to the sea. Similarly, a person's earthly sojourn is limited; a human must eventually die, and the soul must return to its place of origin, which is divinity. As was pointed out to me, also relevant to this interpretation is the Nage idea according to which souls of the dead proceed to the sea (Forth 1998a: 257; 1993b: 52–55).

Evidently related to this metaphorical use of *manu mesi* are other usages representing human beings, or human souls, as chickens (or domestic fowls, *manu*) of divinity. Thus, another song of lament compares death to God collecting all his chickens together to place them in an enclosure or coop (see Appendix 1, text 27). As is stated at the end of the lament, from this fate there can be no escape. *Manu*, it should be noted, also serves as a figurative reference to large livestock used as sacrificial victims, especially buffalo. The Nage belief that death can result from spirits slaughtering humans in buffalo form was mentioned earlier, and is extensively explored in Forth (1998a). The identification of fowls with humans or human souls appears to inform one designation of the cult house (*sa'o waja*) of the Nage clan Mudi. This is called Kodo Mudi, *kodo* being the term for 'chicken coop' (see Plate 5.1).[12] Since *kodo* is also applied, metaphorically, to a buffalo corral (*kopo*), also implicit in the name is the notion of humans as spirit buffalo.

A possible augural significance of *manu mesi* came to light when I once observed what looked like a heron with reddish plumage flying low over paddy fields near the Nage settlement of Ola Kile. Being unable, from my report, to identify the bird other than as a 'sea fowl', Nage commentators later linked my experience with the death of a prominent man – in fact, the highest ranking of the Bo'a Wae leaders – just a few days afterwards. Their reaction to this apparently anomalous sighting of a bird is somewhat reminiscent of the widespread Indonesian aversion to mixing or confusing things belonging to the coast and interior respectively (Forth 1989: 104; cf. Valeri 2000: 248). However, I am now convinced that the interpretation of my report as a portent of a particular death was quite opportunistic, even though it was undoubtedly influenced by the metaphorical usage whereby the 'sea fowl' is associated with human mortality.

Plate 5.1 Kodo Mudi ('Mudi Coop'): the cult house (*sa'o waja*) of the clan Mudi in Tiba Kisa village, undergoing renovation, July 2001

Other possible avifaunal manifestations of deceased souls: kolo, kolo dasi

Earlier I noted how any sort of bird can contextually be taken as embodying a free spirit. As the case of *manu mesi* suggests, it is similarly possible that Nage situationally identify a variety of birds as manifestations of souls of the dead. According to the survivors of a renowned spiritual practitioner (*toa mali*; Forth 1991a), shortly after this man's death in the 1960s, there appeared two doves (*kolo*) which briefly alighted on the roof of his house before flying off in the direction of the Ebu Lobo volcano. The deceased's son described the birds more specifically as domestic pigeons (or Rock doves, *Columba livia*, Nage *kolo dasi*), introduced birds that were rare in the region at the time. As he added, no one knew where the birds had come from and, after their brief sojourn, they were never seen again.

Since the volcano is another place Nage identify as the destination of deceased souls, it is an easy inference that the doves (or one of them) were the dead man's soul.[13] Yet people I questioned did not explicitly make this connection; nor in funerary or other contexts do Nage attach regular augural significance to any bird classified as *kolo*. At the same time, the deceased in this case was a famous spiritualist, and it was highly implicit in the story that the appearance of the doves was not only connected with the man's death but was testimony to his extraordinary powers.

Also noteworthy in this connection is a verse from a song of lament which, following Nage commentary, refers to a dead person's soul as a 'pigeon that is seaward by the waves at Bai (a place on the north coast of Flores)' (*ana kolo dasi lau bata Bai*). In fact, the verse can be paired with the one noted just above, which invokes the 'sea fowl' (*manu mesi*) as another representation of a deceased soul (see Appendix 1, text 26). Although the particular kind named *kolo dasi* may be recently introduced, the expression nevertheless provides additional evidence of an identification of birds called *kolo* with human souls. It is also consistent with the previously mentioned idea that souls of the dead go to the sea. Yet another connection of doves with souls is found in the Keo region, immediately to the south of Nage, where a creation myth tells how the apical ancestress (Ine Ga'e) was impregnated by Kolo, a man taking the form of a dove.

Also in Keo, stylized wooden bird figures called 'doves' (*kolo*) commonly decorate the tips of the branches of forked sacrificial posts (see Forth 2001, Plate 14, showing the post in Kota Pau). While I never heard a coherent rationalization of this usage, it is interesting that, in parts of Ngadha where similar wooden figures are found, the dove has mythical significance as the provider of seeds of the *hebu* tree, from which sacrificial posts are carved throughout central Flores (Arndt 1954: 192). In response to my questions, Keo sometimes spoke of the wooden 'doves' as generalized birds, while on one occasion they described them as symbolizing domestic fowls, considered as chronological indicators.[14] The first evaluation is consistent with the appearance of *kolo* in *peti kolo*, referring (in both Nage and Keo terminology) to birds in general (Chapter 2); indeed, the occurrence of the category *kolo* in other contexts of Nage symbolic usage may be understood in the same way; that is, as a reference to a bird of no particular sort.

Analysis

The ideas reviewed above support a number of generalizations. First, with the single exception of the Bare-throated whistler (*kete dhéngi*), all spiritual birds – that is, bird kinds Nage associate with either free spirits (including witches) or deceased souls – are ominous, or of some augural significance. In this regard, one is reminded of the Latin sources of English 'augury' and 'auspice', both incorporating 'avis' ('bird') and referring originally to observation and interpretation of the song or flight of birds as indications of divine will or approval.

Among Nage, a large majority of spiritual birds manifest themselves as such vocally rather than visually. The single exception are large diurnal raptors (*jata*, *jata jawa*). But this is only a partial exception, since Nage include these birds in the category of *po*-sounders; hence the same spiritual character that can be manifest visibly is expressed in an auditory mode as well. Recalling Southeast Asian symbolic contrasts explored by Löffler (1968; see also Lurker 1983), it is interesting that, among Nage, visible manifestations of both free spirits and souls – including the temporarily detached souls of living human beings – are thought to reveal themselves more often as creatures other than birds, including snakes, fish, insects, and arachnids (Forth 1998a: 50). Even though sounds produced by some insects are also regarded as spiritual revelations, this contrast nevertheless underscores the special connection between birds and spiritual beings grounded particularly in the vocal quality of aviformes.

Yet, as I began to show in the preceding chapter, although particular birds are mostly represented as vocal manifestations of spirits, what links birds with spiritual beings appears to be visual features of morphology and behaviour more than particular auditory qualities of their calls. As demonstrated in the case of the 'witch birds', the group that includes *po*-sounding birds, all members are either nocturnal (or reputedly so in the case of Falconiformes producing *po* sounds at night) or have black plumage. Raptors also possess a fearful appearance and several morphological features obviously facilitating their hunting and killing. Yet another general visible attribute of this group is of course a carnivorous diet, especially as it concerns domestic fowls (*manu*) which, as noted, Nage link metaphorically with humans and human souls (*mae*). It is significant, then, that Nage similarly describe witches and malevolent free spirits as preying on the souls (*mae*) of human victims (Forth 1998a: 56–60, 73–74).

Although the cuckoo-shrike (*cio woza*) has a black face, and the Bare-throated whistler and *deza kela* have heads that are entirely or partly black, shared physical features are not so firmly or consistently attested among birds specifically associated with deceased souls – even though in Nage, as in many other societies, the dead are associated not only with the night (Forth 1998a: 253) but also, in funerary symbolism, with the colour black (Forth 1993b: 49). But then the group of 'soul birds' is not large in any case. For reasons already explained, neither the 'sea fowl' (*manu mesi*) or doves (*kolo*) are unequivocal instances of empirical birds regularly identified, in their phenomenal manifestations, with human souls. At the same time, we should not forget that – excluding the latter two categories – birds that Nage identify with dead souls manifest this quality as much in the auditory mode as do birds associated with free spirits and witches.

For comparative purposes, it is useful to look ahead and consider another group of omen birds – a series of eight categories that are not identified with spiritual beings, which I describe in the Chapter 6. Although at least half of these birds are similarly significant as auditory phenomena, they are not vocally significant to nearly the same extent as are the spiritual birds. Thus, three or four of the eight (one, the Pied bushchat, *tute péla*, is ominous when it calls while flying across the path of a nocturnal hunter) present themselves essentially as visual omens. Also, with flocks of cockatoos (*kaka kea*), another non-spiritual omen, it is the birds' breaking into flight, as much as their calling in the night, that is meaningful for Nage.

Non-spiritual categories differ from spiritual omen birds in other ways. With the single exception of the largely black male of the Pied bushchat (*tute péla*), none has dark plumage. In addition, unlike most of the birds identified with witches, just three (the nightjar, *piko du'a*, and tiny bats) are nocturnal. On the other hand, two mainly diurnal birds (the bushchat and cockatoo) acquire ominous significance only when they manifest themselves, in an unusual way, at night. In regard to morphology, including size and plumage, the non-spiritual omen birds are moreover an extremely variable congeries of avifaunal kinds, and factors motivating their augural significances appear to be similarly various. Even so, as will be shown in the next chapter, these motivations are arguably based, directly or indirectly, on visual features rather than properties of particular sounds.

The largely auditory nature of Nage spiritual birds, especially, raises the question of onomatopoeia. The first thing to recall is that virtually all birds identified with free spirits and witches are designated with names which, in part at least, are onomatopoeic. But this observation requires immediate qualification. As the name of an ethno-ornithological taxon, *po* refers specifically to owls. On the other hand, birds that reputedly produce *po* sounds also include diurnal birds of prey and, with one exception (the Moluccan kestrel, called *iki* or *iki titi*), these birds are not named after their usual, diurnal vocalizations. Yet it is for the most part not in what might be called their ordinary, visible forms that diurnal raptors are represented by Nage as embodiments of free spirits. The exception, moreover, is large hawks seen flying high in the daytime, which are then identified not by the term *po* but by their usual names (*jata, jata jawa*).

In relation to birds associated with free spirits, onomatopoeic naming is less prominent among birds identified with souls of the dead. For example, although often referred to simply as *mae ata mata* ('soul of a dead person'), the little bird called *deza kela* ('enters among giant reeds') is named after a characteristic behaviour rather than the vocalization that is considered a manifestation of a dead soul. What is more, the behaviour that informs the name apparently has no relevance for the bird's spiritual representation. On the other hand, the first part of the name *cio woza* (cuckoo-shrike) and, according to different local interpretations, either both components or the second part of the name *kete dhéngi* (Bare-throated whistler) are onomatopoeic. Neither *manu mesi* nor *kolo* (or *kolo dasi*) have onomatopoeic names but, in any case, and as already remarked, only in a very qualified sense are these birds associated with souls.

It therefore appears to be particularly among omen birds which Nage do not identify with spirits that augural significance does not accompany onomatopoeic naming. As I explain in the next chapter, among eight categories only *koka* (friarbird), *witu tui* (unidentified), and the second part of the more elaborate form of the name of the *bama cea* (Russet-capped tesia) replicate birds' calls. Moreover, although *witu tui* is an onomatopoeic name, it is not the call of this bird, but its reputed behaviour, that is ominous. Nage speak of *kea* (which also means 'to scream, cry out'), the name of the cockatoo, as onomatopoeic, but on comparative grounds this seems doubtful (cf. Verheijen 1963: 687, s.v. *kéka*).

Yet even though onomatopoeia is less prominent in names of non-spiritual omen birds than in those of spiritual kinds, such naming is nevertheless more pronounced among the totality of ominous categories than among birds in general. If we ignore names of individual diurnal raptors associated with the category *po*, and if we discount *manu mesi* and *kolo*, 11 of 19 names denoting birds of augural significance, or nearly 58 per cent, are at least partly onomatopoeic. This compares with a figure of 21 of a total of 79, or 27 per cent, for all Nage bird names.[15] Of course, the difference is even more striking if one counts only the spiritual categories – birds associated with either free spirits or souls – and ignores non-spiritual omen birds. For of the 11 instances of these, eight, or nearly 73 per cent, have onomatopoeic names. Either way, the evidence suggests that birds are more likely to be named after their characteristic vocalizations if these are culturally significant in some way. And since it is more particularly sounds associated with spirits that find expression in onomatopoeic naming, the comparison provides additional support for the significance of sound as an index of spirituality in the Nage cosmology of birds.

Nevertheless, spiritual association is clearly not the only cultural value of bird sounds that may be signalled by onomatopoeic naming. Not only are the names of the non-spiritual *koka*, *witu tui*, and *bama cea* onomatopoeic, but of seven equally non-spiritual birds whose cries provide chronological signs in respect of either the daily or annual cycle (see Chapter 1), three are named onomatopoeically while the names of another two metaphorically describe their characteristic calls.[16] On the other hand, onomatopoeia is not invariably associated with cultural values of any kind. Among the 79 Nage bird names in Table 1.1, at least six wholly or partly onomatopoeic terms are applied to birds that are neither omens nor chronological indicators. These include *ceka* (fantail), *cici ko'i* (Tree sparrow), *ie wea* (Hill mynah), *koko wodo* (Orange-footed scrubfowl), *papa* (Chestnut-capped thrush), and *toto* (Lesser coucal). In addition, there are two more whose possible auditory significance is not generally accepted, namely *iki* (Moluccan kestrel) and *zeghi*, or *jeghi* (bee-eater).[17] In these six or eight cases, then, onomatopoeia may provide little more than a convenient way of identifying and naming particular avifaunal kinds. This is not to say, however, that these names function only as labels. For example, as the scrubfowl (*koko wodo*) is a bird valued for its large eggs, *koko*, the onomatopoeic component of its name, could convey useful information about the call and hence the location of nests.

How far inherent qualities of avifaunal sounds may explain their cultural, and especially spiritual, significance is difficult to determine. Nevertheless, it is a point of some interest that the onomatopoeic names *céce* and *cio woza*, both designating spiritual birds, contain /c/, pronounced approximately as /ch/ in English 'chirp', and corresponding to several hissing, rasping, or harsh whistling sounds. While these are only two instances, additional evidence is suggested by *bama cea* and by *uci* and *po ci*, terms referring to varieties of nocturnal *po* sounds associated with owls and other raptorial birds (see Chapter 4). Similarly attributed to malevolent spiritual beings, *uci* is compounded with *meci*, the onomatopoeic name a kind of cricket, to form the expression *po ko, uci meci*, which designates the totality of ominous nocturnal sounds Nage identify with witches. There is, then, some suggestion that the /c/ sound reproduces a series of arresting, mostly nocturnal noises that Nage immediately link, if not always with maleficent beings, then with unfavourable possibilities. On the other hand, /c/ also appears in *ceka* (fantail) and *cici ko'i* (Tree sparrow), onomatopoeic names of birds whose calls do not possess any spiritual or other ominous significance.

Non-ornithological meanings of bird names, where these are discernible, appear rarely to be connected with a bird's augural or spiritual significance. The components of *kete dhéngi* can be construed as referring respectively to the cool elevations at which the bird is found and the sorrowful quality of its song. But this has at most an indirect bearing on the bird's spiritual association, which in any case is purely categorical and not augural. Apparently clearer instances are to be found in the names of two non-spiritual birds which I discuss in the next chapter: the Pied bushchat (*tute péla*), insofar as *péla* can mean 'to cut in, interrupt' and, according to one local interpretation, the bird called *witu tui*.[18]

Although spiritual associations are largely informed by perceptual, and then mostly visual, features, details of individual spiritual birds confirm that these do not together compose a unit of Nage ethnotaxonomy. Most notably, neither the group of spiritual birds as a whole, nor any of its apparent subdivisions, coincides with any of the intermediate taxa described in Chapter 3. At the same time, spiritual birds might suggest a taxonomic structure of sorts inasmuch as they comprise distinct series of kinds associated, on the one hand, with free spirits and witches and, on the other, with human souls. Also, the group of witch birds includes both notionally *po*-sounding birds and birds that 'do not *po*' (such as the two corvines), thus implicating a taxonomy of at least three levels. But while it is comprised of named categories (more specifically, folk generics) drawn from Nage ethnotaxonomy, this mode of conceptually associating birds is essentially a classification not of avifauna but of spirits. As such, it no more composes a taxonomy of systematically included levels than do the separately named categories of beings that make up the Nage classification of spirits (Forth 1998a: 323–26). The point becomes clearer when it is realized that the 'soul birds' – a category whose boundaries, as we have seen, are hardly unequivocal – are constituted simply by a belief that they embody, or situationally can embody, human souls. But, in this respect, the birds are not distinguished from other animal ethnotaxa (for example snakes). And since these other ethnozoological categories are similarly believed to manifest not only souls but also free spirits, the point applies equally to birds associated with the second sort of spiritual beings. This of course underlines the general point, noted earlier, that the Nage contrast of free spirits (*nitu, bapu*) and souls (*mae*), which defines the most inclusive distinction among the spiritual birds, is itself not absolute.

As a configuration of symbolic representations, the classification of Nage spiritual categories appears to confirm Needham's assessment of symbolic classification as something fundamentally distinct from taxonomy (1980: 41–62). But there is a further point. As it concerns living kinds, the classification demonstrated in this and the previous chapter pertains less to birds as perceptual wholes than to parts of birds. That is to say, it is typically not a whole bird but some component of a bird – its voice, a particular behaviour, the circumstance of its sighting, or perhaps a specific part of its plumage – which conveys symbolic significance and hence links a bird category, symbolically, with other birds. In this regard, the several categories that incorporate *manu* – including the mystical *manu ke'o*, which incorporates physical features of a bird and a reptile – may be seen as but extreme, and thus especially obvious, instances of a more general phenomenon.

Chapter 6

Birds as omens and taboo

As we have just seen, with a single exception (the Bare-throated whistler), Nage regard 'spiritual birds' as ominous. For the most part, moreover, they convey negative omens. Thus, as a resident of the Nage village of Légo once stated: 'Many birds provide signs (*tau tada*) and many of these are bad signs (*tada 'e'e*)'. Writing on the Kantu' of Borneo, Dove characterizes bird augury in this society as 'based on the belief that the major deities in the spirit world have foreknowledge of events in the human world and that, out of benevolence, they endeavour to communicate this knowledge to humans' (1996: 559–60; see also Metcalf 1976: 112). Similarly, Valeri (2000: 231, 244) describes Huaulu animals that are ominous, or the subject of taboos, as being generally linked with spirits of the dead. Nage evidently differ from both the Kantu' and Huaulu to the extent that Nage regard as equally ominous a number of other birds, which they do not consider as manifestations of any sort of spiritual being. These non-spiritual omen birds, as they may be called, form the main topic of the present chapter.[1]

Non-spiritual omens

Bird categories falling under this heading comprise the following:

Bama or bama cea (Russet-capped tesia, or Russet-capped stubtail, Tesia everetti)

Regularly described as a 'tailless' bird, the *bama cea* is among the most frequently remarked of Nage omen birds. The little bird, a low flyer typically encountered close to the ground, is known for producing a chirring or whirring sound – apparently an alarm call – on a person's approach. Reputedly uttered only when it sees a human, the element *cea* in the longer form of the name reproduces this call.[2]

According to Nage, if a traveller should hear the call of a *bama cea* coming from the left (*bama cea kago sala*), then the object of a journey (for example, making a request or securing a loan) will not be fulfilled, and it would be pointless to continue. By contrast, if the call comes from the right (*bama cea kago molo*), then the sign is good, and the journey's success and safety are assured. Occasionally, the value contrast is interpreted in terms of the opposition of front and back, as in the case of a traveller hearing a cuckoo-shrike (*cio woza*; see pp. 86–87). Thus, if a *bama* is heard calling in front, one should immediately turn back, whereas if the bird calls from behind, then one should proceed with haste.

The *bama cea* also resembles the cuckoo-shrike in the more general respect of its cry not invariably being inauspicious. On one or two occasions, Nage suggested that the little bird might be associated with witches. For example, one man stated that the *bama* may manifest a witch when it calls at midday. As noted earlier, this is the hour when Nage consider not only the cuckoo-shrike's call to be especially significant, but spirits of all sorts to be particularly active.[3] However, whereas the ambiguous nature of the cuckoo-shrike can be ascribed to this bird's association with souls of the dead (who are by no means invariably ill-disposed to the living), the morally variable character of the call of the *bama*, which is good or bad according to its relative location, is hard to reconcile with an identification of the bird with such categorically maleficent beings as witches. I am therefore inclined to discount the report.

Kea or Kaka kea (*Yellow-crested cockatoo*, Cacatua sulphurea)

A flock of cockatoos suddenly breaking into flight and screaming (*kea kea*) in the middle of the night can presage the death of a person of high rank. What connects this bird with high-ranking people is not immediately obvious. One clue is available from the compound *kaka ha*, 'cockatoos and crows', which associates the two kinds as pestilential flocking birds that voraciously consume ripening maize. On this basis, the expression refers metaphorically to people who engage in conspicuous consumption, especially in the context of sacrifice and ritual feasting – as people of nobility are indeed more likely than others to do. Another possibility concerns the cockatoo's crest (*odu*), which might recall the headdresses (*lado*) worn by men of high rank on public occasions; the same term, *lado*, further refers to decorations erected on the roof ridges of ritually important buildings controlled by high-ranking people. Yet, despite the cockatoo's brilliant white plumage, it may be the bird's contextual association with the Large-billed crow, the blackest of Nage birds and one of several physically similar kinds identified with witches, that specifically constitutes the negative augury. It should be remarked as well that the death omen involves diurnal birds suddenly becoming active at night, a relatively unusual occurrence. Nevertheless, Nage do not speak of the cockatoo as a form assumed by witches or other spiritual beings. According to Arndt, a flock of cockatoos 'screaming' indicates a witch both in Ngadha (1954: 448) and among the Sikanese of eastern Flores (1932: 319). But for neither group does he clarify whether the shrieking birds are thought to embody witches or, by way of their vocalizations, simply to respond to their presence.

Koka *(Helmeted friarbird,* Philemon buceroides*)*

As a herald of the dawn, the ubiquitous friarbird is one of several species that serve Nage as chronological signs. Yet the bird's noisy, clanking calls possess augural value as well. Although *koka* is considered an onomatopoeic name, Nage also acknowledge the variability of the bird's vocalizations and, in ritual contexts, discern particular meanings in these (usually, if not always, concerning the ultimate cause of a violent death). In fact, this is about the closest Nage come to a systematic use of bird calls as oracles.

An example of the foregoing is provided by a widely known account of a procedure followed after a Bo'a Wae nobleman met his death in a hunting accident. To determine what might lie behind this, it was decided that a ritual expert should interrogate his horse. When a variety of possible causes where mentioned, the animal remained silent, as did all of surrounding nature: 'no wind stirred the trees and not a single bird was singing'. But when it was suggested that the death might have something to do with the dead man's mistress (*ana bu'e*), the horse began to whinny, raise its head, shake violently, and urinate and defecate. At the very same time, a friarbird flew across the village calling *iko ako ma ke ma ke ma ke*, 'iko ako, that's it, that's it, that's it'.[4] More specifically, the nobleman's death was interpreted as resulting from the ill will of his mistress's father, who was a witch. After hearing the outcome of this divination, the man is said to have fled in terror, never to be seen again.

The notion that the 'speech' of the *koka*, as Nage sometimes describe it, can convey definite messages appears to inform references to the friarbird in songs and other poetic genres (see Chapter 8 and Appendix 1). In no context is the bird represented as an embodiment or servant of a spiritual being. Nevertheless, the vocal qualities that underlie the friarbird's oracular and metaphorical functions also illuminate its role in origin mythology, where by defeating the Imperial pigeon (*zawa*) in an oratorical competition, the bird determines the length of night and day and other aspects of the present order of the world (Forth 1992). If not an actual spirit or divinity, therefore, the friarbird appears nevertheless to be conceived as a sort of culture hero.

As both a chronological indicator and a sometime oracle, the friarbird resembles the domestic fowl (*manu*). In cases of violent death (when questions are alternatively, and probably more often, put to the corpse rather than the deceased's horse as in the case described above), the crowing of a cock can equally indicate which of a number of recited alternatives was the origin of a person's demise. A similar significance is mentioned in one variant of the myth of Tupa Lélu (Chapter 9), in which a crowing cock reveals a particular deceit, as well as in the history of the Keo village of Keo Ondo, when a cock's crow was interpreted as approving a decision to move the settlement to another location (Forth 2001: 153).[5]

Also of interest in relation to Nage ideas regarding vocalizations of the friarbird (*koka*) is the Keo characterization of this particular cock crow as a 'sign of ancestral approval'. Yet one should not hereby infer that either Keo or Nage invariably regard domestic fowls, or their cries, as manifestations of ancestors or other spirits, even though Nage identify fowls in general with human souls. As in the case of woodpeckers, interpreted as manifestations of *nitu* spirits (see pp. 84–85), it seems that any bird might be associated situationally with a spiritual being. Once again, then, we see how, by contrast to ethnotaxa, symbolic classes like 'spiritual birds' and 'soul birds' – or indeed 'non-spiritual omen birds' – are not invariably bounded in regard to the folk generics they might comprise.

Leba (Savannah nightjar, Caprimulgus affinis; see Figure 6.1)

The nightjar is inauspicious specifically in the context of night hunting, conducted when the moon is bright and mostly in less elevated regions to the north of Bo'a Wae. If one hears the bird's cry when proceeding to the field, Nage say, one might just as well go home, for the hunt will surely be fruitless. Noteworthy in this connection is the circumstance that the omen, for which there is no antidote, only affects hunting conducted at night by individuals or small groups. It does not concern the annual hunt (*to'a lako*) conducted in the daytime, over a period of several days, by large groups of men. What is more, the nightjar, although a nocturnal bird, is not a raptor. Unlike owls and Falconiformes, it is not one of the birds that Nage credit with producing the ominous *po* sounds, nor is it otherwise associated with witches.

One man described the *leba*, or rather its call, as 'obstructing' hunters, and also as informing game animals that 'an enemy is coming'. The second suggestion, however, probably reflects an individual interpretation. It is an easy inference that any vocalization warns animals, and for this reason alone such a representation is unlikely to be the origin of the omen. As I explain in the next chapter, the nightjar's particular significance in regard to night hunting may be attributed to the fact that, while in the Nage view it closely resembles avifaunal hunters, the nightjar does not hunt. Indeed, not only does it lack the talons and sharp beak of a raptor, but the bird possesses a very small bill, combined with a very large gape and, according to a common Nage report, is lacking in legs altogether.

In these respects, it is interesting to note how the nightjar's cry appears as a symmetric inversion of the nocturnal sound identified as *po keo* (Chapter 4). Produced by a nocturnal bird of prey, the latter is associated with potentially harmful spirits, whereas the vocalization of nightjar is not. Furthermore, although usually an inauspicious portent, in the context of hunting *po keo* is a good omen while the nightjar is of course bad.

In recent years, the symbolism of the nightjar appears to have become extended, so that the negative significance of nocturnal encounters with the bird is now more generally construed. For example, several Nage described an incident involving two lorry-loads of Bo'a Wae people travelling at night to the eastern Flores town of Maumere, to attend a football tournament sometime in the late 1980s. About an hour after their departure, a nightjar flew up from the

Figure 6.1 Savannah nightjar (*Leba*)

road, striking a passenger in one lorry, who instinctively grabbed and killed it. Soon after the bird's death, the lorry broke down and could not be made to start again. Thus the passengers all returned home, and only the second vehicle continued on to Maumere. Although informants could not elucidate how this consequence followed from the encounter with the nightjar, that they perceived a connection was obvious from the way they related the tale. In addition, the story immediately recalls the idea, mentioned just above, that the bird can 'obstruct' hunters on their way to the chase.

Tute péla (*Pied bushchat,* Saxicola caprata)

As an omen for nocturnal human hunters, the Pied bushchat, a diurnal passerine which nevertheless sometimes flies and sings at night, is identical to the nightjar. Also like the nightjar, the bushchat is a bird often encountered in open country and savannah. If it should fly across a hunter's path, or if the bird should call in front, then any further effort will be futile.[6] According to some reports, the nocturnal call of a bushchat is also not a good sign for the annual collective hunt (*to'a lako*), which is conducted in the daytime, but in this case the hunt is never abandoned.

While the nightjar and bushchat are identically ominous in the context of hunting, in view of the marked physical and behavioural dissimilarity between the two birds, their inauspicious significance is probably differently motivated. For Nage, the Pied bushchat is otherwise valued positively as a bird whose early morning song, replicated as *ci cea*, is heard before all others, a half hour or so before the dawn, and so predicts the approach of daylight. In this way, the bushchat resembles the friarbird (*koka*) in that the bird figures contextually as both an omen and a chronological sign. A *tute péla* encountered either vocally or visually in the middle of the night – and in the context of hunting, usually an hour or two before midnight – therefore suggests an instance of categorical confusion, a quality which in itself may be sufficient to account for its inauspiciousness.

Piko du'a ('highland quail')

Piko du'a refers to an unidentified bird that calls at night. This is one of several birds that Nage say is only heard and never seen. People generally thought it was probably not a variety or instance of the Brown quail (*piko*), and several suggested it was not anything like a quail. At the same time, no one could say why the bird might be called *piko*. The component *du'a*, on the other hand, is probably to be understood in the sense of 'highlander', and more specifically as a pejorative applied by Nage to their reputedly coarser and less sophisticated western neighbours, the Ngadha. Among numerous other attributed faults, Nage commonly characterize Ngadha as inveterate livestock thieves. It appears relevant as well that *du'a* occurs in other, euphemistic references to animals. For example, on encountering a Russell's viper (*nipa ba*), one should not use the proper name but refer to the deadly snake instead as a 'parang handle of a Ngadha man' (*ceki codi hoga du'a*). In the same way, a scorpion might be called *bedi hoga du'a*, 'fire-arm of a Ngadha' (or alternatively, a 'spirit's fire-arm', *bedi nitu*). These comparisons thus suggest that *piko du'a* is also to be understood as a euphemism, except in this case the bird apparently possesses no other name.

For Nage, the nocturnal call of the *piko du'a* (variously imitated as 'krik krik', 'frik, frik, frik frik friiiik' or 'ku ku ku ku ku') indicates that someone is about to steal livestock.[7] In addition to taking the usual preventative measures, immediately the sound is heard one should tap on a salt container (*tuku pazo*) or scratch with one's nails on a hard surface and recite the phrases 'leaf spines of the wona tree (and) spilled water, belonging to short (worn down) fingernails (and) blistered back' (*toko wona ae ti'o, ko'o kungu bubu logo una*). The reference of the first phrase is unclear, but the second ('worn down fingernails and blistered back') is a metaphor for hard work. It could, therefore, conceivably allude to the labour expended in raising large livestock.

Witu tui (unidentified; some local descriptions suggest the Great tit, Parus major, while others contradict this identification)

All birds discussed so far are ominous in the sense that, mostly through their calls, they reveal some sort of hidden knowledge or presence. The *witu tui* differs from all of these inasmuch as it is the bird's reputed behaviour, or rather the consequence of this behaviour, which is ominous. According to Nage, if this onomatopoeically named bird should pick up, or 'steal', a person's hair clippings or strands of combed hair, and carry them to its nest or simply to the top of a tall tree, then the person will become mentally deranged (*bingu*, meaning 'intoxicated' and 'dizzy' as well as 'insane'). For this reason, Nage recommend that shorn hair should be hidden under a tree, shrub, or stone, so that the bird cannot find it. Similarly, a child's first hair clippings should always be placed inside a sealed bamboo container, which is then hidden beneath the raised house.

The motivation for these beliefs is fairly apparent. The *witu tui*, Nage say, can never keep still and is always in motion – flitting from one spot to another, circling a branch, or moving its body while perched (behaviours which, incidently, suggest *Parus major*). Accordingly, to say that someone is 'like a *witu tui*' means that the person's behaviour is, at best, unpredictable, inconstant, or irregular. It would therefore appear that, by stealing head hair, the bird transfers its own character to the owner of the hair. According to another idea, the bird's taking hair to its nest, or to the top of a tree, will cause the hair to sway in the wind, which will then result in the person becoming similarly unstable (that is, mentally rather than physically). Although abusing a victim's hair clippings is the sort of activity characteristic of a witch, Nage do not, it should be emphasized, classify the *witu tui* as a 'witch bird'.

Insofar as the belief concerning the *witu tui* focuses on the action of a bird and its unfortunate consequence, the representation resembles Nage ideas regarding the Brown quail (*piko*) and a category of tiny bats (*'ighu*). As these provide instances of the Nage concept of *pie* ('mystically dangerous', 'taboo'), however, the two categories are better discussed in the following section, together with other avifaunal instances of *pie*. At the same time, it is noteworthy that one Nage also described the *witu tui* – or more exactly the possibility of its stealing shorn hair – as *pie*.

Omens and taboo

With respect to birds, one interest of Nage *pie* (cf. western Keo *piye*; Ngadha, Endenese *pire*; Manggarai *pireng*, Sikanese *pireng*) is the way it cuts across the distinction of 'spiritual' and 'non-spiritual', thus once again suggesting the non-taxonomic character of this contrast. As I explain just below, while *pie* applies to at least two categories not associated with spiritual beings, the concept equally pertains to several ominous birds that are indeed identified with free spirits or witches. *Pie* possesses at least two distinguishable, although ultimately related, senses. First, in reference to the actions of humans *vis-à-vis* birds (and, for that matter, a variety of other things), the Nage term can be translated as 'taboo'; that is, 'prohibited' or 'restricted'. Thus, several Nage bird categories are *pie* inasmuch as it is forbidden to eat their flesh. Secondly, the possible actions of birds are characterized as *pie* because they are, in some special sense, considered 'dangerous' for human beings. This combination of meanings, it should be noted, also inheres in the language of the Huaulu of the Moluccas, more particularly in the term *maquwoli* (Valeri 2000); hence there is reason to believe that it may have a wider occurrence in Indonesia, or Austronesia.[8] Be that as it may, referring to situations in which the ultimately uncontrollable actions of animals create a situation of danger for humans, the second sense of *pie* can be seen as inclusive of the first, since what is 'taboo' is equally threatening insofar as a breach also exposes transgressors to misfortune.

Among animals, it is only particular birds whose flesh is taboo (*pie*) for all Nage.[9] These birds, moreover, coincide with the symbolic class of 'witch birds'; that is, owls (*po*) and other notionally *po*-sounding raptors, as well as the Large-billed crow (*ha*), drongo (*céce*), the Flores crow (*héga hea*), and the *koa ka*.[10] Being identified with malevolent spiritual beings, the taboo on eating such birds is hardly surprising. Yet it is important to note that it is specifically consuming their flesh that is taboo, and that simply killing them is not itself prohibited. Also, whereas breaching some other taboos is linked with quite specific consequences (the extinction of a house, or particular ailments), the consequence of eating forbidden bird flesh is generally not specified by Nage. Perhaps connected with this, although still recognized as a traditional taboo (*pie*), at present the prohibition on eating raptors, especially diurnal birds of prey, is sometimes breached with impunity. Several Nage claimed to have consumed the flesh of eagles (*kua*) and to have found it not only tasty but quite harmless. From this, at least two people inferred that eating eagles, or raptors in general, should not be considered *pie*. To some extent, and following comments by Nage themselves, this change appears to reflect the recent availability of air rifles and hence the greater ease with which raptorial birds are nowadays killed. Certainly, there is no evidence that Nage beliefs about witches, and other maleficent beings believed to manifest themselves as tabooed birds, have undergone a parallel decline.

There is just one instance of a bird being taboo (*pie*) for a single Nage clan (*woe*). This is the clan Saga Enge, resident in several settlements not far west of Bo'a Wae. Bound up with a myth describing how one of their ancestors escaped capture by enemies with the assistance of such a bird, the Sage Enge people are forbidden to eat the flesh of the cuckoo-dove (*'owa*), lest their bodies become covered in itching sores. The same myth rationalizes another taboo unique to Sage Enge, namely, a prohibition on using salt when cooking meat on certain major ritual occasions. Should Saga Enge people inadvertently consume cuckoo-dove meat, the solution is relatively simple. The offender takes a few *'owa* feathers (or feathers represented as such) and pretends to begin eating them, but suddenly desists when a companion cries out 'hey, that is taboo' (*ha ta'a pie*) and pulls his hand from his mouth. Any ill effect of breaching the prohibition should then disappear. Called simply *weda walo* ('to pull back'), this same procedure is in fact employed to counter the negative consequences of a variety of Nage prohibitions (for example, prohibitions on burning the wood of several kinds of trees), and in effect to reinstate the taboo (expressed with the Bahasa Indonesia phrase *haramkan kembali*).

Discussing the myth, Saga Enge people suggested that the cuckoo-dove that saved their ancestor might have been an embodiment of even earlier ancestral spirits, or souls of the dead, and that they taboo the bird for this reason. The flesh of other birds which Nage in general identify with deceased souls, however, is not taboo. Nor is that of the several other ominous kinds that Nage do not identify with spirits (for example, the nightjar or the *witu tui*). One man maintained that one should never kill a cuckoo-shrike (*cio woza*; see Chapter 5), but that to do so was not actually taboo (*pie*). The same man stated that, as a youngster, he had always been told that it was *pie* to catch or throw stones at a paradise-flycatcher (*lawi luja*) and that, if one did this, one's house might burn down; but no one else I questioned had ever heard of this idea.

For Nage in general, then, the only forbidden meat is that of the several, mostly raptorial 'witch birds'. Nage explicitly rationalize the prohibition on raptor flesh with reference to the carnivorous diet of these birds, and particularly their reputation as stealers and consumers of domestic fowls. That they do so lends support to Hunn's critique (1979) of Douglas's interpretation of the abominations of Leviticus, particularly as the biblical series includes many of the same sorts of birds as compose the group of tabooed Nage witch birds. Indeed, the majority of birds mentioned in Leviticus are diurnal or nocturnal raptors. Douglas (1966), it may be recalled, construes ritual significance attaching to animals as a function of anomaly deriving from a pre-conceived categorization of life-forms. As shown in Chapter 4 (see pp. 74–77), as birds that resemble non-birds, and even human beings, owls can to that extent be characterized as anomalous birds. However, with reference to the fact that 18 or 19 of the 20 birds proscribed as food in Leviticus are meat- or fish-eaters, Hunn argues that these are forbidden not because they are anomalous but precisely because of their feeding habits (1979: 111). The Nage case also supports Hunn's interpretation insofar as diurnal birds of prey, the largest single group of Nage tabooed categories, cannot be deemed anomalous for Nage; in fact, the several named raptors are among the most central, or focal, in relation to the 'bird' taxon (Chapter 3).

At the same time, it would seem that it is not simply because they are flesh-eaters that Nage taboo similar birds, but also because of the way this links them, in Nage cosmology, with witches. As noted previously, particularly with regard to raptors, it is their preying on fowls that evokes a parallel to human witches and other malevolent spirits, beings that are believed to kill and consume human beings, who in turn are linked metaphorically with domestic fowls (*manu*). Similar behaviours, actual or reputed, of other, non-raptorial 'witch birds' (notably, the crows and the drongo) which connect them with raptors and hence rationalize their inclusion in the symbolic class, were also discussed earlier. The 'cannibalistic' character of birds of prey, a trait which is arguably attested by a view of them as 'birds that eat other birds' (thus ignoring differences of species or folk generic kinds), finds further representation in myth, where an eagle is depicted as killing and eating a human being (Chapter 9). Conceivably, therefore, it is what might be called the biggest Nage food taboo (*pie, ka ta'a pie*) of all, namely, consuming human flesh, that explains why the Nage, whose diet is extremely catholic and who are subject to few dietary restrictions of any kind, place a particular misapprobation on eating the flesh of birds identified as witches. For to do so could be considered as indirect anthropophagy, or cannibalism once removed. Underlining the status of these birds as a special focus of *pie*, it is appropriate to recall that Nage have no aversion to consuming the carcasses of pet birds that die in captivity (see Chapter 1).

Quite apart from the symbolism of birds, Nage thought reveals a generally close connection between the concepts of *pie* and *polo* ('witch'). Sometimes interpretable as a simple statement that witches 'are *pie*', but also implying a declaration that a person is not a witch, or is incapable of becoming one, the standard phrase *polo pie* may in fact entail a partly distinct sense of *pie*. On the other hand, the expression evidently synthesizes the two other senses of the term distinguished above. The Nage witch is the very model of a being that, with impunity, transgresses – or is impervious to – *pie*, understood as a reference to both 'taboo' and 'mystical danger'.[11] Accordingly, the two major ways in which a Nage person might become a witch (a condition represented as far more often achieved than hereditary) are by breaching taboos (*pie*) on eating human flesh and on talking to or laughing at animals (Forth 1989, 1993a).

It is consistent with all of the foregoing that the category of *po*, understood either as a specific reference to owls or to the larger group of *po*-sounding birds, is identified with *pie* in both of the senses identified earlier. Thus, not only is the flesh of these birds taboo (*pie*), but sounds designated as *po* heard close to a dwelling or, indeed, underneath a house, and interpreted as manifesting a witch out hunting for victims, are also designated as *pie*. The phrase *po pie*, which expresses these ideas, might therefore mean either that owl flesh is prohibited or that especially proximate nocturnal vocalizations of the sort designated as *po* are ominous or of dangerous import.

In regard to birds, an instance of the second sense of *pie*, as distinct from the first, is of course the possible characterization as *pie* of a *witu tui* bird picking up human hair cuttings, a notional misuse of a human body part which, as noted, parallels the behaviour of a witch. Whereas in this case it is not certain that *pie* is a general attribution, however, Nage are quite definite that the Brown quail (*piko*) and tiny bats they call *'ighu* are *pie*, or that their possible actions are ominous in regard to the harmful consequences they portend for affected humans.[12]

Nage consider it an ill omen if a covey of quails (*piko*) – at least four or five birds, according to one estimate – should fly into a village. Described as a rare occurrence, the event presages the breakup of the settlement and the dispersal of its inhabitants, unless a remedial ritual is performed. In one opinion, settlement breakup may happen owing to internal strife that follows the quails' appearance. According to another view, a village thus visited might as a result burn down; therefore, if quails are seen inside a settlement, people should be exceptionally careful with fire.

An understanding of these ideas may be gained by first noting that quails, while something of an agricultural pest, are a valued food that men seek in the wild and introduce into habitations as dead game. Indeed, quails are among the most preferred of edible wild birds, an evaluation consistent with the application of the binary compound *piko kolo* (quails and doves) to a larger class of game birds. Characteristically occurring in groups, Brown quails also suggest a social quality; in fact, in poetic idioms quails (*piko*), more than other birds, serve as a metaphor for human sociability (see Appendix 1, texts 13–16).[13] It is possible, therefore, that what Nage find unsettling in the unusual entry of a covey of quails into a major social space, the village, is partly bound up with the birds' very resemblance to humans. As one man put it, the belief (in which he personally did not place much credence) implies that 'the quails drive us (that is, humans) out' (*piko wika kita*); in this regard it seems significant that *wika* can refer to an attack on a village by human enemies.[14]

Of course, many kinds of wild birds are seen in villages, either flying overhead, alighting on the ground, or perched on buildings or in nearby trees. Nage remarks, however, suggest that quails only begin to appear regularly within the bounds of a settlement when it has become partly abandoned, if not entirely deserted. It may therefore be this natural fact that provides the association that forms the basis of the Nage belief. At the same time, by way of a kind of metonymic reasoning, a consequence of settlement breakdown (invasion by birds) not only stands for another consequence (abandonment), but also becomes a predictor of its future occurrence. By the same token, failure to maintain a settlement can reflect social disunity, and thus presage a prospective abandonment also linked symbolically with quail incursions. Alternatively or additionally, a collection of such 'sociable' birds as quails leaving the wild to enter human settlements could arguably call to mind its inversion – humans abandoning their villages. Also relevant to this hypothetical inversion is the phrase 'swarm like flocking quail' (*ligho bhia piko wio*), which in requests addressed to beneficent spirits refers to human fertility and fecundity, thus the very opposite of the settlement disappearance supposed to result from quail invasions.

Further support for this line of interpretation is found in the fact that Brown quails (the specific referent of Nage *piko*) are the kind of bird most likely to appear inside villages – that is, more or less at eye level rather than high overhead – in sizeable groups.[15] In addition, the flocking behaviour of *piko* may be what distinguishes these birds, as an instance of *pie*, from junglefowl (*kata*, a category commonly paired with *piko* in parallelistic idioms). For although Nage also mention the *kata* as another bird that may enter partly deserted settlements, the junglefowl does not typically occur in flocks. Nor, unlike *piko*, does it fly, in groups, close to the ground.[16] In regard to the possibility of their entering villages in fairly large numbers, then, Brown quails are the kind of bird most able to challenge the human–animal boundary protected by the series of other taboos against treating animals like human beings (by speaking to them, playing oddly with them, laughing at them, and so on). Since breaching these prohibitions can turn a person into a witch (Forth 1989, 1998a), it is further relevant that Nage identify invasive coveys of quails with the operation of witches insofar as the remedial ritual, designed to ward off their negative consequence – the breakup of a village – is explicitly predicated on the idea that the inauspicious intrusion has been, or might have been, brought about by a villager who is a witch, and who has 'summoned' the birds. It is interesting, moreover, that Arndt lists the quail (*Wachtel*) as one of numerous bird forms assumed by witches among the neighbouring Ngadha (1954: 448).

This implicit connection with witches would appear to represent an important qualification to the characterization of quails as instances of 'non-spiritual' birds; that is, as ominous kinds not associated with free spirits or human souls. Although Nage do not explicitly identify *piko* with witches (as they do for example with raptorial birds), in view of the close link described earlier between these partly human beings and malevolent free spirits (*nitu*, *bapu*), the ultimate attribution of quail incursions to witches recalls representations of vengeful spirits (*nitu*) rendering human settlements uninhabitable through invasions of land snails (*boko lo*) or caterpillars (*ngota*; Forth 1998a, 2001). Of course, while such invasions are typically located in the mythical past, quail incursions are present-day possibilities. Nevertheless, in both instances one encounters malevolent unseen beings destroying human groups through a mystical manipulation of wild creatures.

A possible identification of quail incursions with the operation of witches also illuminates the relation between *pie* as applied to actions over which Nage have control – by observing taboos on them – and events over which humans have no control, such as birds flying into a village. For although witches are in one respect a variety of spiritual being, they are simultaneously a special, negative type of human being. In this respect, it is also noteworthy that the complete Nage expression 'it is *pie* for quails to enter a village' (*piko pie kono one bo'a*) is grammatically identical to expressions of taboos applying to humans (see e.g. *demu pie poza 'owa*, 'they are forbidden (to eat) flesh of the cuckoo-dove'). In other words, Nage appear to say that there is a 'taboo' that applies to quails entering settlements (and, as we shall presently see, bats entering houses) in the same way that there is a taboo on people eating certain birds. Nevertheless, although only the second case circumscribes human action, it is humans who suffer the consequences of 'transgression' with both sorts of 'taboo'.[17]

In general outline, the Nage evaluation of quails entering a village parallels their application of *pie* to tiny bats (*'ighu*). According to Nage, if such a creature enters a house it must never be allowed to alight, since the inhabitants would then die out. When an *'ighu* flies into a dwelling (by no means an uncommon occurrence), therefore, the occupants should quickly drive it away. No one was able to explain why such an event should have this consequence. What is certain is that, in spite of their nocturnal nature and other features that might suggest a connection, Nage do not associate bats of any kind with witches or other spiritual beings, a rather remarkable fact that is further discussed in Chapter 7. Also, they do not speak of the two other named bat categories (*méte*, flying fox, and *gébu*, medium-sized bats) as in any way harmful or inauspicious.

The belief that a tiny bat (*'ighu*) should never be allowed to alight inside a house evidently differs somewhat from the Nage representation regarding quail invasions. For one thing, the former obviously approaches more closely a use of *pie* as a reference to a prohibited human act, although the independent action of a 'bird' is also involved. In this respect, moreover, it resembles ideas concerning the *witu tui*, since what may be considered *pie* in this case – the bird's theft of human hair clippings – can easily be prevented by hiding the hair. At the same time, as this parallel suggests, what is *pie* is not failure to drive intrusive bats away, but the bat's action of alighting inside a dwelling. Hence the similarity of this idea with that concerning flocks of quails is greater than might at first appear. Also, while Nage do not explicitly associate bats with witches, inasmuch as witches are able to manifest as virtually any sort of creature, it is not inconceivable for Nage that they could take the form of a tiny bat, or order the creature to alight inside houses.[18] Also noteworthy in this connection is the application of *pie* to dogs and goats entering houses and, in the first case, perhaps more explicitly to a bitch whelping inside a house – occurrences which, like a tiny bat alighting inside a dwelling, are both somewhat preventable and can lead to the extinction of human inhabitants. In fact, dogs appear to be the focus of Nage *pie* to a greater degree than any other four-legged animal.[19] Throughout eastern Indonesia, dogs are similarly prominent in taboos bound up in the 'thunder complex' (see Forth 1989: 92, 95, 101, 102).

Together with indications that Nage thought subsumes all bats as instances of a single kind, this last observation permits the speculation that their ideas regarding *'ighu* may be predicated on an association with dogs. As noted in Chapter 3, the three Nage bat generics compose an intermediate grouping most closely identified with *méte*, denoting flying foxes, the largest bats. While bats are recognized as differing in several particulars from other 'birds', *méte* in particular are described as having faces like dogs. What is more, Nage hold that flying foxes, themselves transformations from a smaller kind of bat (*gébu*) which itself originates in the smallest kind (*'ighu*), eventually change into Palm civets, animals (and 'non-birds') that are described not only as facially resembling dogs but also as dogs belonging to free spirits (*nitu*; Forth 1998c: 286).

Linked with their perceived resemblance to dogs, it is further possible that the Nage aversion to tiny bats alighting inside houses owes something to the marginal status of all the bat categories in relation to the ethnotaxon of 'bird' (see further Chapter 7). Unlike diurnal raptors, bats are anomalous 'birds', and in this case anomaly may indeed contribute to the symbolic value of invasive *'ighu*. That other bat categories (*méte*, *gébu*) are not implicated in this representation might then simply be attributed to the fact, articulated by Nage themselves, that these larger kinds never enter houses. On the other hand, *'ighu* bats are the only wild 'birds' that are likely to enter houses (thus not counting the domestic fowl, which is not only not wild but, as previously explained, is not clearly a 'bird'), and this circumstance may itself account for the danger associated with their entry. In other words, in this context, tiny bats may stand for all wild birds, a possibility contingent, not on their anomalous or marginal character, but indeed on their being fully classified as birds.

Although other explanatory possibilities are available in this case as well, anomaly cannot be ruled out as a component of the Nage representation of invasive quails. As I elaborate in the next chapter, Nage maintain that if a *piko* (Brown quail) were to alight or defecate in a tree, the bird would die. While Brown quails are by no means the only ground-dwelling birds known to Nage, this idea never-theless associates *piko*, especially, with the ground and, at the same time, opposes the bird to all others (although in myth especially to the paradise-flycatcher). In addition, the belief supports the recognized resemblance between quails and human beings which, as suggested, also contributes to the Nage evaluation of quails entering villages. Although *piko* do of course fly, in regard to this notional difference from all other avian kinds – which moreover constitutes the Brown quail's 'simple distinctive feature' (see Table 2.1) – the bird might even be con-sidered as a reduced symbolic equivalent of a fully flightless bird, the cassowary, in Moluccan and Melanesian cultures.

Obviously, by no means all ominous avifaunal behaviours are *pie*. Nor does *pie* in any way define a category of birds about which all Nage are in complete agreement. I have already mentioned the uncertainty surrounding the status of the *witu tui*. Similarly, while the inauspicious call of a nightjar seems generally not to be considered *pie*, one of my best informants on matters ornithological thought it could be so described. Unfortunately, I failed to enquire whether a *bama cea* calling to the left of a traveller was *pie*. In view of other, partly comparable applica-tions of *pie* that do not refer to birds (for example regarding the significance of sneezing as one sets out on a journey), one can see how it might be.

To determine the special sorts of danger implicated by the Nage concept would require a comprehensive survey of instances of *pie* such as the one Valeri (2000) has provided for the comparable Huaulu concept of *maquwoli*. Nevertheless, this brief review of applications of *pie* to several kinds of birds does suggest, as a predominant theme, the transgressing of major spatial and conceptual bound-aries. More particularly, the boundaries are defined by the house and the village, the predominant human spaces. In this respect, one might recall the idea that nocturnal sounds called *po* are *pie* specifically when they are heard unusually close to human habitations, as well as Nage ideas regarding transgressive quails and bats. As I have demonstrated at length in my book on Nage cosmology (1998a, see especially Chapter 6, Sections 3 and 4, regarding tutelary spirits that guard against *polo*), the bounds of the house and village not only separate the human domain from that of wild animals, but they equally divide the world of humans from that of malevolent spirits. Since Nage witches are beings that characteris-tically violate and obscure these boundaries – just as they incorporate features of such spirits while retaining the appearance of human beings (see also Forth 1993a) – this observation further illuminates the peculiar connection that exists between various instances of *pie* and the category of *polo* (witches).

Questions of symbolism

To say that a representation involving a bird is symbolic – as, for example, when it is suggested that the idea that certain kinds manifest spiritual beings is symbolic – is not to imply that empirical birds are selected as a means of express-ing a pre-existing concept. In regard to 'spirits', birds (or features of birds, and especially although not exclusively their vocalizations) participate in concepts of spirit; albeit partially (since these concepts have other components), birds constitute rather than merely articulate them. Thus, to state that some birds 'manifest' spirits, as I have done in translating Nage thought about the matter, can only mean that birds present themselves as one of several kinds of perceptual components of a complex of ideas labelled 'spirit', or rather, of ideas concerning several named categories of spirits.

The relation, moreover, is asymmetric. That is, Nage spirit categories are not in the same way a component of individual bird categories, or of the covert life-form category 'bird'. As ethnotaxa, these are the objects of an 'encyclopaedic' knowledge (Sperber 1975) that is cognitively quite separate from ideas linking birds and spirits and, for that matter, from any sort of symbolic knowledge pertaining to birds (including 'non-spiritual omen birds'). Accordingly, a number of individual bird categories are not subject to any sort of symbolic representation (see Chapter 8). Conversely, there appears to be no Nage spirit category (see *bapu, ga'e, mae, nitu, noa, polo*; Forth 1998a) which is not, at least prospectively or situationally, associated with birds.

Like 'religion', to which the concept is clearly connected, 'symbol' (or 'symbolism') is an odd-job word, a polythetic label that has obvious utility yet has perennially defied all attempts at definition. Partly to avoid adding to this catalogue of failure, I shall not endeavour to develop or defend any particular theory of symbolism. Instead, in the remainder of this chapter, I want to demonstrate how the standard contrast of 'symbol' and 'sign', sometimes equated with an opposition of 'metaphor' and 'metonymy' (see Leach 1976; Sperber 1975; Fernandez 1991), is useful in elucidating and articulating certain general distinctions inherent in Nage bird symbolism, and particularly ideas concerning spiritual and ominous birds.

In anthropology and elsewhere, symbolism in a more specific sense has regularly been conceived as a conceptual relation requiring exegesis and thus susceptible to a variable interpretation. Sign relations, on the other hand, implicate a code-like relationship, generating meanings that are specific and relatively fixed. Paralleling this contrast is the distinction of Nage spiritual birds, whose phenomenal manifestations typically signify general misfortune affecting unspecified victims, and non-spiritual omen birds, which signal specific outcomes or consequences (for example, lack of success in hunting, the extinction of a particular house group, derangement for a specific individual).

These distinctions bear on a question recently raised by Dove (1996: 565) with reference to bird augury among the Kantu' of Borneo, concerning the extent to which augural birds independently effect human action, as opposed to being used selectively to rationalize action or explain outcomes after the fact – as Freeman (1960: 79) has suggested. By contrast to Bornean bird augury, which is inextricably bound up in the practice of swidden agriculture (see also Metcalf 1976: 108; Sutlive 1988: 70–71), Nage bird omens do not for the most part prescribe particular courses of action. Rather, they point to some outcome of an action, mostly negative, or more often, they simply presage misfortune, which often cannot be countered by an antidotal ritual. Nevertheless, Nage omens still bear comparison with those of other Indonesian societies. While this is not a matter I have been able to investigate as thoroughly as has Dove, the vocal or visible appearance of some birds can certainly have a coercive effect on Nage behaviour, as shown by reactions I have witnessed to the call of a cuckoo-shrike (*cio woza*; see Chapter 5), or the flurry of ritual activity that followed the entry of a flock of quails into the Nage village of 'Abu. At the same time, my impression is that non-spiritual omens generally have a more direct and coercive effect on behaviour than do manifestations of birds associated with free spirits and witches. Similarly affecting behaviour are the calls of certain birds that have chronological significance; for example, the Channel-billed cuckoo (*muta me*) and Common koel (*toe ou*), whose cries indicate the time of the year when one should prepare and plant fields.

Partly illuminating this difference between spiritual and non-spiritual birds is a principle Nage themselves explicate; namely, that individual members of the avifaunal kinds generally identified with free spirits do not always manifest spiritual beings. In other words, sometimes sounds called *po* are simply the cries of an owl. From this it follows that, while the calls of spiritual birds – and perhaps most notably, those that produce *po* sounds – are subject to situational interpretations which may require the intervention of religious experts, the meanings of non-spiritual omens are immediately given and are known to everyone.[20] Invoking another classical anthropological distinction, one might say that spiritual birds have a 'religious' significance, whereas bird omens not linked with spirits are 'magical' in character. At the same time, this contrast is discernible within the group of spiritual birds itself; for in regard to the specificity and immediacy of their meanings, manifestations of birds identified with deceased souls (particularly vocalizations of the cuckoo-shrike and *deza kela*) more closely resemble those of non-spiritual omen birds that do avifaunal manifestations of free spirits and witches.

The distinction of symbol and sign (or metaphor and metonymy) illuminates other differences among relationships between particular birds and associated spirits. Nage statements suggest that spiritual birds of all kinds either embody the beings with which they are identified or control or command them. Consistent with this, 'witch birds' – birds identified with both witches and malevolent free spirits – inform cultural representations of the beings they are thought to incorporate through physical resemblance. As they, so to speak, resemble these representations, the identification of such birds with particular kinds of spiritual agents of misfortune is sufficiently motivated by their physical appearance (sharp talons and hooked bills, frightening faces, dark plumage) or behaviour (nocturnal activity, predatory habits, carnivorous diet), and possibly also by inherent qualities of their harsh, eerie, or otherwise arresting calls.

Although the identification of some birds with souls of the dead similarly owes something to the quality of their calls (in the case of the *deze kela* and Bare-throated whistler at least), on the whole this association is less obviously motivated by phenomenal features of the kinds in question. In accordance with this distinction, while fearful-looking, or fearful-sounding, birds are identified with malevolent spirits conceived as the agents of misfortune, the call of the cuckoo-shrike, one of the two birds consistently identified as manifesting a dead soul, simply announces a death among the living or, at most, summons a living soul to the land of the dead. With regard to the same contrast, it should also be recalled that the event presaged by a cuckoo-shrike's call is not invariably bad. In a similar vein, the vocalization of the *deza kela*, while revealing the presence and pitiful condition of a deceased kinsman, implies no particular consequence for the living. Although the call signals a request for food, Nage say they give this out of pity (*mesu*) rather than as a definite obligation, and I never heard that failure to provide this should result in misfortune.

If the connection between particular birds and souls of the dead is less obviously motivated, and thus apparently more arbitrary, than the identification of other birds with malevolent free spirits and witches, then in this respect as well these 'soul birds' resemble non-spiritual omen birds. By the same token, one can say that members of both series figure more as generally inauspicious 'signs' than as creatures that, in their perceptual (and especially visual) forms, 'symbolically' evoke free spirits. The meanings of certain non-spiritual avifaunal signs (e.g., the nightjar, cockatoo, and Brown quail) also appear to be linked with empirical features of the bird in question. However, in these instances, the physical resemblance pertains not to a presumed spiritual agent, but rather to the human targets – one might also say 'victims' – of the negative portents. For example, as a palpable 'pseudo-raptor', or false hunter, the nightjar parallels the luckless human hunter whose failure its call predicts. Similarly, the 'sociable' and relatively earth-bound quail resembles the human groups whose destruction invasive coveys are thought to ensure, while the behaviour of the unstable *witu tui* is reflected in the consequent derangement suffered by a person unfortunate enough to have his hair clippings stolen by this bird.

Among Nage ideas pertaining to ominous birds, one might thus discern a scale, with symbolic relations (in a specific sense) arrayed at one end and sign functions at the other. One extreme, of course, is occupied by birds associated with free spirits and witches, and the other by omen birds that Nage do not identify with spiritual beings of any sort. Consistent with their mixed character, birds associated with souls of the dead occupy an intermediate position. That they should do so, moreover, may be ascribed to a general feature of Nage cosmology, which links the dead, or deceased souls (*mae*), both with free spirits – from which they are virtually indistinguishable in certain contexts (Forth 1998b: 51–53) – and with living people (or their souls), the objects of death omens of all kinds, and the targets of other sorts of misfortune signalled by non-spiritual omen birds. Also displaying a mixed character are invasive quails which, although not explicitly identified with spirits as are the 'soul birds', might nevertheless be controlled by witches, beings which themselves appear intermediate between free spirits and humans.

As indicated above, to the extent that they conform more closely to 'signs' than 'symbols', some ominous birds should further be compared with the several species that figure as chronological indicators in regard to the daily or annual cycle (see Chapter 1). Nage themselves appear not to distinguish such chronological signs from augural signs. In fact, they apply the same term, *tada be'o* (cf. Indonesian *tanda*, 'sign, token, mark', Echols and Shadily 1989; *be'o*, 'to know'), not only to both of these but to relations we would call 'symbolic' as well. Nevertheless, chronological signs unquestionably differ from augural signs insofar as they directly reflect naturally occurring physical associations. Friarbirds (*koka*) really do call at sunrise, the Channel-billed cuckoo (*muta me*) really does become especially vocal when the wet season is near, and so on.

All the same, these signs are not simply reducible to inevitable 'natural' phenomena. They may be 'natural indices' as per Leach's (1976: 12) usage; yet as Leach notes, such indices are 'selected (as an index of something) by human choice' and in this sense are fully cultural. Also, they are not absolutely essential to associated socio-economic processes, for which other natural indices (for example, astronomical and meteorological phenomena) can, and indeed do, serve just as well; and their value would therefore appear to lie chiefly in their concurrence with significant human activities. Moreover, as the case of the friarbird especially demonstrates, a bird can figure as a 'symbol', as well as a 'sign' of some regular event (in this instance, daybreak or the dawn). Thus, in myth, the friarbird can be understood as a metaphor for the entire temporal order of the present world, and as the symbolic origin of what Nage regard as a cycle of birth and death (Forth 1992). As the friarbird's mythical rival, the Imperial pigeon then functions as a symbol of the opposite values.

Indications that chronological signs, as an instance of 'natural signs', are not so very different from other signs raise the question of possible materialist, or ecological, explanations of certain bird omens, especially omens of the non-spiritual kind. In fact, something of the sort has already been suggested in the case of quails, which are more likely to invade half-abandoned or neglected villages than other settlements. In a similar vein, it is not inconceivable that natural factors, such as meteorological conditions, that might make nightjars especially vocal could also reduce the availability of game. Nightjars and game animals, however, are equally parts of nature, and it is far more difficult to imagine how such an explanation could apply, for example, to the link Nage posit between a Russet-capped tesia (*bama cea*) calling on the left and an unsuccessful journey, or the nocturnal shrieking of a flock of cockatoos and a noble death, or a bat alighting in a house and the extinction of inhabitants. As these illustrations should make clear, regardless of a representation's potential material motivation, and in spite of the importance of percepts for symbolic construction generally, nothing symbolic in the broadest sense (thus including signs as well) can be fully explained with reference to empirical phenomena alone.

Chapter 7

Hibernating swallows, kite stones, and the legless nightjar: some curiosities of Nage bird knowledge

It is already clear that Nage articulate ideas concerning birds which either conflict with, or derive no support from, contemporary scientific knowledge. In this chapter, I review a variety of such ideas and consider what their basis may be in Nage culture or experience. I do not mean to suggest that only faulty knowledge is to be explained culturally or sociologically. Yet it is where cultural knowledge is in egregious conflict with empirical evidence that the influence of cultural factors can be most clearly identified and gauged.[1]

It will be evident that I believe it not only possible, but also necessary, to state that certain cultural beliefs (standard ideas, received notions) are empirically incorrect. I also maintain that modern scientific knowledge must be the standard against which such judgements are made. At the same time, I allow for the possibility that local people make accurate observations of which western ornithologists have yet to avail themselves, and which might even be hindered by prevailing scientific theory. I will not further defend this position here. By way of an example drawn from another folk tradition, however, I would just point out that the belief, encountered until quite recently in European societies, that Barnacle geese develop from barnacles or the fruit of certain trees is quite plainly wrong and is easily countered by ornithological evidence. This illustration is apposite, for the belief was evidently based in part on an ignorance of the actual breeding habits of these birds and was arguably sustained by culturally constructed values and interests – in this case pertaining to Lenten food prohibitions.

How far comparable Nage ideas can similarly be accounted for is a major question considered in what follows. Another concerns the relation of such notions to ethno-ornithological classification. I begin by reviewing individual cases in the alphabetical order of their local names. As Nage ideas about the nightjar (*leba*) present special problems and possibilities, I discuss these in a separate section.

Remarkable birds

Bele teka *(a falcon, probably including the Peregrine falcon)*

As noted in Table 1.1, the name of this bird literally means 'sharp wing'. Nage say that the falcon, an extremely swift and powerful flier, kills its prey not by seizing with the talons but by striking and often decapitating its victim with the wing. It would seem, therefore, that an ornithologically inexact idea (raptors do decapitate prey, but not with the wing) may have determined the name of the bird and, to that extent, possibly the separation of the species credited with hunting in this manner from other birds of prey, and thus more generally the classification of diurnal raptors. Yet it is also possible that the name, 'sharp wing', simply reflects the observable shape of a falcon's wing, resembling as it does a sickle or some other bladed implement. In that case, the name may have given rise to, or encouraged, ideas concerning the way the bird kills its prey.

Ebu titu *(swallows and swifts)*

According to Nage, birds they call *ebu titu* remain for part of the year inside caves on the higher slopes of the Ebu Lobo volcano, from where they emerge only when rain is near. Hence their appearance in large numbers is one sign of the approach of the wet season. The fact that the birds are not present during several months of the year is evidently due to the fact that some species of Hirundinidae and Apodidae (including the common Barn swallow, *Hirundo rustica*) are migrants. Like many other people, however, Nage appear to have a poor understanding of bird migration.[2] As discussed elsewhere, the association of swallows and similar birds with Ebu Lobo may be explained by the common nomenclatural element *ebu* (Forth 1998a: 240): the component further occurs in Ebu 'Egu, the name of a large boulder with strong mystical associations, and in *ebu gogo*, which designates an extinct population of coarse, dull-witted wildmen who are supposed once to have resided high up the slopes of the Ebu Lobo volcano. In at least some of these contexts, *ebu* possesses something of an honorific sense. Although it is not certain that this applies as well to the term for swallows and swifts, since these birds predict the appearance of so vital a phenomenon as the annual rains (see the alternative name *awe uza*, 'rain summoner'), the interpretation is not implausible.

A probable empirical basis for the association of *ebu titu* with the volcano is readily found in evidence that two of the Apopidae – the Edible-nest swiftlet (*Collocalia fuciphaga*) and the Little swift (*Apus affinus*) – do indeed nest inside caves on the higher slopes of Ebu Lobo. In fact, these caves are among several places where Nage have searched for edible birds' nests (see p. 12). Since birds identified as *ebu titu* occur in large numbers only during wetter parts of the year (a fact partly attributable to meteorological conditions conducive to the appearance of flying insects on which they feed), it is then not an unreasonable inference that, during other times, they as it were hibernate in the same caves.[3]

Jata (Brahminy kite) or kua (eagle)

The reader will already be familiar with the Brahminy kite from the variety of symbolic ideas and metaphorical usages in which the bird participates. Nage also speak of a 'kite's talon grindstone' (*dhédhe kanga jata*; Forth 1998a: 288). Obtainable only from the nest of a Brahminy kite, this is a stone for sharpening knives employed in palm tapping; when used on a tree that has yet to yield, the knife will immediately cause palm juice to flow. Some Nage speak instead of an otherwise identical 'eagle's talon grindstone' (*dhédhe kanga kua* or *dhédhe kua*). In order to obtain a stone of either sort, one must keep one's eyes closed while placing one's hand in the nest, for if one were to look the stone would never be found. According to one report, if one grasped the stone and then looked, one would find one had grasped a fledgling. Similar ideas, concerning powerful stones discovered inside the nests or body parts of eagles and other birds, are encountered in the Moluccas, or at least were so in Rumphius's day (Rumphius [1705] 1999: 344–46).

That these ideas derive from the exceptional sharpness of a kite's (or eagle's) talons is borne out by Nage descriptions of large raptors using the stones for sharpening their talons. Comparable ideas from European tradition concern 'eagle stones', which eagles were thought to keep in their nests in order to assist their egg-laying or to protect their eggs and offspring (Brown 1936: 72–73; with regard to ancient Greece, see Pollard 1977: 15, 23).[4] The Nage idea appears to be rooted in an inference more reasonable than the European notion of eagle stones (since stones are more obviously connected with sharpening than with laying or preserving eggs); yet it is still empirically unfounded. There is, moreover, the additional notion that in order to obtain the stone one must not look inside the nest. This seems to be a stipulation of universal distribution applying to things that contain special power or confer special advantage on persons able to obtain them. Insofar as gaining access to a large raptor's nest should be difficult enough in the first place, the stipulation emphasizes the rarity and limited availability of such grindstones and thus enhances their value.

A question arises as to why it is specifically kites or eagles, and not other diurnal raptors, from whose nests such stones might be obtained. An answer may be found in the fact that these are the largest of common daytime birds of prey known to Nage, in which respect it may be recalled that their compounded names, *kua jata*, are employed as a general term for large raptors. As shown in Chapter 4, raptors, and the Brahminy kite in particular, are considered manifestations of mostly malevolent spirits called *bapu*. Also, it is from certain spirits so classified that favoured individuals are able to obtain special powers, particularly in regard to healing and wealth (Forth 1998a: 177–78). Hence the concept of 'kite's (or eagle's) claw grindstones' is conceivably of a piece with a larger series of ideas concerning spiritual beings as sources of unusual power. What is more, such powers are often secured in the form of stones, including stones derived from the bodies of snakes and wild mammals (ibid.: 262, 286–7).[5]

Je (an unidentified raptor)

As explained in Table 1.1, Nage credit the *je* with a peculiar method of stealing fowls. Described mostly as an owl, this raptorial bird is said characteristically to alight in the night near a roosting hen with young, make a piping noise like a chick while sidling up to its intended prey, and then seize a young bird and carry it off. As Nage recognize, it is after this hunting strategy that the bird is named *je* ('to advance slowly toward, to steal up on').[6] They also identify its behaviour as the source of the metaphorical expression *je podi we'e* ('*je* pretends (in order) to get close'), which refers to a person who becomes close to another in order to take advantage. Just one man, who described the *je* as resembling a falcon, said that the bird will sometimes decapitate hens, a method of killing that Nage attribute to the *bele teka* (see also Chapter 4, note 5 regarding *po pate*). At the same time, with respect to whole prey, he stated that it was able to fly off only with chicks.

In contrast to ideas concerning some other raptorial birds (*bele teka, jata, kua*), the behaviour attributed to the *je* appears quite plausible. However, I have been unable to discover firm ornithological evidence for a Southeast Asian species hunting in this manner. This uncertainty is one factor preventing a secure scientific identification of the Nage category. Like the majority of Nage, I have never seen a *je*. Most people who have (and some who have not) describe it as having the form of an owl, while others say that, despite its nocturnal hunting, it resembles a diurnal hunter (and, in all but one case, a falcon). Probably the most reliable account was provided by a man who, discovering that the offspring of his hens were disappearing each night, lay in wait for the culprit and encountered and killed a *je*. He described the specimen as having an extremely 'ugly' (or 'angry', *'e'e*) face almost identical to an owl (*po*), plumage similar to that of the Moluccan kestrel (*iki*), and short legs, which however ended in sharp talons. (Another man spoke of the *je* as resembling a nightjar, which Nage also liken to the kestrel.) He further claimed that the bird had a very small crest in the centre of its head. Except for this last, rather enigmatic detail, the description, like those of several other informants, most strongly recalls the Brown hawk-owl (*Ninox scutulata japonica*).[7]

The fact that hawk-owls (also called 'boobooks') lack the distinct facial discs of most owls could account for some Nage describing the *je* as (or as resembling) a Falconiforme. King *et al.* thus portray *N. scutulata* as looking like a 'dumpy hawk' (1975: 196) – a characterization possibly also illuminating a report of the bird as having short legs. In relation to the bird's reputed behaviour, another source of this last idea may be the Nage identification of chicken-stealing with Falconiformes more than Strigiformes (owls, including hawk-owls) – even though there is the general, albeit not universally accepted, idea that owls (*po*), too, will prey on domestic fowls. On the other hand, it is not entirely ruled out that the predatory behaviour after which Nage name the bird may indeed be that of a falcon (see Table 1.1). And in this case, it may be the bird's nocturnal habit that suggests to Nage a Strigiforme.

On the other hand, there is no reason to believe that the Nage report of the *je*'s behaviour is entirely imaginary, or that it is an artifact of a culturally specific nomenclature or classificatory practice. As regards classification, if the referent is the Brown hawk-owl, then it is somewhat surprising that the bird occupies a separately labelled taxon while all other owls (including members of the Strigidae and Tytonidae) are named together as *po*. Seemingly consistent with this is the report that the *je*, unlike a variety of raptors, does not make the nocturnal *po* sounds (see Chapter 4), and moreover that it produces no vocalization other than the imitative piping mentioned above. If the bird is the hawk-owl, a winter visitor mostly present on Flores between October and March, then its reputed lack of a voice accords with Verhoeye and Holmes's description of this bird as 'being silent in winter quarters' and thus 'perhaps overlooked' (1999: 31). But if it is not the hawk-owl, then, regardless of the accuracy of the Nage view of the *je*'s vocal capacities, the taxonomic distinction of *po* and *je* can more readily be explained on morphological grounds.

All things considered, the most parsimonious explanation of Nage ideas about the *je* is that they directly and, to some degree accurately, reflect universally available percepts. In regard to the category's most likely avifaunal referent, it is noteworthy that western ornithologists still know very little about the habits of the Brown hawk-owl (Hails and Jarvis 1987: 95); hence it would not be surprising if Nage were more knowledgeable. Ornithological accounts of *Ninox scutulata* inhabiting forest edge and lightly wooded cultivation, and being active at dusk (Coates and Bishop 1997: 362), accord with Nage descriptions of the *je*. Also, the *japonica* sub-species, to which Flores hawk-owls belong, is described as hunting small wild birds (König *et al.* 1999: 408), though not domestic fowls.

According to Verheijen (n.d.), in more easterly parts of Flores, the Brown hawk-owl is the referent of cognates of Nage *manu miu* (see Chapter 5). Nage apparently do not make this connection, nor do they associate *manu miu* with the category *je*. It may be noted, however, that if these two terms did in fact refer to the same bird, then we should have a further instance of double naming (see pp. 41–42), with one name (*manu miu*) referring to a vocalization and another to a behaviour.

One more peculiarity of the *je* is worthy of mention. This concerns the naming of the category. As noted, Nage interpret the standard metaphor *je podi we'e* as '*je* pretends to be close' (*podi*, 'to pretend'; *we'e*, '(to be, become) close'). Yet it appears that the phrase could be translated, more simply, as 'to advance (or "come close") in pretence', thus omitting reference to the bird altogether (see Appendix 1, text 39). It is not impossible, then, that, rather than the bird's reputed behaviour informing the expression, as Nage believe, the expression is the source of the use of *je* as a name for a nocturnal bird with regard to its peculiar method of nocturnal hunting. However that may be, on comparative grounds it appears to be ruled out that *je* in the sense of 'to advance gradually' (or 'to steal up on') derives from the name of a bird.

Lawi luja (*Asian paradise-flycatcher*) and piko (*Brown quail; see Figure 7.1*)

Apparently more fantastic than the preceding are Nage ideas concerning the *lawi luja*. Nage say that this bird never alights or defecates on the ground. If its excrement falls towards the earth, it is, in some unspecified way, always able to retrieve it, whereas should the bird itself alight on the ground, it would soon die. (In order to drink, therefore, the flycatcher must swoop down and scoop up water, presumably after the manner of a swallow.)

The notion of a bird for whom the earth is anathema is not unknown to European thought. Citing the Spanish Dominican Luis Uretta, the early seventeenth-century English writer Edward Topsell describes a kind of Ethiopian 'bird of paradise' which 'never lights on the earth till it dye' and so 'sleepeth in the aer and feedeth on flies and the dewe of heaven' (1972: 111). Concerning a species which nowadays Nage also describe as a 'bird of paradise' (Indonesian *cenderawasih*), it is just possible that their representation of the paradise-flycatcher derives from the extraordinary long white tail feathers of the male, which may be thought to prevent it from landing on the ground.[8]

However that may be, Nage conceive of the flycatcher in this context expressly in opposition to the quail (*piko*) which, on pain of death, must never perch in a tree or defecate on a branch. Noteworthy in this connection is the statement of one Nage man, who suggested conducting an experiment by placing a quail in a tree to see if the bird would indeed die. While this experimental attitude is in itself remarkable, it also indicates that the man (who possessed an

Figure 7.1 Asian paradise-flycatcher (*Lawi luja*) and Brown quail (*Piko*)

above-average formal education) did not definitely discount the traditional idea. A brief popular tale – amounting to little more than a statement to this effect – describes how the flycatcher and the quail once swore an oath obligating them to assume their present characters. As it concerns the quail, the Nage representation is more readily reconciled with ornithological fact than are the complementary ideas regarding the paradise-flycatcher, since quail are ground-dwelling birds. Since the stubby, almost tailless quail is also morphologically very different from the flycatcher, it is arguable that the contrasting character attributed to the latter derives largely from this perceptual contrast.[9]

Neither the account of the compact between the two birds, nor any other Nage story, describes how the flycatcher acquired its extraordinarily long tail. Although the quail (*piko*) is of course an ominous bird whose possible negative behaviour instances the concept of *pie*, the Asian paradise-flycatcher has no comparable symbolic or religious value that might account for ideas concerning its antipathy to the earth. Although, as mentioned in the previous chapter, one Nage man stated that it was taboo (*pie*) to catch or pelt a *lawi luja*, no one else was familiar with this idea. Also, while I once heard the bird described with the Indonesian (Bahasa Indonesia) term *sakti* ('supernaturally powerful, sacred'), this appeared to refer to no more than the ideas reviewed above. Nage often remark that, if caught, paradise-flycatchers will quickly die in captivity, but this observation applies as well to any number of other birds. As noted, in Nage taxonomic thought the paradise-flycatcher is associated with the drongo (*céce*), since both birds possess long and forked tails. Obviously, however, this association is more readily attributed to morphological resemblance than to any of the notions recounted above.

Manu wodu (unidentified)

Nage describe the *manu wodu* as a wild bird resembling a dark-coloured hen, with a crest (*odu*, from which derives *wodu*) in place of a coxcomb. The creature is said occasionally to enter villages, where some Nage claim to have seen it, and to mix with domestic fowls, thus causing them to become prolific – although not unequivocally through breeding. Possessing a crest apparently similar to the one Nage describe, and well-known for its very large eggs, the Orange-footed scrubfowl (*wodo, koko wodo*) might conceivably provide a partial inspiration for the image.[10] Nevertheless, the *manu wodu* is almost certainly an imaginary creature. In other words, the representation refers to something that does not exist, at least not as an avifaunal kind separate from domestic fowls or the scrubfowl.

Underlining its fantastic character, the idea of the *manu wodu* as an exogenous creature promoting the fertility of domestic hens parallels Nage ideas pertaining to other sorts of livestock. Being identical in most respects to the spiritually powerful creature called *manu ke'o*, which combines features of a bird and a large serpent, the *naga bhada* – or 'buffalo snake' – is described as a being that can take the form of a male buffalo and mate with cows, thereby causing them to calve frequently and successfully (Forth 1998a: 143–44). Similarly, a type of lizard named *mapa bonga* is believed to have intercourse with sows, to the same reproductive effect.

Méte *(flying fox) and other bats* (gébu, 'ighu)

As discussed elsewhere (Forth 1998c), Nage subscribe to a belief in animal metamorphosis, whereby creatures of one kind regularly transform (*bale*) into creatures of another kind. No such idea pertains to true birds. One of the best-known instances, however, concerns all three of the Nage bat generics. Briefly, although there are sceptics, many Nage claim that the smallest bats (*'ighu*) develop from grubs (*ule*) found in bamboo. After a time *'ighu* then turn into *gébu* (medium-sized bats), and these are eventually transformed into *méte* (large fruit bats, or flying foxes). Finally, flying foxes, when they have grown old, lose their wings and become Palm civets (*bheku, Paradoxurus hermaphroditus*). It should be stressed that, for Nage, none of these categories denotes the infant stage of the category which (as it were pseudo-ontogenetically) succeeds it.

As various possible empirical bases of these ideas have been discussed in my earlier paper (1998c), I shall not repeat myself here. One factor adduced in my earlier analysis, however, concerns the status of bats as marginal members of the covert category 'bird'. As Nage recognize, unlike true birds, none of the bat kinds lays eggs, a circumstance evidently linked with the idea that the smallest kind (*'ighu*) derive from grubs. On the other hand, they describe the two larger kinds, *méte* and *gébu*, as giving birth live (*dhadhi ana*) and as possessing navels (*puse*), ideas which obviously reflect close observation but which are not immediately reconcilable with the notion that the larger bats are transformations of *'ighu* (but see Forth 1998c: 276). The foundation of the belief in bat transformation therefore appears to pertain to the origins of the smallest kind. Yet, given the general resemblance that Nage recognize among members of all bat categories, in combination with the idea that the smallest, *'ighu*, derive from quite a different sort of creature (a grub), it is not unreasonable to posit that the two larger bat kinds (or at least those individuals which do not have a placental origin) may also develop from an ethnotaxonomically different kind and, moreover, retain the ability to undergo further metamorphosis.

The fact that Nage transformation ideas apply to all three categories of bats but not to any other 'bird' could indeed be a function of the classificatory position of bats in relation to aviformes. More particularly, it may be connected with the fact that the three bats closely resemble one another in precisely those respects that distinguish them from all other birds. Yet this does not mean that a fully formed, monolithic classification, even if catalysed by empirical observation (including the common habitats of small bats and grubs, and resemblances between small bats and moths; see Forth 1998c: 277) straightforwardly gives rise to an explanation of bat genesis in terms of metamorphosis. In fact, while bats for Nage are yet in some sense 'birds', the idea that bats, unlike other birds, derive from transformations would appear to contribute to, or reinforce, their ambiguous character and thus peripheral position in Nage classification. In other words, the relation between classification and ideas about reproduction – a type of ethnozoological knowledge – is, in this case, very probably one of mutual reinforcement.

As I have argued more fully elsewhere, Nage transformation ideas – or, more specifically, notions of 'contemporary zoological transformation' – are similar to scientific ideas. By the same token, they are distinguished from metamorphoses found in myth and religious ideology. Positing regular, permanent, and irreversible transformations, they differ, for example, from the idea that a witch or malevolent spirit can temporarily turn itself into a bird, before assuming some other form, or the notion that a little girl was once transformed into a Bare-throated whistler. To that extent, transformation ideas concerning bats are not usefully considered as symbolic; they are propositions provisionally maintained which are subject to revision, or even rejection, on empirical grounds (Forth 1998c: 289–90). Furthermore, there appears to be no necessary connection between these ideas and the previously described notion that an *'ighu* bat alighting inside a house produces harmful effects for the human inhabitants.

Although no less extraordinary, another apparently unrelated idea is that flying foxes (*méte*), the largest sort of bats, lack an anus and must therefore expel waste by continual vomiting. When questioned, Nage said that this applies as well to the smaller *gébu*; but *méte* is unequivocally the focal category in this regard, as in other contexts where the two bat categories are identified.[11] Interestingly, comparable ideas concerning the absence of the anal orifice among bats in general are found in New Guinea (see Bulmer 1968: 636; Dwyer, pers. comm. 2000; Healey, pers. comm. 2000) and possibly Australia.[12] In yet other traditions, the same physiological feature is attributed to different animals (for example, the sloth in South America, Lévi-Strauss 1985). Writing in the seventeenth century, Topsell described the Ethiopian 'bird of paradise', mentioned above, as having 'no excrementary or hole behinde' (1972: 115).

Among Nage, the idea that larger bats (*méte*) cannot defecate appears firmly rooted in observation of their anatomy, behaviour, and diet. Not only are flying foxes eaten, but their flesh is reckoned to be excellent, especially the internal organs. As this should suggest, Nage do gut the animals before cooking and consuming them (contrary to what Bulmer, 1968: 636, reports for the New Guinean Karam), and when doing so, they report, faeces are never found in the intestines. This observation most likely reflects the flying fox's diet of fruit and nectar. This results in faeces which are barely distinguishable from urine (P. Dwyer, pers. comm. 2000), and are quite possibly the 'vomit' found near roosting sites and described by Nage as being light in colour and containing the pits of arenga palm fruit.[13] Yet further support for the idea that flying foxes expel waste orally rather than defecate is adduced by Nage from the fact that they characteristically hang upside down, a behaviour which they explicitly link with the animal's propensity to vomit, if not their lack of an anal orifice (cf. Bulmer 1968: 636).

Given the Nage recognition of bats as odd in certain morphological respects, and more specifically as peculiar 'birds' that share several features with mammals, one should not be surprised to discover features of their diet and metabolism being attributed to equally odd, albeit unsubstantiated, features, such as the lack of an anus. For the anthropological analyst, however, bats present another puzzle. Sleeping suspended upside down during the daytime, bats may appear to be the very model of the sorts of inversions Nage attribute to witches and other spiritual beings. Yet despite their nocturnal and inverted behaviour and generally dark (or 'black', *mite*) colouring, and regardless of their marginal and ambiguous status in relation to the taxon of 'birds', Nage do not identify bats as embodiments of witches or other malevolent beings. Nor in fact do they associate the creatures with any other kind of spirit and, with the obvious exception of the tiny *'ighu*, Nage do not consider bats as in anyway ominous.[14]

In the general context of Nage symbolic thought, however, the 'non-spiritual' character of bats is quite easily explained with reference to two empirical features of all Flores Chiroptera. Unlike the 'witch birds' – to which symbolic category they might otherwise be thought to belong – bats are not carnivorous (as are the raptors and scavengers that constitute the majority of birds Nage identify with malevolent spirits), nor do they produce the same sorts of arresting calls. The importance of a carnivorous diet is underlined by the fact that, for essentially the same reason, Nage also do not classify the nightjar as a witch bird, despite its nocturnal habit and falcon-like form and plumage (see pp. 130–33). With regard to vocalizations, as Nage themselves remark, sounds made by flying foxes and lesser bats are quite different from those of other 'birds', being not only smaller and softer but of a quite different quality as well.[15]

Turning as it partly does on differences between bats and true avifauna, this analysis serves to underline earlier conclusions concerning birds Nage identify with witches and malevolent spirits; namely, that the focal criteria of this symbolic class are the habit of killing or consuming flesh and the production of ominous calls. As eastern Indonesian bats do not hunt or eat meat, it would therefore appear that bats are, perhaps ironically, disassociated from malevolent spirits not because they are taxonomically peripheral to the life-form 'bird', but because, like the majority of true birds, they do not eat meat. In addition, while bats (and among 'birds', only bats) are thought to undergo metamorphosis, the comparison with birds whose physical and auditory forms witches and maleficent spirits are believed to take further underlines fundamental differences between the two types of postulated transformations which I discussed at length in my earlier essay (Forth 1998c).

Muta me (Channel-billed cuckoo)

The *muta me* is a very large cuckoo that parasitizes both Large-billed crows (*Corvus macrorhynchos*) and Flores crows (*Corvus florensis*). Nage articulate a number of ideas consistent with this reproductive behaviour. But how far these accurately or adequately describe parasitism in birds is another matter.

Describing the bird as the 'child of the crow' (*ana ko'o ha*), Nage claim that young cuckoos and crows hatch from the same clutch of eggs. At least two Nage I questioned were quite sure that these eggs were laid by crows, with one man stating that the cuckoo is unable to lay eggs (*mona ngala ta telo*), while others were less certain. Whatever the Nage opinion on the derivation of eggs, the notion of crow parentage appears to have less to do with biological connection than with the common report that *muta me* are 'fed', or 'reared' by crows (*ha ti'i ka; ha ta'a pagha*). At the same time, one man described the cuckoos and crows as being 'of the same stock' (Bahasa Indonesia *rumpun*). Moreover, referring to the Nage idea (which is probably ornithologically correct) that the *muta me* is heard only during the early part of the wet season, another man offered the remarkable – and perhaps unusual – opinion that, after this time, the bird 'may again take the form of a crow'. This of course recalls the Nage attribution of metamorphosis to several animal categories, including all three named types of bats (cf. Dwyer 1976: 197). It is further reminiscent of an ancient Greek belief, also found in England until quite recent times, to the effect that the migratory and equally parasitic European cuckoo (*Cuculus canorus*), at summer's end, turns into a sparrow-hawk, and that in the spring such hawks change into cuckoos (Swann 1913: 68; Brown 1936: 56–57).

The standard Nage description of the *muta me* includes other features consistent with the status of the Channel-billed cuckoo as a brood parasite of crows. In early October, when the bird begins to utter the loud, harsh calls from which it takes its name (see Table 1.1), it is commonly seen on the wing and then always, Nage say, followed by several pursuing crows. Although I have witnessed this myself, whether the phenomenon involves adult females being driven away by reluctant crow hosts or newly mature birds being expelled from nests by corvine foster-parents is not clear. Nevertheless, it is the penetrating cry of the cuckoo, heard throughout the day and just before the wet season begins in earnest, that serves Nage as a major chronological indicator, and more particularly as a sign that one should begin preparing fields for planting. When planting is finished in December, Nage say, the bird becomes mute (*ngongo*); from that time until the end of the dry season, the *muta me* remains, inactive, in a nest to where crows bring it food. Then, before the beginning of the following rainy season, the bird leaves its treetop home and begins searching for its own food, whereupon it begins to call again.[16]

Nothing Nage say about the *muta me* suggests that they are fully aware that the bird lays its eggs in the nests of crows. Thus one must conclude that their understanding of the cuckoo's parasitic habit is incomplete. On the other hand, none of their statements about the bird appears to be grounded in anything other than observation of its actual behaviour, or that of its crow hosts. Of all cases described so far, therefore, this representation is the one most in accord with scientific ornithology and, by the same token, the one most independent of factors of symbolism or features peculiar to Nage ethnotaxonomy. On the other hand, their interpretation of the bird's association with crows (more particularly the Large-billed crow, *ha*) has evidently influenced their inclusion of *muta me* in the ornithologically mixed intermediate taxon of 'crow-like birds' (Chapter 3).

As a final note, I would just mention that, while Nage represent *muta me* and *toe ou*, the Common koel, as complementary calendrical signs, and in one context as a metaphorical pair (see Appendix 1, texts 1–3), they appear to be unaware that the koel, also, is a brood parasite of crows (both the Large-billed and Flores crow).[17] Since both birds belong to the hypothetical covert taxon of 'crow-like birds', this would moreover suggest that the koel's inclusion is based mainly on its morphological resemblance to crows – the male koel being all black and not much smaller than the Large-billed crow (see Figure 7.2). At the same time, it cannot be ruled out that the classificatory association with the Channel-billed cuckoo (*muta me*) is based on the seasonal salience of their respective vocalizations, at roughly the same crucial point of the agricultural year. Noteworthy here is the fact that, on the island of Komodo (immediately west of Flores) it is specifically the koel, there called *mori urang*, 'master of the rain', that local people associate with the first rains, and which they speak of as 'fighting with crows' (Verheijen 1982: 245, 255 note 2), a phrase reminiscent of Nage descriptions of the *muta me*. Indeed, the koel may sometimes be the referent of the name *muta me* in Nage usage as well.

Tiwe *(sunbird; see Figure 8.1)*

Nage describe the tiny sunbird as bold and aggressive (*bani*), even more so than the drongo (*céce*). The *tiwe*, they say, will chase away eagles (*kua méze*), and will steal eagles' feathers to line its nest. The eagle is unable to catch the

Figure 7.2 Channel-billed cuckoo (*Muta me*) and Common koel (*Toe ou*)

tiwe because it is too small. All this is reminiscent of ideas concerning the equally aggressive wren, among the smallest of European birds, and its opposition to the eagle – the rival 'king of birds' – in European tradition (Lawrence 1997). Describing the Olive-backed sunbird, the focus if not the sole referent of the category *tiwe*, Coates and Bishop characterize the tiny nectar-feeder as 'conspicuous, active, vocal, nervous and pugnacious' (1997: 482). It is no doubt these traits that inform the Nage representation. At the same time, the perceptual features are arguably catalysed as a symbolic motivation by the bird's diminutive size – a fact that lends this image, like that of the European wren, a touch of irony – while its size is of course highlighted by setting the sunbird in opposition to the eagle. As indicated in Table 2.1, the extreme sizes of the two birds constitute their respective 'simple distinctive features'.

The boldness of the sunbird also finds expression in the Nage story of the Imperial pigeon and the friarbird (Forth 1992), where both birds are portrayed as being afraid of the *tiwe*, which moreover succeeds in releasing the friarbird from bondage. That the tiny bird sides with the friarbird may reflect phylogenetic linkage. Friarbirds are large members of the Meliphagidae (or Honeyeaters), whereas sunbirds belong to the Nectarinidae. While ornithologists disagree as to how closely related the two families might be (Cameron and Harrison 1978: 232; cf. Coates and Bishop 1997: 480), small honey-eaters closely resemble sunbirds in form and behaviour; accordingly, Nage appear to include small honey-eaters (genus *Lichmera*), together with sunbirds, in the category of *tiwe* (see Table 1.1). However closely related they may be ornithologically, friarbirds and sunbirds, both nectar-feeders, have similar diets and, despite the difference in their sizes, resemble one another in a tendency to aggressiveness (Coates and Bishop 1997: 473, 482).

Toto (Lesser coucal)

In the older literature, coucals are called 'crow-pheasants', a name that quite accurately describes these mostly dark and rather corvine birds, which otherwise bear some resemblance to gamebirds. They are also weak fliers and so remain close to the ground, where they nest in tall grass or reeds. Nage describe coucals as producing two characteristic calls: one which lends them their onomatopoeic name and another, lower-pitched vocalization locally imitated as 'guum, guum' or 'tuum, tuum'. According to Nage, whereas the higher-pitched vocalization comes from the bird's mouth, the *toto* produces the lower-pitched sounds with its anus. The two sorts of sound then alternate.

The coucal's anus is the focus of another extraordinary idea. Nage claim that, during the wet season, this part of the bird's anatomy becomes infested with 'maggots', or 'worms' (*ule*), a feature described in the standard expression *toto 'obo mou*, '*toto* with a rotten anus'.[18] Then, with the onset of the dry season, the bird each year undergoes a remarkable recovery: the anus 'dries out' and the maggots disappear. With reference to this reputed phenomenon, Nage employ the phrase '*toto* with a rotten anus' as a simile for a person who seems to become ill only when there is work to be done. As one man remarked, this ability to recover completely from such a serious condition distinguishes the coucal from all other creatures, since these would surely die from a comparable bodily deterioration. The condition thus figures as the *toto*'s 'simple distinctive feature'.

Other than the fact that anal infestation and anal 'vocalization' refer to the same part of the bird's anatomy, it is not clear how the two ideas might be related. The notion that the bird calls anally – an idea I also encountered among eastern Sumbanese – probably derives from the quality of the sound. Although I never actually heard it formulated in this way, the sound, in other words, may be thought to resemble flatus. Another Nage expression, *toto wolo gobe*, 'toto drowns in a water container', refers to its resemblance to the gurgling sound of water poured from a large vessel. Describing the same bird on Java and Bali, McKinnon (1991: 176) characterizes the 'several deep hollow "boop" notes' of the Lesser coucal as 'like water pouring from a bottle'.

While having some basis in auditory qualities the idea that the *toto* vocalizes anally is surely incorrect. On the other hand, the report of infestation of the anus probably reflects accurate observation of some natural condition.[19] Although I have found no ornithological source that could substantiate it, as Nage describe the bird as easily caught, especially during the wet months, they presumably have ample opportunity to observe its anatomy. Different informants described the infested anus as smelling either like diarrhoea or a rotting chicken carcass. This is consistent with Mason and Jarvis's description of the Lesser coucal as giving off 'a rather disagreeable smell' and as tasting 'foul' (1989: 29). Even if justified, however, the latter assessment does not prevent Nage from partaking of the bird's flesh, at least during the dry season.

Other than as the source of a particular simile, the coucal holds no symbolic value for Nage, and thus no occult connection that might inform, or be informed by, the bird's peculiar anal associations. Nor do the latter illuminate the classification of the bird, which is not grouped with any other, nor separated from other birds with which one might expect it to be connected on perceptual grounds. (In regard to bird taxonomy, one informant thus described it as 'standing alone'.) Conversely, the bird's classificatory status does not point to any obvious source of the ideas about its anus.

Witu tui *(possibly the Great tit,* Parus major)

The *witu tui* was described in the previous chapter as a bird that reputedly picks up human hair, thus causing madness or mental derangement (*bingu*) in the human owner. How far this idea is empirically grounded turns partly on a question of ornithological identification, similar to the one involved in assessing the Nage representation of the behaviour of the raptor they call *je*. As noted, consistent with the particular consequence of a *witu tui* stealing a person's head hair, Nage describe the bird as restless and irregular in its movements. This description fits well the hyperactive Great tit, in fact titmice (including North American 'chickadees') in general. In addition, the idea of the bird picking up human hair may be based in an actual use of hair, or some similar material, as nesting material.

It should be stressed that some Nage are sceptical about the *witu tui*'s reputed habit of stealing human hair. Some were even doubtful about any bird using hair for making nests – a habit which, in regard to mammal hair, is ornithologically well documented. Nevertheless, Nage are familiar with birds using such similar materials as palm fibre for nest building. It is also noteworthy that, in Europe at least, Great tits, like other members of the Paridae, use animal hair to line their nests (Richards 1979: 163). Local descriptions of the bird's plumage accord with the Great tit as the referent of *witu tui*. On the other hand, the characteristic call, from which the Nage name is derived, while just conceivably motivated by vocalizations of the Great tit, is not entirely consistent with these. In fact, Nage imitations and descriptions of the *witu tui*'s cry, as well as my own observations of what I took to be the actual call, suggest a rather larger bird, perhaps a sub-species of the locally unnamed Elegant pitta (see Table 1.1, s.v. *witu tui*). Referring to a Nage dialect other than that of Bo'a Wae, Verheijen (n.d.) identifies a cognate name, *'itu tui*, with the Brush cuckoo (*Cacomantis variolosus*). However, not only does this species not clearly occur on Flores, but if the Nage idea regarding the *witu tui*'s nest-building habit has any basis in fact, the bird is obviously excluded by virtue of its parasitism. On the other hand, another member of the genus, the Rusty-backed cuckoo (*Cacomantis sepulcralis aeruginous*), does occur, and descriptions of its call given by Coates and Bishop (1997: 349) appear to match that which Nage ascribe to the *witu tui*. But, insofar as this cuckoo is also a brood parasite, its reproductive technique similarly lends no support to the Nage representation of the *witu tui*.

Some evidence suggests that it may be the bird's onomatopoeic name, as much as the erratic behaviour of the Great tit or some other species, that has informed an association of the *witu tui* with mental derangement or instability, and perhaps even its reputed behaviour in regard to hair clippings. To begin with, the first component of the name is reminiscent of *titu* which, in the compound *bingu titu* ('deranged, insane'), refers to the mental condition that supposedly results from the bird's habit of picking up shorn hair. In fact, one man suggested that *bingu titu* could be understood as an abbreviation of *bingu witu tui*. Although apparently equally idiosyncratic, another possible support for this interpretation is the opinion of another man, who insisted that the bird which steals hair and thus causes madness is not the *witu tui* but the *ebu titu* ('swallow' or 'swift'). Also attributing a semantic value to the bird's call and linking it with the bird's reputed behaviour, the first man further glossed the second component, *tui*, as 'to pick up and carry away'. *Witu*, moreover, means 'bush, undergrowth', thus something which is not entirely dissimilar to hair, and which birds do indeed use as nesting material.

Whatever the precise balance of factors contributing to the representation of the *witu tui*, it is likely that observation of actual bird behaviour, both visual and vocal, plays a considerable part. It is also possible that the representation is based on observations of two distinct species – one being the Great tit, and the other the call of a quite different bird. At the same time, the belief that the appropriation of human hair by a bird, of any kind, can result in mental derangement is quite clearly symbolic insofar as it obviously cannot be reduced to its empirical supports, whatever these might be. I would conclude by noting European and Euro-American parallels of Nage ideas regarding the *witu tui*. Ingersoll (1923: 9) cites an unnamed 'Baltimore folklorist' as warning 'every lady against letting birds build nests with the combings of her hair, as it will turn the unfortunate woman crazy'. This notion the author then ascribes to a European 'saying' to the effect that 'if a bird uses human hair in its nest the owner of the hair will have headaches and later baldness'. Comparable ideas linking bats and human hair are also well known in the west (cf. Lawrence 1993: 327–28). Obviously, there is quite a lot one could say about these kinds of beliefs, but probably not much that would significantly expand an understanding of the specifics of the Nage representation of the *witu tui*.

The luckless hunter and the legless nightjar

As mentioned in the previous chapter, Nage describe the Savannah nightjar (*leba*) as legless, or footless (*taga mona*).[20] The idea has an obvious empirical basis in the possession, by the Caprimulgidae generally, of short legs and very small feet (Coates and Bishop 1997: 364). Also, when these nocturnal birds are encountered during the daytime, sleeping on the ground or on a low tree branch, their legs and feet are normally not visible. The representation might therefore be characterized as a hyperbole, or standard exaggeration. Consistent with this, some Nage more exactly describe the nightjar as 'having legs but very short ones' (*taga bhoko*) At the same time, others, in fact most people I spoke with, either simply asserted that, as far as they knew, the bird was legless or insisted that this was so.

For the most part, the notion of the legless nightjar appears to be a product of incomplete observation predicated on the bird's nocturnal habits and its plumage, which provides very effective camouflage during the daylight hours. Nage also describe the bird as very difficult to catch; even when spotted on the ground, it breaks into flight before one can make one's move, setting down again some distance away. At the same time, as I indicated previously, the advent of paved motor roads, on which nightjars have become in the habit of resting at night, has resulted in the birds regularly being caught in the glare of headlights or even killed by vehicles, and has thus provided Nage with more opportunities for observation.[21] Three men described how they had been able to obtain nightjars, either dead or alive, while travelling by motor vehicle. This, then, may account for qualifications of the standard representation of the *leba* as a legless bird. I encountered no clear pattern, in regard to age or ethno-ornithological expertise, between advocates of the categorical and the qualified views of the nightjar's leglessness. In fact, older people described the bird's legs as very short, rather than non-existent, at least as often as did younger informants, while the most insistent proponent of the categorical view was an older man who claimed to have inspected a carcass.

The nightjar provides a good illustration of how local knowledge of a bird, including in this case a quasi-empirical characteristic, contributes to its symbolic value. The nightjar's notional leglessness constitutes its 'simple distinctive feature'. Yet in regard to the bird's significance as a negative omen for nocturnal hunters, other physical features of the bird appear equally relevant. With considerable frequency, as well as ornithological accuracy, Nage spontaneously describe the nightjar as closely resembling, in size, form, and plumage, a small falcon – the Moluccan kestrel (*iki*).[22] What this suggests is that, like bird's supposed leglessness, Nage themselves find the resemblance between nightjars and falcons quite 'remarkable'. It is a reasonable inference that they do so because in other respects, the two birds are very different.

The main difference of course lies in the fact, of which Nage are well aware that, unlike falcons and other raptors, the insectivorous nightjar is not a hunter. Indeed, not only does it lack the talons of a bird of prey, but in the standard Nage image, the nightjar lacks legs and feet (*taga*) altogether. This combination of empirical fact and quasi-empirical local imagery, I suggest, sufficiently motivates the Nage symbolic association of the nightjar with lack of success in hunting. The nightjar looks very much like a raptor – in fact, a diurnal bird of prey – yet this nocturnal bird lacks the means to seize prey and hence never kills a single victim. It is, in a word, a pseudo-hunter.

Other features distinguishing the nightjar from birds of prey are its small weak bill and gaping mouth. Well-suited to catching flying insects, the second trait is reflected in European names for the nightjar (specifically *Caprimulgus europaeus*), including French *engoulevent* (literally 'wind-swallower') and *tête chèvre*, German *Ziegenmelker*, and the older English name 'goatsucker' (Lévi-Strauss 1985: 50).[23] In conjunction with features associating the nightjar with birds of prey, moreover, the gape, especially, could suggest to Nage a disproportion between large consumption and an inability to provision evoked both by a tiny beak and small or absent feet that are inadequate to gripping or cutting into flesh – and hence a hunter whose appetite always exceeds his kill. One is thus reminded of Lévi-Strauss's remarks (1985) about greed as a general attribute of nightjars (or 'goatsuckers', as he calls them) in New World mythology. Of particular interest is the way Californian Indian myths depict the nighthawk, one of the American nightjars, as a 'bad hunter' (to use Lévi-Strauss's phrase, 1985: 85) who unsuccessfully tries to pass himself off a 'great hunter', the eagle.[24]

Another important contrast between nightjars and raptors concerns the fact that, as the highest and strongest of flyers, falcons and other diurnal birds of prey are associated with the sky. Although certainly capable of flight, the nightjar, which sleeps and nests directly on barren ground, is most decidedly associated with the earth. Another bird whose call constitutes a negative hunting omen, the Pied bushchat, is also associated with the earth, since Nage accurately characterize it as a low flyer that nests in low shrubs and rockeries. Yet, in the case of the nightjar, it is arguably the contrast that an earthly association strikes with the aerial environment of high-flying raptors which renders the former trait relevant to the nightjar's significance as a negative hunting omen. In other respects as well the nightjar and Pied bushchat are very different birds, a circumstance that tends to preclude their characterization as members of a single symbolic class. Among other things, the bushchat's link with the earth inheres largely in its nesting inside earthen or rock cavities, a feature it shares with the bee-eater (*zeghi*), a bird whose call one man, apparently idiosyncratically, also described as a negative sign for hunters (see Chapter 5, note 17). In contrast, relying on camouflage, the nightjar nests on top of the earth, in open and relatively exposed sites. Hence the bushchat's inauspicious significance for hunters may derive from a sympathetic similarity with game animals (such as porcupines, Giant rats, or wild pigs) which might, likewise, remain in burrows or nests, or may otherwise take cover at the hunter's approach. The symbolism of the nightjar, on the other hand, consists in its similarity to a failed hunter.

So far I have endeavoured to show how Nage empirical knowledge of the *leba*, and their representation of its physical features in relation to those of partly similar birds (specifically raptors), informs their image of the legless nightjar as a symbol of a luckless hunter, and its predictive call as a sign of an unsuccessful hunt.[25] As the comparative component of this process should suggest, the same empirical features also affect the place of the nightjar in Nage ethno-ornithological classification. More particularly, the hyperbolic idea that the nightjar lacks legs – the birds 'simple distinctive feature' – expresses a crucial distinction between the nightjar and otherwise similar birds of prey. What is more, this ethnotaxonomic function could contribute to the persistence of an idea which is, strictly speaking, contrary to ornithological fact.

This is not quite to argue, however, that the Nage idea is – to invoke an analytical contrast central to recent cognitive anthropology – completely counter-intuitive or contradictory to common sense (see Atran 1990; Boyer 1994a, 1994b; also Sperber 1994: 62, who uses 'reflective' as the opposite of 'intuitive'). Not only does the legless nightjar have an obvious basis in local experience (as partial as this may be), but the notion is also glossed by some Nage commentators as a reference to the bird's lower appendages being very short. Following Sperber's usage, it might therefore be characterized as a 'figure' – and more precisely a hyperbole – rather than a 'belief' (1975: 105). On the other hand, some Nage do indeed seem to accept the nightjar's reputed leglessness, either as a simple fact or as something like a 'dead metaphor'.[26] This raises the further question of whether Nage, or anyone else, might conceive of the possibility of a bird being legless, after the manner of snakes, earthworms, or whales, without thereby constructing a special 'mythico-religious' representation (Atran 1990: 219) to this effect. I should say that they can, and moreover that their acceptance of a legless nightjar is not itself a religious idea, even though it contributes to the symbolism of the nightjar in regard to hunting augury.[27]

Insofar as the express notion goes beyond perceptual experience, or is so to speak 'hyper-empirical' as opposed to simply inaccurate, it does so as a function of an ironic contrast with raptorial birds which informs not only the nightjar's value as a sign for nocturnal hunters but also its ethnotaxonomic status. In regard to its apparent utility as a mnemonic stereotype or aid to classification – a relative distinction rendered categorical by hyperbole – it should further be noted that the nightjar's reputed leglessness is by no means the only 'simple distinctive feature' whose expression involves an exaggeration of empirical reality. For example, Nage commonly describe the *bama cea* (Russet-capped tesia) as tailless (cf. Verheijen, 1977, who records the same notion for Rembong), whereas the bird, as Nage are aware, only has a very short tail. Similarly, Nage characterize the Bare-throated whistler (*kete dhéngi*) as a bird that is heard but never seen (*mona tei*); in fact, some people have seen it and are able to give an accurate, albeit sketchy, description of the bird's appearance.

Since in a number of previous cases I have mentioned western parallels to Nage representations, I shall close by noting how the idea of a 'legless', or more exactly 'footless', bird is by no means foreign to European tradition. One instance relates to the previously mentioned misconception, promoted by no less a figure than Linnaeus, concerning birds of paradise, and reflected in the scientific naming of one species, the Greater bird of paradise, as *Paradisaea apoda*, or 'footless paradise bird'. Another example is the old belief that swifts (or sometimes swallows) lack feet. Similarly enshrining this notion is the scientific name of the swift family: Apodidae, the 'footless ones'. Interestingly enough, this group reveals a close evolutionary relation to the Caprimulgidae, the family of nightjars. It is further noteworthy that the swift's supposed footlessness – possessing roughly the same empirical basis as the Nage nightjar's leglessness – secured for the bird a place in English heraldic symbolism. Thus, under the rubric of 'martlet', the swift came to be adopted as 'the mark of cadency of the fourth son of a house'. Drawing on an unacknowledged source, Blair explains the motivation as follows:

> [fourth sons] . . . being in a manner like unto that bird that lacketh feet wherewith to settle upon land, and they lacking land whereon to set their feet, may be thereby reminded of the necessity wherein they stand of earning unto themselves an estate by prowess of arms and their own endeavours.
>
> (Blair 1957: 42)

It is not stretching things too far to discern in this a close parallel to the relationship between the nightjar, which shares the environment of a night bird's prey but lacks the hunting appendages of a raptor, and the luckless Nage hunter, who possesses weapons but can kill no game. By the same token, it is also not difficult to see how the symbolic function of the European bird might have buttressed the representation of the swift as a footless bird.

Empiricism, symbolism, and classification

The majority of ideas reviewed in this chapter appear firmly grounded in observations of physical features or behaviour of the kinds concerned. The extent of this empirical foundation, however, varies from case to case. Thus, while the notion that kites or eagles use grindstones to sharpen their talons is obviously linked with their undisputed sharpness, the belief itself consists in an incorrect inference. Similar assessments apply to flying foxes' lack of an anus and falcons decapitating prey with their 'sharp' wings. At the other extreme, Nage statements about the behaviour of the Channel-billed cuckoo (*muta me*) appear on the whole accurate. To the extent that such representations are inaccurate (for example, in suggesting that cuckoos and crows hatch from eggs laid by the same bird), they derive from observations that are incomplete and fail to provide a full or exact account of the phenomenon to which they relate (in this case, parasitism).

A functionalist approach would require that such ideas, insofar as they are not fully substantiated empirically, should be explained in relation to other ideas about birds, in particular ones bound up with specific cultural or symbolic values. In fact, the foregoing review reveals relatively few connections of this sort. Most of the birds discussed above have no major symbolic value for Nage. The Brahminy kite and other large raptors certainly do, by virtue of their association with malevolent spirits; but this association has no necessary connection with ideas about the grindstones. In contrast, the notion that nightjars lack legs can indeed be seen to possess a symbolic function. Yet, according to the analysis advanced above, in this case it is an empirically grounded representation which informs a particular symbolic value (the nightjar as hunting omen) and then only in an indirect and partial way, rather than a pervasive cultural symbolism (such as an identification of raptorial birds with malevolent spirits) informing an empirically unfounded belief.

Following the approach of Sperber (1975), who treats as 'symbolic knowledge' any statement that is not strictly rational (accurately 'encyclopaedic' or 'semantic'), some Nage ideas about birds might appear to be 'symbolic', or hypothetically so, in the simple sense that they are difficult to reconcile with present ornithological knowledge. Yet this also varies considerably among different instances. For example, while it is entirely possible that coucals (*toto*) do annually suffer from a condition that gives the appearance of anal infestation, the notion that paradise-flycatchers never alight or defecate on the ground seems empirically less likely. However, if this second belief is symbolic, it is so precisely because it appears significantly influenced by another, symmetrically inverse (though empirically probably better grounded) idea; namely, that quails never perch or defecate in trees. At the same time, to quite a remarkable degree, the majority of Nage ideas about birds appear plausible, even when they are not supported by findings of western ornithology. And where this is so, it is quite possible that Nage observations are further advanced than those of their scientific counterparts. The most that Nage can be accused of is not regularly subjecting their ideas to systematic experimentation, although as I noted with regard to the opposing characterizations of quails and paradise-flycatchers, an experimental spirit is certainly not absent among them.

As indicated above, some cognitive anthropologists have labelled symbolic ideas, especially ones pertaining to religion, magic, and myth, as counter-intuitive, or contrary to a universal common sense. Not emerging as it were naturally from normal experience of the world in the course of an individual's cognitive development, such ideas, being part of a cultural tradition, have to be specially learned and perpetuated. This characterization probably applies to Nage representations concerning the *manu wodu*, apparently an imaginary creature, and the *witu tui*, a category possibly based on percepts relating to two different empirical birds. It also applies to symbolic ideas discussed in the previous chapter, concerning for example the several kinds of birds Nage identify with witches. However, it is questionable whether the majority of ideas reviewed in this chapter can be called counter-intuitive. And even if the designation could be justified in some instances, this would not necessarily mean that the ideas were symbolic, let alone religious. All cultures develop and maintain representations which do not accord with, and may even appear to contradict, everyday experience, and which culture members themselves would regard as pertaining to things extraordinary or remarkable, if not utterly fantastic. Yet, as several authors have shown, counter-intuitive ideas – notions that appear to run in the face of everyday common sense – are as much a feature of modern science as they are of religious and mythological representations (Wolpert 1992; Sperber 1994: 62).

In regard to Nage ethnozoology, I have argued elsewhere (Forth 1998c) that ideas concerning 'contemporary zoological transformations', whereby creatures of one kind are supposed to turn into creatures of another kind, bear a greater resemblance to scientific ideas than to symbolic or religious ones. As further demonstrated in that paper, the extent to which Nage are convinced of such metamorphoses corresponds directly to their degree of empirical support. For example, the transformation of *ana fe* (tadpoles) into *pake* (frogs) – which Nage classify as different kinds of animals – is accepted by everyone (or nearly everyone); it is also the metamorphosis whose process is most elaborately described. On the other hand, not all Nage accept the transformation of one kind of bat into another (or of flying foxes into Palm civets), while still other locally reported metamorphoses receive even less support. Although it is sometimes convenient to designate them as such, these latter notions are thus not 'beliefs' in the sense of ideas firmly adhered to by all or most members of a community; indeed, they are more like scientific hypotheses.

The foregoing applies to many of the ideas reviewed in this chapter. As noted, some Nage understand the representation of the legless nightjar as a reference to the bird having very short legs. And even though the reputed leglessness informs a symbolic notion – a negative hunting omen – it is arguable that this function would be subserved nearly as well by the observation that the bird's legs are extremely small and weak. In a related vein, inexact ideas about swifts and swallows (*ebu titu*), the Channel-billed cuckoo (*muta me*), and the Peregrine falcon (*bele teka*), and perhaps also flying foxes and the coucal (*toto*), appear simply to explain Nage experience of natural phenomena such as migration, parasitism, and the hunting methods of raptors; and it would make little if any cultural difference if they were to obtain a more accurate understanding of these phenomena. Such ideas do not in any way impinge on Nage religious or magical thought. They do not obviously link with other common cultural ideas; and to that extent no useful purpose is served by labelling them as 'symbolic'.

In contrast, something quite different applies to beliefs that can be characterized as spiritual. For example, the notion that certain birds, or their calls, can manifest witches appears to be a representation that all Nage accept and never seriously question. Universally accepted in the same way are portents deriving from the entry of tiny bats or quails into human habitations or the cry of the nightjar which, although not spiritual, are nevertheless symbolic. By the same token, as I pointed out in my discussion of equally non-spiritual transformation ideas, while these ideas are often doubted by individual Nage, no one I spoke to ever questioned the existence of free spirits (*nitu, bapu*) or witches (Forth 1998c: 288–89).

In one respect, the various ideas reviewed above would appear to relate to ethnotaxonomy in quite a fundamental way. For nearly all refer, directly or indirectly, to 'simple distinctive features', those most frequently mentioned empirical, or quasi-empirical, characteristics of birds that set each apart from other kinds (see Table 2.1). Possessing an evident mnemonic function, and in a few instances reflected in a bird's name, these features compose stereotyped images that contribute to the cognitive representation and hence definition of folk generics. On the other hand, simple distinctive features do not in any way illuminate relations between generic categories, which for the most part compose the terminal taxa of Nage ethno-ornithological taxonomy. Thus, they have no bearing on the *form* of the classification; that is, relations of inclusion or the composition of (mostly unlabelled) higher-order groupings.

In most other respects as well, features of classification seem not to be closely connected with curious ideas about birds. In a couple of instances, the attribution of unattested behaviours may be traced to nomenclature (see *bele teka* and *witu tui*). But whatever the force of particular interpretations, nomenclature is not the same as classification. A stronger argument for the influence of classification might be made in the case of bat metamorphosis, in regard to the marginal position of all bats in relation to other 'birds'. Yet, as indicated earlier, this too requires qualification.

Insofar as the notion of bat transformations can be ascribed to an ornithologically incorrect inclusion of Chiroptera in a covert life-form category of 'birds', this case lends support to Bulmer who, writing on similar notions among the Karam of New Guinea, endeavours to demonstrate how 'erroneous' ideas 'tend to go with' 'zoologically inadequate taxonomy' combined with 'social, and perhaps psychological pressures, largely expressed in mystical beliefs, which inhibit observation, or the rational interpretation of observation, or both' (1968: 636, 638). In a similar way, the inclusion of the Channel-billed cuckoo (*muta me*) in a covert grouping of 'crow-like birds' may be linked to Nage ideas about the crow parentage of cuckoos, while the notion that migratory swallows and swifts hibernate in caves can be partly ascribed to their imprecise placement of these birds in the same named taxon (*ebu titu*) as resident swifts of the genus *Collocalia*, which do inhabit caves. However, other Nage ideas about birds, although equally 'erroneous', cannot so readily be attributed to features of their ethnotaxonomy. Nor, where inaccuracy appears simply to reflect inadequate observation, does the latter typically follow from 'mystical beliefs' – even though I have allowed that the symbolic function of the nightjar's notional leglessness might reinforce this representation of its morphology. Bulmer's argument thus finds little confirmation in Nage ideas about birds. By the same token, Ellen's essentially similar treatment of Nuaulu transformation beliefs as functioning to 'legitimate' or 'confirm' a prevailing classification of animal categories as central and peripheral members of a single class (1993a: 170–71) does not resonate in the Nage data.

At the same time, Bulmer does allow that observations which could qualify or invalidate inaccurate ideas may be restricted, not only by 'mystical beliefs' but by practical difficulties as well (1968: 636). Indeed, I would suggest that, among Nage, such difficulties (for example, the virtual impossibility, entailed by a simple technology, of observing the reproductive habits of species that parasitize crows, which nest high up in tall trees, or of determining where migratory species go during part of the year) are the main factor accounting for inaccurate statements about birds. In other words, one usually does not require recourse to particular features of either ethnotaxonomy or local symbolism to account for such notions. Nevertheless, it is possible to glimpse another, diachronic connection between empirically unsubstantiated notions and both bird symbolism and ethno-ornithological classification. Many of the ideas discussed above can be described as occupying an epistemologically intermediate position between, on the one hand, the sort of fully intuitive or perceptual knowledge on which ethnotaxonomic distinctions are typically based and, on the other, symbolic or religious ideas. As I have suggested in regard to transformation beliefs (1998c: 289–90), over time such ideas might as it were turn in one direction or the other, and become implicated either in a more consistent empiricism or in religious or mythical thought. In the first case, they could thus be subject to further investigation and thence revised or, if empirical support is lacking entirely, be abandoned altogether. In the second, they might evolve into, or become fully incorporated as crucial components of, symbolic representations.

Chapter 8

Birds in myth and metaphor

In Chapter 4 I showed how nocturnal and diurnal birds of prey are related metaphorically to malevolent spiritual beings in the sense that behavioural and associated morphological features of the former are also attributed to the latter. Expressed another way, one may say that these birds serve as models for spirits that typically cause harm to human beings, metaphorically linked with domestic fowls. At the same time, the spiritual beings themselves – and especially those called *polo* ('witches') – are for a large part conceived anthropomorphously. In what follows, I review the Nage use of birds as metaphors of another kind; that is, as sources of proper names and as tropes for human characteristics, partly physical (as in the case of many similes) but mostly social and psychological. After that, I introduce the topic of birds in Nage myth, a symbolic genre in which birds are linked metaphorically with spirits, but at the same time interact in significant ways with human beings.

Birds and proper naming

Thus far, considerable attention has been given to Nage naming of birds. In this section, I review Nage naming of persons, places, and social groups after birds. With regard to persons, as shown in Appendix 2 (see 'Personal names'), bird names appear to occur significantly more often as names (*ngaza*) of men than of women. Since these lists are opportunistic, however, and not definitely complete, this impression may not be accurate. With the same qualification, it may be noted that bird names given to men refer on the whole to larger and more powerful birds than do those given to women. Particularly noteworthy is the fact that three of the ten male names are those of raptors while three of the four female names denote favoured game birds (quails, buttonquails, and the ground-dove). The fourth (*peti*) is the name of a variety of small passerine birds, but this is also used as a male personal name. An association of small birds, especially, with human females is further reflected in several poetic idioms (see pp. 143–44) as well as in the story about a little girl who turns into a Bare-throated whistler (*kete dhéngi*; see pp. 150–52).

As regards the derivation of such names, one man suggested that they probably originated as nicknames or aliases (*sédho*) given to children who are frequently ill or pine constantly. In the course of time, they may then have become permanent, being inherited in the usual Nage manner by grandchildren and descendants of the person named. Since aliases of this sort are indeed often the names of wild creatures, this local hypothesis is perfectly credible. There is, in any case, no other obvious explanation of why some Nage personal names are bird names. Female personal names are often place names, especially village names; but since there are very few settlements named after birds, this transfer of place names can hardly account for the use of bird terms as women's names.[1] Nevertheless, and in spite of the opportunistic nature of the lists, it may be worth noting that of the 14 male and female personal names, as many as six also occur as place names, the total of which in Appendix 2 (see 'Place names') is also 14 (counting doubtful cases such as Gako). The six names are Iki, Jata, Kata (which occurs three times as a place name), Leo, Koka, and Kolo (which occurs at least once and possibly twice). Other than the fact that these are all names of well-known birds, I can offer no explanation of this coincidence.

As indicated in Appendix 2 ('Place names'), Nage give proper names to a great variety of places and locations. Most probably, those named after birds are so designated because of the presence of the ornithological kind, perhaps in especial abundance or nesting in the place. Of the names given in the appendix, it is interesting that three include *kata* (junglefowl), while two appear to include *kolo* (dove). As both names designate favoured game birds, and another, *wodo* (scrubfowl), refers to a bird that lays exceptionally large eggs, the choice of these names may reflect utilitarian factors. But this does not apply to the majority of the names. As Appendix 2 reveals, by far the majority of such places are not settlements but uninhabited sites or, in a couple of instances, whole regions (e.g. Gako, 'Owa) rather than single locations. Why this should be so is not obvious, particularly as Nage villages and hamlets often retain the names that were given to the sites they occupy prior to settlement (see e.g. Nata Iki). It may be supposed, however, that birds present in a particular spot will disappear or become less evident soon after humans begin to settle there, and that, in consequence, the initial avifaunal association will cease to be meaningful. This obviously does not apply to villages named after nearby trees, other vegetation, or landscape features – all of which are far more common sources of site names (and hence settlement names) among Nage.

While Nage recognize a number of places named after birds, they are usually unable to give a definite reason for the naming. One apparent exception is the place name 'Owa ('cuckoo-dove'; Rowa in the local dialect), which is mythically rationalized by the association of an ancestor of the Rowa people with a cuckoo-dove. As I presently explain, however, the evidence in this case suggests that the myth may have been borrowed from elsewhere to provide an *ex post facto* explanation of an existing place name.

A large number of Nage clans, probably more than half, are named after present or former villages where clan members reside or once resided. Since settlements are not commonly named after birds, it should therefore come as no surprise that names of birds rarely appear as names of clans or other social groups either. The same observation can be made in respect of animals of all kinds, since names of wild mammals, reptiles, insects, and fish are similarly rare among Nage clan and village names.[2]

Construed as a clan name, Mude Wodo (Appendix 2, s.v. Lebi Wodo) is the only instance I encountered in the vicinity of Bo'a Wae, of a group being named – and then only in part – after a bird.[3] Although not reflected in its name, another Nage clan – Saga Enge – maintains a special ancestral relationship with the cuckoo-dove ('owa), even to the extent that members are forbidden to eat the flesh of this bird (see p. 104). The relationship, moreover, is explained by a myth identical to the one the people of Rowa ('Owa) tell when accounting for their district name. This is the only instance of anything like a 'totemic' relationship linking a clan with a bird in Nage. In fact, with the noteworthy exception of prohibitions several clans maintain on burning certain kinds of wood, 'totemic' relationships involving any kind of natural species are uncharacteristic of Nage, so that the Saga Enge people's connection with the cuckoo-dove is more unusual than might at first appear.[4]

By contrast, Arndt reports clan 'totems' for Ngadha and East Flores. The Ngadha clan Manu ('fowl') resident in Belu is described as having the fowl as a totem; thus all women of the clan are forbidden to eat chicken while they are still childless (Arndt 1954: 224). Two other Ngadha clans, Dizi and Biru, maintain a similar regard for the 'voko-bird' (ibid.: 233), apparently a reference to the Elegant pitta (Verheijen n.d., s.v. woko). In East Flores, several clans in the village of Labao regard raptors (including, apparently, the Brahminy kite and the White-bellied sea-eagle) as totems, and two in particular as apical clan ancestors. Men belonging to a section of one clan maintain a special relationship with two sorts of doves and the kewikit (Moluccan falcon, Verheijen n.d.), but only so long as they are without children (Arndt 1940: 53).

Birds in figurative language

Bird metaphors mostly occur in the parallelistic idioms of Nage speech, song, proverb, and ritual (especially offertory) speech. Forty examples from the vicinity of Bo'a Wae are recorded with English translations in Appendix 1. Also included are exegetical commentaries of individual usages. As these reveal, most employ empirical features and associations of particular bird categories (nearly all in fact, folk generics) in order to make statements about human characters, qualities, or situations. For example, the first text, a planting song, contrasts two pairs of birds – the Channel-billed cuckoo and Common koel, and the cockatoo and crow – as useful signs for cultivators and as crop pests. Yet the text also reflects on the human condition, in particular the fact that human effort (represented by the first two birds) is not always rewarded, while at the same time some people (represented by the second pair) profit unfairly from the efforts of others.

As this case also illustrates, many of the texts, in fact 18, or 45 per cent, refer to birds which serve as chronological indicators of either the annual or daily cycle. Besides the two just mentioned (*muta me* and *toe ou*), these include the friarbird (*koka*), Imperial pigeon (*zawa*), Pied bushchat (*tute péla*), swifts and swallows (*ebu titu*), the domestic fowl (*manu*) and, in a qualified sense, the fantail (*ceka*). In fact, the only 'chronological' bird categories that are not mentioned are *kuku raku* and *lako lizu*, although the first of these occurs as a standard simile (see Appendix 3). If nothing else, this prominence would appear to reflect the obvious importance of chronological birds in human affairs. At the same time, not in all poetic contexts where these terms appear is the bird's chronological significance necessarily relevant (see for example, the friarbird in texts 5 and 6, and the bushchat in text 35).

A similar point applies to birds otherwise associated with spirits. For example, the appearance of three raptors (*kua*, *sizo*, and *jata jawa*) in songs of mourning (texts 24 and 25) can be interpreted as reflecting the general association of such birds with death-dealing spirits. But while the cries of the *kua* and *sizo* are mentioned in the text, it is not these that Nage regard as death omens, but rather the *po* sounds that such birds are also reputed to make. Also, the identification with malevolent spirits does not motivate the mention of the kestrel (*iki*) in text 23 where, according to Nage commentary, this small falcon represents not a spirit, but 'good people in general'. Similarly, in text 9, the appearance of the Brahminy kite (*jata*) as a foil to the friarbird and Imperial pigeon does not obviously draw on the bird's spiritual associations. Nor, in the first text, does the reference to the Large-billed crow (*ha*), one of the 'witch birds', and a form taken by *noa* spirits, or the drongo, another witch bird, mentioned in text 5.

These remarks attest to an important general point. Nage bird symbolism admits several distinct modes, which are most fundamentally discernible in the relation between symbolic birds and their standard interpretations. Thus, with kinds identified with spirits, manifest most often as inauspicious sounds, the bird is conceived as – and, moreover, is believed to be – either an embodiment of a spiritual being or a creature controlled by such a being. By contrast, in poetic or figurative usage, birds, including sometimes birds otherwise identified with spirits (as in the case of the kestrel, cited just above), are represented as resembling, not malevolent spirits, but aspects of ordinary human beings. For example, the crow mentioned in the first text is not of course considered an actual embodiment of a fortunate person who gets to eat without working (nor, as remarked just above, is the bird here conceived as a harmful spirit), but figures simply as an allegorical reference to such a human possibility. A similar observation pertains to non-spiritual omen birds (Chapter 6), including the cockatoo mentioned in the first text, with the crow. Also, while in Nage augury a flock of quails (*piko*) is a negative omen portending the breakup of a village, in figurative language the same bird symbolizes the positive values of fecundity and sociability (see texts 13, 14, and 15). In fact, here one glimpses a general parallel between figurative usage and the symbolism of non-spiritual omens which, as shown in Chapter 6 with regard to the nightjar, appear to derive their augural symbolism from a resemblance to human 'victims'. On the other hand, not all spiritual birds have a different significance in poetic idioms from that which applies in other symbolic contexts. In particular, most of the 'souls birds' (including *cio woza, manu, manu mesi, kolo dasi,* and *kete dhéngi*) retain their spiritual, or more specifically mortuary, associations in dirges and planting songs (see texts 26, 27, 29, 30, and 32).[5]

While, with many usages, the source of a metaphor relates directly to well-known empirical features of a bird – and is then often articulated by Nage themselves – with others, possible meanings require a special interpretation. Indeed, sometimes the import is completely obscure, not only to the present author but, apparently, to Nage as well. Although the figurative use of bird categories need not have anything to do with their spiritual or mythological association, these associations can nevertheless provide clues to possible meaning. For example, in text 5, the joint appearance of the drongo and friarbird is conceivably motivated by the fact that both are noisy birds. Yet whereas the drongo is an ominous witch bird, the friarbird is a herald of the dawn and – largely on account of this characteristic behaviour – figures in myth as a sort of culture hero. Furthermore, inasmuch as the drongo can be considered as possessing inherent power (albeit of a maleficent kind), then the friarbird strikes a contrast as a representation of someone who (as is explained in the commentary to text 5) must rely on his own achievements – or 'sing for his supper' – and does so with consistent success.

In a similar vein, the song concerning the Bare-throated whistler (*kete dhéngi*, text 29) refers to the myth describing how a small child once changed into such a bird (see pp. 150–52), a transformation that accounts for the bird's association with infant souls. Albeit less directly, the same representation may also inform text 30, where the whistler is paired with the Hill mynah (*io wea* or *ie wea*), owing perhaps to a vocal similarity between the two birds.[6] On the other hand, while the sunbird (*tiwe*; see Figure 8.1) makes an appearance in the story of the friarbird and the Imperial pigeon (Forth 1992), this appears to have no bearing whatsoever on references to the bird in texts 36 and 37.

As these examples demonstrate, in poetic usage one encounters metaphors drawing directly on perceptual features as well as ones exploiting symbolic associations of birds pertaining to other (for example, religious) contexts. While, on the whole, metaphors rooted directly in perception may appear to dominate, the distinction is not always easily made, not least because other symbolic forms are similarly grounded in percepts. Empirical features of the friarbird undoubtedly inform references to the bird in texts 4, 6, and 7, as they do in text 5. In particular, the representation of the friarbird as sending a message (in text 4)

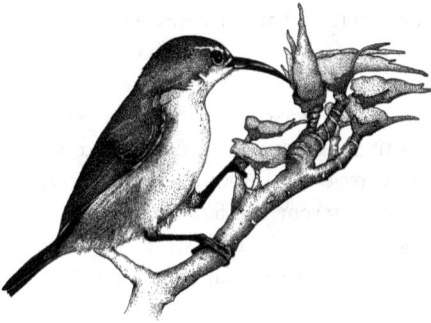

Figure 8.1 Olive-backed sunbird (*Tiwe*)

and 'not revealing the news' (in text 6) evidently turns on the bird's garrulous nature. Yet it also recalls the belief that its varied vocalizations can have oracular value (even though in the second example, the bird in fact acts contrary to this characteristic, by staying silent). On the other hand, why the friarbird should in two instances be contrasted specifically with the oriole (*leo*) remains unclear. Most likely, this selection is motivated mainly by metrical considerations, and in text 6 more particularly by the fact that the oriole's name *leo* (or *léro*, as this is sometimes pronounced) rhymes with *be'o*, 'to know'.

More readily interpreted on empirical grounds is the pairing of the fantail (*ceka*) and the Russet-capped tesia (*bama* or *bama cea*) in text 7. Known to ornithologists also as the 'stubtail', and to Nage as the tailless bird (see Table 2.1), the *bama* contrasts visibly with the *ceka* which, as its English name suggests, possesses a very prominent tail which it is able to open and close like a fan. The reference to the fantail being present at noontide, according to some Nage, reflects a general association with the middle of the day. This is also indicated in text 10, where the chronological association is presented as comparable to that of the friarbird with the first morning light. Other Nage commentators, however, disagreed with this identification, and although the fantail is a diurnal bird, the figurative connection has no obvious empirical support. Whether the refusal of the *bama* to address the fantail, in text 7, draws on the idea that the tesia's call is especially inauspicious when heard in the middle of the day is an open question. The fantail appears again in text 38 where, according to the local interpretation, the bird represents a fickle woman, a symbolism that may draw on the bird's coquettish posturing with its tail.

Not only are possible meanings of a number of usages quite obscure, but sometimes the selection of particular birds appears to be largely arbitrary. In addition to the oriole (*leo*) mentioned above, this would seem to apply to birds named in the two or three 'nonsense rhymes' (see texts 12, 22, and 38). On the other hand, by their anthropomorphous actions, the five birds mentioned in text 38 all evidently represent human characters, while the interpretation of one of these, the fantail, is probably inspired by the above-mentioned behavioural feature of the bird. It is a point of some interest that, in cases where gender appears to be germane (see the Spotted dove, fruit-dove, bushchat, and fantail in texts 17, 18, 35, and 38), three bird figures are locally interpreted as female while the fourth (the fruit-dove) can stand for a person of either sex pursuing someone of the opposite gender. (In all other figurative contexts where a bird represents a human character, sex is apparently irrelevant.) Another possible instance is the sunbird (*tiwe*) in text 37, which may represent the female genitalia.

Although I do not claim that the texts in Appendix 1 illustrate the entirety of figurative uses of Nage bird categories, as a relatively large sample they are likely to be quite representative. As such, they provide a sufficient basis for making several generalizations about Nage bird metaphors.

Not counting two doubtful cases (see *je* and *bio* in texts 39 and 40), 31 bird categories appear in songs, proverbs, and other poetic idioms.[7] These then comprise about 40 per cent of the categories listed in Table 1.1. Not surprisingly, all the terms refer to common birds that are well known to Nage. For example, the friarbird, which appears in no fewer than nine texts, is likely to be the first exotic bird to catch the ear, if not the eye, of the western visitor to eastern Indonesia. At the same time, as is also illustrated by the ubiquitous friarbird – and more generally by birds of chronological importance – this is not simply a matter of regular phenomenal occurrence, but can reflect cultural significance as well. What is more, there are a number of other relatively well-known birds (for example, *bébe ae*, *detu*, *feni*, *koko wodo*, *po*) that are not mentioned in the texts.

In 12 of the texts, bird names occur in pairs, while another three contain two pairs. Since a few of these pairs appear in more than one text, the total number of distinct pairs is 13. At the same time, it will be noted that some terms occur in more than one pair; thus *koka* pairs with *céce*, *leo*, *zawa*, and *ceka*; *piko* pairs with *kolo* and *kata*; *ceka* with *koka* and *bama*; and *kolo* with *piko* and *muke*. *Piko* (quail), it may be recalled, also appears in two mundane pairings, *piko kolo* and *peti kolo* (Chapter 3); the first of these is replicated in texts 15 and 16. Most figurative pairs occur in songs and proverbs. There are relatively few instances of bird names participating in the sort of strict canonical parallelism typical of ritual speech, though this genre is as much characteristic of Nage offertory address as it is of cognate eastern Indonesian traditions. In Appendix 1, a ritual speech couplet is clearly exemplified only in text 14. Text 36 also evidences ritual parallelism, but here *tiwe* (sunbird) is combined with a binary phrase, itself parallelistic, which incorporates the names of two wild mammals.

As this last example shows, bird categories can further occur in sets of three terms, as also in text 9. Another trio (text 19) combines a bird term (*ebu titu*, swifts and swallows) with two other expressions of indefinite reference. These are discussed in the accompanying commentary.

With regard to bird terms occurring singly in the texts, it may be noted that some of these form pairs in other contexts. For example, *iki* (kestrel, text 23) combines with *jata* (Brahminy kite) to form *iki jata*, a general reference to diurnal raptors. Similarly, *bopo* (fruit-dove) is paired with *zawa* (Imperial pigeon) when referring to larger Columbiformes (*bopo zawa*). This second case is particularly instructive since, in poetic genres, *zawa* is regularly combined with *koka* (friarbird; see texts 8 and 9), the two birds then appearing as closely successive chronological signs rather than perceptually similar exemplars of a wider, quasi-taxonomic grouping.

As already indicated, some texts combine names of birds with names of other animals. Of the two examples recorded in Appendix 1, the more elaborate is obviously text 38, the lyric of a song that conjoins five bird terms with three non-birds categories: 'stick insect', 'crayfish', and 'fish'. 'Crayfish' also occurs with 'crab' (*moga*) in text 39, but as explained in the commentary, whether this song lyric also makes reference to a bird (the *je*) is equivocal. As the entire contents of Appendix 1 should suggest, combining bird and non-bird categories is rare in Nage figurative language. For the most part, this reflects the apparent fact that categories referring to animals other than birds are relatively uncommon in Nage poetic usage generally. In other words, Nage appear to make greater metaphorical use of birds than they do of other life-forms. A variant of text 14, a prayer that pairs *kata* (junglefowl) and *piko* (quail), combines the first bird term with a category of fast-growing and prolific waterside plant (*mako ae*). But, as one might expect, combinations of bird and plant terms are rarer still.

Even so, the possibility of combining birds and non-birds (or animals and plants) in figurative speech further distinguishes this kind of conceptual connection from Nage ethnotaxonomic thought. By the same token, while in a few instances metaphorical pairs comprise taxonomically related kinds (for example the two Columbiformes, *kolo* and *muke*, in text 13 and the raptors *kua* and *sizo* in text 24), on the whole, this too is not common, and arguably occurs only to the extent that ornithologically similar kinds, displaying morphologically and behaviourally similar features, convey the same, or similar, symbolic significance. More often, indeed, figurative pairings express contrasts, symbolized by perceptual differences (e.g., the two pairs of birds in text 1; see also the commentary to text 13). Although the friarbird and Imperial pigeon, as chronological indicators, possess similar significances both in the texts recorded in Appendix 1 and in origin mythology, in myth these are traced to a conflict commensurate with marked vocalic and physical differences between the two birds, as I explain below.

In view of the frequent occurrence of pairs and other combinations of bird terms in Nage songs and proverbs, it might be thought that these would significantly affect patterns of free recall. The evidence of the recall lists, however, suggests that such combinations have far less influence on the order in which bird terms are mentioned than does general taxonomic association. For example, *leo* (Black-naped oriole) was listed immediately before or after *koka* (friarbird), the term with which it is associated in texts 6 and 7, by just three of 24 informants. Similarly, *koka* was mentioned with *céce* (drongo, see text 5) by just five people, while *koka* and *zawa* (Imperial pigeon) were listed in succession by just two. This last result is especially surprising, not only in view of the association of the two birds in the well-known origin myth (Forth 1992), but also because the calls of the two birds as associated as chronological indicators in the daily cycle. On the other hand, as many as eight Nage listed *leo* in succession with *ie wea* (Hill mynah), the bird with which Nage tend to group the oriole explicitly on the basis of yellow plumage. Similarly, the Imperial pigeon, the friarbird's mythical opponent, was usually mentioned with other Columbiformes. Comparable findings for *kaka* (*kaka kea*, *kea*) and *ha*, and *piko* and *kolo*, paired terms that also occur as components of mundane binary compounds, were detailed in Chapter 3.

Similes

In addition to their use in songs, proverbs, and parallelistic ritual speech, Nage employ individual bird names to describe human physical or behavioural types. For example, to describe a man as resembling a *gako tasi* or *o ae* (two heron categories) means that he is exceptionally tall and slender. Further illustrations are recorded in Appendix 3. As can be seen from a comparison with Table 2.1, the majority of similes make reference to a bird's 'simple distinctive feature', while just under a third of such features motivate similative usages.

The use of birds as similes is comparable to their employment in songs and proverbs insofar as similes, too, associate particular birds with human beings rather than identifying birds with spirits. At the same time, Nage similes mostly refer to physical attributes of humans, whereas proverbs and songs, when they make implicit reference to humans, allude entirely to human behaviours and dispositions, or to social situations. Several birds linked with spiritual beings (see *ha*, *jata* and *wole wa* – both diurnal raptors), or otherwise regarded as ominous (see *kaka kea*, *piko*, *witu tui*), are also invoked as similes. Yet in each case their significance in this idiom has no necessary connection with their spiritual or ominous associations in other contexts. For example, the observation that kites wait to feed on flying insects driven into the air when vegetation is burned, and that this habit of kites resembles human opportunism (see *jata tei nu api*, Appendix 3), is not at all dependent on the idea that kites embody harmful spiritual beings; nor, conversely, does the spiritual association draw crucially on this aspect of kite behaviour. The one arguable exception to this generalization concerns the possibility that the ominous significance of nocturnal cries of cockatoos (*kaka kea*) draws on an association of nobility with conspicuous consumption (see Chapter 6).

Three birds employed as similes – the friarbird (*koka*), waterhen (*kuku raku*), and Channel-billed cuckoo (*muta me*) – are also valued as chronological signs. However, only the vocalizing behaviour of the friarbird is identically involved in the bird's similative function. Finally, it may be noted that several bird categories used as similes do not have any other figurative uses (that is, they do not occur in songs, proverbs, or ritual language), nor are they identified with spirits or as non-spiritual omens. These include the coucal (*toto*), herons (*gako tasi* and *o ae*), kingfisher (*fega*), and waterhen (*kuku raku*) – though, as just noted, the last kind does have significance as a marker of seasonal change.

I have already remarked on how Nage make less metaphorical use of other animals, including insects, reptiles, and mammals, than they do of birds. We might conclude this section by briefly addressing the question of why, in this culture, birds are apparently preferred as symbols. One obvious factor is the number and variety of birds reflected in named folk generics. If one includes the three bat categories, there are nearly 80 of these (see Table 1.1). By contrast, the number of both wild and domestic mammals is far fewer.[8] Rivalling, indeed surpassing, the total of labelled generic bird taxa are Nage ethnotaxa comprising insects and similarly small creatures.[9] Yet the generally small size of such creatures, and to some extent their less varied appearances, may render them less suitable than birds for symbolic exploitation. Moreover, where one finds colour and variety in the insect world – for example among butterflies and dragonflies – one encounters just a single term (e.g. *bhébha*, 'butterfly') applied to all – a situation that would seem partly to reflect the fact that, despite morphological diversity, their behaviour is quite uniform.

All the same, some insect categories do of course occur in Nage parallelistic speech and other forms of figurative language (see the expression *po ko, uci meci*, discussed in Chapters 4 and 5, as well as the stick insect mentioned in text 38, in Appendix 1). Also, as creatures identified with spirits and souls, insects, as well as snakes and fish, are symbolically comparable to birds. In regard to insects, it is noteworthy that many share with birds the ability to fly, one factor associating them with spiritual beings and entities that are ultimately free of physical forms and credited with the ability to travel quickly from one place to another. But a more important similarity may lie in the ability of many insects, like birds, to produce sounds. Indeed, it would seem to be mostly in respect of their calls, and moreover the variety, volume and quality of these, that birds are distinguished among life-forms as symbolic vehicles. Accordingly, many references to birds in Nage songs and proverbs – in fact, about 19, or nearly half, of the texts in Appendix 1 – make explicit or implicit reference to their calls. The point is further brought out by the myth of the Imperial pigeon and the friarbird, which I analyse below. In addition, as demonstrated in earlier chapters, it is mainly by way of their vocalizations that certain birds are thought to manifest spirits and souls, or to reveal omens – even though, as I have also argued, identification of birds with particular kinds of spirits or auguries derives primarily from visible features of the kinds in question.

Birds in myth

Bird categories occur with some regularity in mythical texts I collected in the Bo'a Wae region.[10] Several times already I have mentioned the story of the friarbird (*koka*) and Imperial pigeon (*zawa*), a tradition accounting for the present order of the world, whose variants are widespread in eastern Indonesia (Forth 1992). Disputing with the pigeon over the proper length of night and day, the friarbird advocates a day and night that are of short duration and alternate rapidly. The bird further argues that humans should die, but also reproduce and thus continually replace themselves with new generations. In contrast, the Imperial pigeon wishes the world to remain in darkness, if not eternally then for a very long time, so that day should succeed night very slowly. The pigeon also deems it undesirable that humans should be prolific, arguing that seven men and seven women will be sufficient to populate the earth. The friarbird, of course, wins the contest, so that life is as we know it today.

By virtue of their both calling early in the morning and again in the late afternoon, as chronological signs the pigeon and the friarbird reveal an equivalence facilitating a primordial contest that emphasizes their differences. As partly demonstrated in my previous analysis (Forth 1992), the myth turns on a series of oppositions connected with the contrasting empirical features of the two birds; these are finally resolved by the defeat of the pigeon which, in terms of vocal significance, becomes the subordinated surrogate of the friarbird.[11] Motivating the friarbird's advocacy of rapid alternation of day and night – and thence of death and birth, providing a continual replacement of the dead by new humans – is the fact that, as Nage recognize, the friarbird calls before the Imperial pigeon, both in the early morning and the late afternoon. As Nage also express this, the friarbird is 'faster' than the 'slow' pigeon.[12] Another vocalic opposition concerns the high-pitched, noisy clamour of the friarbird, contrasting radically with the deep, mellow, resonant voice of the Imperial pigeon, which one source describes as 'a lovely deep coo . . . somewhat like a cow mooing in the distance' (King *et al.* 1975: 171). Also noteworthy is the contrast between the pigeon's monotonous call and the friarbird's variable (and contextually prophetic) cries; the latter moreover typically comprise binary vocalic contrasts, reproduced in the Nage names for the bird and its call (*koka* and *iko ako*), which arguably parallel the regular and rapid alternation of day and night advocated by the bird in the myth.

Although apparently of less importance than vocalic contrasts, the two birds also differ sharply in regard to visible differences of morphology and behaviour. Considered the least edible of avian kinds, the friarbird is a scrawny creature whose emaciated appearance Nage link with its vociferousness (see Appendix 3 and Figure 8.2). By contrast, the larger Imperial pigeon is round and plump, and its flesh is among the most favoured of wild bird meats. Mostly a nectar feeder, the friarbird – like the sunbird (*tiwe*) to which it is related symbolically if not ornithologically (see pp. 126–27) – is also an active and pugnacious bird, whereas the Imperial pigeon is quite different in regard both to behaviour and diet.

A noteworthy feature of Nage variants of the eastern Indonesian tale of the pigeon and the friarbird is the way it links the origin of the present temporal order with the origin of death, or a cycle of death and birth. Of comparable cosmological import is a rather longer and more complex narrative concerning

Figure 8.2 Helmeted friarbird (*Koka*)

a series of mostly raptorial birds, which I examine in the next chapter. Besides the friarbird (*koka*), Imperial pigeon (*zawa*), and the *po*-sounding diurnal and nocturnal raptors – a group which in principle comprises nine of the named categories listed in Table 1.1 (including the *je*) – birds mentioned in Nage myths include the Large-billed crow (*ha*), sunbird (*tiwe*), cuckoo-dove ('*owa*), Bare-throated whistler (*kete dhéngi*), drongo (*céce*), quail (*piko*), and paradise-flycatcher (*lawi luja*).

Mentioned briefly in Chapter 5, the myth regarding the drongo illuminates the taboo (*pie*) on its flesh and connects the bird with a particular sort of malevolent spirit. The story relates how a *noa* spirit (*ana noa*) was once playing on a flute, which bothered a nearby herd of buffalo. Angered by this, the owner of the herd took the flute from the spirit and broke it. In retaliation, the spirit then reduced the man to a very small size and, in the form of a drongo, swallowed him. Thus it is that one should not eat drongo flesh.

Also as embodiments of *noa* spirits, Large-billed crows (*ha*) make an appearance in a story concerning an ancestor of the Nage clan Nila, named Muga Uma, who is said to have visited a village of such spirits. There he meets a man with one eye who, he eventually learns, was one of a flock of crows that stole his ripe papayas, and which he had therefore shot in the eye with his blow-gun. After spending the night in this village, the Nage ancestor further discovers that its mundane form is a rookery, high in a tree, where the *noa* manifest themselves as a flock of crows (Forth 1998a: 100–01).

In the Keo region, immediately to the south of the Nage, a myth describing the earliest generations of humans mentions an ancestor who is identified with a dove (*kolo*; Forth 2001: 28). An unpublished collection of texts by the missionary linguistic Karl van Trier (n.d.) contains three stories with bird characters. One of these concerns a quail (*piko*) and a Brahminy kite (*jata*), and was recorded in Hobo Nio, in the far western Nage district of Rowa. Another, recorded in the western district of Solo, is about a small bird (*ana peti*) and a deer. The third, also recorded in Solo, is a variant of a clan myth I recorded in Bo'a Wae, which I discuss below.

Virtually all of the Bo'a Wae narratives I collected that concern birds can be described as origin myths. In some, birds appear, mostly in an anthropomorphous representation, as major characters who play a part in constructing the present order of the world or the emergence of particular traditions or practices. For example, one story tells how the sunbird (*tiwe*) – the friarbird's redeemer in the Nage origin of death myth – introduced the art of palm wine manufacture by dropping a blossom of the *ko'u* tree, a fermenting agent, into a container of arenga palm juice.[13] In contrast, stories regarding the 'origin of species' – that is, how particular bird kinds acquired their present physical forms or other characteristic features – appear to be virtually absent from the Nage mythical corpus, as Nage I questioned about such tales verified. This applies in Bo'a Wae at least. In the far western district of Rowa, one of the narratives recorded by van Trier (n.d.) relates how a quail (*piko*) kicked a water buffalo in the teeth, an act that explains why buffalo no longer have upper teeth. In retaliation, the buffalo pulled out the quail's tail feathers, thus shortening the bird's previously long tail.[14]

Although it concerns behaviour rather than physical features, perhaps the closest approximation to such a myth in Bo'a Wae is the story of Tupa Lélu discussed in the next chapter, since this is often presented expressly as an account of how raptorial birds came to prey on domestic fowls. Also reminiscent of the genre is the story concerning the contrasting environments and defecatory habits of the paradise-flycatcher and quail described in Chapter 7. As noted there, however, these habits are represented as deriving simply from a pact between the two birds and are not explained, as in similar stories elsewhere, as a result of particular incidents or actions. In a variant of the story I recorded in western Keo, the Imperial pigeon (Keo *rawa*, Nage *zawa*) takes the place of the flycather. The pigeon, moreover, is able to alight on the ground by carrying a twig, while the quail can perch in a tree so long as it brings with it a little soil – details which seem to obviate the categorical opposition of the two birds to the earth and trees respectively posited in the Nage tradition.

Apart from the Rowa story of the quail and the buffalo mentioned above, the only trace I encountered of a tale pertaining to the acquisition of actual physical features is another Keo narrative in which a kingfisher (*fega*), in order to trick a gullible monkey, claims to have obtained his red bill by chewing a large quantity of betel and areca. Quite apart from the fact that the idea is presented as no more than a ruse, however, I never came across any similar tale in Nage.[15]

The previously mentioned story featuring the Bare-throated whistler, which describes how a small, neglected child was once transformed into a whistler, is also not clearly an origin myth since it does not unequivocally document the origin of all birds of this kind. People I asked thought it unlikely that all Bare-throated whistlers derived from this child. As one man put it, 'there probably already were whistlers' before this transformation to place. The story line is simple:

> A little girl refuses to light a fire for her mother on a cold and rainy day. After kindling the fire herself, the woman repeatedly casts the child out into the rain and refuses to allow her back into the house. Following several attempts to return, in order to warm herself by the fire, the girl turns into a whistler. Remorseful, the mother then endeavours to call her back, beckoning her with a cradling cloth. But by this time, the girl, now a bird, has flown up to the roof ridge of the house. She flies from house to house until she reaches the head (or landward extremity) of the village, where she disappears high up the mountain-side and is no longer seen. All that can then be heard is her voice, the voice of a bird.

How this story relates to the Nage association of the Bare-throated whistler with aborted foetuses and infant souls was discussed in Chapter 5. Nevertheless, it is worth recalling how the character of the whistler, encapsulated in its 'simple distinctive feature' (Table 2.1) as a bird that is far more often heard than seen, befits its spiritual nature as an embodiment of immature human souls – as of course does the bird's association, made explicit in the myth and supported by its melancholy song, with a pathetic child. Even more obviously, the child's rejection by her mother illuminates the association of the bird with aborted foetuses, while the meteorological setting of the story, a cold and rainy day, is consistent with the cool and damp higher elevations – 'halfway up the mountain' as the song has it (see Appendix 1, text 29) – in which the *kete dhéngi* is found, and also with a possible interpretation of one part of the bird's name (see *kete*, 'cold, to feel cold').[16]

If this story is not intended as an aetiological account of the origin of Bare-throated whistlers in general, the mythical transformation can yet be understood as a prototype for the current belief according to which immature deaths become whistlers. Otherwise expressed, the narrative theme of transformation does not inform a sort of quasi-evolutionary development so much as it symbolizes a connection between two quite various things – a physical bird encountered mostly as a disembodied voice and insubstantial infant souls. In that case, we appear to encounter here a quasi-phylogenetic notion comparable, though not identical, to the quasi-ontogeny of Nage contemporary transformation beliefs – for example, that concerning the derivation of tiny bats from bamboo grubs.

One more representation concerning the Bare-throated whistler is worthy of attention. This draws on the bird's well-deserved reputation as a superb mimic, able to imitate all sorts of things including the sounds of dogs and wild pigs and human voices. Both Nage and Keo tell how the whistler was once found near the south coast. There, the bird endeavoured to reproduce the sound of ocean waves, but finding their roar too loud, gave up and fled to the highlands. If this report reflects a separate myth, I never heard a full version. Nevertheless, people also simply state that the whistler is a bird able to imitate 'everything except waves'. Obviously, the idea turns upon an opposition of mountain and sea, or seaward and landward directions, which is so fundamental to the organization of social space in central Flores (see Forth 1991b, 2001). That the whistler should thus find the sea anathema is again consistent with its character as a rarely seen bird of high places that is never encountered in lower elevations.

Earlier I noted how the only instance of a clan food taboo found among Nage in the Bo'a Wae region concerns the clan Saga Enge and the 'owa, or cuckoo-dove (probably *Macropygia ruficeps*). Interestingly, a story linking the bird and the clan explicitly rationalizes not the prohibition on cuckoo-dove's flesh but a taboo on the use of salt when cooking meat in the context of major rituals. Entitled *Hozo pau pazo* ('Hozo runs away with salt'), it relates the adventures of a young man named Hozo, an ancestor of Saga Enge but not the clan's apical or founding ancestor. The tale may be summarized as follows:

> During the performance of a teeth-filing ritual (*koa ngi'i*), Hozo is sent to fetch salt for cooking. Unaccountably, he proceeds all the way to the north coast of Flores, where there are extensive salt-beds, and obtains (or steals) a handful of salt. On his return journey, Hozo is stopped by men who intend to take him captive. When asked if he is alone, he replies he is travelling with several companions who are close behind. Following his captors' instructions, Hozo then feigns to summon these non-existent companions, shouting *wuu ane* ('hey comrades'; or *wuu hoga*, 'hey people'). Fortunately, his cry is answered by a cuckoo-dove ('*owa*) calling *wuu*, the bird's characteristic vocalization, which resembles a human exclamation of acknowledgement. The young man is thus left unharmed by his assailants. But since he is unable to return home with the salt, as this has long since dissolved in his hand, his descendants – people of clan Saga Enge – refrain from using salt for cooking at commensal rituals (particularly the major life-cycle ceremonies, *koa ngi'i* and *tau ngi'i ae*) to the present day.

The story of Hozo is well known in the vicinity of Bo'a Wae. As noted, it is also known in the far western Nage region of Rowa. In fact, Rowa people, who are not associated with the clan Saga Enge, claim that Hozo was their ancestor and, moreover, that it is from the cuckoo-dove, Hozo's incidental saviour, that the territory of Rowa – a dialectal form of '*owa* (cuckoo-dove) – takes its name.[17] It is a point of interest, however, that neither the story as told in Rowa, nor a variant recorded by van Trier (n.d.) in Solo, immediately to the east of Rowa, mentions a prohibition on salt. Nor, despite their claim regarding the district's name, do Rowa people regard the cuckoo-dove as taboo. This, then, suggests a closer connection of these traditions with the Nage clan Saga Enge.

Symbolic birds

Employing 'symbolic' in a broad sense to describe a use of birds, consciously or unconsciously, to represent humans or anthropomorphous spirits, we might conclude this discussion by addressing the question: 'How symbolic are Nage birds?' By this, I simply mean how many of the named bird categories listed in Table 1.1 occur as components of Nage religious belief, augury, ritual language, song, proverbs, or myth – the symbolic contexts of Nage thought concerning birds described in this and earlier chapters.

In Chapters 5 and 6 I described 26 Nage categories that refer to kinds interpreted either as spiritual birds or non-spiritual omen birds.[18] If to these one adds birds mentioned in mythical narratives and other speech idioms (including similes), as well as birds employed as chronological signs, then a fairly precise answer can be given to the above question. Excluding several doubtful cases, at least 55 out of 79 Nage ethno-ornithological categories, or nearly 70 per cent, possess symbolic value. As is already abundantly clear, moreover, some categories participate in more than one variety of symbolic usage, and more often than not, the symbolic value of a single category will vary accordingly. The use of bird terms as proper names does not affect the above total since all terms employed in this way also occur in one or more of the symbolic genres specified above.

On the other hand, about 18 of the 79 Nage categories possess no symbolic value at all. Many of these are less well-known birds. But some certainly are not: for example, *bébe ae* (wild duck), *detu* (woodpecker), *feni* (parrot), and *koko wodo* (scrubfowl).[19] Together with other sorts of evidence, these instances of 'non-symbolic' birds should dispel any suggestion that symbolic value is a major factor determining recognition of ethnotaxa or the form of Nage ethno-ornithological classification. I have already shown how categories like 'spiritual birds' and 'witch birds' – although undoubtedly components of Nage thought – do not refer to units of Nage ethnotaxonomy. In addition, the ethnotaxon 'bird' does not coincide with a discrete symbolic class; for as manifestations of spiritual beings, for example, animals of other kinds (reptiles, fish, and insects – not to mention sacrificial buffalo and Cassia trees) are identically or comparably significant (see further Chapter 9). Birds are obviously an important focus of Nage symbolic thought. But other kinds of cognition involving birds operate quite independently of bird symbolism.

The story of Tupa Lélu, or how birds of prey became chicken thieves

Members of the symbolic class focused on nocturnal and diurnal birds of prey are assembled in the story of Tupa Lélu, a myth that Nage present as an account of the origin of the raptorial habit of killing and consuming domestic fowls. The appearance of these birds, as members of a single mythical collectivity, confirms my earlier demonstration that owls and Falconiformes – bird kinds dissociated in a generalized, ethno-ornithological classification of avifauna – are associated in spiritual contexts. A particular aim in what follows is to show how possible meanings of the myth can be fully grasped only through a consideration of the significance of carnivorous birds in Nage culture generally, and more specifically as manifestations of a symbolic category of spiritual beings. It should also become clear that any attempt to reduce the myth to an aetiological text, a simple attempt to explain why certain birds prey on domestic fowls, largely misses the point (see Sperber 1975: 6).

The longest and most detailed version of the myth concerning Tupa Lélu was recorded in July 1988. Entitled 'The reason why birds of prey are the enemies of domestic fowls to the present', this was narrated by Gregorius Doa Mite, a resident of the village of Wolo Mako, a short distance to the west of Bo'a Wae. The following is a summary of his text:

Once there was a man named Nala Alu, whose wife was pregnant. The woman, called Lélu Béna, was about to deliver when the man announced that he had had an inauspicious dream. In his dream, Nala Alu had learned that, if his wife were to bear a daughter, the child must be killed, otherwise he would die prematurely. He then announced that he was going on a long journey, and he told Lélu Béna that, were she to give birth to a daughter, she must cut the child to pieces. After Nala Alu's departure, the child was born. It was a girl, and her mother called her Tupa Lélu. Having pity on her infant, Lélu Béna did not follow her husband's instructions. She hid Tupa Lélu in the loft of her house. She then informed fellow villagers that she had killed her daughter, and she made a false grave.

When Tupa Lélu was about three years old, her father returned. Nala Alu asked his wife if she had borne a boy or a girl. Lélu Béna replied that it was a girl, and pointing to the false grave, told him that she had hacked the child to death and buried her. Sometime later, the couple were taking a meal inside the house, when Nala Alu discovered something dripping from the loft onto his plate. Lélu Béna said it was probably just rainwater that a mouse had shaken down. But Nala Alu smelled it and discovered that it was urine. Consumed with anger, he inferred that his wife had indeed given birth to a daughter and was hiding her in the loft. To this Lélu Béna finally confessed. He enquired after the girl's name and her age. Declaring that the child was truly wicked, as she had urinated onto his plate, Nala Alu took his parang and sharpened it. He called to Tupa Lélu to come down from the loft. Weeping in the knowledge that her father intended to kill her, however, she made the excuse that she was busy sweeping out her mother's loft.

Thus thwarted, it was some time before Nala Alu again summoned Tupa Lélu from the loft. In the meantime, the child went about her work, ascending and descending to and from the loft every day. The second time her father called for her to come, she explained that she was sweeping the floors of her mother's house.[1] Nala Alu become saddened and put off killing Tupa Lélu. He made a number of further attempts but each time the girl had another excuse. First, she was sweeping the area beneath the raised floor of the house. Then she had to sweep the forecourt. Later she protested that she was clearing the path from the house to her mother's garden. Later still, she had to sweep out her mother's field hut.

By this time, Tupa Lélu was about ten years old. When her father tried again to kill her, she pleaded with him to do the deed by a leafless tree. But when they reached the tree, the girl implored Nala Alu to postpone the killing until they had reached the site of a pair of 'twin stones' (*watu ta'a doa zua*), located seaward (*lau*) of the mother's garden. So he took her to this place. Then Tupa Lélu pleaded that he should not kill her until they reached a spot, located landward (*zéta*), where there grew swaying Imperata grass. It was finally at this place that Nala Alu hacked his daughter to death. He returned to the village and told her mother what he had done.

Afterwards, several birds of prey (*kua, jata, iki, sizo, bele teka* and *je*) smelled the blood of Tupa Lélu and flew to the spot where she had been murdered. Speaking with authority, the eagle (*kua méze*) took the lead and instructed the other birds each to take a piece of the girl's flesh. This they did until her body was completely reassembled, whereupon they fanned it with their wings. The eagle then ordered the other birds of prey to carry Tupa Lélu to their nest at the top of a tree. Again the eagle spoke to the other birds, instructing them to steal pots of cooked rice, honey, and meat, as well as cotton, yarn, and weaving instruments, so that Tupa Lélu would be provided for and could weave. The eagle then fanned Tupa Lélu again until she woke up (that is, came back to life).

After a year or so, Nala Alu and Lélu Béna went with their three sons to cut Imperata grass to repair the roof of their house. They arrived at the site of Tupa Lélu's murder, but Nala Alu did not recognize it. About midday he instructed his sons to light a fire so they could cook a meal. But whenever they struck their flints and kindled a flame, the fire went out. Their father then instructed them to go and look for fire elsewhere. Eventually they came to a tree and, looking up, saw a rude hut with smoke rising from the top. The boys called out to the householder, who turned out to be Tupa Lélu. She had been weaving. When she emerged from the hut, they recognized her as their elder sister. To stay their hunger, Tupa Lélu gave them packets of rice (*tupa hau*) and dried meat. When they had eaten these, she threw down some more to be given to her parents.

Returning to their parents, the three sons told them what had transpired. Nala Alu did not believe they had encountered Tupa Lélu. But when he opened a rice packet and bit into the rice, he discovered a white bracelet Tupa Lélu had hidden inside, and thus he realized the truth of their claim. The family then went to retrieve Tupa Lélu. At first she refused to recognize Nala Alu as her father, but eventually they become reconciled. The family went in search of a climbing pole to bring her down from the treetop. However, while they were erecting the pole, the eagle swooped down and pecked at them. When Nala Alu explained what they were doing, the eagle exclaimed that Tupa Lélu was no longer his child, as they, the birds of prey, had looked after and raised her. Nala Alu then offered the eagle water buffalo, horses, and golden objects in exchange for Tupa Lélu. The eagle agreed to the exchange, but declared that the birds were not interested in these things. Instead, the eagle demanded that they must hang a coop with a hen and chicks from each of the 100 footholds (*saka pe'i*) on the climbing pole.

Agreeing to this, the family searched everywhere but could produce only 99 coops. The eagle then declared that, since Nala Alu and his family had not been able to provide all they had asked for, from then on the birds of prey would themselves go out in search of hens and newly hatched chickens, and that humans should not abuse and insult them for swooping down and seizing domestic fowls. The family acquiesced and were thus able to recover Tupa Lélu, whose return to the village they celebrated with the slaughter of goats, pigs, and buffalo. However, since this time and to the present day, eagles (*kua*), kites (*jata*), falcons (*iki, sizo*) and owls (*po kua, je*) have been the enemies of domestic fowls.

After recording the preceding text, I heard two less elaborate versions. I also discovered a variant of the Nage story in the literature on the Lio people, to the east of the Nage (Heerkens 1943). The two Nage versions may be summarized as follows:

Variant 1, told by F. Lowa, 'Abu

Formerly, birds of prey (*kua jata* or *iki jata*) were afraid to steal fowls from humans. Once there was a nobleman with six wives, all of whom bore him only daughters. So he took a seventh wife. He then went on a journey, leaving instructions with a servant that, if the seventh wife bore a daughter, he was to kill both the woman and her child. When her child turned out to be another daughter (that is, Tupa Lélu), the woman kept postponing the execution. Her final plea was that the killing should take place only at a spot where there were twin boulders and a leafless tree. The servant eventually found such a place and carried out the execution. But the mother was either spared or escaped, and only the daughter was killed: she was cut to small pieces (*dota*). Later, several birds of prey (*kua jata*) appeared. Observing the birds from her place of hiding, the mother thought they had come to eat the girl's flesh. But instead they gathered the body parts together in a pile and fanned them. Thus the child was brought back to life. Seeing this, the mother fled. The birds then raised the girl to maturity in the leafless tree. After the girl had grown into a beautiful young woman, she was discovered by a young nobleman. He gave his followers instructions to abduct her. But every time they approached the tree, they found her gone. Finally, the young nobleman's parent's decided to request her hand in marriage, with an offer of bridewealth. The birds agreed, but they demanded a large number of chickens which they should attach to the footholds of seven climbing poles. They assembled many fowls but were unable to provide fowls for three of the footholds. Thus, they gave the birds of prey leave to search for fowls themselves. And ever since, they have simply seized people's fowls.

Variant 2, told by P. Lape Ga'e, Ola Kile

A couple had only sons. The man's wife became pregnant again. But before the child was born, the father went on a journey. Before leaving, he specified that, if the child was a girl, she should be killed and her liver preserved, so he could consume it on his return.[2] The mother gave birth to a daughter, who she named Tupa Lélu. Instead of killing her, however, the woman and her brother (that is, Tupa Lélu's mother's brother) hid her in the loft. When the father returned, they served him a goat's liver, claiming it to be the girl's liver. But a crowing cock (*manu*) informed him of this deceit. Eventually, he also discovered the girl's whereabouts. She made various excuses in order to postpone her execution, but finally her father killed her at the place of 'the twin boulders and the leafless tree'. After her murder and dismemberment, an eagle came and piled up her body parts and fanned them. (The other birds – described as followers of the eagle – only make an appearance later in the story. As well as several kinds of raptors, they include a crow, *ha*.)

Living in a tree top, Tupa Lélu was later discovered, as an adult, by her elder brother. He had been fishing and needed fire to cook his fish. He saw smoke rising from the tree house. But to him and to others, the tree in which Tupa Lélu was kept by the birds looked like an ordinary house. The brother was struck by Tupa Lélu's beauty, but he also recognized that the woman resembled his dead sister. He wished to marry her. But his mother put him off, claiming that they had no goods for bridewealth. The mother later went to visit her daughter, but Tupa Lélu told her that, while she could look at her, she must not touch her body, because she was the 'soul of a dead person'.

A nobleman from an eastern region (*mosa laki ta'a wisa zale*) also encountered Tupa Lélu and wished to marry her. Tupa Lélu's father endeavoured to receive his request. But the eagle, claiming that the request should be directed to him, confronted the father. Taking the form of a human being (*bale kita ata*), the eagle killed the father and ate his corpse. The eagle then gave the nobleman leave to marry Tupa Lélu. But the bird demanded bridewealth consisting of seven climbing poles with a coop containing a hen and chicks suspended from each of the footholds. The nobleman was able to provide all of these except one. Hence he invited the birds to search for fowls themselves. Thus it is that they steal chickens to the present day.

Ethnographic preliminaries and cultural clarifications

My intention here is not to analyse all aspects of the myth. I restrict my remarks to points of ethnography that are essential to an understanding of the plot, the structure of the story, and the relationship these entail between human beings and birds. The narrative features three named human characters: a father, mother and a daughter. Although Nage personal names are often analysable, the father's name, Nala Alu, has no meaning clearly relevant to the myth. Nage recognize the mother's first name, Lélu, as meaning 'cotton', a detail that is conceivably significant in regard to Tupa Lélu's association with weaving. The appearance of Lélu as the heroine's second name follows a regular pattern of Nage surnaming, whereby the mother's first name is appended to a child's first name.

The heroine's first name, Tupa, appears apposite to the character, as it also occurs in *tupa hau*. Designating packets made of coconut boughs in which cooked rice is wrapped (cf. Bahasa Indonesia *ketupat*), *tupa hau* are what Tupa Lélu gives to her hungry family after she is discovered by her brothers. As a source of food for her family, Tupa Lélu in fact recalls the 'rice maiden', a mythical character encountered in many Indonesian cultures, including Nage who, like the young girl in the present story, is murdered by her father or brothers (Forth 1998a: 237; cf. Kohl 1998). As rice and other crops then grow from different parts of her body, the myth – and particularly the primordial human sacrifice – accounts for the origin of cultivated plants, especially rice. In fact, although some people I questioned disagreed, other Nage identified Tupa Lélu with the mythical rice maiden, and more particularly with a female sacrifice which, according to their tradition, took place on Mount Dota (Kéli Dota), a mountain in Lio territory. *Dota*, significantly enough, means 'to chop up, cut into small pieces', and is the term used to describe Nala Alu's method of infanticide.

The point of departure of the Tupa Lélu story is obviously the father's dream. From this, he learns that, in order to avoid a premature death, he must kill his newborn child if the child is female. Why a female birth should have this consequence is never explained in the myth. Nage commentators, however, linked it to the notion of *waka*, 'forehead', which also refers to an individual spiritual force or power that affects a person's – and particularly a man's – fortune and social success. More to the point, a father's *waka* can conflict, or be in competition, with that of his son to the extent that the one whose *waka* proves the weaker may die or suffer misfortune as a result (see Forth 1998a: 48, note 2). By contrast, a mother's *waka* never conflicts with her child's, and a daughter's never presents a danger to that of her father. Discussing the father's dilemma in Tupa Lélu, one man thus remarked how it was actually better if a man's first child were a girl, since in that case the child's *waka* could not be superior to his. It is evident, therefore, that the story of Tupa Lélu starts with an inversion of a normal state of affairs, and this sets in motion a train of events that involves further inversions. Arguably, the most egregious of these is a parent's murdering his own child.[3]

In the longest version of the story, Tupa Lélu's father finally kills her at a spot marked by two large stones. Before this, they linger near a leafless tree. In the two other versions, the stones and tree are named together as a single place, while in one the leafless tree is the location of the raptor's nest that becomes Tupa Lélu's home after her revitalization. As regards the 'twin stones' (*watu doa*), one narrator specified this as the Watu Doa mentioned in the epic tale of Lalo Sue (Forth 1998a: 38–45) – a location seaward of the Nage region where two ancestral brothers once received extraordinary powers from a *bapu* spirit. As I further explain below, the raptorial birds who bring Tupa Lélu back to life can be understood as embodiments of precisely this category of spirits.

The specification of Tupa Lélu, in one of the shorter versions, as a 'soul of a dead person' (*mae mango ata mata*) obviously accords with her murder. Yet it seems to be contradicted by her having been brought back to life by the birds. The implications of this are discussed presently. For the time being, it may be noted that Tupa Lélu's admonishing her mother only to look at her, and not to touch her, reflects the general idea that, at one time, the dead remained visible to the living so long as they did not have physical contact (Forth 1998a: 248).

Tupa Lélu's later dealings with other members of her family also invite comment. In the longest version of the story, her younger brothers encounter her while searching for fire, which they repeatedly fail to kindle themselves. In another version, just a single brother is mentioned; he is older than Tupa Lélu and needs fire specifically to cook fish. Tupa Lélu's possession of fire – an element of civilized life which the first people in origin myths commonly lack, and which they must obtain from an external source – echoes the rice maiden's gift of cultivated food.[4] Among Nage (as in Keo, Forth 2001: 97), kindling fire is also a metaphor for the gift of continuing life and well-being which wife-givers provide to wife-takers. Tupa Lélu's brothers, therefore, may be understood as failed wife-givers. By the same token, their receiving cooked food, if not actually fire, implies an inversion of the affinal relationship linked with other, comparable, social inversions. As all variants in different ways make clear, in the role of wife-giver, the place of the girl's brothers and father is taken by the nurturing birds of prey, from whose 'hut' – the collective nest of the several raptors – the brothers see smoke rising.

Considerations of affinal alliance also illuminate references to Tupa Lélu's weaving. The girl's introduction to this activity could simply symbolize her increasing maturity. Yet it is also noteworthy that she begins to weave only after being revived and taken in by the birds of prey, who provide her with a loom. Since woven textiles are goods Nage wife-givers give to wife-takers, this detail further contributes to an understanding of the raptorial birds, in relation to the errant father, as comparable to affines of the first sort.

Implicit themes

The recovery of Tupa Lélu from the dead – or from a state that succeeds death – and her return to the living, recalls the Orpheus myth. However, in regard to the father's obligation, stemming from an evidently spiritual source, to kill his daughter – and perhaps to offer her as a human sacrifice (a principle made explicit in the Lio variant) – one is reminded more of Oedipus and of God's demands on Abraham in respect of Isaac.[5] Similar themes occur in other Nage myths. In the story of Lalo Sue (Forth 1998a: 41), an errant child pulls a silk cloth from a bamboo tube but cannot replace it. In a dream, his father then learns that, in order to fit the cloth back in its container, he must cut the child's throat and smear the blood on the cloth and tube – an instruction he follows, with immediate results.

As intriguing as these comparisons may be, they do not in themselves take us much further in understanding the story of Tupa Lélu, particularly with respect to the possible significance of the birds. To this end, one needs to consider the structure of the Nage tale. Structural analysis has often been criticized as a method resulting in the discovery of patterns that the analyst is already inclined to see. In this case, however, it would be difficult to disagree with the observation that the narrative is predicated on an inversion of social and spiritual norms: a father whose own life depends on his killing his child, and who does indeed kill his child, or has her put to death.

Once the deed is done, one is then immediately presented with an opposition entailing a further inversion which, by all appearances, returns the murdered girl to her previous, living state. Acting contrary to the paternal norm, the father kills his daughter. Yet she is brought back to life by birds of prey that similarly behave in a manner entirely contrary to the usual nature of raptorial avifauna. For rather than dismembering and devouring prey they have killed, or consuming another's kill as carrion, they reassemble a human corpse whose death is the act not just of her own kind but of her own father. Noteworthy here is the statement in one of the shorter versions of the myth that Tupa Lélu's mother, observing the birds' arrival, thought that they had come to eat the girl's flesh. The narrator of the other version even remarked how the eagle's act of bringing Tupa Lélu back to life, rather than eating her corpse, appeared entirely contrary to the nature of such birds.

In the longest version, the story is concluded when the father, apparently at last reconciled not just to his daughter's birth but to her rebirth as well, attempts to recover her in exchange for wealth. In both of the shorter versions, by contrast, it is a request for Tupa Lélu's hand in marriage that occasions the exchange, and in one version it is in the context of this request that her father endeavours, unsuccessfully, to reclaim the status of father and hence of wife-giver. But, whatever the circumstances of the exchange, the birds' demand cannot quite be fulfilled. Hence their dissatisfaction defines their present predatory nature: they continuously steal domestic fowls from human beings who, in exchange for Tupa Lélu, continue to be in their debt. By the same token, they remain for all time the enemies of fowls (*manu*) which, as previously noted, figure as metaphors for human beings, or human souls.

One Nage variant differs from the others insofar as, in this version, after revitalizing Tupa Lélu the eagle, the leader of the raptorial birds, kills and consumes her father. The bird does so, moreover, after taking the form of a human being, a metamorphosis which arguably attests further to the creature's spiritual character. This act of killing and anthropophagous consumption may serve to emphasize how the inverted behaviour of the raptors pertains exclusively to their treatment of Tupa Lélu. The eagle's murder of the father can be further understood not only as a means by which the bird establishes once and for all his claim to be the girl's rightful parent (and the wife-giver in the context of the proposed marriage), but also as revenge for the father's act of infanticide. As subsequent remarks by the narrator of this version revealed, however, the eagle's eating of human flesh may have yet another significance. For in this specific regard, he described the bird as, or as being like, a 'witch' (*polo*). Since the bird consumes the errant father only after assuming human form, the behaviour, and the narrator's interpretation, recalls the Nage representation of a witch as, primarily, a human (or quasi-human) cannibal. What is more, in this same version of the myth, the father too is represented as a cannibal: not only does he order that his daughter be killed, but he further intends to consume her liver.[6]

The narrator's remark thus points to a possible mythological foundation for the general notion that eagles (*kua*), like all raptorial birds, are 'witch birds'. In the same vein, the man went on to claim that it was because of the bird's anthropophagous act that the flesh of eagles was taboo (*pie*), although he recognized that the prohibition also applied to the flesh of all birds 'that steal fowls' (*ta'a naka manu*). As previously shown, the Nage identification of raptorial birds with witches also implicates an analogy. Just as witches prey on humans, or human souls, so raptors prey on fowls. And as mortal beings, human beings are expressly represented as domestic fowls, and more particularly the chickens of the divinity (*ana manu déwa*).[7] It is, I suggest, this analogy – a sort of avifaunal cannibalism paralleling and evoking a sort of human cannibalism – rather than the mythical anthropophagy attributed to the eagle in one variant, that motivates both the Nage identification of raptors as witch birds and the concordant prohibition of their flesh. The point may seem to require qualification, since birds, both domestic and wild, which fall prey to raptors are of course non-raptorial kinds. Yet it can be argued that for Nage, similarities between raptors and other birds outweigh their differences, thus supporting a view of the former as, in effect, cannibalistic. In fact, raptors are cannibalistic to the same extent as witches, since witches, too, possessing a special spiritual property that distinguishes them essentially (although not visibly) from other people, similarly differ in kind from ordinary, moral humans.

As is already clear, Nage associate birds of the sort that bring Tupa Lélu back to life not just with human witches but equally with harmful *bapu* spirits, described as fundamentally similar to witches. Prominent among the *bapu* are beings that reside near the top of Ebu Lobo, the active volcano that defines the centre of Nage country. Besides manifesting themselves vocally, by way of the *po* sounds, such spirits can also assume a visible, corporeal guise, appearing as diurnal birds of prey. This they do, moreover, when engaged in their definitive nefarious activity – slaughtering human beings whom they sacrifice in the form of (spirit) water buffalo. It is thus believed that a high-flying Brahminy kite (*jata*) or large hawk (*jata jawa*) manifests such a mountain spirit out in search of sacrificial victims. Although the eagle (*kua*) is the leader in Nage versions of the myth, it is noteworthy that comparable stories from Komodo and Dhawe (in north-eastern Nage) feature the Brahminy kite as their sole avifaunal character.

In view of all these considerations, the birds' reassembling and revitalizing of the dismembered corpse of Tupa Lélu can be seen to involve a double inversion, or an inversion operating on two planes. On the one hand, their behaviour is, as Nage recognize, contrary to the nature of birds that characteristically kill, tear apart, and consume flesh, more specifically non-human flesh.[8] On the other hand, the actions of the raptors controvert the spiritual nature of the beings that such birds both audially and visually incorporate: witches (*polo*) and *bapu* spirits, both of which kill and consume human beings.

Since the inverted behaviour of the raptors pertains to an imagined relation with a human being, it is obviously the spiritual rather than the empirical (or ethno-ornithological), character of the birds that is basic to the story of Tupa Lélu. Accordingly, the manifest, aetiological theme – explaining why mundane raptors steal mundane chickens – can be considered a superficial and secondary concern. By the same token, the birds' actions are symmetrically opposite to those of the homicidal father, just as anthropomorphous and anthropophagous *bapu* spirits – the 'people on the volcano', as they are also called – are opposed to moral humans who, in sacrificing (earthly) buffalo, cause the destruction of the malevolent spirits (Forth 1998a). In other words, by killing his daughter, the father is doing what the *bapu* do (when they kill humans in buffalo form), while the *bapu*, identifiable with the raptorial birds, do what a proper father does – that is, sustain and provide for a human child.[9]

Noteworthy here is the eagle's claim, when Nala Alu attempts to recover his daughter in the longest version of the myth, that Tupa Lélu is no longer her father's daughter but now belongs to the birds. Seemingly accepting this, the man then offers the raptors goods comprising buffalo, horses, and gold. Being the principal forms of traditional wealth, these goods can be used as exchange media in several kinds of transactions, including the payment of ransom and fines. Their major use, however, is as bridewealth and, indeed, by assuming the status of the recipient of bridewealth in the two shorter versions, the eagle, as leader of the birds of prey, confirms his status as Tupa Lélu's father. Yet it is not simply in respect to exchange roles and domestic nurturance that the raptors are able to claim the parental status; by bringing Tupa Lélu back to life, they have, in a substantial sense, created and given birth to her.

Although in all versions the birds reject the large livestock and golden objects, in return for Tupa Lélu they nevertheless demand a good that Nage wife-takers are equally obliged to give to wife-givers: domestic fowls. Whenever wife-takers visit wife-givers, they must present a gift which minimally consists of a fowl and palm wine (or gin). This obligation can never be completely discharged, just as the gift of life provided by wife-givers, in the form of brides, can never be fully reciprocated. Here, the parallel between wife-givers and raptorial birds is particularly striking. For on account of the errant father's treatment of his daughter, the debt humans incur to the birds, taking the form of fowls, is not only substantially identical but is identically continuous. Also relevant in this connection is the previously mentioned possibility of substituting a fowl (*manu*) for a larger sacrificial animal, as well as the verbal use of *manu* as a euphemistic reference to more valuable sacrificial victims, especially water buffalo. Less valuable goods can therefore stand for more valuable goods; but both can also stand for their owners, or, in the context of exchange relations, their donors. In that case, the numerous fowls demanded by the raptors in return for Tupa Lélu are identical to the human victims continually demanded by *bapu* spirits, who Nage identify in various ways with raptorial birds. As for water buffalo, the equation is even more explicit: wife-givers demand buffalo from wife-takers (both as bridewealth and as part of an ongoing obligation) just as the spirits sacrifice humans in buffalo form.

In other respects, the birds obviously suggest spirits of the dead, and their nest (which they transform into a treetop house) the Nage land of the dead. Pertinent here is Tupa Lélu's description of herself, in one version of the myth, as a 'dead soul'. What is more, among various possible destinations for the deceased, Nage mention large trees as well as the top of the Ebu Lobo volcano; and the top of the volcano is of course also the place where man-killing *bapu* spirits reside. As shown in Appendix 1, Nage songs of mourning are redolent of possible connections of raptorial birds with spirits of the dead, or the abode of dead souls. Recalling the treetop home of Tupa Lélu, one of these thus describes the grave as a nest atop which sits a hawk (*jata jawa*) – one of the kinds that can manifest a malevolent spirit out in search of a human victim. Another song describes the cries of eagles (*kua*) and goshawks (*sizo*) as omens presaging a premature death.

Facilitating an identification of *bapu* spirits and the dead is a general form of Nage spirit classification (Forth 1998a), where *bapu* is implicitly subsumed by the category of *nitu*. Thus, Nage also call *bapu* spirits *nitu bapu*, if not simply *nitu*. Although usually applying to free spirits (and thus glossable as 'earth spirit' or 'nature spirit'), as noted earlier, *nitu* can be seen to encompass spirits of the dead as well, most notably by virtue of the idea that dead souls enter the domain of *nitu*, or even become *nitu* (Forth 1998a: 259–65). From a regional perspective, we might at this point appear to have completed an analytical cycle. For in the Lio variant of the story of Tupa Lélu (there called Tepa Lélu), the girl's father is required to sacrifice his daughter to spirits called *nitu*, or more exactly *nitu pa'i*. According to Arndt (1933), when qualified by a possessive pronoun, *nitu pa'i* refers to a person's 'guardian spirit'; yet the same term can otherwise denote a malevolent being (ibid: 513 s.v. *ule*), evidently comparable to the Nage *bapu*. Can one therefore identify the raptorial birds as the spiritual source of the onerous obligation communicated in Nala Alu's dream? Since Lio are culturally quite distinct from Nage, the suggestion would seem to take us beyond the bounds of permissible inference. Nevertheless, the Lio variant identically features nurturing raptorial and scavenging birds; and after the homicidal father consecrates his daughter's dismembered body as an offering to the spirits, it is these birds that immediately come and collect the pieces.[10]

As suggested earlier, the myth begins with an inversion that 'sets off' other inversions – in a dream a female child is specified as a danger to a father, a danger normally represented, in Nage belief, only by male children. If the source of this initial inversion is spiritual, then it fully accords with the general Nage depiction of free spirits as inverted beings and beings that invert (Forth 1998a: 65).

The bird characters

As demonstrated in Chapter 4, Nage identification of certain birds as manifestations of *bapu* spirits implicates a spiritual class which, contrary to Nage ethnotaxonomy, unites diurnal raptors with nocturnal raptors. Symbolically, these are all conceived by Nage as birds that produce sounds designated as *po*, a term which, in ethno-ornithological discourse, exclusively labels a folk generic category of 'owls'. It is therefore of particular significance that the birds in the story of Tupa Lélu similarly comprise both diurnal raptors (eagles, falcons, hawks) and nocturnal birds of prey, designated as *po* (or more exactly *po kua*) and *je*. That these various kinds compose a single group is emphasized in the myth by their apparent sharing of a single nest, which becomes a treetop hut – the abode of Tupa Lélu. In the longest version, members of the group are more explicitly indicated, in different parts of the story, by varying combinations of names. These include: *kua, jata, iki, sizo, bele teka, po* and *je* (see Table 1.1).

A qualification is in order with regard to the inclusion of the Large-billed crow (*ha*) in one of the shorter variants of the Nage tale. Together with raptors identified simply as 'eagle' and 'falcon', a crow is also mentioned in Heerkens's Dutch translation of the Lio variant of the myth (1943). The crow of course is not a raptor, nor is it one of the *po*-sounding birds. Nevertheless, owing partly to its carnivorous and scavenging habits, it is a member of the more inclusive category of 'witch birds' and, like other such birds, is further identified with malevolent free spirits. Far from controverting an interpretation of the birds in the Tupa Lélu story as a specifically symbolic class, the appearance of the crow, like the appearance of the owl (*po*), actually confirms it, since the crow, too, is classified separately from raptors in Nage ethnotaxonomy.

It is a point of some interest, and perhaps also of concern, that the owl (*po*) is in fact mentioned just once in the longest version of the Nage story, and right at the end. Nevertheless, the particularly symbolic combination of nocturnal and diurnal birds of prey is further attested by the appearance of the *je*, another kind of nocturnal raptor (possibly the Hawk-owl; see Chapter 7), which is mentioned twice. In response to my question, Nage confirmed that the inclusion of an owl (*po*) among Tupa Lélu's protectors was no mistake. Also, in 2001, more than a dozen years after I first recorded the tale, I was again able to question G. Mite Doa, the narrator of the longest version, regarding the composition of this assembly. Apart from several diurnal birds of prey, he mentioned *po koba* and *po kua*, terms which, as I have explained elsewhere, equally designate the single Nage ethnotaxon 'owl'.

The admittedly minimal reference to *po* alternatively invites a more positive explanation. In the myth, the birds appear as an exclusively visible group – no reference at all is made to their calls – even though, in spiritual or mystical contexts, *po* designates a predominantly auditory category. Thus the owl (*po*), while definitely a member of this category, in fact its focal instance, figures as a marginal instantiation when the class is represented visually – as it also is, for example, when malevolent spirits manifest themselves visibly as high-flying hawks or kites. In other words, the fact that *po* is explicitly mentioned just once is about what one might expect from the analysis offered in Chapter 4.

In one respect at least, the main mythological significance of this collection of birds is their status as 'chicken thieves' (*naka manu*). Even the crow (*ha*) fits this category, albeit in a marginal way, since Nage describe crows as stealing hens' eggs. Some Nage also describe owls (*po*) as preying on domestic fowls; yet as noted previously, others were doubtful on this point. Thus, in this respect as well, *po* (owls) may be considered peripheral to the avifaunal assembly manifest in the story of Tupa Lélu.[11] Consistent with this interpretation is another peculiarity of the longest text – namely, the appearance of just one of the three synonymous binomials incorporating *po* to specify 'owl'. This is *po kua*, a term

Nage explain as identifying owls by reference to a similarity of plumage with eagles (*kua* or *kua méze*). Of course, one of the other two binomials, *po tadu*, equally refers to a morphological feature: the 'horns' (*tadu*) possessed by scops-owls (genus *Otus*). Yet the preference for *po kua* finds a possible motivation in the prominent part taken by the eagle (*kua*) in the myth. It might even be argued that, by conjoining terms that separately denote owls and eagles, the usage not only underlines the absence of distinction of nocturnal and diurnal raptors in this symbolic context, but also implicitly transfers some of the eagle's dominance to the owl. At the same time, an exclusive use of *po kua* is clearly not a necessary feature of the story, and as noted above, the narrator of the longest version mentioned *po koba* ('vine po') as an alternative to *po kua*.

It is also noteworthy that the eagle's leadership appears to be specific to the Tupa Lélu story. That is, Nage articulate no general representation of the eagle as a symbol of power or authority, as found for example in the European tradition of the eagle as 'king' of birds. Another sort of hierarchy can be discerned in the frequency with which particular bird categories are named in the longest version of the myth. Thus, apart from the eagle (*kua*), the most often mentioned are *jata* (Brahminy kite) and *iki* (kestrel), then *sizo* (goshawk), then *je*, and finally *po kua* and *bele teka* (the peregrine falcon). (The crow, *ha*, is mentioned only in one of the shorter variants.) Since none of the other birds plays a special role in the story, however, no symbolic significance can be ascribed to this frequency. In fact, the predominance of *kua*, *jata*, and *iki* appears to reflect no more than the relative prominence of these three kinds in Nage experience, as well as the influence of the binary compounds *kua jata* and *iki jata* (see Chapter 3). In regard to the eagle's mythological leadership, moreover, it should be noted that, in two variants of the story I discuss immediately below, the sole raptorial character is the Brahminy kite (*jata*).

Comparisons: regional and internal

Besides the myth from Lio, two other texts from the Flores region, while in certain respects quite different from the Nage story of Tupa Lélu, are sufficiently comparable to be considered as variants. The more similar of the two was related by T. Doa Gamo, a man from Dhawe, in the north-eastern part of the colonial district of Nage. The following is a summary translation:

> Originally, Brahminy kites (*jata*, or *jata ulu bhara*, 'white-headed *jata*', in the Dhawe dialect) only caught grasshoppers and the like. There was once a woman who gave birth to a daughter whom she could not look after. A kite came along and caught the child and took her to its nest high in a tree. It gave her food and drink and raised her. When she was grown up, she wanted to come down from the tree but could not, because the kite had looked after her. All the people gathered, to find a way to secure the woman's release. But the kite refused; it considered her its daughter. The

people proposed to erect a climbing pole reaching to the top of the tree, to which they would tie fowls, from bottom to top. This they did, using seven lengths of bamboo.[12] But eventually they ran out of fowls. Thus, they gave the Brahminy kite leave to search for fowls itself.

One difference between this tale and the versions recorded at the beginning of the chapter is that, here, the child is forsaken (although only implicitly) by her mother rather than her father. Another is the reduction of the group of raptorial birds to a single member, the Brahminy kite. In this variant, it is also the girl herself who wishes to leave the raptor's nest, although, as in the Bo'a Wae narratives, it is implicit that she is obliged to remain, having been raised by the bird, who considers her its daughter. Consistent with the unnamed girl's desire to leave the kite is what appears to be the most importance difference – namely, that in the Dhawe story the girl is not killed by a parent nor is she brought back to life by a bird. Like other features of the tale, this suggests an abridgement of the Bo'a Wae story; indeed, the act of suspending fowls from a climbing pole is not completely intelligible without reference to the latter. The Dhawe story thus adds little to our understanding of the Nage symbolism of birds, even though it underlines the status of the Brahminy kite as, arguably, the most spiritual of Nage birds, and the only kind, besides the similarly named *jata jawa*, that can visibly manifest malevolent *bapu* spirits.

Recorded by Verheijen (1982: 55–59), a narrative from the island of Komodo, off the western tip of Flores, resembles the Dhawe story insofar as it too features the Brahminy kite and a mother (or a mother more than a father) who mistreats a young daughter. The following is a summary of Verheijen's Dutch text:

Once there was once a girl named Amina. When she was still young, her mother was invited to a feast. She locked the girl inside the house with no water, so she was obliged to drink coconut oil. After a while, the girl bore a human child. When her parents returned, they asked her how it was that she had given birth. She told her mother that she had become pregnant from drinking coconut oil. But the mother did not believe her, claiming that this was impossible and that she was a trollop. To disprove her mother's accusations, the girl took a container and laid her child in it. She swore an oath, saying: 'Oh, my child. If you really derive from the coconut oil, then liquefy like coconut oil. But if a man has used me, then you shall remain a human being.' The child then gradually melted away and turned into oil. The girl gave the oil to her mother, and went inside her compartment. There she made herself a pair of wings. Flapping the wings inside the compartment, she heard her mother ask what she was doing. She said she was doing nothing. A while later, the girl fluttered up to the loft, and when asked what she was doing in the loft, she replied that she was only clearing away the remains of her weaving. More time passed, and she flapped her wings again and flew up to the roof ridge. Her mother followed her outside the house and, seeing what had happened to her daughter, she broke into tears. By this time the girl was perched in a tree. She had flown up into the tree and had turned into a Brahminy kite. The mother called to her child, imploring her to come back. But the girl had gone. Thus it happened, because of the guilt of the parents, that the bird called *amina* (the Brahminy kite) came into existence.

One interest of this story is the theme, common in Indonesia, whereby a thirsty woman becomes pregnant after drinking some sort of liquid. Among features that bear more directly on the Nage story of Tupa Lélu is a parent's mistreatment of a daughter. Although the intention is different, the Komodo girl's confinement inside the house by her mother recalls Tupa Lélu's mother hiding her inside the loft. In addition, the girl eventually enters a loft where, like Tupa Lélu in her treetop hut, she is evidently engaged in weaving. The story also resembles the Nage myth in that, as a result of parental mistreatment, a daughter becomes effectively lost to her family. What is so arresting about the Komodo story, however, is that the girl is not simply adopted by birds of prey but actually transforms into such a bird. She does so, moreover, following the destruction – by liquefication – of her unwanted child (unwanted particularly, it would appear, by her mother), a detail comparable to the murder – by cutting to pieces – of Tupa Lélu who is herself an unwanted child (unwanted specifically by her father).

As an act separating her absolutely from her family, the Komodo girl's transformation can be understood as an extreme form of the transfer to, and subsequent identification with, raptorial birds in the story of Tupa Lélu. Yet in this case it serves superficially to rationalize the ordinary naming of a bird. For, according to Verheijen (1982), the Komodo term for 'Brahminy kite' (*Haliastur indus*) is *amina*. This is curious, especially since Amina looks rather like a Muslim (or Arabic) female name. However this might be explained, the metamorphosis recalls another mythical transformation into a bird, also involving a young girl and also occasioned by a mother's mistreatment. I refer, of course, to the Nage story of the Bare-throated whistler (*kete dhéngi*).

This is an appropriate place to compare the group of mostly raptorial birds in the Nage myth of Tupa Lélu with avifaunal characters occurring in other Nage narratives. As illustrated especially by the friarbird, several other bird characters appear in the positive role of helpers of humanity. The birds that bring the slain Tupa Lélu back to life are obviously similar in this respect. Yet their assistance is clearly contrary to the ordinary representation of these birds as empirical killers and consumers of bird flesh, and their symbolic representation as malevolent spiritual killers of human beings. In this latter respect, the birds' extraordinary behaviour provides a good illustration of how myth can involve inversions not only of ordinary experience – or common sense, intuitive knowledge (cf. Atran 1990: 219) – but also of standard religious ideas. (A similar case might be made with regard to the Imperial pigeon, a bird represented in myth as opposed to human interests, but which in the present day, owing to its eventual subordination to the friarbird, is almost as positively valued as its mythical rival.)

In contrast to the unexpected benevolence of Tupa Lélu's raptorial saviours, the mythical blessing of the friarbird is both consonant and continuous with the bird's present-day status as a useful chronological sign. Indeed, if raptors and other 'witch birds' are considered the most 'spiritual' of avian kinds, the friarbird is undoubtedly the most human. In regard to helpfulness, therefore, any resemblance between the birds that assist Tupa Lélu and birds occurring in other myths may seem superficial. Nevertheless, considered in the broader context of Nage bird symbolism, the story of Tupa Lélu and the myth of the Imperial pigeon and the friarbird reveal an intriguing parallel. One result of the friarbird's victory is of course the origin of death, whereas all the story of Tupa Lélu appears to account for is the fowl-stealing habit of birds of prey. Yet insofar as Nage symbolically equate humans with domestic fowls, and raptorial birds with death-dealing malevolent spirits, the Tupa Lélu myth might be understood identically to that of the avian rivalry. Indeed, it is in this, rather than in those aspects that approximate a 'just so' story regarding behavioural features of certain birds, that one finds a comprehensive relevance for the tale of Tupa Lélu.

For students of myth, it will come as no surprise that elements of the Tupa Lélu story recall Nage narratives which do not feature bird characters. Yet to compare these will not take us completely beyond the realm of ethnozoological discourse, since the myths in question happen to include other sorts of animals as essential components. A particularly striking comparison concerns the story of Wégu the Orphan and Pénu Ga'e. This may briefly be summarized as follows (see also Forth 1998a: 83–84):

A woman named Pénu Ga'e committed incest with her brother. Overcome by shame, she drowned herself in a river, whereupon her body was transformed into a large fish. The fish was eventually caught by Wégu, a poor orphan residing in Dhawe (in north-eastern Nage). Instead of killing the fish, he kept it alive in a pot of water in his house. Eventually, the fish turned into a beautiful woman – the revitalized Pénu Ga'e – who became his wife. She told him to plant pumpkins. A giant snake ate the leaves of the pumpkins. Pénu then instructed Wégu to kill the snake and leave its body to decompose. From the carcass, myriad maggots emerged. Implicitly through Pénu Ga'e's intervention, the maggots were then transformed into water buffalo, making Wégu an extremely rich man and, eventually, the major ancestral figure in Dhawe.

In several respects, the Wégu story suggests a mirror image of the myth of Tupa Lélu. For example, whereas in Tupa Lélu a father–daughter relationship – thus a consanguineal connection – is negative and leads to the death of the female partner, in Wégu the Orphan a husband–wife relationship – thus a marital connection – is positive and beneficial to the male partner. My main interest in the present context, however, concerns the fact that Pénu Ga'e, too, is killed (albeit by her own hand) and then transformed into a fish which later is turned back into a human female. Pénu Ga'e's fate is thus quite similar to that of Tupa Lélu, who is also revitalized and who, in a social sense if not by way of an explicit metamorphosis, becomes one of a group of birds but is later recovered (as a human daughter in one version of the myth, as a human wife in others). In addition, whereas the fish into which Pénu Ga'e is transformed can be understood as an embodiment of a dead soul (which of course is what the woman is at this stage of her career), the raptorial birds in Tupa Lélu similarly evoke spirits of the dead, while in one version of the story, Tupa Lélu actually refers to herself as a dead soul.

At this point, however, the resemblances mostly end. Although in one respect obviously identified with the dead, the fish, like Pénu Ga'e herself as a beautiful woman and wife to the hero (Wégu), conforms to the general Nage representation of a *nitu* spirit, more particularly the unmarked or focal kind of *nitu* (Forth 1998a: 84). In other Nage myths as well, spirits of precisely this kind are represented as sources of wealth, just as is Pénu Ga'e in this story. While commonly embodied as fish and other aquatic creatures, the animal form they most often assume in Nage thought is that of a snake. Accordingly, the most direct source of Wégu's wealth is a large snake.

The contrasts between these creatures and the birds of prey in the story of Tupa Lélu should already be apparent. By giving her life, the birds assist Tupa Lélu in a way comparable to the fish and snake, both identified with the wealth-giving Pénu Ga'e. Yet, far from being sources of wealth, the birds not only receive wealth from humans in the myth but, as chicken thieves, forever after become a constant drain on human resources. A comparison of the two myths thus appears to confirm Löffler's thesis (1968) regarding a regular opposition in Southeast Asian symbolism between birds on the one hand and fish, snakes, and similar creatures on the other. Among Nage, of course, the opposition is more generally attested on the spiritual plane, in the contrast between nefarious, death-dealing, and symbolically masculine *bapu* spirits, associated especially with the Ebu Lobo volcano and embodied vocally and visually in both nocturnal and diurnal birds of prey, and *nitu*, predominantly feminine free spirits identified largely with bodies of water which, although not invariably well-disposed towards humans, are regularly associated with life, beauty, and wealth (see Forth 1998a: 170–72).

What this seems to show, then, is that the most inclusive contrasts in Nage mythology, as in their symbolic thought generally, pertain to an opposition of life-forms (e.g., birds and fish) rather than one of different sorts of birds. Raptors and scavengers may virtually exhaust the kinds identified with witches and malevolent spirits; yet the remainder of bird categories (with the exception of the few 'soul birds' described in Chapter 5) are not identified with spiritual beings of any sort, and these 'non-spiritual' birds certainly do not compose a comparable symbolic class to which the flesh-eating birds are systematically opposed. What is more, the fact that the raptors in Tupa Lélu suggest features of dead souls (*mae ata mata*), even while they are mostly to be understood as representations of witch-like free spirits called *bapu*, reveals how this contrast, also, is not consistently made in regard to different kinds of birds.

As regards symbolic contrasts between life-forms, the morphological and ecological sources of such an opposition are palpable: reptiles and fish, which in several respects resemble one another, are distinguished from birds in regard to body form and locomotion as well as the more general or abstract distinctions of sky and earth (or sky and water) and above and below. Yet this symbolic dualism, too, is by no means absolute. As well as birds, Nage souls of the dead can manifest themselves as reptiles, insects, and fish (the form initially assumed by Pénu Ga'e). Similarly, while most often identified with snakes and water creatures, *nitu* can also take the guise of birds (as in the story of the woodpeckers related in Chapter 5), while the *bapu* spirit of a *hebu* tree – a sort of being otherwise most closely identified with raptors – can, in one ritual context at least, take the form of any kind of bird.[13]

Confirming a general variance between symbolic classification and ethnotaxonomy, the foregoing remarks – like complementary observations offered in previous chapters – point to one conclusion. Symbolic associations and contrasts revealed in Nage mythology, though expressed in terms of named bird and other folk generics composing Nage ethnozoological taxonomy, are not identical to ethnotaxonomic inclusions and exclusions. In other words, while different folk generics are implicated in the composition of one or more symbolic classes, the latter do not exactly coincide with ethnotaxa at the intermediate or any higher level. Accordingly, particular birds, fish, and snakes are to be understood as no more than instances of symbolic (and spiritual) categories that additionally comprise quite different things. Thus, besides raptorial birds, *bapu* spirits are identified with sacrificial buffalo and certain trees, and can also appear in the guise of human males. In the same way, Nage speak of *nitu* as assuming the form, not only of snakes and water creatures, but of beautiful young women. It is noteworthy, moreover, that while *nitu* spirits are most often identified with snakes, fish, eels, and other aquatic creatures, these natural kinds, also, do not constitute a single ethnozoological taxon. All snakes are *nipa* (which corresponds to English vernacular 'snake', Forth 1995), while fish are separately classified as *ika* (fish), and eels are included in neither category.[14] Concerning members of several other life-form categories, this example provides an obvious parallel, at a more inclusive level of classification, to the 'witch birds', a symbolic class that brings together ethnotaxonomically separate Strigiformes and Falconiformes, as well as several other birds besides.

Chapter 10

Comparisons and conclusions

Reflecting mythical traditions found in one case in several parts of the Flores region, and in the other throughout eastern Indonesia, the story of Tupa Lélu and the tale of the Imperial pigeon and the friarbird suggest that birds of certain kinds are mythologically prominent not only in Nage but over a wider area. From published ethnography, it is difficult to determine precisely how uniform bird symbolism might be among eastern Indonesian societies. Similarly beyond the scope of the present investigation is a comprehensive comparison of eastern Indonesian ethno-ornithological nomenclature and classification. Nevertheless, largely on the basis of Verheijen's terminological records (n.d.), it is possible to indicate, in a general and preliminary way, the likely results of a comparative study of eastern Indonesian bird taxonomy[1] and, with reference to the older literature, to draw provisional conclusions concerning symbolic continuities as well.

Comparisons

With regard to the 76 Nage names for birds (excluding bats) listed in Table 1.1, Verheijen's data indicate that 24 have cognates in Flores languages belonging to both the Bima-Sumba group (including Manggarai, Ngadha, and Lio) and the Ambon-Timor group (Sika and the Lamaholot languages of eastern Flores; see Map 2).[2] The terms are: *ana peti, bama, bébe ae, bi, céce, cio woza, ha, iki, kata, kea, koka, wodo* (see *koko wodo*), *kolo, lawi luja, manu, manu miu, muke, piko* (provisionally or hypothetically), *po, tiwe, toe ou, toto,* and *zawa*. At least nine of these 24 terms (*bi, ha, iki, kata, koka, wodo, manu, toto, zawa*) are further related to bird names in Sumbanese languages (Forth 2000), also members of the Bima-Sumba group, while cognates of perhaps as many as seven Nage terms (*bi, iki, kea, koka, manu, muke, toto*) occur in Tetum (see Hull 2001), an Ambon-Timor language spoken on Timor. Two Nage terms, *manu* and *zawa*, appear to reflect Proto-Austronesian forms, as does *bébe ae* (assuming *bébe* is not a Malay loan). *Muke* is a Proto-Malayo-Polynesian reflex (Clark 1994: 82, citing Blust 1983), while *ha* may be associated with a Proto-Hesperonesian (western Austronesian) reconstruction (Zorc 1994: 576). In view of evident cognates in Bahasa Indonesia (see *teuweuw*, MacKinnon 1991), *toe ou* apparently reflects another Proto-Malayo-Polynesian form, as does *piko* in regard to Western-Malayo-Polynesian cognates (e.g. Malay *pikau*, Winstedt 1965). The first component of *lawi luja* (paradise-flycatcher) also reflects a protoform at this level (**lawi*, 'tail feather', Zorc 1994: 581); the second component recalls the bird's name in Iban (*langgai lemujan*, Richards 1981).

Reviewing the birds named by the 24 Nage terms, it is difficult to discern what features these might share. In the Nage region at least, all are relatively common and well-known birds. Yet there are equally familiar birds that are not designated by any of the 24 names (for example, the Brahminy kite, which is quite variously labelled throughout Flores). Several kinds are prized for their flesh – for example, the domestic fowl (*manu*), three kinds of pigeons (*kolo, muke, zawa*), the junglefowl (*kata*), and the Brown quail (*piko*) – while the scrubfowl (*koko wodo*) is valued for its unusually large eggs. The Imperial pigeon (*zawa*) and the friarbird (*koka*) are of course prominent in eastern Indonesian origin mythology. Yet, again, it is not difficult to find examples of birds equally possessing these characteristics, whose names are rather more localized. Among the 24 terms are the names of several birds whose cries or appearance are ominous (*céce, cio woza, ha, po*), or mark seasonal change (*toe ou*). Interestingly, the available ethnography suggests that all of these possess comparable significance outside of Nage. Yet, while suggestive in certain particulars, the register of bird names widely reflected on Flores and elsewhere in Indonesia is equivocal in regard to any general pattern of culture it might express.

With respect to semantic features of the 24 Nage names, it may be mentioned that the majority (15, or 62.5 per cent) have no analysable meaning other than as names for birds.[3] If onomatopoeic terms are counted as non-analysable, then the figure rises to 100 per cent. Since the terms hypothetically reflect Austronesian, Malayo-Polynesian, or Central-Malayo-Polynesian protoforms, this is hardly surprising, for while the original forms may have referred to perceptual features of bird morphology or behaviour, in the course of time these connections are likely to have become obscured. What is more remarkable is the fact that as many as 37.5 per cent of the names (nine of 24) are onomatopoeic or partly onomatopoeic. This figure should be compared with the 22 instances of onomatopoeia (constituting 29 per cent) among the total of 76 Nage names for birds (not including bats) listed in Table 1.1. What these comparisons suggest, of course, is that onomatopoeic names retain their form in the course of language change to a greater extent than do names which describe perceptual characteristics of bird categories.

Distinct from cognatic relationship, different Flores languages also incorporate bird names that are comparable on purely semantic grounds. For example, the Nage naming of the Pale-headed munia (*Lonchura pallida*) as the 'Brahminy kite munia' (*ana peti jata*), owing to the resemblance between its plumage and that of the kite (*jata*), is replicated in terms for the same bird in Manggarai, Rembong, Ngadha, Endenese, and Lio (Verheijen 1963, 1977, n.d.).[4] Other instances of semantic parallelism include the compounding of terms for doves and munias to denote a utilitarian category of birds that do damage to ripening crops (see Nage *peti kolo* and eastern Sumbanese *mbàra manginu*, 'doves and munias'), and the naming of swallows and swifts in various Flores languages after 'rain' (see Nage *awe uza*, 'rain summoner'). Also noteworthy in the latter regard are Iban *layang ujan* (*ujan*, 'rain'), a reference to wood swallows (*Artamus* sp., Smythies 1960: 548), and the term for swallows and swifts in the non-Austronesian Tobelo language of Halmahera, which translates as 'rain caller' (Taylor 1990: 120).

Formal similarities and differences of bird classification between Nage and speakers of other eastern Indonesian languages are less easily summarized, although in respect of form, continuity appears on the whole more pronounced than discontinuity. In all these languages, productive binomials commonly take the form 'Ax', where this denotes the single contrast to 'A' (see Nage *jata* and *jata jawa*). Available evidence also suggests a recognition of similarly constituted intermediate categories. In fact, in regard to at least four Nage intermediates – small passerine birds (and especially Estrildine finches), Columbiformes, Falconiformes, and quails and buttonquails – one encounters quite a remarkable consistency of classification, especially with other languages in the Bima-Sumba group. Noteworthy here are eastern Sumbanese *manginu*, Manggarai *cik*, and Sikanese *ti* (all categories closely comparable with Nage *ana peti*); eastern Sumbanese *rawa*, which appears in several compounds denoting pigeons or doves; *ikitu*, a general Sumbanese term for several large diurnal raptors; and Manggarai *but*, denoting quails or buttonquails (Verheijen 1963, n.d.; Forth 2000). On the other hand, a general formal difference between Bima-Sumba and Ambon-Timor bird terminologies is suggested by the somewhat greater occurrence, within the latter, of productive binomials and the extensive use, in the construction of these, of *manu* and *kolo* (or cognates), terms which in Ambon-Timor languages translate, explicitly or implicitly, as 'bird'.[5]

Although evidence for symbolic and spiritual values attaching to particular birds is limited, what information is available (mainly from missionary writers like Arndt and Verheijen) suggests that, among different eastern Indonesian societies – and between speakers of Bima-Sumba and Ambon-Timor languages – there may be at least as much continuity as there generally appears to be in forms of naming and ethnotaxonomy. In regard to their association with witches and malevolent spirits, Nage ideas concerning diurnal and nocturnal raptors are broadly similar to representations encountered not only elsewhere on Flores (e.g. Sika, see Arndt 1932: 319, and Ngadha, see Arndt 1930: 829) but also on neighbouring islands, including Solor and Adonara (Arndt 1951: 191), Sumba (Forth 1981: 113; 2000: 173, 183), and Komodo (see Komodo *bungga sétang*, 'devil's dog', referring to the Brown hawk-owl, Verheijen 1982: 245, 255). Particularly the identification of diurnal as well as nocturnal birds of prey with spiritual malevolence moreover suggests the existence of variants of the Nage symbolic class of 'witch birds' in other eastern Indonesian societies, as do ideas linking crows with witches.[6] Further attesting to a spiritual category comparable to Nage 'witch birds' are remarks by Arndt indicating that the drongo (Nage *céce*) and the Flores crow (*héga hea*) are forms that witches identically assume among the neighbouring Ngadha (Arndt 1954: 448, s.v. the categories transcribed as *sisé jié* and *xéga réca*).

This is not to suggest that the class of 'witch birds' is everywhere the same. According to identifications provided by Verheijen (n.d.) of local categories recorded by Arndt (1932: 297, 319; 1951: 133), the pitta (*woko*) is identified with witches in Sika and East Flores – both Ambon-Timor speaking regions – while in Sika the Collared kingfisher (*kedur*) is regarded in the same way. By contrast, neither bird possesses any sort of spiritual significance among Nage. As noted in Chapter 6, similar differences pertain to interpretations of particular behaviours of cockatoos and quails, birds linked with witches in Ngadha and Sika but not in Nage. Nevertheless, despite local variations, it is evident that symbolic representations of birds comparable to ones encountered among Nage occur not only among speakers of other Bima-Sumba languages (such as Ngadha and Sumbanese), but also among speakers of Ambon-Timor languages (for example, Sikanese).

At the same time, while much of this symbolic uniformity may be attributed to common cultural heritage, some resemblances are quite general and coexist with variable local interpretations. What is more, just as similarities between Bima-Sumba and Ambon-Timor speakers in regard to the categorization of birds may reflect universal tendencies in ethno-ornithological taxonomy, several symbolic ideas could just as well be ascribed to an extremely widespread, if not universal, symbolism. Instances include the association of owls and other nocturnal birds with malevolent spiritual beings, and thus the evaluation of their cries as negative omens. Although not always construable as expressions of an unequivocally symbolic thought, other quite specific resemblances between Nage ideas concerning birds and beliefs encountered in other parts of the world, including Europe and native North America, were discussed in Chapter 7.

Given that variations are encountered between eastern Indonesian societies in regard to both symbolism and ethnotaxonomy, the question naturally arises of a possible connection between the two sorts of difference. Provisionally at least, the question may be answered in the negative. Languages in the Ambon-Timor group differ from Bima-Sumba languages in regard to the occurrence, in the former, of numerous binomial terms incorporating *kolo* or *manu* (or cognates of these). Yet in view of the great diversity of ornithological kinds named in this way, it is would be difficult to argue that either of the terms labels, or provides evidence for, an intermediate ethnotaxon.[7] By the same token, there is nothing to suggest that the birds in question form single symbolic classes. As I have remarked elsewhere, there are noteworthy differences between Nage and eastern Sumbanese in the naming of Columbiformes, particularly with regard to the use of Sumbanese *rawa* and *mbàra* in binary compounds (Forth 2000: 168–69, 177, 178–79). Simultaneously, pigeons and doves appear somewhat more prominent in eastern Sumbanese symbolism (ibid.: 181–84, 185–86). Yet one cannot derive one sort of difference from the other, not least because, in spite of the contrasts in nomenclatural form (and in that sense in classification), both societies nominally distinguish the same folk generic taxa.

Throughout this book, I have emphasized how symbolic ideas are, like ethnotaxonomy, ultimately grounded in perception of empirical birds. As demonstrated, Nage classification incorporates several, mostly unnamed intermediate taxa, including diurnal birds of prey (Falconiformes), pigeons and doves (Columbiformes), a category of crow-like birds, quails and buttonquails, small passerine birds, and bats. It will already be clear how these taxa also figure prominently in Nage spiritual ideas, augury, mythological narratives, and poetic idioms – although in certain cases it is a particular generic taxon subsumed in an intermediate category that is involved (see, for example, Nage ideas concerning *piko*, *'ighu*, and *ana peti jata*). Relative differences in Nage and eastern Sumbanese treatment of Columbiformes notwithstanding, pigeons and doves, Falconiformes, and crows or crow-like birds appear to be of roughly equal importance in the symbolic life of other Flores societies, as well as in the symbolism of other eastern Indonesians for whom evidence is available. As shown, diurnal raptors and Columbiformes compose the two best-attested covert intermediate taxa in Nage bird classification. At the same time, several of these groupings – although, again, especially Columbiformes, diurnal birds of prey, and quails and buttonquails – appear similarly to compose intermediate taxa in the ethnotaxonomy of other eastern Indonesian societies. Hence, not just for Nage, but for a larger group of eastern Indonesian societies, there is a suggestion that symbolic importance correlates with classificatory prominence.

Yet this observation requires qualification. For despite the symbolic importance of Falconiformes in Nage representations of malevolent spirits, symbolic classes like 'spirit birds' and 'witch birds' do not in fact coincide with any of the intermediate categories discernible in Nage ethnotaxonomy. From the available ethnography, it would appear that Falconiformes and Columbiformes account for much of the uniformity in eastern Indonesian thought concerning birds. Given the widespread salience of 'hawks and doves', both symbolic and classificatory, in a variety of the world's cultures, however, it is difficult to explain eastern Indonesian instances exclusively with reference to a peculiar regional form of folk ornithology, as resemblances between individual societies could alternatively be attributed to a universal symbolism. Also tending towards the universal is the category of 'dicky-birds', named by Nage as *ana peti* and focused on munias and other Estrildine finches. Yet while conceivably motivated in part by utilitarian factors relating to cereal cultivation, *ana peti* does not correspond to any symbolic class. Marginally included in the symbolic class of *po*-sounding birds, the *ana peti jata* (Brahminy kite munia) might seem exceptional in this regard. Tellingly, however, this bird derives its symbolic value not from its status as a member of the ethnotaxon *ana peti*, but from a quite different (and empirically more selective) sort of identification with a raptor, the Brahminy kite.

Conclusions

Even on the basis of this limited review, it may be concluded that linguistic sub-grouping has no pronounced effect either on ethno-ornithological classification or bird symbolism. Since groups speaking both Bima-Sumba and Ambon-Timor languages occupy a variety of ecological zones, ethnotaxonomy and symbolic usages would similarly appear to transcend environmental differences – except, of course, insofar as the absence of species would naturally preclude both their classification and symbolic employment.

Much the same conclusion must be drawn with regard to social structure. Nowadays, it is unlikely that even an extreme relativist would defend the position of Durkheim and Mauss ([1903] 1963), according to which animal and plant taxonomies originate in the organization of social groups. At any rate, it is quite clear that the present study lends no support to the famous theory. As Verheijen's unpublished records attest, Nage closely resemble their Ngadha neighbours in regard to both bird classification and symbolism. Yet traditional forms of social organization differ considerably between these two groups. Thus, unlike Nage, Ngadha communities do not for the most part favour patrifiliation of offspring, practise asymmetric affinal alliance, or prohibit marriage between parallel cousins. On the other hand, societies resembling Nage in all of these respects – notably Ambon-Timor speakers in eastern Flores and the Solor region – are less similar in regard to ethnotaxonomy and (albeit perhaps to a lesser extent) to symbolic representations as well.

Nevertheless, there are at least two areas of Nage folk ornithology that appear to manifest particular cultural principles, and even to recall features of social morphology. One concerns the ubiquitous friarbird. As I demonstrated in my previous analysis of the bird's mythical contest with the Imperial pigeon (Forth 1992), being more closely identified with the value of alternation than his rival, the friarbird symbolically subsumes values associated with the pigeon, which the bird in fact eventually subordinates. Since nowadays the friarbird always calls before the pigeon, moreover, the ultimate relationship of the two birds entails an asymmetric order of precedence representing the proper order of the world, so that the outcome of the myth is a binary relation combining precedence and encompassment that is redolent of dualistic forms which, as I have copiously demonstrated elsewhere (Forth 2001), are pervasive in central Flores society.

Described in Chapter 3, a second instance of this sort of isomorphism concerns the form of dualistic nomenclature instanced in such binary compounds as *peti kolo*, *piko kolo*, and *kua jata*. As noted, these usages also correspond to a pervasively dualistic principle of Nage social structure. Yet social dualism further parallels, and indeed is articulated by, a ubiquitous binary tendency of Nage language in general; hence its particular manifestation in the naming of congeries of birds is not at all surprising. It should not be forgotten, either, that compound expressions like *kua jata* are metaphorical (or, specifically, synecdochal), and while composed of names denoting folk generic taxa, they do not directly designate units of ethnotaxonomy. Pertaining to nomenclature rather than classification – a distinction necessarily made in several other contexts – apprehending this feature of Nage bird naming as an instance of a general pattern of culture and language thus does not contradict a view of ethnozoological classification as a phenomenon or process that functions mostly independently of local social structure and a particular cultural tradition. Nor, of course, do social structural parallels of the mythical connection of the Imperial pigeon and the friarbird. Accordingly, the independence of ethnotaxonomy from symbolic forms remains the major conclusion of the present investigation.

Appendix 1:
Birds in Nage songs and proverbs

1   Channel-billed cuckoo, koel, cockatoo and Large-billed crow (a planting song, *pata joki*)

Muta me, kau ta 'éghe 'éghe, foko o héde
Cuckoo, you shout a great deal, but your throat is sore in vain
Toe ou ta ohu ohu, mona mewi sa puju dho'u
The koel coughs and sputters, but does not get a single handful
Kasa kasa ko'o ngata kea ne'e ha
Most fortunate of all are the cockatoo and crow
Ta'a heta pau ko'o ngata
Who both stay silent
Ulu mewi holo dala
But are the first to get star maize

Commentary: The Channel-billed cuckoo (*muta me*) and the Common koel (*toe ou*) call noisily in the early part of the rainy season, thus announcing the time for planting. But they get nothing for their efforts. In contrast, the cockatoo and crow produce no useful vocalizations and yet feast upon ripening maize (or 'star maize'; that is, maize cobs with widely spaced kernels). At the same time, as one commentator pointed out, referring implicitly to the fact that the Channel-billed cuckoo is a brood parasite of crows, young *muta me* feed on maize that is brought to them by their foster parents.

2   Channel-billed cuckoo and koel (planting song)

Muta me négha éghe
The cuckoo has already cried out
Toe ou négha polu
The koel has already called
Kau tei tei noa
You see what looks easy
Kau wudha wa'a koba
You strike against vines
Kau tei tei zala
You find a path to follow
Kau boba wa'a ngaba
You fall into a ravine
Féke poma ko négha koba
The creeping plant has already put out runners
Mélu wole ko négha wonga
The spadix has withered and already blossomed

Commentary: The lyric mocks lazy people who have yet to prepare their fields when it is already time to plant, as indicated by the calling of the two birds. *Féke poma* is the name of a wild plant.

3   Channel-billed cuckoo and koel (planting song)

Muta me kau ta'a sezu pawe
Cuckoo, you speak well
Napa de wula joki pase
Presently in the month of planting and dibbling
Toe ou kau ta'a polu poa
Koel, you call in the morning
Ke 'iwu négha mo'o we'e joki oa
Then the masses are already near planting and broadcasting

Commentary: Broadcasting is the method of planting various cultigens after maize and several other crops are planted by dibbling. The phrases thus express the specific idea that the Channel-billed cuckoo calls somewhat before the koel. 'In the morning' can also be understood as 'on the following day'. The cuckoo's cry indicates that people should begin to prepare the fields for planting, while the call of the koel means that the wet season rains are imminent and that planting should commence.

4   Friarbird (a children's song)

Ana koka zéta Ae Boa
The friarbird up at Ae Boa
Kai toda mo'o kami sa kola
Goes to tell us that he wants us to attend school
Toda wali mo'o kami sa rani
Lets us know as well that he wants us to become Christians
O ea o ea oe
O ea o ea oe

Commentary: Originating in the colonial period, the song obviously encourages youngsters to go to school and convert to Christianity (two processes by no means entirely distinct during the first half of the twentieth century). The lyric draws on two features of the friarbird (*koka*). The first is the idea that the bird's vocalizations can convey all sorts of messages and hidden meanings. The second is the *koka's* role in determining the order of the natural world (especially the length of day and night; see Chapter 8). In this case, modern education and the Church, following in the wake of the colonial incursion, heralded indeed a new world order arguably comparable, in some respects at least, to the original creation. Ae Boa, the name of a stream, appears to have no particular significance in this context.

5   Drongo and friarbird (a planting song)

Ana céce ma nabu ne'e
The drongo is in possession (of something)

Ana koka ma nabu mona
The friarbird has yet to obtain (anything)
Ana koka iko ako
But the friarbird calls 'iko ako'
Tei noa noa talo
And gets (whatever he wants) with ease

Commentary: The friarbird personifies someone of good fortune who, while he may not be wealthy, is always successful in his endeavours. As 'friarbird' refers metaphorically to a vociferous and persistently vocal person, something akin to the English notion of the 'squeaky wheel always getting the oil' is also implied. (*Talo*, which usually means 'to be unable (to do something)', is to be understood here as an emphatic, indicating that the bird cannot fail in his efforts.)

6   Friarbird and oriole (a proverb)

Ana koka mona toda
The friarbird does not reveal the news
Ana léro me'a be'o
The oriole has discovered it himself

Commentary: The phrases describe a situation where a person has yet to tell another something, but it does not matter as the latter already knows. *Léro* as the name of the Oriole (*leo*) exemplifies the occurrence of /r/ in idiomatic language (including songs and chants) in Nage dialects from which the sound has disappeared in ordinary speech. In the present context, however, the term is alternatively pronounced as *leo*. Similarly, *toda* ('to inform', 'convey information') is recognized in Bo'a Wae as a dialectal word. As such, it illustrates another common practice of Nage poetic speech.

7   Friarbird, oriole, fantail, and tesia (a planting song)

Wai poa ke kau ana koka
In the morning, it is you, friarbird
Ana koka poa, ana leo dia mona
The friarbird is here in the morning, but the oriole is not present
Wai leza ke kau ana ceka
At midday, it is you, fantail
Ana ceka leza, ana bama bhia mega
The fantail is here at noontide, but the tesia bird does not wish to address (him)

Commentary: The meaning is unclear, but the phrases evidently associate different birds with different parts of the day. The friarbird's call announces the sunrise (see just below). The call of the *bama* (the Russet-cappet tesia) is inauspicious when heard at midday. Nage also associate the fantail with the middle of the day (see below), though this does not have the same empirical support as the friarbird's association with the dawn.

8   Friarbird and Imperial pigeon (song and proverb)

Ana koka ola pea poa
The friarbird is the one who heralds the morning
Ana zawa ola pea da
The Imperial pigeon is the one who points to the daylight

Commentary: The reference is to the calls of the two birds, heard early in the morning, signalling the approach of daybreak.

9   Friarbird, Imperial pigeon, and Brahminy kite (a song)

Poa kau ana koka
In the morning you are there, friarbird
Ana koka ola polu poa
The friarbird who calls in the morning
Napa kau ana zawa
Later it is you, Imperial pigeon
Ana zawa ola pea da
The Imperial pigeon who points to the dawn
Haba 'é'e ana jata méze
Of no value at all is the big kite
Zéle koba léke
Up on the great vine
Tau ie ghéghe ie ghéghe
Who cries and utters harsh sounds

Commentary: The song describes the Brahminy kite as possessing cries which, unlike the calls of the friarbird and Imperial pigeon, are of no use as indicators of daily time. The adjective *méze* ('big'), after *jata*, appears semantically gratuitous, merely producing a vocalic rhyme with *léke* and *ghéghe*. *Léke*, here translated as 'great vine', refers to the liana *Entada phaseoloides*. As a compound, *ie ghéghe* is a general reference to the cry of the kite. *Ie*, however, specifically refers to a high-pitched, whinnying sound while *ghéghe* denotes a harsher call.

10   Friarbird and fantail (song and proverb)

Ana koka polu poa
The friarbird calls in the morning

Ana ceka pea leza
The fantail indicates (that it is) midday

Commentary: A variant of text 7, expressing an association of the fantail with midday comparable to the friarbird's link with the morning and sunrise.

11   Friarbird and domestic fowl (a proverb)

Koka sedho sa wedho
The friarbird gives but a brief cry (cries for an instant)
Manu kako be'o pau
The cocks straightaway know (are able) to crow

Commentary: The phrases allude to the relation of the friarbird's calls to the early morning cock crows.

12   Munia (a play song of small children, *mébho ana éno*)

Ana peti to mo zéle lima lobo
Little red munia bird up on the side of the volcano
Kedho ko mogo, fio nodho nodho
Pecks a whole (unsliced) chilli pepper, sniffs from its strong spiciness
Tei lobo uta, tengu mo'o bua
Sees the tip of a vegetable, the stalk is going to break
La'a zili mesi, ghae ghedhi ghedhi
Goes down to the sea, scratches the earth like a fowl

Commentary: *Ana peti to* was said to refer to the Pale-headed munia (*ana peti jata*). In this context, *lobo* can be understood as referring specifically to the great Nage volcano, Ebu Lobo. The song is described as a simple nonsense rhyme.

13   Ground-dove and Spotted dove, quail and junglefowl (a song)

Zéle wolo muke ne'e kolo
Up in the hills, the ground-dove and the Spotted dove
Dému zua dhesi papa moko
The two of them live in friendship side by side
Lau mala piko ne'e kata
Down in the plain, the quail and the junglefowl
Dému zua bana sama sama
The two of them always travel together

Commentary: The metaphor is comparable to the English proverb 'birds of a feather flock together', meaning that people seek the company of others like themselves. The parallelistic structure of the Nage phrases, however, contrasts two pairs of birds as well as two sorts of environments. The association of the two pairs (*muke//kolo* and *piko//kata*) appears motivated by the combination of *piko* (quail) and *kolo* (Spotted dove) in a binary compound (*piko kolo*) that refers to common and preferred kinds of game birds (see further examples below). In the first pair, *zawa* (Imperial pigeon) can be used in place of *muke*.

14   Junglefowl and quail (from a prayer)

Bi lala bhia kata mala
Reproduce like junglefowl in the plains
Ligho bhia piko wio
Swarm like flocking quails

Commentary: The phrases are recited when requesting fertility and fecundity – in both humans and livestock – from beneficent spirits. I initially recorded the second line as *liwo bhia piko wigho* which, while not definitely incorrect, defies direct translation. The gloss of *wio* as 'flocking' reflects informant responses to questioning; however, the usage is also reminiscent of *pi wio*, a phrase that denotes a quail's call.

15   Quail and Spotted dove (a proverb)

Piko ta'a wito io
The quail that takes along others
Kolo ta'a 'isi moko
The Spotted dove that urges on his friends

Commentary: The reference is to a person who seeks companionship or desires the support of others in some undertaking. The pairing of the birds is consistent with the flocking habits of quails and the fact that Spotted doves, also, are commonly encountered in pairs or small groups. At the same time, *piko* and *kolo* form a standard compound. A third line can be added to the foregoing. This is *manu ta'a edho bédho*, 'the domestic fowl that pulls up the parson's nose', a reference to one fowl following close upon another.

16   Quail and Spotted dove (a proverb, or simple binary expression)

Kolo co, piko bhebhe
Dove flies (away), quail sets down (on the ground)

Commentary: The phrases refer to an area of land occupied by agricultural fields belonging to various parties (in contrast to a collection of adjacent fields belonging to a single owner or members of the same house or clan). The metaphor also suggests the idea of replacement over time as the cause of this pattern; that is, one party abandons a field ('flies away'), whereafter another begins cultivating there. An apparently synonymous expression is *ja kéla, manu ke'o*, 'mottled horse, speckled fowl', the second component of which otherwise refers to the fantastic creature combing the features of a cock and a snake (see Table 1.1).

17   Spotted dove (a planting song)

Kolo ku zéle mai lobo
The Spotted dove coos high up on the summit
Tei ke'o ko'o ata lebi Geo
Sees Job's tears of people on the hillsides of Geo
Teku eku kau ne'e podi éngo
'Teku eku' you say pretending and deceiving
Teku eku podi éngo
'Teku eku' pretending and deceiving

Commentary: This is sung by males making fun (*néke*) of females. The dove is a woman, while 'Job's tears' refers to a man or men. Geo, or Géro, is a region to the north-east of Bo'a Wae. *Teku eku* is one vocalization of the dove.

18   Fruit-dove (a planting song)

Ana bopo co zéle lima lobo
Fruit-dove flies up to the volcano
Tei nunu ta'a li'e wale wunu
Sees a banyan full of leafy fruit
Co ko'a mona peta poa
Flies and alights never missing a single morning

Commentary: *Wale wunu* refers to the fruit of the banyan tree which characteristically grow close to the leaves. This can be understood as a metaphor for a person of the opposite sex, to whom an individual – represented by the fruit-dove – is attracted. The song refers to a man who continuously visits a woman, or alternatively a woman who is constantly drawn to a man.

19   Swallows and swifts (a song, including a planting song)

Ebu titu leo lizu
Swallows and swifts wander the sky
Ana ja paka laba
'Little horse' beats the drum
Ine to dhégo go
'Mother Red' strikes the gong

I dhono, i dhono
(Imitation of a percussive sound)

Commentary: The lyric describes impending rains and the approach of the wet season, indicated by flights of swifts and swallows and the sound of distant thunder (thus the beating of the drum). The referents of 'little horse' (an informant's gloss) and 'mother red' – or 'red mother' (*ine to*; 'To' is also a common female personal name) – are obscure, though the latter, sometimes conflated with *ana ja* to become 'Ine Jawa', was interpreted as a reference to a figure named Ine Géna, a personification of rain. In addition, some motivation for combining the three terms is apparent from the inclusion in each of a kin term. Although in *ana ja* it is best glossed as 'little', *ana* is also 'child', while *ine* of course refers to the female parent. Similarly, whereas the significance of *ebu* is unclear as a component of a bird name, the term's most common meaning is 'grandparent, grandchild'. In regard to the kin referents of all three terms, the lyric may further entail a pun. A variant of the first line is *ebu titu watu wula*, 'swallows command (control) the months (season)'.

20 Bushlark or pipit (*ana go*) and swallows or swifts (a song)

Ana go dhégo go
The pipit strikes the gong
Ana ja paka laba
Little horse beats the drum
Ebu titu leo lizu
Swallows and swifts wander the sky

Commentary: This was reported as an alternative to the more common variant recorded as text 19. Although the association with a gong (*go*) accords with the homonymous name of the pipit, the fact that this element is repeated in the first line suggests that this is not the preferred version.

21 Bushlark or pipit (*ana go*) and kestrel (from *déro tua*, songs performed at annual pugilistic competitions called *etu*)

Ana go sa iki mea e
The pipit speaks to the shy kestrel
So kupe sa rada mala
Saying the *kupe* tree shades the plain
Nage sa fa'o tana
The tamarind casts a shadow on the earth

Commentary: The translation is provisional. *Iki mea*, 'shy kestrel', is itself the name of a chant (more completely known as *iki mea, 'ago talo ana*, 'shy kestrel, unable to embrace a child') accompanied by hand-clapping and dancing. The chant is included in the agricultural rites *po'o wete* and *po'o uta*, performed respectively when dry rice has ripened and after the harvest. One group (either of the same sex or mixed) will chant and clap their hands while another group dances. The dancers hold small pieces of cloth in their hand which they wave, imitating the flight of the kestrel. The performance was once described as a sort of collective courting ritual.

22   Bushlark or pipit (*ana go*) (a children's song)

O ana go, ana go e
O pipit, pipit e
Laga ngala tada tuga jara Mado Mala
Only the horse named Mado Mala is able to cross the finish line
Kema ngala uma tuga ema Jago Kuda
Only Jago Kuda is able to work the field(s)

Commentary: Mado Mala is explained as the name of a racing horse that once belonged to the last raja of Nage, J. Juwa Dobe. Jago Kuda (or, in his own dialect, Jago Kunda), was a famous leader in western Keo and a colonially appointed administrator contemporaneous with the Nage raja. The song thus originates in the colonial period (early twentieth century). Otherwise no exegesis is available. With regard to the horse, however, it may be relevant that the bird called *ana go* has thin and relatively long legs and is inclined to run along the ground.

23   Kestrel (from a planting song and circle-dance song)

Ko modhe ana iki e
A good sort is the little kestrel
Ana iki ta'a wolo mena
Little kestrel on the western hill
Co leo ta siba leta
Flies circling continuously going directly onward

Commentary: In this lyric, the kestrel was described as representing 'good people in general'. It may also be taken to refer to the singers themselves, as they work or dance. The sense of the third line is that the circling flight of the kestrel continues until the bird disappears, never to return. Commentators thus suggested that the lyric may allude to lost love; but conceivably it could refer to the impermanence of any good thing. (*Mena*, glossed here for convenience as 'western', actually refers to a rightward direction as one faces a central point of orientation, which in much of Nage is the Ebu Lobo volcano, mostly to the south.)

24   Eagle and goshawk (a song of mourning, *pata kasi*)

Kua no'i lau lobo koli
The eagle calls seaward from the tip of a lontar palm
Mesu ame ulu mata po'i
Have pity on father who died before his time
Sizo io zéta lobo nio
The goshawk cries upstream from the top of a coconut tree
Mesu ine ulu mata 'ibo
Have pity on mother whose death was premature

Commentary: The song mourns the victim of an early death. Since eagles, hawks, and indeed all raptors belong to the class of birds associated with ominous *po* sounds, reference to these birds may more specifically imply the death of a relatively young person caused by spiritual malevolence. In an alternative version, *sizo* (goshawk) is replaced by *mole sio*, a dialectal name for the cuckoo-shrike (*cio woza*). This is consistent with the significance of the cuckoo-shrike's call as a possible death omen (see text 32).

25   Large hawk (a song of mourning, but also performed as a planting song)

Ana jata jawa zéta wawo sa
The high-flying hawk sits atop the nest
Angi wa wéjo ate zéze zeo
The wind rocks the heart making it unsettled and sad
Mesu é wai azi nga'o nebu ke
Have pity on my younger brother of former days
Ghubu ne wai ku
His roof ridge is of grass
Naja ne wai tana
His walls are of earth

Commentary: *Azi* is 'younger sibling', but any relationship, and thus any kin term, can be used in the third line. The song mourns a long deceased relative. *Ate* is 'liver' but metaphorically translates as 'heart'. An alternative to the second line is: *Te'e wai tana, lani wai watu*, 'The sleeping mat is of grass, the pillow is of stones'. The structure of grass and earth, comparable to a building, refers to the grave, which is probably also the referent of 'the nest'. The 'high-flying hawk' may be an allusion to a death omen, although one Nage commentator interpreted the phrase as referring to the spirit of the deceased which hovers distantly like a hawk.

26   Domestic pigeon (*kolo dasi*) and 'sea fowl' (*manu mesi*) (from a song of mourning)

Ana kolo dasi lau bata Bai
The pigeon who is seaward by the waves at Bai
Ana manu mesi polu kasi weki
The sea fowl calls pitying himself

Commentary: The two lines can be sung separately in mourning songs. Consistent with the recent introduction of birds called *kolo dasi*, a Nage commentator explained that *dasi* is inserted to correspond with Bai, a place name which, also in recent times, has come to be used to denote the north coastal region generally. (*Kolo* alone can specify the Spotted dove.) He might also have mentioned the parallel, or partial rhyme, with *mesi* in the third line. The reference to the north coast accords with the Nage idea that deceased souls proceed to the sea. As Nage pointed out, both 'sea fowl' and pigeon (*kolo dasi*) can be understood as references to dead souls. The usual meaning of *weki* is 'body' and, according to local interpretations, can be translated as such here, with the sense of 'mourning over the body'. 'Sea fowl' refers to a seabird that for a time frequents inland places but must eventually return to the sea, just as human souls must ultimately return to their place of origin upon death.

27   Domestic fowl (from a song of mourning)

Kita ana manu déwa
We are fowls of divinity
Déwa dua poi
Divinity comes down to gather (his fowls) together
Mona be'o lozi
(They) know no escape

Commentary: *Poi manu* refers to the act of calling or gathering fowls together, in order to place them in an enclosure or coop. The lyric describes humans as like the fowls of god, who comes to collect them at death, from which there is no escape.

28   Domestic fowl (refrain sung when carrying large pieces of wood, *pata bhe kaju*; untranslated)

Manu ɟéka
Manu ɟéka ee
Ee ee manu ɟéka
Roɟa manu ɟéka

Commentary: *Géka* occurs in the expression *fu bha géka*, referring to hair that is completely white or the feathers of a cockatoo. *Roga (= hoga) manu géka* can denote a light-skinned person, like a European. No further exegisis is available.

29   Bare-throated whistler (a song, including a planting song)

Ana apa ai ai
What child is that?
Kau ta'a éngi éngi
You who always peer down
Bhila ana dhéngi
Like a sad child lamenting
Ma zéle kisa kéli
Halfway up the mountain
Léle pau ta'a sezu sezu
The voice is always heard
Ta'a weki mona tei tei
But the body is never seen

Commentary: The song refers to the myth of the Bare-throated whistler (*kete dhéngi*). Lines two and four allude to the fact that the bird inhabits high elevations. *Ana dhéngi* in line three is alternatively interpretable as a form of the bird's name, more completely rendered as *ana kete dhéngi*, 'cold, lamenting child'. In accordance with the contextual use of *ana* for 'bird, creature' (see Chapter 3), the first line could alternatively be glossed as 'what (kind of) bird is that'.

30   Bare-throated whistler and Hill mynah (a planting song)

Ine kete ana dhéngi menge
Cold mother and lamenting sweet-smelling child
Polu ana apa dhewe
Whatever child is it that you care for
Ana io wea mara dobhe déna
The mynah bird still turns its head from side to side
Ana io wea
(So it is with) the mynah

Commentary: The first two passages allude to the myth of the child transformed into a Bare-throated whistler, and her mother who did not care properly for her. The first line illustrates a common syntactical feature of Nage formal speech, whereby terms of a compound phrase (*ine ana*, 'mother and child, mother–child relationship') are separated by, in this case, a compound name (that of the bird, *kete dhéngi*) which in this context functions as a modifier. The complete expression might therefore alternatively be glossed as 'sweet (fragrant) whistler (bird) mother and child'. Unfortunately, this does not shed further light on the intent of the lyric. *Dobhe déna* refers to the mynah's habit of regularly turning its head from side to side, as if to listen. No further exegesis was obtained.

31   Hill mynah (a song of mourning)

Ie wea polu dobhe déna
The mynah calls tilting its head to one side
Mesu é wai ine nga'o nebu ke
Have pity on my mother of old
Ghubu ne wai ku
The roof ridge is of grass
Naja ne wai tana
The walls are of earth

Commentary: This is a variant of text 25, which substitutes the mynah for the hawk (*jata jawa*). The significance of neither the bird nor its habit of tilting the head is clear in this context.

32   Cuckoo-shrike (from a planting song)

Cio woza sezu
The cuckoo-shrike speaks
Lu mata me'a bedhu
Tears just fall

Commentary: The lyrics refer to the call of the cuckoo-shrike heralding bad news, including a death (see commentary to text 24).

33   Pied bushchat (proverb)

Tute ci cea
Bushchat cries 'ci cea'
Ola mo da
(Expressing) a desire for daylight

Commentary: The expression refers to the early morning call of the bushchat, before sunrise, and so is comparable to texts referring to the friarbird and this bird's association with the dawn. Here and in the following song, the bushchat's usual name, *tute péla*, is abbreviated to *tute*, as it is in other contexts (for example, the place name Wolo Tute, 'Bushchat Hill').

34   Pied bushchat, friarbird, and Imperial pigeon (song lyric)

Tute ci cea
Bushchat cries 'ci cea'
Koka polu poa
Friarbird calls in the morning
Zawa pea da
Imperial pigeon points to the daylight

Commentary: Here the comparison of the bushchat's cry with those of the friarbird and Imperial pigeon is made explicit (see texts 8 and 33).

35   Pied bushchat (a song)

Ana tute lau tolo watu
Little bushchat seaward sits on top of a stone
Ate weta dhiku dheka pau
The lady's heart goes pitter patter
Tutu rumu pau ne'e wunu muku
Cover up and conceal with a banana leaf
Toda ine négha wula wutu
Let mother know it is already four months
Piri néde pau ne'e wunu réje
Screen off and hide with a watermelon leaf
Toda ine wula négha we'e
Let mother know that the month is already near.

Commentary: This is performed by young men, teasing (*néke*) young women. The lyrics refer to a woman, represented by the bushchat, who has become pregnant after an affair and is attempting to conceal it. The woman is also denoted as *weta*, a general term for female relatives of male ego's genealogical level. Representing earlier and later stages of pregnancy, 'banana' and 'watermelon' evidently contrast the differing distension of the abdomen at these times. (The compound *piri néde*, 'to hide', appears to be a deliberate distortion of the ordinary language phrase *pére nidi* (or in most dialects *pe nidi*). In another recorded version, *tutu rumu* and *piri néde* were replaced respectively with the nonsense phrases *tunu runu* and *téte réne*.)

36   Sunbird (from the rite *zi'a tua mata utu*, performed to promote the growth and well-being of newly tapped Arenga palms)

Tiwe mole
The sunbirds swarm around
Kogha poma, wawi jola
The deer soak themselves, the wild pigs take a bath

Commentary: The phrases describe creatures coming together to nourish and cool themselves and allude to a plenitude of palm juice. The *tiwe* is mentioned because the bird likes to sip the juice. As part of the *zi'a tua* rite, the officiating elder may lower and raise his head three times in imitation of the bird sipping – or stealing – palm juice, an act described as a way of making fun of the owner of the tree.

37 Sunbird and (in one variant) friarbird (a song performed when breaking new ground, *pata woka*; a song of ridicule (*néke*) in two parts sung by men and women respectively)

Men's chant:
Tiwe mata gibe
The one-eyed Sunbird
Zili (or *lau*) *tolo nige*
Down (or seaward) at the top of the *nige* tree
Nana padu tau
Juice of the papaya makes it
Emi a'u pau
Blink indeed

Women's riposte:
Tua kau sa eo
Your palm wine (container) is a single internode
Ne'e manu ege weo
And your fowl has feathers only around the tail
Nara na mai
Brother comes and goes
Mo réwo a'i
Will get tired in vain

An alternative women's riposte:
Beu koka napa dewe poa
Drowsy the friarbird waited until morning
Nebu lu pizu nguzu nguzu
Last night embraced rubbing noses
Izu ne'e wunu mumu
With nose and lips (as well)

Commentary: The phrases, particularly of the men's chant and women's first riposte, evidently refer to the female and male genitalia and the act of intercourse, although when directly questioned Nage often denied this. The linking of palm wine and a fowl in the women's riposte accords with the fact that these items, common components of prestations made to wife-givers, and thus in effect 'male' goods, are regularly given together. Palm wine and gin are stored in containers of bamboo which may be one or more internodes in length. The imagery of the alternative riposte is less clear, although it is significant that this introduces the friarbird. Both drinkers of palm juice, the two birds are also linked in the Nage creation myth described in Chapter 10. 'Beu' was explained as a personal name or epithet; its translation as 'drowsy' is provisional.

38   Fantail, fruit-dove, goshawk, cockatoo, and crow (a song of the type named *oe doko*)

Lako lao taso babho
The stick insect comes to make a request
Ana ceka bhia ngazo
The fantail does not want to agree
Ceka pi'u pebha pebha
Fantail hobbles to the left and right
Ceka sodho ne'e bopo
Fantail gives instructions to the fruit-dove
Bopo ughu agha bholo
Fruit-dove merely makes threats
Bopo wito ne'e sizo
Fruit-dove requests assistance from the goshawk
Sizo énga ne'e kea
Goshawk calls the cockatoo
Kea bele li'o lénga
Cockatoo moves his wings back and forth
Kea ghata ne'e ha
Cockatoo gives orders to the crow
Ha ughu agha agha
Crow threatens and intimidates
Ha a'i ana kuza
Crow catches the crayfish
Ana kuza mona me'a tau
Crayfish does not follow his own wishes
Ana ika noto watu
It is the fish who instructs him.

Commentary: Generally considered amusing, these lyrics belong to the genre called *néke*, which refers to a teasing or mild ridicule of the opposite sex with metaphors of a sexual import. At the same time, what these may be in the present case is largely unclear. The fantail is understood to represent a woman, more specifically a fickle woman who quickly changes her mind. Here, she is the object of the stick insect's request, made on behalf of another.

39 The raptorial bird named *je* (a planting song)

Moga lowo Doga
Crab in the river Doga
Je podi we'e
Je advances slowly in pretence
Kuza Au Galu
Crayfish at Au Galu
Medhi léwa latu
Retreats a long way

Commentary: Nage, who cited the foregoing as an instance of lyrics mentioning a bird, stated that *je* was to be understood as a reference to the raptor so named. However, the term is more readily translated simply as 'advances', and in fact the song makes more sense in this way, with the verb then describing the action of the crab. Doga is the name of a stream near the village of Bo'a Gu. Au Galu denotes a place located downstream.

40 Estrildine finch (*bio*) (lyrics sung when carrying large pieces of wood, *pata bhe kaju*)

Ana bio
Ana bio
Bido bido
Moves the upper body up and down (when carrying heavy objects)
Ana bao
Ana bao
Bado bado
Moves to the left and right (when travelling, pulling a load)

Commentary: *Bio* is understood by Nage as denoting the kind of small bird so named. *Ana bao* is also assumed to refer to a bird, but one of an unknown identity. However, not only is *bao* very improbable as a bird name but in this context *bio* may well also have another reference.

Appendix 2:
Bird terms as personal
and place names

Personal names

Detailed identification of the Nage terms is given in Table 1.1. Some of the terms listed below are homonyms of other words; hence inclusion of a name implies only a possible derivation from a bird term.

Male names

Bi   (Red-cheeked parrot)
Iki   (kestrel)
Jata   (Brahminy kite)
Kaka   (see *kaka kea* = *kea*, cockatoo; *kaka daza*, dollarbird)
Kata   (junglefowl)
Kea   (cockatoo)
Koka   (friarbird)
Kolo   (dove)
Kua   (eagle)
Leo   (oriole)
Peti   (see *ana peti*, small passerine birds; also female)

Female names

Bewu   (buttonquail)
Muke   (Emerald ground-dove)
Peti   (see *ana peti*, small passerine birds; also male)
Piko   (Brown quail)

Place names

1   Ana Ha, (Little) Crow, a place in the district of 'Awe (Rawe).

2   Bo'a Manu, Chicken Village, a hamlet near the village of Wolo Bidi Au, inhabited by people of clan Mudi.

3   Deko Kata, Junglefowl Dale (*deko* = Bo'a Wae *dhegho*, 'dip, depression'), a location just north of the village of Wolo Wawo.

4   Gako, an area to the west of Bo'a Wae now largely converted to wet-rice cultivation. Possibly named after *gako tasi* (herons), many of which were once found in this region. Alternatively, the name may be connected with Bao Gako (*bao*, 'shade, shelter'), the name given to the decorated roof ridge of an ancestral house (or 'cult house', *sa'o waja*) belonging to the clan Tegu ('Thunder'), the largest landowner in the Gako region. The name also occurs in Gio Gako, a reference to Tegu territory mentioned in military diatribes (*kadha*).

5   Hobo Tute, Bushchat Valley, a low-lying area adjacent to Wolo Tute (see below).

6   Kuyu Kata, Junglefowl Pasture, a grassy area (*kuyu*, 'grass', 'pasturing area') in western Keo.

7   Lebi Wodo, Scrubfowl Slope (see Table 1.1, s.v. *koko wodo*), a former ritual site belonging to the clan Mude, now in Pago Nage but once resident in Bo'a Jigha and, before that, in Wai Keo. Lebi Wodo is located not far from the last village. Many scrubfowls are said once to have nested near the site, which may thus explain the name. Owing to their association with this place, people of clan Mude established in Pago Nage are distinguished from Mude elsewhere as 'Mude Wodo'; Nage therefore describe Mude Wodo as a 'clan' rather than a 'village' name. The name may also have been applied to that section of Bo'a Jigha occupied by clan Mude.

8   Leo Wea, (Golden) Oriole, a spot near the river Bhia, in the vicinity of the village of Ola Kile.

9   Lia Kolo, Dove Cavity, an uninhabited spot near Ola Ewa. (*Lia*, 'hole', denotes a natural cavity, vent, or passage.)

10   Lia Po, Owl Cavity, a place in the far eastern Nage district of Doa (Ndora).

11   Mala Kata, Junglefowl Plain, a flat area where the river Léle flows into the river Ae Sésa.

12   Mala Talo Kolo, a place in 'Awe, the name of which might literally be translated as 'plain where a dove failed, was unable (to do something)'. In this context, however, Kolo could be a personal name.

13   Mala Tute, Bushchat Plain (see Table 1.1, s.v. *tute péla*; see also Wolo Tute, below).

14   Manu Ko'a, Fowls Perch (more exactly '(place where) fowls alight, perch'), a location near wet-rice lands belonging to residents of Ola Kile.

15   Mata Koka, Friarbird Spring, a water source and site above the Nage village of Ola Ewa.

16   Nata Iki, Place of the Kestrel (*nata* denotes a flat area suitable as a settlement site), a former village occupied by the clan Kisa Ola. This appears to have been the name of the site before a village was built there.

17   'Owa (Rowa), Cuckoo-dove, a district in far western Nage, possibly also a former single village, named after the mythical association of an ancestor with a cuckoo-dove (*'owa*, locally *rowa*).

18   Sa Jata, Kite's Nest, a site of wet-rice fields near the river Bhia, in the vicinity of Ola Kile.

19   Toto, Coucal, now the name of a district, but apparently once the name of a single village. Whether the place so designated is named after a bird, however, is unconfirmed, as the name is susceptible to other interpretations.

20   Wolo Tute, Bushchat Hill, a hill several kilometres to the south of Bo'a Wae village.

Appendix 3:
Similes incorporating bird categories

All of the following terms appear in similes referring to humans. Typically, they occur in expressions describing a person as resembling or being like (*bhia, bhia ko'o*, or *bhia na'a*) the bird in question. The numbers correspond to those given in Table 1.1.

1   *ana go* (bushlark or pipit). Describes someone, especially a young child, with very thin, spindly legs; also used in banter among young adults. The usual expression is *kau taga bhia ko'o ana go*, 'you have legs like a bushlark'.

12   *ceka* (fantail). To have hair like the 'tail of a fantail' (*weo ceka*) refers to very curly or frizzy hair that tends to stick or spread out, and so is not easily secured in a knot or bun, nor easily combed.

18   *fega* (kingfisher). 'To have a mouth like the bill of a kingfisher' ((*wunu*) *mumu bhia ko'o fega*) refers to a person whose lips are stained with red spittle from betel and areca chewing, or more recently to women who wear red lipstick.

20   *gako tasi* (large heron). Someone who is exceptionally tall (*jaga léwa*); thus synonymous with *o ae* (see below).

26   *jata* (Brahminy kite). *Jata tei nu api*, 'kite (that) sees smoke from a fire' refers to someone who sees a chance of profit in a situation, and – somewhat like 'vultures' in the western metaphor – proceeds to exploit it. The simile alludes to the tendency of Brahminy kites and other raptors to gather in large numbers when forest is burnt, in anticipation of feasting on insects driven up by the flames and smoke.

28   *je* (unidentified raptor). The expression *je podi we'e*, '*je* (hawk-owl?) pretends to be close (or advances in pretence)', describes someone who becomes friendly with another in order to gain an advantage (see Chapter 7).

29   *kaka daza* (dollarbird). A person with a raucous laugh is described as sounding like a dollarbird, a bird with a harsh cry.

31 and 21   *kaka kea* and *ha*. *Kaka ha* (Cockatoo and crow; *kaka* abbreviates *kaka kea*, cockatoo). The standard compound can refer to people gathered in great numbers, but can also describe someone who behaves in a disorderly or mindless manner 'like an animal' (in which regard the combination is synonymous with *lako wawi*, 'dogs and pigs'). Possibly connected with this, *lea kaka ha*, 'to discard (things) like the cockatoo and crow' denotes wanton consumption, for example eating while idly discarding unwanted portions of food. Somewhat more positively, the expression further refers to conspicuous consumption, and to individuals or groups that are wealthy enough to engage in this – for example, by slaughtering large numbers of animals regardless of cost. All of these meanings draw on the phenomenon of cockatoos and crows descending, in large numbers, on fields of ripening maize and consuming maize kernels rapaciously, with many falling to the ground. Accordingly, the time of the year about late February or early March, when maize ripens, is called *wula kaka ha*, 'month of the cockatoo and crow'.

30 *kata* (junglefowl). 'Junglefowl who alights in undergrowth' (*kata ko'a koba*) refers to a vagrant or wanderer, someone not permanently present or resident in a particular place. Nage describe the junglefowl as always moving from place to place. One searches for the bird in a concealed spot only to find that it has already flown to another.

34 *koka* (friarbird). Describes someone who is simultaneously thin and loquacious. The usage draws on the idea that the friarbird, whose calls are loud and repetitive, owes its slender build to the energy it expends in continuous vocalization.

40 *kuku raku* (waterhen). Describes someone with long legs (and, perhaps, also large feet), thus largely synonymous with *gako tasi* and *o ae*.

55 *muta me* (Channel-billed cuckoo). A shiftless person who receives food from others. The simile draws on Nage representations of the parasitic habits of the Channel-billed cuckoo, which lays its eggs in crows' nests and whose young are thus fed by crows.

57 *o ae* (heron or egret). Someone who is exceptionally tall; synonymous with *gako tasi*.

61 *piko* (quail). Someone of short stature, more specifically described as *piko pada*, 'short, squat quail'.

68 *toto* (coucal). To be like 'a coucal with a rotten anus' (*toto (ta'a) 'obo mou*) describes a person who is, or claims to be, ill only at particular times, especially when there is work to be done. The usage is based on the idea that the coucal suffers an infestation of the anus during the wet season, but miraculously, as it were, always recovers during the dry season. The wet season is the part of the year when most agricultural labour is required.

72 *witu tui* (unidentified; perhaps the Great tit). A person who is unstable or restless and inconstant in his behaviour (see Chapter 7).

73 *wole wa* (a hovering raptor). To dance like a *wole wa* describes a method of dancing with the arms outstretched like a raptor while hovering.

79 *méte* (flying fox). Describes a youngster who eats continually and frequently vomits. The simile draws on the idea that flying foxes lack an anus and therefore cannot defecate, but instead expel food waste by vomiting. One man, who rejected this idea, claimed that 'to be like a flying fox' described a child that eats and defecates continually. Another man explained the phrase *bhia ta'i méte*, 'like bat shit', as a reference to something that is spilled or scattered on the ground. While he further described the phrase as curious in relation to the idea that bats do not defecate, it seems that *ta'i* may be understood here in the more general sense of 'waste'. The expression *ciku méte*, '(to have) the elbow of a flying fox', refers to a man who is sturdy and tough, especially in the context of pugilistic competitions (*etu*). Fine hair at the back of a person's neck, which is light or variable in colour, is called *fu méte*, 'flying fox hair'.

Notes

1 Introduction

1 In this regard, Hunn (1999: 48) even speaks of 'rigorous and systematic data collection and analysis' resulting in a 'substantial consensus among ethnobiologists'.

2 Hunn describes 'ecological salience' as 'reflecting the biogeographic and phenological interactions of a population of organisms to be classified and the human population classifying them' (Hunn 1999: 48). As it concerns the environments a human group characteristically enters, exploits, or is otherwise familiar with, ecological salience possesses an obvious 'cultural component' (ibid.). Nevertheless, Hunn treats ecological salience as a factor distinct from 'cultural salience'.

3 Some ethnobiologists appear to reduce cultural salience to virtually any sort of recognition of an animal or plant by a human population. In such a broad conception, Turner even describes 'culture significance' (or an organism's 'importance within' a culture) as being influenced by factors of 'perceptual salience' (two of which are 'size' and 'conspicuousness', 1988: 277). If this is accepted, then it hardly makes sense to debate whether culture or perception is more important in shaping folk classifications. On the other hand, such a linking of culture with perception does in a way accord with my analysis of Nage bird symbolism as firmly grounded in empirical, and then especially visual, features of the kinds in question.

4 A distinctive utilitarian value is exemplified by the Black-naped oriole (*leo*), killed for its bright yellow feathers. But while Nage classify the oriole with the Hill mynah as a member of an unnamed category of 'yellow birds' (Chapter 3), this association does not derive from this specific utility, since the mynah is not exploited for its feathers.

5 Also possible is a finer distinction involving 'folk varietals', but these are mostly found in the classification of plants rather than animals, and then largely with reference to domesticates. Since 'folk generics' often coincide with categories identified in scientific biology as 'species', Berlin has found it necessary to defend his use of 'generic' (1992: Ch. 2, especially pp. 74–75). I find his argument convincing, and therefore continue to employ '(folk) generic' throughout.

6 Referring to the larger part of Wallacea comprising Nusa Tenggara (that is, the modern Indonesian provinces of West Nusa Tenggara and East Nusa Tenggara, to which Flores belongs) and the islands of the Moluccas (or Maluku), Jepson describes this region as 'a major centre of global bird diversity', possessing 672 recorded species, including a total of 144 endemics (1997: 830).

7 I leave out of account Valeri's splendid monograph on the Huaulu of Seram (2000). While Valeri provides much insight into Huaulu animal classification and symbolism, focused on local concepts of 'taboo', his book does not comprise a systematic treatment of either ethnotaxonomy or local knowledge of zoological kinds.

8 *Modho piko kolo* instances a use of *piko kolo* ('quails (and) doves'), as a general reference to birds favoured as food. More specific terms include *modho bopo, modho kolo,*
   modho piko, modho kata, modho bewu, and *modho ana go.* Nage recognize that snares
   must be somewhat differently constructed to trap different kinds and sizes of birds.

9 Following the statements of several informants, I previously recorded the idea that
   the friarbird should not be killed or eaten because of its significance as a herald of
   the dawn (Forth 1992: 428). Further field material, however, suggests that the bird
   is not strictly prohibited. If it ever was in earlier days, then Nage certainly no longer
   observe such a prohibition.

10 Simply because they find them curious, and sometimes specifically in order to please
   young children, Nage will occasionally acquire, through capture or purchase, colourful
   birds such as pittas and kingfishers, which typically do not live long in captivity. When
   these die, the birds usually find their way directly to the pot. On a more general note,
   all this suggests that people can keep animals as 'pets' without the immediate development of a distinct ontological and moral category of 'pet' (cf. Leach 1964).

11 For the same reason, the birds have for a long time been scarce in many parts of
   eastern Indonesia (Jepson, in Monk *et al.* 1997: 830–32). After visiting Sumba in
   1925, K.W. Dammerman (1926: 24) could already report the local extinction of
   cockatoos in the vicinity of Waingapu, the main port town on Sumba's north coast.

12 The Chestnut-capped thrush is *Zoothera interpres.* A similar member of the same genus,
   Z. dohertyi, the Chestnut-backed thrush, also occurs on Flores, but I have no direct
   evidence of this bird being captured as well.

13 At present, Nage call the pitta *burung matahari,* 'sun bird', a national language term
   probably introduced by Bimanese. Verheijen (n.d.) gives *'oko* as the Bo'a Wae term
   for the pitta (cf. *woko* in Ngadha and some languages spoken to the east of Nage,
   including East Flores and Sika), but no one I questioned had ever heard of any such
   name. Interestingly, Verheijen provides no term for the pitta in any other Nage dialect
   either. A western Keo man identified a live specimen of *Pitta elegans* as *boko lowo,*
   a bird he described as crying 'ko wo, ko wo' or 'o wo, o wo'.

14 According to one man, although local people, notably inhabitants of the district of
   Mula Koli, have endeavoured to obtain nests from caves near the top of the volcano,
   none has so far been successful, even though swifts are numerous there.

15 Nage told me that, although the nests can fetch a high price, the supply in central
   Flores is so limited that visiting traders often do not find the business worthwhile.
   When Nage first became involved in the collection of nests is unclear: different accounts
   placed this in the 1960s and the late 1990s. According to one account, swift guano
   is also collected and sold, but I have been unable to verify this.

16 That the expression is of recent coinage is clear from the derivation of *mado* from
   Malay (or Bahasa Indonesia, the Indonesian national language) *mandor* (or *mandur,*
   'foreman'), a term denoting a native official of the colonial era.

17 This phrase does not definitely refer to anything different from 'middle cock crow'
   (*manu kako kisa*), an expression that may be applied in a general way to cocks crowing in the middle of the night, or the early hours of the morning. The tripartite series
   beginning with *manu kako sa pa'u,* however, evidently articulates the transition from
   night to daytime.

18 Some claim that it is specifically bats called *gébu* that steal juice from suspended
   containers, and that it is these, rather than *méte,* that are likely to fall in and drown.

19 According to one local report, the dollarbird is most vocal in the Nage region in the
   early part of the rainy season, about the time planting commences. But this seems to
   find no support in the ornithological literature, and other Nage contradicted it.

20 Scrubfowl (*koko wodo*) seem always to have been more common in parts of the Keo
   region, near the south coast, than in Bo'a Wae. However, in the western Keo village

of Guyu Wolo, I was told that the birds, once valued for their large eggs, had not been seen in the vicinity for over twenty years.

2 Ethno-ornithological classification: generic categories and ethnotaxonomy

1 The list of 61 was provided by a younger man who insisted on writing the names. Another literate informant also produced a written list of forty names. The largest number provided orally was 41. The mean total was 25.44, the median 26, and the mode 20.

2 The free recall procedure is also known as 'free listing'. As Weller and Romney note (1988: 16), the procedure 'provides a strong source of cognitive data in terms of frequencies and the order properties of the individual lists'.

3 The list of 79 names expands the list of 69 names (including three bat terms) published in Forth (1996a). The additional names include: *bi, deza kela, lako lizu, manu wodu, mata to,* and *sizo awu.* The expanded total, deriving from field research conducted in July and August 2001, however, has not significantly affected the analysis offered in Forth (1996a).

4 The Nuaulu figure should be seen in relation to the 195 species reported for Seram.

5 For the Jopu dialect of Lio, also to the east of Nage, Verheijen (n.d.) lists just 42 names for birds. In Arndt's Lio dictionary (1933), however, I have discovered at least 59, excluding synonyms and terms for bats.

6 Since Nage sometimes resort to the national language in referring to local birds, and probably do so most often when describing a bird to outsiders, it should also be noted that Bahasa Indonesia is of exceedingly limited value in obtaining identifications through translation of Nage categories. Not only are Nage usually unfamiliar with Indonesian names for particular bird kinds (and hence may employ them incorrectly), but a standard bird nomenclature is mostly lacking in the national language (but see MacKinnon 1991: x).

7 Conceptualization of basic (folk generic) categories in terms of simple distinctive features may be the empirical foundation of generalizations, such as that of Descola, who claims that 'animic systems' treat animals and plants 'as proper persons, as irreducible categories' (1992: 114). At the same time, this does not rule out their simultaneous functioning as 'privileged operators of taxonomic thought' (ibid.). In fact, I suggest that the two characteristics are connected.

8 An exception might be the Green imperial pigeon (*zawa*), a bird whose call and behaviour serve a chronological function (see Chapter 1).

9 Arguably, some non-empirical kinds could be included insofar as they too can be succinctly described in a way that suggests the simple distinctive features of empirical kinds. For example, the *manu ke'o* is represented as a creature with a snake's body and the head of a cock.

10 Apart from the cockatoo, the Bare-throated whistler, *kete dhéngi*, a rather plain bird that is rarely seen and whose appearance Nage are therefore usually unable to describe in detail, was nevertheless once characterized as having a beak somewhat like that of a parrot. Indeed, the bird's bill does have a slight crook at the tip.

11 Whether or not they distinguish a bird category relatively or absolutely, single distinctive features, considered as the principal members of short lists of empirical traits that serve to identify a bird and distinguish it from other birds, are comparable to the features, or 'field marks', employed in western ornithological 'field guides'. For any given species, these marks are also typically few in number, and they are designed to delimit, as far as possible, the range of species to which a bird observed in the field (that is, a single specimen) might belong.

12   Although most Nage regard *bopo* and *bopo soi* as synonymous labels for an undivided category, a few similarly interpret the terms as distinguishing a larger kind (also specified as *bopo méze*) from a smaller (and implicitly differently coloured) kind. A formally comparable interpretation of *bopo zawa* as a reference to the bird usually labelled simply as *zawa* is recorded in Table 1.1.

13   The recent introduction of the Rock pigeon explains the optional specification of *Streptopelia chinensis*, the kind simply called *kolo*, as *kolo méze*, 'big *kolo*', even though the pigeon, *kolo dasi*, is slightly larger.

14   These are *ana go, deza kela, je, lako lizu, manu ghebhe, piko du'a, sizo awu, witu tui* and *wole wa*. The figure errs on the side of caution. For example, the usual referent of *ana go* is one of two or three ornithological species. Also, *sizo awu* and *wole wa* both refer unequivocally to Falconiformes.

15   Two men from the Kebi region, to the west of Bo'a Wae, mentioned a category named *fega céhi*, with one contrasting this to two others called simply *fega* and *fega méze*, 'big kingfisher'. Although one man, apparently idiolectically, applied *fega céhi* to a live specimen of the Elegant pitta (*Pitta elegans*), the other man's description suggested the name might refer to the bee-eater (see *zeghi, jeghi*); but this could not be confirmed. In view of the close phylogenetic relation between kingfishers and bee-eaters, it is also interesting that Verheijen (n.d.) gives *teghi* (or in one instance *jeghi*) as the term for the Collared kingfisher in several Ngadha dialects.

16   Just three Nage listed large flying insects in free recall. One mentioned *naku ae*, 'dragonfly', another mentioned *poi*, a category of large grasshoppers and locusts which includes several named types, while a third mentioned *poi ce*, a particular instance of this category known mostly from its nocturnal sound.

17   On one occasion, the bird called *je*, probably the Brown hawk-owl, was classified as an *ana peti*.

18   In a British context, if one were to substitute 'wren' – another common, small bird – for 'robin', one could further cite the opposition, deriving from European folklore, of wren and eagle, especially as expressed in their contest over the status of 'king' of birds (see Lawrence 1997, who also discusses the association of English robin and the wren in traditional contexts).

19   *Manu ghebhe* appears to be an exception to this. Yet this category was known to just two informants, who could not moreover provide sufficient information to link it with any particular scientific species or genus. Also, others suggested that the term might be an alternative designation for the scrubfowl (*koko wodo*).

20   Some association of turtles and birds is suggested by the fantastic image Nage designate as *kepi* or *kepi kea*, a spiritually powerful being appearing in highland villages and assuming the form of a turtle or young hen (Forth 1998a: 141–42). But while this appears to confuse birds and reptiles, much in the same way as does the image of the *manu ke'o*, it does not specifically link turtles with cockatoos. An intriguing English parallel to the homonymy of Nage *kea* concerns the archaic use of 'turtle' both for the bird now called 'turtle dove' and for the marine reptiles. As the name of a bird, 'turtle' is onomatopoeic (*Shorter Oxford English Dictionary* [*SOED*]; cf. Nage *dhoro* in *kolo dhoro*, Spotted dove, a species very similar to the European turtle dove). In reference to the reptile, on the other hand, *turtle* may derive from *turckle*, a native Bermudan name (*SOED*), though the dictionary also relates the word to French *tortue*. Also worth mentioning in this context are 'Greenland turtle' and 'Sea turtle', seventeenth-century terms for the Black guillemot (a seabird belonging to the Alcidae).

21   That the mole cricket is called a 'dog' probably refers to its habit of digging in the ground, from which the insect gets its English name. In Indonesian (Bahasa Indonesia), the insect is similarly, and presumably for the same reason, named *anjing tanah*, 'earth dog'. 'Sky' in the Nage name most likely refers to the insect's ability to fly.

22 According to Verheijen (n.d., 1963), the Black-naped monarch is named in So'a, to the north-west of Nage, where it is called *si rére* or *ana mae*, and also in Manggarai.

23 The moorhen seems usually to be identified as *wi* (see Table 1.1), although some Nage recognize it to be different from other birds labelled *wi*.

24 Just as this book was going to press, there appeared a paper by Fleck *et al.* (2002) demonstrating convincingly how the Matses Indians of Peru recognize numerous covert, or 'sublexemic', categories of bats. While the authors do not speak of 'covert generics', but refer mostly to unnamed 'kinds' and 'species', it is nevertheless clear that the morphological and behavioural distinctions recognized by Matses are of the sort that generally define folk generics. Also relevant to the present discussion is the authors' consideration of the scant attention so far paid by ethnobiologists to unnamed categories at this level, as opposed to more inclusive levels, and the importance of language study, including grammatical analysis, in discovering covert generics.

25 Although some people know the name from association with south-western Nage, *mapa bewa* should probably not be regarded as a Bo'a Wae bird term. At the same time, the name is also known as that of a mimic bird in Wudu, just to the east of Bo'a Wae, and in western Keo. Verheijen (n.d.), who provides no name for the Bare-throated whistler in any Nage dialect, does not record the term *kete dhéngi*. He gives *mapa bewa* only for the western Keo district of Sawu, as the name of the Collared kingfisher, but this is surely incorrect.

3 Intermediate categories, binary associations, and nomenclature

1 In making this computation I count only four birds as *ana peti*: *ana peti jata, bio, cici ko'i,* and *naka bo*. If *ana peti* were to be regarded as a much more inclusive, though less clearly defined, intermediate group of 'small birds', or 'dicky-birds', then the figure would come to well over 50 per cent.

2 The separation of water birds into pairs was suggested by one man who grouped bird terms into several categories labelled with Indonesian national language terms. These included a group called 'herons' (Bahasa Indonesia *bangau*) and a separate category of 'wild ducks' (*belibis*; cf. Nage *bébe ae*) which, the informant claimed, contained two unnamed varieties.

3 It is not always clear, moreover, that when Nage speak of *méte* they do not sometimes also, implicitly, include *gébu*. In that case, *méte* might be construed as a polysemous term admitting a specific and a general sense and then one more general still, insofar as the term may, contextually, also subsume *'ighu*. Consistent with this interpretation, Nage tend to describe *gébu* as differing from *méte* only in regard to smaller size. Also, characters they attribute to *méte* will be found, upon questioning, to apply as well to *gébu*, most notably the notional lack of an anus (see Table 2.1 and Chapter 7).

4 Figures for other Falconiformes were *sizo* (15), *bele teka* (12), *wole wa* (four), and *jata jawa* and *sizo awu* (one each).

5 It is not clear how *sizo awu* may fit into this tripartite series, although implicitly it is subsumed, as a folk-specific, by *sizo*. In fact, I only encountered the term *sizo awu* late in my research, and after I had recorded this idea.

6 This is not to say that only members of clearly defined intermediate categories are central to the life-form. Some other well-known and frequently mentioned birds, however, such as the friarbird (*koka*) and cockatoo (*kea*), arguably do not form part of intermediate groupings owing to their manifest singularity.

7 Although his formulation was perfectly idiosyncratic, one man went so far as to describe the birds as two kinds of *leo*, specifying the oriole as *leo te'a*, and the Hill mynah, simply, as *leo*.

8 The association of the oriole and mynah appears to find support in free recall, where their names were listed in succession in seven of the 16 instances when both were mentioned. Although the evidence is less supportive with regard to the drongo and the paradise-flycatcher, which were mentioned together just five out of 18 times, nevertheless Nage frequently compare the two in respect of their remarkable tails when talking about birds. In the Ngadha dialect of Wogo, the oriole and the drongo, named respectively as *sésé lézo* and *sésé jié*, are apparently associated by virtue of a common nominal element (Verheijen n.d.), one moreover that appears to be cognate with the Nage name of the drongo.

9 I also encountered the idea that, further constituting a common kind with the two rails, was the less common and less well known sort named *mata to*. Here, as elsewhere, one may be dealing with a nascent intermediate.

10 Ellen (1993a: 56–58) discusses this sort of compounding under the heading of 'juxtaposed uninomials'. He correctly characterizes such binary formation as a general feature of Austronesian languages.

11 Nowadays, Nage often substitute Indonesian (Bahasa Indonesia) *biasa*, 'common, ordinary, usual', for *bholo*. Whereas *biasa* therefore specifies the otherwise unmarked member of a pair, however, I twice recorded *kolo dasi* referred to as *kolo biasa*, or 'common pigeons', and once as *kolo méze*, 'big *kolo*'. This may suggest, then, that the domestic pigeon is taking over from the Spotted dove (*Streptopelia chinensis*) as the lexically unmarked, and indeed focal, instance of *kolo*. As regards the modifier *bholo*, it should be noted that in the expression *ana peti bholo*, referring to small, passerine birds that are not specially named (see Chapter 2), *bholo* identifies a residual category rather than otherwise unmodified prototype.

12 In regard to vocalic variation, see also *ceghi*, *jehi*, and *jéhi*, alternative pronunciations for the onomatopoeic name of the bee-eater, more often pronounced *zeghi* or *jeghi*).

13 For the same reason, I do not count *o ae* as a binomial. The Ngadha and Manggarai cognates *oro* and *orong* suggest that *o* derives from a more complex protoform by way of a general loss of /r/ in Bo'a Wae, as in most Nage dialects. At some point, therefore, *ae* ('water') was most likely added to disambiguate the name.

14 Examples include *ana fe*, 'tadpole'; *ana gu*, 'house lizard' (*Hemidactylus frenatus*); and *ana bo* and *ana tebhu*, two kinds of freshwater fish.

15 I have only one record of Nage, employing Bahasa Indonesia, describing physically similar birds being 'descendants' (*turunan*) of the same ancestors. This concerned the Large-billed crow and Flores crow which, as noted earlier, are generally spoken of as being closely related, or as members of a single kind. Nage also describe the Channel-billed cuckoo (*muta me*) as *ana ko ha*, 'child of the Large-billed crow', but this reflects an imperfect knowledge of the cuckoo's status as a brood parasite of crows (see Chapter 7).

16 Whether or not *bébe ae* ('water *bébe*', wild duck) follows this pattern is equivocal. Although *bébe* is nowadays employed alone for recently introduced domestic varieties, Nage explained this usage as reflecting the influence of Indonesian *bébék* ('duck'), which became widely known about the same time as the introduction of the domesticated bird.

17 According to Verheijen (1963: 696), *léros*, a cognate name for the oriole in some dialects of Manggarai, also means 'yellow'. Comparative evidence, however, suggests that, as a colour term, the word is derived from the bird name. Also relevant here is the Nage use of *leo* as a qualifier in the names of other creatures with mixed yellow and black colouring, similar to the plumage of the Black-naped oriole. Instances include

goka leo, the Timor python (*Python timoriensis*, Forth 1995: 52), and *ika leo* (or *ika léro*), a freshwater fish.

18 The fact that 22 and 36 total 58 rather than 57 is accounted for by *ie wea*. Since the first component is onomatopoeic and the second describes a visible feature, the term is counted twice.

4 Things that go *po* in the night: ethnotaxonomy and symbolic classification

1 Unprompted mentions of *po*, either by itself or in a binomial, occurred in ten of 24 recall lists.

2 Except when informants were prompted with a question asking for the names of night birds, *po* was often mentioned alone in free recall; that is, not in a series with the names of other birds. When the term was listed with others, it was either named with *je*, a term many Nage understand as a reference to another Strigiforme, or, in three cases, with a diurnal bird of prey (*iki* or *jata*). When given in response to a prompt, *po* was only ever mentioned with other night birds (including *je*), and (as one should expect) never with diurnal raptors.

3 Only one Nage man ever spoke of the three terms as referring to bird 'kinds' (Indonesian/Bahasa Indonesia *jenis*). This was the educated informant referred to in the previous chapter who, unlike his contemporaries, spontaneously classified a variety of birds into several generic categories employing national language terms such as *elang* (hawk) and *burung hantu* (owl).

4 Things may be different in other parts of central Flores. In the Keo region, to the south of Nage, *po pate* refers to a bird of prey that swoops down on domestic fowls and severs (*pate*) their heads with its sharp wing. Although the description is reminiscent of falcons that Nage designate as *bele teka* (see Table 1.1), the characteristic decapitation in this case is said always to be performed at night, and some Keo seemed sure the bird was an owl, not a Falconiforme. In fact, the described behaviour recalls that attributed to the *je* (see Chapter 7), a bird term not known in Keo. For what it may be worth, Arndt (whose ornithological identifications leave a great deal to be desired) records a Lio expression, *po pate manu*, which he glosses as 'the owl bites the fowl (*manu*) to death' (1933: 379). In Lio, as well as in Nage and Keo, *pate* means to 'cut off' and *po* means 'owl'. No one I questioned in Bo'a Wae, however, had ever heard of the term *po pate*.

5 Although *je* appears to be a relatively well-known bird term, only five of 24 informants recalled the name without prompting. Others only mentioned *je* in response to a prompt specifying 'night birds'; but in all instances the term was listed in close proximity to *po*. It is also worth noting that the name resembles those of several diurnal raptors, in referring to a behavioural attribute, rather than the bird's vocalization, as does the onomatopoeic *po*.

6 As discussed elsewhere (Forth 1995), Nage *bhia ko'o*, 'kind of', '(to possess the) form of', can express both class inclusion and resemblance. Yet to describe a daytime raptor as *bhia ko'o po* could, I was assured, only mean that the bird resembled an owl, either physically or vocally.

7 In free recall only one informant gave one of the sound terms – *po bapu* – as the name of a bird. This, moreover, he speculatively identified with the *je*, or Hawk-owl. Given that sounds classified as *po* are probably made exclusively by owls, including indeed the Hawk-owl, it is not impossible that, through observation, individual Nage have come to link particular sound categories with particular species of Strigiformes. This, however, is contrary to the general pattern, whereby all *po* sounds are attributed to all (or nearly all) raptorial birds. It is also contradicted by the doubts of some

informants about the ability of the *je* to produce any such sound. One usually knowledgeable informant furthermore claimed that the *je* was mute (*mona sezu*).

8 Nage associate *po polo* with such a variety of auditory phenomena that it is not possible to link the category definitively with particular species. Vocalizations of two species of *Otus* (Coates and Bishop 1997: 360–61), however, are probably the most usual referents, especially insofar as these consist of a series of repeated calls. One vocalization described for the Eastern grass owl (*Tyto longimembris*), one of the Tytonidae (or barn owls), is another possibility.

9 The 'puff' ascribed to the buffalo horn *po* would appear to correspond to what one man, perhaps idiosyncratically, called *po befu*. This however he attributed to *po polo*, in contrast to the 'strong voice' that identifies *po bapu*. As this may suggest, some of these distinctions are contextually variable in their applications.

10 An association of owls with wild pigs in particular is also encountered in western Flores (Manggarai; Verheijen 1950: 67) and eastern Sumba (Onvlee 1984: 196 s.v. *katua*, *katua wei*).

11 Another possible empirical referent of *uci* is 'a plaintive, rather weak, whistled two note *wheep wheep*' attributed by Coates and Bishop (1997: 247) to the crepuscular Black-winged kite (*Elanus caeruleus*).

12 As a parallelism, *po uci* is further elaborated by interposition to become *po ko, uci meci*. Although apparently more characteristic of other dialects, *po ko* was equated by western Keo informants with *po keo* (an identification which suggests that this term too might be construed parallelistically). Similarly, Nage described *ko* as a variant of *keo*, or as an alternative cry of the bird that also calls *keo*. On the other hand, *meci*, the paired term of *uci* in the more elaborate expression, denotes a nocturnal – and ventriloquistic – sound attributed to a cricket named by the same term. With regard to regional variations, it should also be noted that an informant from north-eastern Nage stated that *po kusi* (= western Nage *po uci*) and *po ko* could be distinguished as auditory manifestations of the anger of ancestors and of witches respectively. This distinction introduces a contrast not found among ideas regarding *po* in western Nage, where the category is not linked with ancestral spirits or the dead. A Keo informant claimed that *ko* denoted an owl smaller than owls named *po* but possessing larger eyes. The same man, however, later described *po*, *ko* and *uci* as references only of different sounds produced by the same birds.

13 Mention of the air rifle in the young man's account suggests that this and perhaps other items of modern technology may allow Nage greater access to the physical form of owls than previously, and thus facilitate a recognition of morphological distinctions tending to contradict the general notion that all birds belonging to the ethnotaxon *po* are of a single kind. In Keo, the term *kero keko*, given as the name of a bird, was later explained as referring more specifically to a vocalization of owls called *po uci*. As *kero keko* indicates the presence of wild pigs, it would seem to be identical to what Nage call *po keo*.

14 This implicit equation of *po lobo* and *po bapu* was confirmed in 2001, when a Nage man defined the latter as 'coming from (the top of) the volcano' (*pu'u ze lobo*).

15 Once I recorded the idea that the kestrel's cry, heard at night, indicates an impending death. This, however, may be attributed to the abnormal nocturnal occurrence of the sound; also it is not clear that the bird, in this context, is considered to manifest a spiritual being.

16 While Feld's analysis of Kaluli knowledge of birds is illuminating in regard to some Nage conceptions of *po*, on the whole he appears to consider visible birds as manifestations of spiritually derived sounds in all epistemological contexts. In contrast, as I have copiously shown in previous chapters, the Nage evidence suggests the existence of a distinct ethno-ornithological domain in which spiritual associations and auditory capabilities are mostly irrelevant.

17 In standard Indonesian (Bahasa Indonesia), by contrast, both *burung suangi* and the synonymous *burung hantu* ('spirit bird') refer specifically to owls. The association of owls with witches and spirits is of course extremely widespread. In European traditions, the connection is reflected, for example, by Latin morphemes from which are derived the scientific names 'Strigidae' and 'Strigiforme'. See e.g. *striga*, 'an evil spirit supposed to howl in the night' (Glares 1982: 1828), 'a woman that brings harm to children, a hag, a witch' (Andrews 1907: 1766), and *strix*, 'a kind of owl, regarded as a bird of ill omen, sometimes as a vampire or evil spirit' (Glares 1982: 1829).

18 A similar interpretation may apply to *keo*. Although I have no record of comparable senses in Nage, included among meanings of the cognate employed by the neighbouring Ngadha are 'to cut off, through' and 'to determine (fate), prophesy, preordain' (Arndt 1961: 238 s.v. *kéco*).

19 In my earlier article on which this chapter is based (Forth 1998b: 204), I remarked that 'as ominous manifestations of spiritual malevolence evoking ritual or other responses that in a general sense can be called practical, the class of *po* sounds and the entities with which they are associated are culturally quite specific, and are arguably bound up with kinds of utilitarian considerations such as avoidance of illness and other misfortune'. I would not now withdraw this observation. However, in order to avoid the imputation of any general equation of 'symbolic' and 'utilitarian' categories, I would qualify my remarks by characterizing *po*-sounding things, as a symbolic class, as simultaneously composing a sort of quasi-utilitarian category. With fully utilitarian categories (such as those comprising avian crop pests), Nage regularly respond in predictable ways, whereas, as indicated above, only in special circumstances do Nage interpret *po* sounds as omens and therefore take action to counteract their maleficent import.

20 I am thinking, for example, of the application of 'cuckoo', originally the name of the European cuckoo (*Cuculus canorus*), to a whole scientific family of birds, by no means all of which produce the sound reproduced by 'cuckoo'.

21 In support of possible connections between taxonomy and visually based literate culture, Ong (1977: 139) points out that English 'species' derives from Latin *specio*, meaning 'to look at, behold'. Contrary to Ong, however, the evidence of the present volume suggests that taxonomic ordering of natural kinds may be based primarily on visual criteria in oral cultures as well.

5 Spiritual birds

1 The use of 'soul' has been subject to continuing criticism in Anglophone anthropology, as has the concept of 'spirit(s)' (see e.g., Valeri 2000: 23–30). I use 'soul' as a convenient gloss of Nage *mae*, a concept I describe at length in my book *Beneath the Volcano* (Forth 1998a). As I demonstrate there, Nage *mae* is not identical, for example, to the Christian concept of 'soul', even though it resembles the latter in several important ways. But then one would be surprised if anthropological readers expected it to be. As a reference to the Nage category, 'soul' is just as good as other English terms, and better than some. 'Spirit' is similarly defensible and, by now, so well established that little is to be gained by replacing it with other terms, such as 'occult power' (see Valeri 2000: 25).

2 Insofar as 'witch birds', a gloss of an Indonesian term, nowadays labels a Nage category, the term might be understood as a synecdoche. For, with the possible exception of the *manu miu*, described on pp. 83–84, there appears to be no sort of empirical bird that Nage conceive of exclusively as a manifestation of a witch and of no other variety of spiritual being.

3 Verheijen (n.d.) gives the name of the drongo in So'a as *ra sie*. Since *ra* is 'blood' in several other languages and dialects of central Flores (including Ngadha, Lio, and some Nage dialects; cf. Bo'a Wae *'a*), the name may thus link the bird with blood. The meaning of *sie* is less clear. In western Keo, the name of the Large-billed crow is *ya* (see p. 82 regarding Nage *ha*), a term that also means 'blood'. However, this may be simply ascribed to homonymy, deriving from the fact that /y/ in this dialect is elsewhere reflected both as /r/ and /h/.

4 Another possible identification is the Common koel (*Eudynamys scolopacea*), a large cuckoo and a brood parasite of the Flores crow and the Large-billed crow. Named onomatopoeically as *toe ou*, the male koel is all black. Vocalizations recorded by Coates and Bishop (1997: 352–53) possibly correspond to the sound replicated by Nage as *koa ka*, as does the fact that the koel sometimes calls at night – according to both Nage and western ornithologists (Forth 1998b: 192). Various sorts of evidence suggest that, like the Flores crow in Nage, the koel is associated with witches in several parts of Flores, including Ngadha (Arndt 1931: 723), Lio (Verheijen n.d.), and East Flores (Arndt 1951: 133), as well as in Kédang (Barnes 1974: 211; pers. comm. 2001) and eastern Sumba (Forth 2000: 175, s.v. *kuu*; 183). Nevertheless, people I questioned in Bo'a Wae denied that the *toe ou* was a witch bird. That they do not conceive of the bird in this way may be connected with the significance of koel vocalizations as a chronological sign and agricultural aid, a value the bird shares with the Channel-billed cuckoo (*muta me*), another species classified as a crow-like bird (Chapter 3) which Nage also do not identify as a witch.

5 This then distinguishes *manu miu* from *po*, in the sense of sounds associated with both owls and diurnal raptors. Also, while *manu miu* is partly identified with kites and eagles, I never heard owls (*po*) described as a source of the sound.

6 For example, descendants of 'Oga Ngole (1860?–1928) related how the famous Nage leader once soaked himself in a particular pool as part of a cure for a skin disease (apparently smallpox). As he did so, 'thousands' of Brahminy kites – specified on this occasion as *ulu bha* ('white heads') – assembled in nearby trees. The birds were witnessed by 'Oga Ngole's sister, who was visiting him at the time. As to the possible significance of this reputed event, I was told only that it was probably a sign of 'divine power' (Indonesian *kesaktian*).

7 Towards the end of this text Arndt (1960: 124) adds that Kua is the same being to whom offerings are made when, about midday, he appears in the form of 'an eagle or a falcon' above a palm-tapping site. This brief remark recalls not only the Nage representation described just above, but also their general belief that free spirits of all sorts are especially active about midday. The noontide further appears as a particularly inauspicious time in ideas concerning the cuckoo-shrike (*cio woza*), described on pp. 86–87.

8 Also redolent of the European basilisk, comparable figures are found throughout Indonesia – including Manggarai (Verheijen 1963: 694, s.v. *manu nggé*), Sika (where the creature is called *naga*; see Arndt, 1932: 153, 318), and Sumba (where it is called *ularu ningu landu*, 'crested serpent') – as well as in mainland Southeast Asia (Forth 1998a: 88–98). An early account of a Sulawesi variant is found in the seventeenth-century writings of Rumphius (1981: 74–75, 81, 129).

9 The cry of the cuckoo-shrike is also regarded as a portent of death among the Sikanese of eastern Flores (Arndt 1932: 319, s.v. *wora*; cf. *sia wora*, Verheijen n.d.). A representation of birds' carrying away the soul of a dead person appears to be more developed among the Atoni of Timor, who also speak of a 'bird soul' (*sman kolo*), or an aspect of the soul that may take the form of a bird in order to escape the body (Schulte Nordholt 1971: 150).

10 In his unpublished comparative lists for Flores, Verheijen (n.d.) does not give *manu mesi* as a Bo'a Wae term. However, he lists it as the name for several large water birds in other Nage dialects and in the Wolo Topo dialect of Lio. In western Keo, the same term refers to sandpipers.

11 Originally, I recorded the second phrase as *polo kasi weki*, where the first term is *polo*, 'witch' (Forth 1996a: 91, note 2). Although this now appears to be wrong, I am not entirely sure that some Nage do not understand the expression as alluding to witches and their reputed common role in human death.

12 In a similar vein, two parties (for example, two sections of a clan) which derive from the same ancestor (or ancestral couple) are described as having 'a dark hen as mother, a red cock as father' (*ine susu mite, ame lalu to*). Here, *susu* and *lalu* abbreviate *manu susu* and *manu lalu*, denoting respectively females and males of the domestic fowl. The colour terms *mite* (dark, black) and *to* (red) connote great age.

13 The fact that there were two birds is not problematic. Like many people, Nage believe that dead souls are collected and accompanied to the afterworld by souls of earlier deceased relatives. Also, one commentator stated that there was just one dove.

14 Carvings of cocks and hens are also found on some forked posts in western Keo, as well as in the centre of a thick plank that lines the front of a Nage cult house (*sa'o waja*). In the latter case, Nage link these figures with the agricultural ritual *pete wole*, described in Chapter 1 (also see Plate 1.1).

15 This is slightly less than the figure of 'between 28 and 32 per cent' reported in Forth (1996a: 103), based on a smaller sample of 69 names.

16 The former three are *kuku raku* (White-breasted waterhen), *toe ou* (Common koel), and *koka* (friarbird), a bird whose cries are also interpreted as omens. The latter two are *lako lizu* (the waterhen or Night heron) and *muta me* (Channel-billed cuckoo), the names of which are analysed in Table 1.1. Chronologically significant birds whose names do not refer to a vocalization are the Green imperial pigeon (*zawa*) and swifts and swallows, designated as *ebu titu*, or less often as *awe uza*, 'rain summoner'. The onomatopoeically named fantail (*ceka*) is associated with the noontide, at least in poetic idioms, yet seems not to be a true chronological sign.

  Although the nocturnal cry of the 'sky dog' (*lako lizu*) is entirely positive for Nage, and while the bird is not identified with any sort of spirit, there is nevertheless an interesting comparison with the 'Gabriel's hounds' of European tradition, if only in the identification in both cases of nocturnal avian vocalizations with dogs. The European representation has variously been ascribed to the nocturnal cries of wild geese and curlews (Swann 1913: 91; Armstrong 1970: 219).

17 One man claimed that the bee-eater (*zeghi*) was a negative hunting omen analogous to the nightjar and Pied bushchat (see Chapter 6). Not least because no one else was familiar with this idea, however, the notion is almost certainly idiosyncratic. As noted in Chapter 4 (note 15), the nocturnal cry of the kestrel (*iki*) was described by one informant as a death omen. Whatever the status of this idea, it seems significant that the one Falconiforme that is named onomatopoeically (after a cry described as a high-pitched 'ki ki ki') is the only one whose own, individual voice may be conceived as ominous.

18 It is also conceivable that the spiritual or augural significance of a few birds may derive from the meaning of words taken to resemble their cries. One example is *kela*, the call of the Flores crow (*héga hea*), which can also mean 'to look at, inspect' and 'to chop, cut (e.g., wood)'. In the second significance, informants compared the word to *wela* and *wéla*, terms that denote slaughtering pigs and buffalo, by incising the head and throat respectively. The phrase *wéla ata*, similarly, refers to killing, or hacking to death, a human with a parang. Comparable possibilities relating to *po* and *keo* (see *po keo*) were recorded in Chapter 4.

6 Birds as omens and taboo

1 'Non-spiritual' omen creatures that are not birds are noticeably less numerous. One example is the gecko (*teke*): whether the creature calls an odd or even number of times indicates wet or dry weather, and hence, towards the end of the dry season, the time when people should prepare to plant. Also, the sound of a small house lizard (*ana gu*) – a 'chirping noise' not unlike that of a bird – can contextually be interpreted as a sign of approval (for example, when a decision is taken), much as can the crowing of a cock, as I describe below. A corollary is that, where animals other than birds are ominous, they are almost always associated with some sort of spiritual being, most often a witch. In fact, this may apply in the aforementioned case of the house lizard. Heard inside a house, the sound of an unidentified creature, possibly an insect, onomatopoeically designated as *ti ti*, is regarded as manifesting a deceased soul in the same way as is the bird named *deza kela* (see p. 87).

2 Noteworthy here is Coates and Bishop's characterization of the Russet-capped tesia as 'strongly territorial and vocal'. They further describe the bird's habit of singing from low perches and scolding people who come near, and its 'curious sideways movement along branches in the undergrowth when disturbed' (1997: 431).

3 Not only is the *manu ke'o*, another spirit manifestation, also encountered most often about midday, but it is similarly ambiguous as it can confer benefits on particular favoured people while proving harmful to others (Forth 1998a: 89).

4 According to another version, the bird cried out *ta kéna de, ta kéna de* 'that's the one, that's the one'. In yet another account, the call was reproduced as *ta bu'e, ta bu'e*, 'the mistress, the mistress'.

5 The equivalence of the domestic fowl and the friarbird is further suggested cross-culturally, in the creation mythology of the Donggo of Sumbawa (Arndt 1952: 483–84). In Donggo tradition, the continuous crowing of a cock gradually transforms an originally dark world into one in which day and night alternate, just as, in Nage mythology, the victory of the friarbird over the Imperial pigeon results in a world in which night and day rapidly succeed one another.

6 These ideas may be related to the bird's name. As noted, *péla* can mean 'to cut in, interrupt', as for example young children are wont to do while adults are speaking. Other senses are listed in Table 1.1.

7 I have sometimes wondered whether *piko du'a* might not in fact refer to the nightjar, partly because local descriptions of the call resemble those of this nocturnal bird, and partly in view of the identical Sumbanese representation of a bird they call *landu witu*, an apparent reference to the nightjar, as signalling the presence of nocturnal thieves (Forth 2000: 176). Nage I questioned, however, denied this identification. As mentioned in Chapter 4, a sound classified as *po*, repeated eight times, can indicate an imminent theft, but there is nothing to suggest that *piko du'a* refers to an owl.

8 *Pie* possesses two other, partly distinct senses. When applied to places or objects, the term can mean 'restricted'; that is, not to be used in particular ways (as when it is forbidden to cultivate an area of land) or by particular categories of people (most notably, women and wife-takers, *ana weta*). In addition, *pie* is applied to individual food avoidances, as when it is said of a person who is averse to eating dog (*lako*) – a meat relished by most Nage – *imu pie lako*, 'he (*imu*) regards dog (*lako*) as *pie*'. Interestingly, in this case the food is neither strictly speaking 'taboo', nor is it considered particularly dangerous. As people with such avoidances pointed out to me, to eat the food in question would not cause them any real harm; rather, they would simply find it – or more particularly the 'smell' of the flesh – unpleasant or disagreeable.

9 By contrast to recent practice, Nage claim that before the colonial period – and particularly before they saw Japanese troops doing so – they never ate snakes. Yet they are quite sure that snake meat has never been *pie*. One man argued that eating

snake is not *pie* because doing so incurs no ill consequence. Another man, however, pointed out, correctly, that this also applies to other acts or behaviours which are equally categorized as *pie*, including individual food avoidances.

10 A couple of informants equivocated about the possibility of eating *héga hea* and *koa ka*. But this may reflect no more than the fact that, whereas Large-billed crows and drongos are common birds, the first bird is rare while the second, a bird that Nage often claim never to have seen, may be the same species as the first. As noted, another category of 'witch bird', the *manu miu*, appears to be imaginary. Although some Nage consider the Pale-headed munia (*ana peti jata*) a *po*-sounder, and to that extent a manifestation of a witch, I never heard that the flesh of this tiny bird was taboo. I also never thought to ask.

11 A cognate idea is that the process of becoming a witch can involve surviving serious illness that kills other, 'normal' people (Forth 1993a: 111).

12 Unfortunately, although my informant, a woman, was one of my best sources of information on all aspects of Nage birds, I never had the opportunity to investigate how general the characterization of the *witu tui* as *pie* might be. Responding to my question, she stated that it was the action of the bird stealing hair that was *pie*, not the human act of carelessly discarding hair clippings, which is merely ill-advised.

13 According to Nage, the Blue-breasted quail (*mu ki*) and buttonquails (*bewu*) – thus other members of the intermediate category of which *piko* appears to be focal (Chapter 3) – do not flock, occurring either singly or in pairs. This difference is also recognized by western ornithologists (Coates and Bishop 1997).

14 At the same time, the situational appearance of a single quail inside a village can evidently be considered ominous. Thus, I was told how, on the day a certain man was buried, a *piko* was seen to alight on the ridge of his house. This caused considerable consternation, in which respect my informant remarked how quails were believed to come to rest only on the ground (see Chapter 7). After this, each year someone of that house passed away, until all male members had died heirless and the group became extinct. As I describe presently, such extinction is also thought to follow an *'ighu* bat alighting inside a house.

15 In the last few years, small flocks of Tree sparrows (*Passer montanus*) have begun to appear in Nage villages. These birds, however, are of very recent occurrence on Flores (see Table 1.1) and even now, in the Bo'a Wae region, seem to prefer larger, more modern buildings and other sites outside of traditional villages.

16 It may initially seem curious that the Nage representation of junglefowl as the domestic fowl of *nitu* spirits (Forth 1998a: 70) appears not to be reflected in ideas concerning *pie* birds. This circumstance is however illuminated by the fact that various wild mammals, including the most prized of game animals, deer and wild swine, are identically regarded as domesticates of the spirits.

17 Comparative ethnography however reveals a class of taboos where harm befalls not the transgressive actor (in this case comparable to the quails) but the person acted upon. An eastern Indonesian example is found in the Sumbanese idea according to which the public use of any name pertaining to the nobility would cause them illness or death (Kapita 1976: 43).

18 Arndt (1954: 444) states that Ngadha witches can cause a bat (*Fledermaus*) to enter a house, thus possibly forcing the inhabitants to abandon the dwelling. They can employ a poisonous snake or a dung beetle in the same way.

19 For example, one should not step over or strike a hunting dog. Dogs, but also other animals (including domestic fowls), should never be allowed to traverse a corpse (*meo lako laga tebo pie méze*), since it might then come back to life.

20 The significance of particular cries of the friarbird (*koka*) might appear to contradict this characterization. However, within the ritual frame which alone confers augural

value on the voice of the friarbird, the bird's cries, which are taken to imitate a word or phrase, are described as always significant – something which cannot be said, for example, of sounds Nage classify as *po*. Moreover, as already noted, if not an embodiment of a spirit, the friarbird is nevertheless represented as a culture hero.

7 Hibernating swallows, kite stones, and the legless nightjar: some curiosities of Nage bird knowledge

1 It will become clearer that the sort of enquiry I pursue here owes a lot to the ethnozoology of Ralph Bulmer, particularly his article entitled 'Worms that croak and other mysteries of Karam natural history' (1968).

2 Bulmer (1968: 637) notes the similar Karam idea that certain migratory birds, notably the bee-eater (*Merops ornatus*), nest on a high mountain, which accounts for their absence for part of the year. The American folklorist, Ernest Ingersoll (1923), devotes a whole chapter to 'The folklore of bird migration'. Noting for example the belief that certain birds, including swallows and swifts, 'hibernated in hollow trees, caverns, or even buried themselves in the mud at the bottom of ponds', he shows how a faulty or imperfect understanding of migration is a widespread feature of folk ornithology.

3 In many parts of eastern Indonesia, an association of swifts and swallows with bats (some of which, of course, also roost in caves) is indirectly reflected in nomenclature. In western Keo, the tiny bat that Nage designate as *'ighu* is called *titu yiyu*, and in Dhawe, in north-eastern Nage, *ana titu*. In addition, cognates of Indonesian (Bahasa Indonesia) *kelawar*, 'bat', are applied to swallows or swifts in some Flores languages. For example, Manggarai *lawar* or *kaka-lawar* denotes the Apodidae and Hirundinidae in general (Verheijen 1963), while *bléku-bléwar* and variants similarly denote swallows (*Hirundo* spp.) or swifts of the genus *Collocalia* in dialects of Sika and East Flores (Verheijen n.d.).

4 A similar European idea concerns hawkweed, a plant reputedly consumed by hawks to maintain their exceptional eyesight (Brown 1936: 72–73). Pollard (1977: 23, 132, 134) attributes the Greek representation of the eagle stone specifically to the poet Dionysius. According to the latter, such a stone, attached to the abdomen of a pregnant woman, would prevent abortion; it could also cool boiling water. In regard to the Moluccan 'eagle stones' described by Rumphius, Beekman (in Rumphius [1705] 1999: 530; notes 1, 2 to Ch. 60) cites the Roman naturalist Pliny.

5 Dismissing the representation, one man maintained that the term 'kite's claw grindstones' simply referred to old stones which, through continual use, have become as small as a raptor's talon. A parallel here may be *ko kanga jata*, 'kite's claw pepper', a small chilli which in English is almost identically designated as 'hawk's claw pepper'. Although this would seem to be an idiosyncratic interpretation, perhaps based on ignorance of a traditional belief, it is not impossible that the general belief in the derivation of the grindstones could owe something to an originally purely figurative usage.

6 According to Arndt (1933), in the Lio language of eastern central Flores, a cognate of *je* means 'to fly obliquely', 'to swoop down', and 'to fly low, close to the ground', as well as 'to approach closely'. From questioning, however, I am assured that the word does not refer to types of avian flight in Nage.

7 Regarding the small 'crest', it may be relevant that MacKinnon (1991: 182) describes the hawk-owl as having a white spot at the front of the crown; other authors describe white lores. Another Nage man, who although generally a very knowledgeable source on birds had never seen a *je*, similarly stated that the bird has 'small horns', by contrast to scops-owls, which possess larger 'horns' (ear-tufts; see Chapter 4, regarding *po tadu*).

8 Contrary to the modern Nage assessment, and elements of its name both in English and Latin (*Terpsiphone paradisi*), the bird is not a true bird of paradise (that is, of the family Paradisaeidae) but a member of the Monarchidae (Monarch flycatchers).

9 An arresting parallel to these ideas is found in the Kédang region of Lembata (Lomblen). There too, a kind of quail, called *boreq*, is said never to fly into a tree lest it die. In this respect, it is paired with a snake called *ular male manuq* ('chicken star snake') which is said to have wings like a bat's, live in tree tops, eat eggs, and to die if it ever touches the ground (R.H. Barnes, pers. comm. 25 May 2001). This idea seems partly to refer to the so-called Flying snake (*Chrysopelea* sp.; Nage *goko*, Forth 1995: 51). Presumably, the paradise-flycatcher and the snake are interchangeable as between the two traditions owing to the long and conceivably serpentine tail of the flycatcher.

10 One man described the crest of the *manu wodu* as resembling that of a cassowary (*kasuari*), a bird evidently known to him through modern media, since cassowaries do not occur on Flores.

11 One man thought that *'ighu* also lacked anuses. Other people I asked stated that these bats were so small that one could not determine whether they did or not.

12 The idea that flying foxes have no anal opening and must excrete through their mouths is reported for Queensland by Lévi-Strauss (1985: 160, note 1), whose source appears to be Ratcliffe (1951: 28–29). Whereas Lévi-Strauss attributes this idea to aborigines, however, Ratcliffe cites only the testimony of an old Australian prospector who is not identified as an aborigine. Referring to the same idea among the Nidula of Goodenough Island, and citing Majnep and Bulmer (1977: 125), Michael Young describes the notion that bats, or flying foxes, lack an anus as a 'widespread belief' (1991: 382).

13 Bulmer (1968: 636) remarks that some fruit bats 'discard the stones and other debris' of fruit that they have carried back to their roosts, 'rather than swallowing these and allowing them to pass through the alimentary tract', thus possibly giving rise to the idea that they excrete all food wastes through their mouths.

14 By contrast, a Trobriand witch can send out a 'double' that may take the form of a flying fox, a night bird, or a firefly (Malinowski 1922: 238). Similarly, among another Austronesian-speaking group, the Nidula of Goodenough Island, bats are regarded as the 'messengers' of sorcerers (Young 1991: 382). Bats are of course associated with witches in European lore. The association is also found among the African Azande, although in this connection one must question their ethnographer's statement that bats are 'universally disliked' (Evans-Pritchard 1976: 236). Elizabeth Lawrence notes how, in China, bats are associated with 'good luck and happiness', and in 'some Pacific island legends' are 'depicted as heroes' (1993: 332, 333). In eastern Sumba, also, bats are not identified with witches. On the other hand, tiny bats called *pahomba* – apparently the equivalent of Nage *'ighu* – are associated with wealth and homonymous life-giving spirits (Forth 1981: 80; 2000: 180) and for this reason should not be killed. By contrast, bats among the Nuaulu share many of the negative associations found elsewhere: they are identified with the dead, and more specifically with people who died a violent death (Valeri 2000: 233). Positive as well as negative interpretations of bats in Mexican traditions, including a Cora myth in which a bat appears as a culture hero, are recorded by Cordry (1980: 1985–86).

15 One informant reproduced the sound made by flying foxes as an unvoiced 'chi ii iii iii' and 'k'chi ii, k'chi ii'. In my field-notes, I describe it as 'like someone pulling a curtain that is suspended with metal rings from a metal rail', and as 'a sort of drawn-out metallic "swish", somewhat reminiscent of the sound of cicadas (*naju*)'.

16 Verhoeye and Holmes remark that, in East Flores, the Channel-billed cuckoo is 'always observed after the first rains', and that 'it is associated with the onset of the rainy season by the local people, at which time it is extremely conspicuous and noisy' (1999:

29). As Nage pointed out, although crows steal ripening maize, they nevertheless feed some of this to the *muta me*, which later provides a useful chronological function; hence there is a certain reciprocity in this relationship.

17 Thus, I was told that koels do make nests, but these are in such tall trees that they are inaccessible. It should be noted as well that, although the Flores crow, *héga hea*, is also a host of the *muta me*, Nage only ever mention the Large-billed crow, *ha*, in this connection.

18 *Ule* is a general term for worms, maggots, grubs, and similar small creatures. According to one man, during this infestation only a single 'worm' is ever seen emerging from the anus. I am not sure, however, whether many other Nage are familiar with this idea, since, despite the fact that singular and plural are not always distinguished in their language, they appeared usually to refer to an infestation involving a number of worms.

19 The condition could be myiasis caused by the Old World screw-worm fly (*Chrysomya bezziana*) or, perhaps more likely, an endoparasite that also affects domestic fowl in Southeast Asia (see Sani *et al.* 1987).

20 *Taga* can be translated as either 'leg' or 'foot'.

21 Writing on Bali, Victor Mason similarly refers to the Savannah nightjar's 'unfortunate habit of sitting at night on roads, eyes reflecting red in the headlights of oncoming motorcars', as a result of which 'a great number are squashed flat' (Mason and Jarvis 1989: 59).

22 Peterson *et al.* (1993, opposite Plate 68) remark how 'all nightjars share a falcon-like silhouette', although they differ from falcons in manner of flight. The similarity of nightjars to Falconiformes is further enshrined in the English dialectal name 'dor-hawk' (Swann 1913) and the North American name for one species of nightjar, the 'night-hawk'. Further afield, the Japanese call the nightjar *yotaka* which, as Lévi-Strauss has noted (1985: 53), literally means 'night falcon'.

23 Referring to the bird's wide gape, and thence the idea, disseminated by Aristotle (Pollard 1977: 51), that the bird was able to suck the udders of goats, the last three terms are all loan translations of Latin *caprimulgus*.

24 Actually, from these narratives, it would appear that the nighthawk could be equally, or better, characterized as a false hunter, or pseudo-hunter. In one Californian myth, moreover, the nighthawk, having failed to secure food for his wives through hunting, 'cuts flesh from his legs' to give to them (Lévi-Strauss 1985: 86). Although Lévi-Strauss does not make the point, it is a reasonable surmise that this narrative detail may reflect the actual small size of the bird's legs, in the same way as does the leglessness Nage attribute to the Savannah nightjar.

25 If the nightjar's symbolic value for hunting is accounted for by the bird's visible morphological and behavioural features, it may be asked why it is not the bird's appearance, but its call (a 'frequently uttered, loud buzzy squeal', Coates and Bishop 1997: 367) that is inauspicious. The simple answer is that the omen is conveyed by the nightjar's vocalization because this is the principal way in which the bird manifests itself at night. In this regard, the representation of the nightjar parallels that of raptorial *po*-sounding birds (Chapter 4) which, as inauspicious portents, similarly manifest themselves vocally even while their association with spiritual malevolence can largely be attributed to their physical form and behaviour.

26 This recalls a Nage account of a male ancestor who refused to consummate an arranged marriage because his bride had 'no breasts' (*susu mona*). Questioning the exact sense of this (since *susu* can sometimes mean 'breast milk'), I was told that the woman probably did have breasts, but they were extremely small. It goes without saying that such expressions also abound in modern English.

27 Whereas Aristotle defined birds as creatures possessing feet, Edward Topsell, in the seventeenth century, disputed this, subscribing to a then current idea that birds of

paradise were footless, or legless (1972: 106). The modern editors of Topsell's work ascribe this notion to the shipping of the birds' carcasses from Asia to Europe with the legs, and sometimes also the wings and head, removed (ibid.: 266).

8 Birds in myth and metaphor

1 For reasons I cannot go into here, it is more likely that women tend to be named after settlements, rather than the other way around.

2 Among the few examples in the vicinity of Bo'a Wae are Lia Kutu (Porcupine Cavity), Ua (Bee) and Fua (Wasp), all long abandoned former villages.

3 In the north-eastern region of Dhawe there is a clan named Gako Tasi (Heron). In the main village of Ola Dhawe, this group is assigned to occupy and guard the 'tail' (that is, the seaward) gate, an association seemingly consistent with the clan being named after a water bird found in abundance in north coastal regions.

4 After the dissolution of the village of Nila, one segment of the homonymous clan, led by the ancestor Koi To, headed westward following a kite (*jata*; or an eagle, *kua*, according to another version) that had seized one of the ancestor's chickens. While following the great bird, they came across a pleasant spot which, Koi To decided, would be a good place to build a new village. This was the site of the village that came to be known as Bo Koi (Koi's granary). Since the segment of clan Nila descended from Bo Koi does not maintain any special relationship with the kite (or eagle), however, totemism is not attested in this case either.

5 Another 'soul bird', the *deza kela*, like three categories of witch birds, *héga hea*, *koa ka*, and *manu miu*, apparently do not occur in songs or other figurative speech genres. For a large part, this might be attributed to the fact that these categories are less well known than others. The same cannot be said, however, of *po* (in the sense of 'owl') or *leba* (nightjar), which also seem not to occur in these genres, at least in the vicinity of Bo'a Wae.

6 Although no match for the whistler in the variety and beauty of its song, the Hill mynah (*Gracula religiosa*) nevertheless possesses a wide vocal repertoire and, like the whistler, is a known mimic (cf. Coates and Bishop 1997: 472). On the other hand, the free recall lists give no hint of any general association of the two birds.

7 I have counted *kolo dasi* (text 26) separately from *kolo*, which in texts 13 and 15–17 refers specifically to the Spotted dove.

8 Nage of Bo'a Wae possess 12 generic terms for wild mammals (including *lako witu*, 'feral dog') as well as eight terms for domestic animals (including *sapi*, 'cattle', a term introduced from Malay about the same time as the animal itself). Even so, by contrast to what one finds, for example, in the ceremonial language of eastern Sumba, the figurative employment of both domestic and wild mammals appears to be lower in Nage than in other eastern Indonesian societies.

9 I have recorded 66 terms for insects (including arachnids). Of these, 17 are binomials incorporating a term for one of 49 folk generics plus a modifier. The total does not include the separate terms for larval forms of insects. Also, as I have paid far less attention in the field to Nage classification of insects and other small creatures than I have to their classification of birds, the total of 66 is almost certainly minimal.

10 I use 'myth' in a broad and inclusive sense, and make no distinction between, for example, 'origin myths', 'folk tales' and 'legends'.

11 Some points registered here derive from a further analysis of materials treated in my 1992 article, which owing to space restrictions could not be included in this volume.

12 Referring to text 5 in Appendix 1, one man remarked how, by contrast to the pigeon, the friarbird likes everything to be done quickly and without difficulty. The friarbird's mythological desire, that night and day should alternate rapidly, informs the Nage

phrase *kobe koka*, 'night of the friarbird'. Relevant to several ritual contexts, this denotes a procedure that can be employed to speed up a lengthy undertaking, and more particularly to dispense with a day of inactivity which should otherwise intervene between component rites of a ceremonial sequence. In order to expedite this, participants pretend to sleep for a while; then someone imitates a cock's crow and everyone rises and continues as though a night had passed.

13 It is the dried bark of the tree that Nage use to render palm juice 'bitter', and to promote fermentation. One version of the myth specifies the sunbird's deposit as a *ko'u* leaf. *Ko'u* is alternatively named *denu* or *ko'u denu*. According to Verheijen's (1990) listings for cognate Ngadha and Ende dialects, the plant, a small tree or shrub, may be *Melochia umbellata*.

14 One woman in her sixties remembered a story of this sort from an old school textbook. This told of how the friarbird has a long neck because it was pulled by the crow. The former then retaliated by smearing charcoal on the crow's feathers, thus making them black. Like other informants, however, she denied that Nage possessed traditional narratives comparable to this. A Sikanese variant of the story of the friarbird and Imperial pigeon, which includes an account of how the two birds acquired their present physical forms, is recorded in Arndt (1932: 24). Instancing the same mythological genre, a Mambai tale from Timor (Hicks 1997) relates how the friarbird, after defeating the pigeon in the primordial contest, kicks the bird, thus causing it to fall on some moss, which changes the colour of its plumage.

15 The Keo narrative is the one briefly alluded to in Forth (1996a: 93), where unfortunately I failed to specify its derivation from Keo.

16 One man described the bird as vocalizing only in cloudy places, or when the weather is cloudy.

17 While interpreting Rowa in this context as the name of a region comprising several villages, informants also suggested that it may specifically have been a former village called Wolo Rowa ('Rowa hill') which took its name from the bird.

18 The figure of 26 includes *po*, considered as a term referring specifically to owls, plus eight categories of diurnal raptors.

19 The scrubfowl is mentioned in Sumbanese similes (Forth 2000: 189, note 23), one of which turns on the bird's peculiar nesting habit. However, while Nage also recognize this peculiarity (see Table 2.1), they do not, so far as I know, exploit it metaphorically.

9 The story of Tupa Lélu, or how birds of prey became chicken thieves

1 These excuses can be rendered in the form of song, but in this version they were simply spoken. The expression *kau wai tupa lélu sale*, 'you are just like Tupa Lélu', refers to someone who speaks nonsense (*bohu*), or more specifically, who is always making excuses.

2 When I asked the narrator why, if the man already had sons, he did not want a daughter, he could offer no explanation.

3 In variant 1, the first of the two shorter versions, the father's desire to kill his daughter might appear to be sufficiently motivated by the fact that none of his several wives has borne him a son. However, the Lio version (Heerkens 1943) involves much the same kind of spiritual compulsion, as does the longest Nage text.

4 In the Lio story, the brothers keep blowing out fires they make, owing to excessive flatulence. The heroine (named Tepa Lélu) then provides them not with cooked food, as in one of the Nage versions, but a firebrand.

5 Closely paralleling the story of Tupa Lélu is a tale from Kisar (Christensen and Christensen 1991) in which a man instructs his pregnant wife to kill a prospective

daughter before he goes on a journey. Finding she has not done so, the father, on his return, murders the girl. But, unlike Tupa Lélu, she is not directly brought back to life. Rather, from her blood grows an areca palm which bears seven fruits; these then transform into six young men and a young woman, who are considered the children of the murdered girl.

6 As described in my earlier book (Forth 1998a), eating human livers is for Nage an attribute of both witches and *bapu* spirits.

7 If God possesses humans as it were in the form of chickens, then he resembles raptors insofar as he too must kill poultry. By the same token, he resembles those malevolent spirits who possess humans in the form of water buffalo, in which respect it should be recalled that *manu*, 'fowl', can contextually refer to a sacrificial buffalo (see Chapter 5). There seems, then, to be much scope for conflating the divinity (Ga'e Déwa) on the one hand and *bapu* spirits and witches (*polo*) on the other. Yet this is an equation that Nage seem never to explicate. As indicated in Chapter 5, Nage do not ascribe positive spiritual value to diurnal raptors, whereas such birds figure prominently in the creation mythology of several other groups on Flores, Timor, and eastern Sumba (Forth 2000: 182). For example, myths found among the Ngadha (Arndt 1954: 194–95), in East Flores (Arndt 1940: 56–57, 61), and on Timor (Laubscher 1975: 216–17, citing Middelkoop 1938) ascribe the creation of the earth to a pair of raptors with contrasting red (or brown) and grey plumage. Comparable traditions concerning a pair of birds, considered as manifestations of creator deities, are also found among the Iban of Borneo (see e.g. Jensen 1974: 73–76).

8 As to this last point, it should be mentioned that Nage do not regard even large raptors as a direct threat to humans. For example, outside of the present mythological context, one does not encounter the idea – apparently still common in the west – that eagles can carry away small children. Nage say the largest prey eagles (*kua*) can take is a piglet.

9 Demonstrating how the White-bellied sea-eagle is conceived simultaneously as a 'super-killer' and a 'super-nurturer' among the Austronesian-speaking Nidula people of eastern New Guinea, Michael Young (1991: 383–84) recounts a tale, which in this connection bears some similarity to the story of Tupa Lélu. Although quite arresting, the resemblances between the two traditions cannot, however, definitely be attributed to a common Austronesian heritage.

10 Comparison with the Nage story highlights another intriguing detail: the Lio heroine is the daughter of a woman named Wonga Wea, whereas in Nage cosmology Wonga Wea is the name of a male spirit (*nitu, bapu,* or *nitu bapu*) who dwells near the peak of the Ebu Lobo volcano.

11 How far Flores Strigiformes do actually prey on poultry is uncertain. Since the composition of a symbolic class is not completely determined by empirical knowledge (let alone by scientific ornithology), however, on this ground alone one need not be too concerned with ornithological fact in the present context. By the same token, the idea that owls steal domestic fowls may be epistemologically equivalent to the notion that diurnal raptors, as well as owls, produce the *po* sounds.

12 This occurrence of seven reflects a preference for this numeral in central Flores and other parts of eastern Indonesia (see Forth 1998a, 2001). Besides other texts summarized above, the number also occurs in the Kisar tale described in note 5 and in variants of the Nage story of the friarbird and Imperial pigeon from Flores and Timor (Forth 1992).

13 As I have discussed at length in *Beneath the Volcano* (1998a), the possibility of such shifting identifications is facilitated by varying applications of the category of *nitu*, and moreover by the encompassment (in the sense of Dumont 1979) of *bapu* by *nitu*. For a large part, therefore, the two spiritual terms describe relatively malevolent and benevolent aspects of a single entity or quality.

14 As shown by the myth of Lalo Sue (Forth 1998a: 38–42), in which a father and two daughters respectively take the form of a large eel and a pair of fish, as manifestations of *nitu* these creatures can compose unitary social groups, even members of a single family. Yet while Nage may subscribe to the veracity of this tale, no one believes that fish are regularly sired by eels. The Nage notion that a certain kind of eel (*tuna balo*) can derive from a transformation of the Russell's viper (*nipa ba*) involves an entirely different sort of representation (see Forth 1998c).

10 Comparisons and conclusions

1 I intend to pursue such a comparative investigation in a future paper.
2 Like 'Bima-Sumba', 'Ambon-Timor' derives from Esser's classification (1938). In their linguistic atlas (1981, Map 40), Wurm and Hattori retain Esser's Bima-Sumba group, while placing the Ambon-Timor languages of eastern Flores and the islands of Solor, Adonara, and Lembata in a 'Flores–Lembata subgroup', which they then classify within a 'Timor Area group'. Moluccan languages included by Esser in his Ambon-Timor group are then included in a separate 'Central Maluku group'. In regard to certain features of bird classification, however, the languages of eastern Flores appear to resemble more closely Timorese and Moluccan languages than they do the languages of central and western Flores and other members of the Bima-Sumba group, hence I provisionally retain Esser's better-known category of 'Ambon-Timor'.
3 Longer forms of some names, for example *bama cea*, *koko wodo*, and *leo te'a*, are partly analysable (*cea* and *koko* are thus both onomatopoeia, while *te'a* is a colour term). However, the components that have cognates in other languages (*bama*, *wodo*, *leo*) are not.
4 In Nage, the visible similarity between the munia and the kite is of course bound up with a spiritual identification of the munia – not just with this bird of prey but with all raptorial birds that are deemed capable of producing nocturnal sounds designated as *po*. Whether similar notions are encountered in other parts of central Flores, however, is not indicated in the ethnographic literature.
5 In Nage and other Bima-Sumba languages, *manu*, when used alone, of course refers only to the domestic fowl, while Nage *kolo* occurs only in names denoting kinds of doves. That *manu* derives from a Proto-Austronesian form meaning 'bird' is well established. Since there is not the space to demonstrate the more inclusive application of *kolo* in other eastern Indonesian languages, it may be sufficient to note Fernandez's reconstruction of **kolon* as a general term for 'bird' in the ancestral language he calls Proto-Flores (1996: 146).
6 For Solor and Adonara see Arndt (1951: 191); for Ngadha, Arndt (1930: 829; 1931: 711); for Sika, Arndt (1932: 297, 319); for Kédang, Barnes (1974: 211); and for eastern Sumbanese, Forth (2000: 184, 183; 1981: 113).
7 For example, Sikanese compounds of *manu* designate diurnal and nocturnal raptors, storks, the nightjar, junglefowl, and koel. Similarly, in Solorese (another Ambon-Timor language), compounds of *kolo* refer to frigatebirds, the Brahminy kite, egrets, sandpipers, terns, the Spotted dove, and the Pied bushchat (Verheijen n.d.). Also worth noting is Manggarai *kaka*, a lexeme occurring in at least 17 bird names, as well as in numerous names denoting generics belonging to several other life-forms. As this should suggest, if the Manggarai term has any single ethnozoological meaning, it is 'animal' rather than 'bird'.

References

Andrews, E.A. (ed.) (1907) *Harper's Latin Dictionary*, New York and Cincinnati: American Book Company.

Armstrong, Edward A. (1970) *The Folklore of Birds* (2nd edn), New York: Dover Publications, Inc.

Arndt, P. (1930) 'Die Religion der Ngad'a', *Anthropos*, 24: 817–61.

—— (1931) 'Die Religion der Ngad'a', *Anthropos*, 25: 353–405, 697–739.

—— (1932) *Mythologie, Religion und Magie im Sikagebiet (östl. Mittelflores)*, Ende-Flores: Arnoldus-Druckerei.

—— (1933) *Li'onesisch-Deutsches Wörterbuch*, Ende-Flores: Arnoldus-Druckerei.

—— (1940) *Soziale Verhältnisse auf Ost-flores, Adonare und Solor* (Anthropos, Internationale Sammlung Ethnologischer Monographien, Vol. 4), Münster i.W.: Aschendorffsche Verlagsbuchhandlung.

—— (1951) *Religion auf Ost-flores, Adonare und Solor* (Studia Instituti Anthropos, 1), Wien-Mödling: Missionsdruckerei St Gabriel.

—— (1952) 'Zur Religion der Dongo auf Sumbawa', *Anthropos*, 47: 483–500.

—— (1954) *Gesellschaftliche Verhältnisse der Ngadha* (Studia Instituti Anthropos, 8), Wien-Mödling: Missionsdruckerei St Gabriel.

—— (1960) 'Mythen der Ngadha', *Annali Lateranensi*, 24: 9–137.

—— (1961) *Wörterbuch der Ngadhasprache* (Studia Instituti Anthropos, 15), Posieux, Fribourg, Suisse: Anthropos-Institut.

Atran, Scott (1990) *Cognitive Foundations of Natural History*, Cambridge: Cambridge University Press.

Barnes, R.H. (1974) *Kédang: A Study of the Collective Thought of an Eastern Indonesian People*, Oxford: Clarendon Press.

Berlin, Brent (1992) *Ethnobiological Classification: Principles of Categorization of Plants and Animals in Traditional Societies*, Princeton, N.J.: Princeton University Press.

Berlin, Brent, J. Boster and J.P. O'Neill (1981) 'The perceptual bases of ethnobiological classification: evidence from Aguaruna Jivaro ornithology', *Journal of Ethnobiology*, 1: 95–108.

Berlin, Brent, D.E. Breedlove, and P.H. Raven (1968) 'Covert categories and folk taxonomies', *American Anthropologist*, 70: 290–99.

Berlin, Brent and J.P. O'Neill (1981) 'The pervasiveness of onomatopoeia in Aguaruna and Huambisa bird names', *Journal of Ethnobiology*, 1: 238–61.

Blair, John (ed.) (1957) *Birds of Field and Garden: A Popular Handbook and Illustrated Guide*, London and Edinburgh: W. & R. Chambers Ltd.

Blust, Robert (1979) 'Proto-Western Malayo-Polynesian vocatives', *Bijdragen tot de Taal-, Land- en Volkenkunde*, 135: 205–51.

—— (1983) 'A linguistic key to the early Austronesian spirit world' (Unpublished manuscript).

Boyer, Pascal (1994a) *The Naturalness of Religious Ideas: A Cognitive Theory of Religion*, Berkeley, Los Angeles, London: University of California Press.

—— (1994b) 'Cognitive constraints on cultural representations: natural ontologies and religious ideas', in L.A. Hirschfeld and S.A. Gelman (eds) *Mapping the Mind: Domain Specificity in Cognition and Culture*, Cambridge: Cambridge University Press, pp. 391–411.

Brown, C.H. (1984) *Language and Living Things: Uniformities in Folk Classification and Naming*, New Brunswick, N.J.: Rutgers University Press.

Brown, W.J. (1936) *The Gods had Wings*, London: Constable & Company Ltd.

Bulmer, R. (1967) 'Why is the cassowary not a bird?', *Man*, 2: 5–25.

—— (1968) 'Worms that croak and other mysteries of Karam natural history', *Mankind*, 6(12): 621–39.

—— (1974) 'Folk biology in the New Guinea Highlands', *Social Science Information*, 8: 9–28.

—— (1979) 'Mystical and mundane in Kalam classification of birds', in Roy F. Ellen and David Reason (eds) *Classifications in their Social Context*, London: Academic Press, pp. 57–79.

Cameron, A.D. and C.J.O. Harrison (1978) *Bird Families of the World*, Oxford: Elsevier–Phaidon.

Christensen, Sylvia and John Christensen (1991) *Yotowawa nin Koirwakar: kumpulan dongeng dari pulau Kisar (Kisar Folktales)*, Ambon: Pusat Kajian dan Pengembangan Maluku, Universitas Pattimura dan Summer Institute of Linguistics.

Clark, Ross (1994) 'Evolution, migration and extinction of Oceanic bird names', in A.K. Pawley and M.D. Ross (eds) *Austronesian Terminologies: Continuity and Change* (Pacific Linguistics Series C-127), Canberra: Department of Linguistics, Research School of Pacific and Asian Studies, The Australian National University, pp. 73–86.

Coates, B.J. and K.D. Bishop (1997) *A Guide to the Birds of Wallacea: Sulawesi, the Moluccas and Lesser Sunda Islands, Indonesia* (Illustrated by Dana Gardner), Alderley, Australia: Dove Publications.

Coley, J.D. *et al.* (1999) 'Inductive reasoning in folkbiological thought', in Douglas L. Medin and Scott Atran (eds) *Folkbiology*, Cambridge, Mass. and London: MIT Press, pp. 205–32.

Cordry, Donald (1980) *Mexican Masks*, Austin and London: University of Texas Press.

Dammerman, K.W. (1926) *Een tocht naar Soemba*, Batavia: Ruygrok & Co.

Descola, P. (1992) 'Societies of nature and the nature of societies', in A. Kuper (ed.) *Conceptualizing Society*, London: Routledge.

Douglas, Mary (1966) *Purity and Danger: An Analysis of Concepts of Pollution and Taboo*, London: Routledge & Kegan Paul.

Dove, M.R. (1996) 'Process versus product in Bornean augury: a traditional knowledge system's solution to the problem of knowing', in Roy Ellen and Katsuyoshi Fukui (eds) *Redefining Nature: Ecology, Culture and Domestication*, Oxford and Washington, D.C.: Berg, pp. 557–96.

Dumont, L. (1979) 'The anthropological community and ideology', *Social Science Information*, XVIII(6): 785–817.

Durkheim, E. and M. Mauss ([1903] 1963) *Primitive Classification*, translated from the French and edited with an introduction by Rodney Needham, London: Cohen & West.

Dwyer, P.D. (1976) 'Beetles, butterflies, and bats: species transformation in New Guinea folk classification', *Oceania*, 46: 188–205.

Echols, J. and H. Shadily (1989) *An Indonesian–English Dictionary* (3rd edn, revised and edited by J.U. Wolff and J.T. Collins with the assistance of H. Shadily), Ithaca, N.Y. and London: Cornell University Press.

Ellen, Roy (1993a) *The Cultural Relations of Classification: An Analysis of Nuaulu Animal Categories from Central Seram*, Cambridge: Cambridge University Press.

—— (1993b) *Nuaulu Ethnozoology: A Systematic Inventory* (CSAC Monographs 6), Canterbury: Centre for Social Anthropology and Computing in co-operation with the Centre of South-East Asian Studies, University of Kent at Canterbury.

Esser, S.J. (1938) 'Talen'; Blad 9b in *Atlas van Tropisch Nederland*, 's-Gravenhage: Martinus Nijhoff.

Evans-Pritchard, E.E. (1976) *Witchcraft, Oracles, and Magic Among the Azande* (abridged, with an introduction by Eva Gillies), Oxford: Clarendon Press.

Feld, Stephen (1982) *Sound and Sentiment: Birds, Weeping, Poetics, and Song in Kaluli Expression*, Philadelphia: University of Pennsylvania Press.

Fernandez, Inyo Yos (1996) *Relasi historis kekerabatan bahasa Flores: kajian linguistik historis komparatif terhadap sembilan bahasa di Flores*, Ende: Penerbit Nusa Indah.

Fernandez, J.W. (ed.) (1991) *Beyond Metaphor: The Theory of Tropes in Anthropology*, Stanford, Calif.: Stanford University Press.

Fleck, David W., Robert S. Voss and Nancy B. Simmons (2002) 'Undifferentiated taxa and sublexical categorization: an example from Matses classification of bats', *Journal of Ethnobiology*, 22(1): 61–102.

Forth, Gregory (1981) *Rindi: An Ethnographic Study of a Traditional Domain in Eastern Sumba* (Verhandelingen van het Koninklijk Instituut voor Taal-, Land- en Volkenkunde No. 93), The Hague: Martinus Nijhoff.

—— (1989) 'Animals, witches and wind: eastern Indonesian variations on the "thunder complex"', *Anthropos*, 84: 89–106.

—— (1991a) 'Shamanic powers and mystical practitioners among the Nage of central Flores', *Canberra Anthropology*, 14(2): 1–29.

—— (1991b) 'Nage directions: an eastern Indonesian system of spatial orientation', in Ole Grøn, Ericka Engelstad and Inge Lindblom (eds) *Social Space: Human Spatial Behaviour in Dwellings and Settlements*, Odense: Odense University Press, pp. 138–48.

—— (1992) 'The pigeon and the friarbird: the mythical origin of death and daylight in eastern Indonesia', *Anthropos*, 87: 423–41.

—— (1993a) 'Social and symbolic aspects of the witch among the Nage of eastern Indonesia', in C.W. Watson and R.F. Ellen (eds) *Understanding Witchcraft and Sorcery in Southeast Asia*, Honolulu: University of Hawaii Press, pp. 99–122.

—— (1993b) 'Ritual and ideology in Nage mortuary culture', *Southeast Asian Journal of Social Science*, 21(2): 37–61.

—— (1995) 'Ethnozoological classification and classificatory language among the Nage of eastern Indonesia', *Journal of Ethnobiology*, 15(1): 45–69.

—— (1996a) 'Nage birds: issues in the analysis of ethno-ornithological classification', *Anthropos*, 91: 89–109.

—— (1996b) 'To chat in pairs: lexical pairing as a pervasive feature of Nage mundane speech', *Canberra Anthropology* 19(1): 31–51.

—— (1998a) *Beneath the Volcano: Religion, Cosmology and Spirit Classification Among the Nage of Eastern Indonesia* (Verhandelingen van het Koninklijk Instituut voor Taal-, Land- en Volkenkunde No. 177), Leiden: KITLV Press.

Forth, Gregory (1998b) 'Things that go *po* in the night: the classification of birds, sounds, and spirits among the Nage of eastern Indonesia', *Journal of Ethnobiology*, 18(2): 189–209.

—— (1998c) 'On deer and dolphins: Nage ideas regarding animal transformation', *Oceania*, 68(4): 271–93.

—— (1999) 'Supplementary notes on Nage bird classification and ethno-ornithology', *Anthropos*, 94: 568–74.

—— (2000) 'Eastern Sumbanese bird classification', *Journal of Ethnobiology*, 20(2): 161–92.

—— (2001) *Dualism and Hierarchy: Processes of Binary Combination in Keo Society*, Oxford: Oxford University Press.

Freeman, J.D. (1960) 'Iban augury', in B.E. Smythies, *The Birds of Borneo*, Edinburgh: Oliver and Boyd, pp. 73–98.

Gardner, P.M. (1976) 'Birds, words and a requiem for the omniscient informant', *American Ethnologist*, 3: 446–68.

Geddes, W.R. (1945) *Deuba: A Study of a Fijian Village* (Memoirs of the Polynesian Society, Vol. 22), Wellington: The Polynesian Society Incorporated.

Gennep, A. van (1960) *The Rites of Passage*, translated from the French by M.B. Vizedom and G.L. Caffee, Chicago: University of Chicago Press.

Ghiselin, Michael T. (1999) 'Natural kinds and supraorganismal individuals', in Douglas L. Medin and Scott Atran (eds) *Folkbiology*, Cambridge, Mass. and London: MIT Press, pp. 447–60.

Glares, P.G.N. (ed.) (1982) *Oxford Latin Dictionary* (Combined edn), Oxford: Clarendon Press.

Hage, P. and W.R. Miller (1976) 'Eagle = bird: a note on the structure and evolution of Shoshoni ethnoornithological nomenclature', *American Ethnologist*, 3: 481–88.

Hails, C. and F. Jarvis (1987) *Birds of Singapore*, Singapore: Times Editions.

Hall, D.G. (1993) 'Basic-level individuals', *Cognition*, 48: 199–221.

Hall, D.G. and S.R. Waxman (1993) 'Assumptions about word meaning: individuation and basic-level kinds', *Child Development*, 64: 1550–70.

Heerkens, P. (1943) 'Noengoenange van Wonga Wea', *Cultureel Indië* 5: 1–24.

Hicks, D. (1997) 'Friarbird on Timor: two Mambai myths of avian rivalry', *Anthropos*, 92: 198–200.

Hull, Geoffrey (2001) *Standard Tetum–English Dictionary* (2nd edn, revised and expanded), Crows Nest, NSW, Australia: Allen & Unwin in association with the University of Sydney.

Hunn, Eugene S. (1976) 'Toward a perceptual model of folk biological classification', *American Ethnologist*, 3: 508–24.

—— (1977) *Tzeltal Folk Zoology: The Classification of Discontinuities in Nature*, New York: Academic Press.

—— (1979) The abominations of Leviticus revisited: a commentary on anomaly in symbolic anthropology', in Roy F. Ellen and David Reason (eds) *Classifications in their Social Context*, London: Academic Press, pp. 103–16.

—— (1982) 'The utilitarian factor in folk biological classification', *American Anthropologist*, 84: 830–47.

—— (1991) 'Sahaptin bird classification', in Andrew Pawley (ed.) *Man and a Half: Essays in Pacific Anthropology and Ethnobiology in Honour of Ralph Bulmer*, Auckland: The Polynesian Society, pp. 137–47.

—— (1992) 'The use of sound recordings as voucher specimens and stimulus materials in ethnozoological research', *Journal of Ethnobiology*, 12(2): 187–98.

—— (1999) 'Size as limiting the recognition of biodiversity in folkbiological classifications: one of four factors governing the cultural recognition of biological taxa', in Douglas L. Medin and Scott Atran (eds) *Folkbiology*, Cambridge, Mass. and London: MIT Press, pp. 47–69.

Hunn, E. and David French (1984) 'Alternatives to taxonomic hierarchy: the Sahaptin case', *Journal of Ethnobiology*, 4(1): 73–92.

Ingersoll, Ernest (1923) *Birds in Legend, Fable and Folklore*, New York and London: Longmans, Green & Co.

Jensen, Erik (1974) *The Iban and their Religion*, Oxford: Clarendon Press.

Jepson, Paul (1997) 'Bird conservation priorities in Nusa Tenggara and Maluku', in Kathryn Monk, Yance de Fretes, and Gayatri Reksodiharjo-Lilley, *The Ecology of Nusa Tenggara and Maluku* (The Ecology of Indonesia Series Vol. V), Hong Kong: Periplus Editions (HK) Ltd, pp. 830–35.

Jesperson, Otto (1921) *Language: Its Nature, Development, and Origin*, London: Allen & Unwin.

Kapita, Oe. H. (1976) *Masyarakat Sumba dan adat istiadatnya*, Waingapu: Panitia Penerbit Naskah-Naskah Kebudayaan Daerah Sumba Dewan Penata Layanan Gereja Kristen Sumba.

King, Ben, Martin Woodcock and E.C. Dickinson (1975) *Birds of South-East Asia*, London: HarperCollins Publishers.

König, Claus, Friedhelm Weick and Jan-Hendrik Becking (1999) *Owls: A Guide to the Owls of the World*, New Haven, Conn. and London: Yale University Press.

Kohl, Karl-Heinz (1998) *Der Tod der Reisjungfrau: Mythen, Kulte und Allianzen in einer ostindonesischen Lokalkultur*, Stuttgart, Berlin and Köln: W. Kohlhammer GmbH.

Lakoff, George (1987) *Women, Fire and Dangerous Things: What Categories Reveal About the Mind*, Chicago: University of Chicago Press.

Laubscher, Matthias Samuel (1975) 'Gottesnamen in indonesischen, vorzugweise ostindonesischen Stammesgebieten', in H. von Stietencron (ed.) *Der Name Gottes*, Düsseldorf: Patmos-Verlag, pp. 209–29.

Lawrence, Elizabeth Atwood (1993) 'The sacred bee, the filthy pig, and the bat out of hell: animal symbolism as cognitive biophilia', in Stephen R. Kellert and Edward O. Wilson (eds) *The Biophilia Hypothesis*, Washington, D.C.: Island Press.

—— (1997) *Hunting the Wren: Transformation of Bird to Symbol*, Knoxville: University of Tennessee Press.

Leach, E.R. (1964) 'Anthropological aspects of language: animal categories and verbal abuse', in Eric H. Lenneberg (ed.) *New Directions in the Study of Language*, Cambridge, Mass. and London: MIT Press, pp. 23–63.

—— (1976) *Culture and Communication: The Logic by Which Symbols are Connected*, Cambridge: Cambridge University Press.

Lévi-Strauss, C. (1985) *La potière jalouse*, Paris: Plon.

Löffler, Lorenz G. (1968) 'Beast, bird, and fish: an essay in South-East Asian symbolism', in *Folk Religion and the World View in the Southwestern Pacific*, Tokyo: The Keio Institute of Cultural and Linguistic Studies.

Lurker, Martin (1983) *Adler und Schlange: Tiersymbolik im Glauben und Weltbilder Völker*, Tübingen: Rainer Wunderlich Verlag, Herman Leins.

MacKinnon, John (1991) *Field Guide to the Birds of Java and Bali*, Yogyakarta: Gadjah Mada University Press.

Macnamara, John (1986) *A Border Dispute*, Cambridge, Mass. and London: MIT Press.

Majnep, I.S. and R. Bulmer (1977) *Birds of My Kalam Country*, Auckland: Auckland University Press.

Malinowski, B. (1922) *Argonauts of the Western Pacific*, London: Routledge & Kegan Paul Ltd.

Malt, Barbara C. (1995) 'Category coherence in cross-cultural perspective', *Cognitive Psychology*, 29: 85–148.

Mason, Victor and Frank Jarvis (1989) *Birds of Bali*, Berkeley, Calif. and Singapore: Periplus Editions.

Metcalf, Peter (1976) 'Birds and deities in Borneo', *Bijdragen tot de Taal-, Land- en Volkenkunde*, 132: 96–123.

Middelkoop, P. (1938) 'Iets over Sonba'i, het bekende vorstengeslacht op Timor', *Tijdschrift voor Indische Taal-, Land- en Volkenkunde*, 78: 392–509.

Molnar, Andrea K. (2000) *Grandchildren of the Ga'e Ancestors: Social Organization and Cosmology Among the Hoga Sara of Flores* (Verhandelingen van het Koninklijk Instituut voor Taal-, Land- en Volkenkunde No. 185), Leiden: KITLV Press.

Monk, Kathryn, Yance de Fretes, and Gayatri Reksodiharjo-Lilley (1997) *The Ecology of Nusa Tenggara and Maluku* (The Ecology of Indonesia Series Vol. V), Hong Kong: Periplus Editions (HK) Ltd.

Needham, R. (1979) *Symbolic Classification*, Santa Monica, Calif.: Goodyear Publishing Company, Inc.

—— (1980) *Reconnaissances*, Toronto, Buffalo and London: University of Toronto Press.

Ong, Walter J. (1977) *Interfaces of the Word: Studies in the Evolution of Consciousness and Culture*, Ithaca, N.Y. and London: Cornell University Press.

—— (1982) *Orality and Literacy: The Technologizing of the Word*, London and New York: Methuen.

Onvlee, L. (1984) *Kamberaas (Oost-Soembaas)-Nederlands Woordenboek*, Dordrecht: Foris Publications Holland/USA.

Peterson, Roger Tory, Guy Mountfort and P.A.D. Hollom (1993) *Birds of Britain and Europe* (5th edn), London: HarperCollins Publishers.

Pollard, John (1977) *Birds in Greek Life and Myth*, London: Thames & Hudson.

Randall, Robert and Eugene S. Hunn (1984) 'Do life forms evolve or do uses for life?', *American Ethnologist*, 11: 329–49.

Ratcliffe, Francis (1951) *Flying Fox and Drifting Sand: The Adventures of a Biologist in Australia* (2nd edn), Sydney and London: Angus & Robertson.

Richards, Alan J. (1979) *British Birds: A Field Guide*, London: David & Charles.

Richards, Anthony (1981) *An Iban English Dictionary*, Oxford: Clarendon Press.

Rips, Lance J. (1975) 'Inductive judgements about natural categories', *Journal of Verbal Learning and Verbal Behavior*, 14: 665–81.

Rosch, E. (1973) 'On the internal structure of perceptual and semantic categories', in Timothy E. Moore (ed.) *Cognitive Development and the Acquisition of Language*, New York: Academic Press.

—— (1978) 'Principles of categorization', in E. Rosch and B. Lloyd (eds) *Cognition and Categorization*, Hillsdale, N.J.: Lawrence Erlbaum Associates, pp. 28–49.

Rumphius, G.E. (1981) *The Poison Tree: Selected Writings of Rumphius on the Natural History of the Indies*, edited and translated by E.M. Beekman, Amherst: University of Massachusetts Press.

—— ([1705] 1999) *The Ambonese Curiosity Cabinet*, translated, edited, annotated and with an introduction by E.M. Beekman, New Haven, Conn. and London: Yale University Press.

Sani, R., M. Harisah, Aini Ideris and M. Shah-Majid (1987) 'Malaysia: fowl diseases', in John W. Copland (ed.) *Newcastle Disease in Poultry: A New Food Pellet Vaccine* (ACIAR Monograph No. 5), Canberra: Australian Centre for International Agricultural Research, pp. 89–92.

Schmutz, E. (1977) *Die Vögel der Manggarai (Flores)*, Ruteng, Flores: Regio S.V.D. (mimeographed).

Schulte Nordholt, H.G. (1971) *The Political System of the Atoni of Timor* (Verhandelingen van het Koninklijk Instituut voor Taal-, Land- en Volkenkunde No. 60), The Hague: Martinus Nijhoff.

Smythies, B. (1960) *The Birds of Borneo*, Edinburgh and London: Oliver & Boyd.

Sperber, D. (1975) *Rethinking Symbolism*, translated from the French by Alice L. Morton, Cambridge: Cambridge University Press.

—— (1994) 'The modularity of thought and the epidemiology of representations', in L.A. Hirschfeld and S.A. Gelman (eds) *Mapping the Mind: Domain Specificity in Cognition and Culture*, Cambridge: Cambridge University Press, pp. 39–67.

Sutlive, Vinson. H. (Jr.) (1988) *The Iban of Sarawak: Chronicle of a Vanishing World* (2nd edn), Prospect Heights, Ill.: Waveland Press, Inc.

Swann, H. Kirke (1913) *A Dictionary of English and Folk-Names of British Birds*, London: Witherby & Co.

Taylor, P.M. (1984) ' "Covert categories" reconsidered: identifying unlabelled classes in Tobelo folk biological classification', *Journal of Ethnobiology*, 4(2): 105–22.

—— (1990) *The Folk Biology of the Tobelo People: A Study in Folk Classification* (Smithsonian Contributions to Anthropology 34), Washington, D.C.: Smithsonian Institution Press.

Topsell, Edward (1972) *The Fowles of Heauen or History of Birdes*, edited by Thomas P. Harrison and F. David Hoeniger, Austin: The University of Texas.

Trier, Karl van (SVD) (n.d.) *Naskah-naskah Nagekeo-Ngada (Danga-Rawa-Sawu, dll.)*, Unpublished manuscript held in the library of the Catholic Seminary at Ledalero, Flores.

Turner, Nancy J. (1988) ' "The importance of a rose": evaluating the cultural significance of plants', *American Anthropologist*, 90(2): 272–90.

Tuzin, Donald (1984) 'Miraculous voices: The auditory experience of numinous objects', *Current Anthropology*, 25(5): 579–96.

Valeri, V. (2000) *The Forest of Taboos: Morality, Hunting, and Identity Among the Huaulu of the Moluccas*, Madison: University of Wisconsin Press.

Verheijen, J.A.J. (1950) 'De stem der dieren in de Manggaraise Folklore', *Bijdragen tot de Taal-, Land- en Volkenkunde*, 106: 55–78.

—— (1963) 'Bird names in Manggarai, Flores, Indonesia', *Anthropos*, 58: 677–718.

—— (1977) *Bahasa Rembong di Flores Barat. I: Kamus Rembong-Indonesia*, Ruteng, Flores: Regio S.V.D. (mimeographed).

—— (1982) *Komodo: het eiland, het volk en de taal* (Verhandelingen van het Koninklijk Instituut voor Taal-, Land- en Volkenkunde No. 96), The Hague: Martinus Nijhoff.

—— (1990) *Dictionry of Plant Names in the Lesser Sunda Islands* (Pacific Linguistics Series D – No. 83), Canberra: Department of Linguistics, Research School of Pacific and Asian Studies, The Australian National University.

Verheijen, J.A.J. (n.d.) 'Vernacular bird names in the Lesser Sunda Islands', Unpublished, in 'Collection Verheijen', Historical Archive of the Koninklijk Institute voor Taal-, Land- en Volkenkunde, Leiden.

Verhoeye, J. and D.A. Holmes (1999) 'The birds of the islands of Flores: a review', *Kukila: Bulletin of the Indonesian Ornithological Society*, 10: 3–59.

Waddy, J.A. (1988) *Classification of Plants and Animals from a Groote Eylandt Aboriginal Point of View* (Vol. 1), Darwin: Australian National University North Australia Research Unit.

Waxman, S.R. (1999) 'The dubbing ceremony revisited: object naming and categorization in infancy and early childhood', in Douglas L. Medin and Scott Atran (eds) *Folkbiology*, Cambridge, Mass. and London: MIT Press, pp. 233–84.

Weller, Susan C. and A. Kimball Romney (1988) *Systematic Data Collection* (Qualitative Research Methods, Vol. 10), Newbury Park (Calif.), London and New Delhi: Sage Publications.

Winstedt, R.O. (1965) *An Unabridged Malay–English Dictionary* (6th edn, enlarged), Kuala Lumpur and Singapore: Marican & Sons (Malaysia) Ltd.

Wolpert, Lewis (1992) *The Unnatural Nature of Science*, London: Faber & Faber.

Wurm, S.A. and Shiro Hattori (general eds) (1981) *Language Atlas of the Pacific Area*, Canberra: Australian Academy of the Humanities in collaboration with the Japan Academy.

Young, Michael W. (1991) 'The sea eagle and other heroic birds in Nidula mythology', in Andrew Pawley (ed.) *Man and a Half: Essays in Pacific Anthropology and Ethnobiology in Honour of Ralph Bulmer*, Auckland: The Polynesian Society, pp. 380–89.

Zorc, R.D.P. (1994) 'Austronesian culture history through reconstructed vocabulary (an overview)', in A.K. Pawley and M.D. Ross (eds) *Austronesian Terminologies: Continuity and Change* (Pacific Linguistics Series C-127), Canberra: Department of Linguistics, Research School of Pacific and Asian Studies, The Australian National University, pp. 541–94.

Index

For Product Safety Concerns and Information please contact our EU
representative GPSR@taylorandfrancis.com
Taylor & Francis Verlag GmbH, Kaufingerstraße 24, 80331 München, Germany